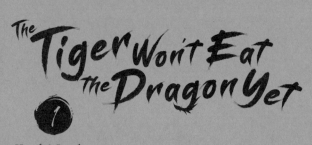

The Tiger Won't Eat the Dragon Yet

1

Hachi Inaba

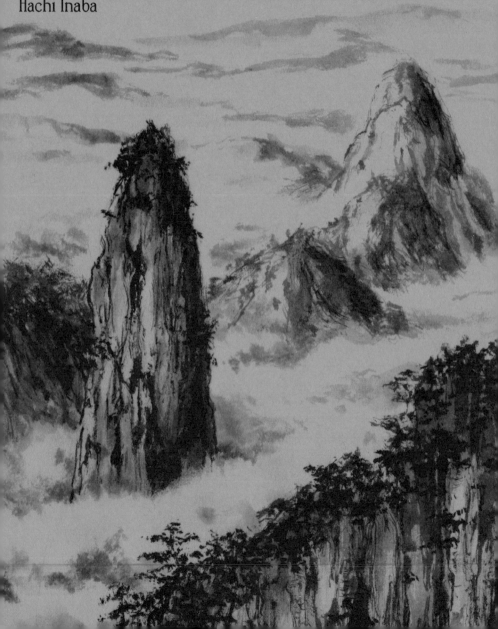

CONTENTS

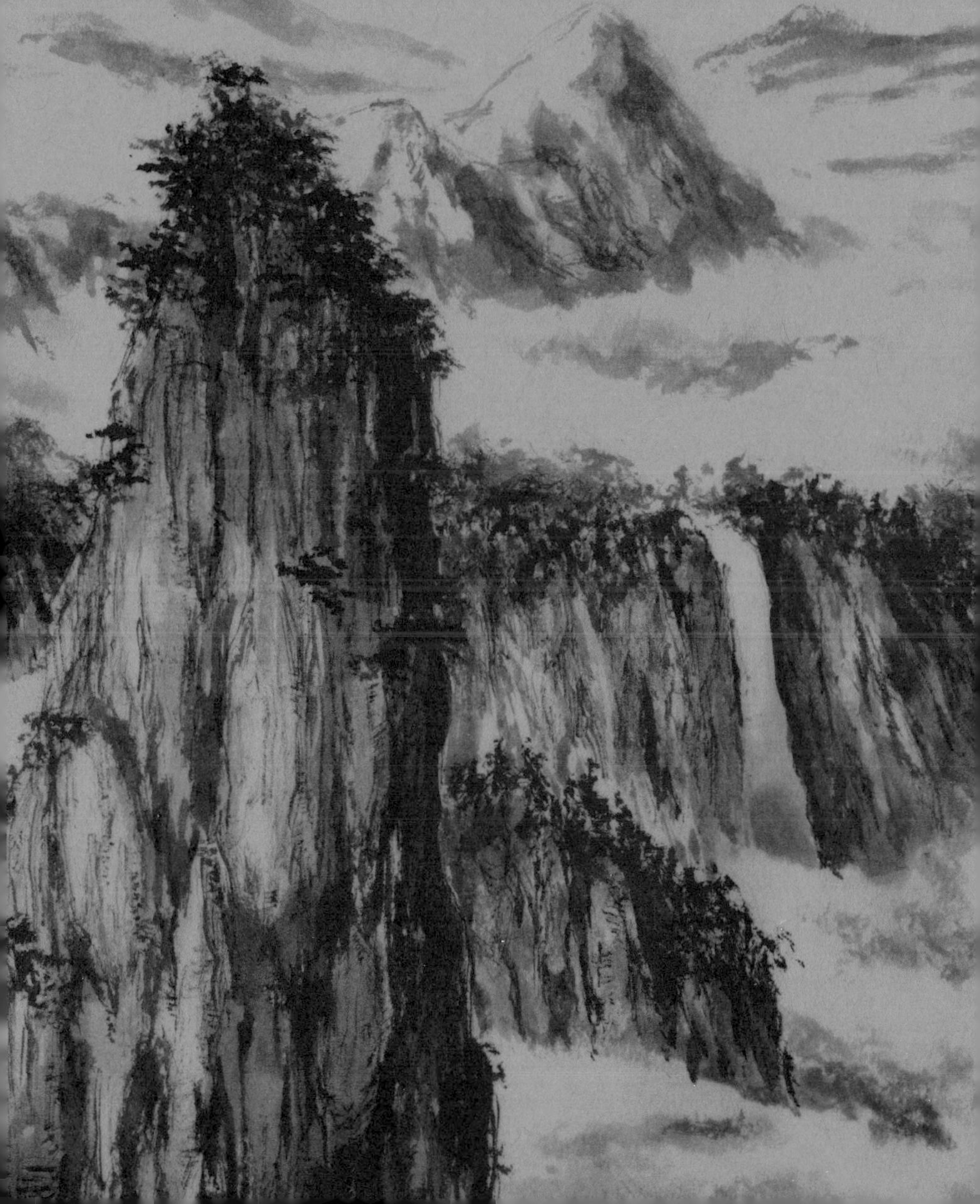

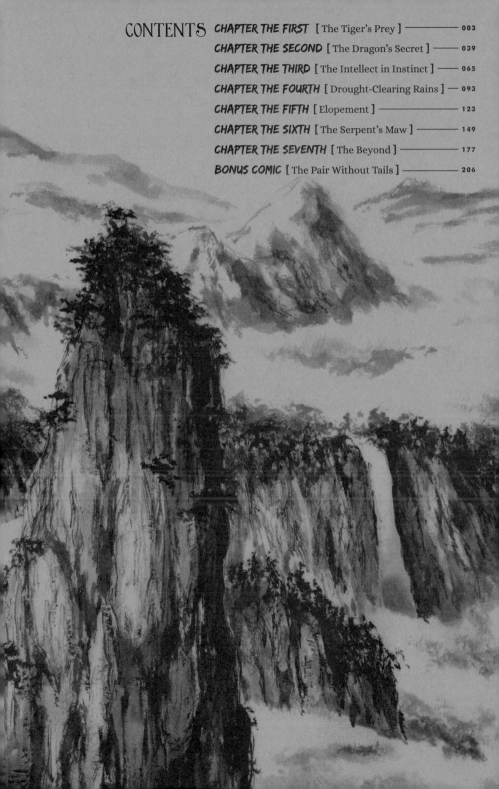

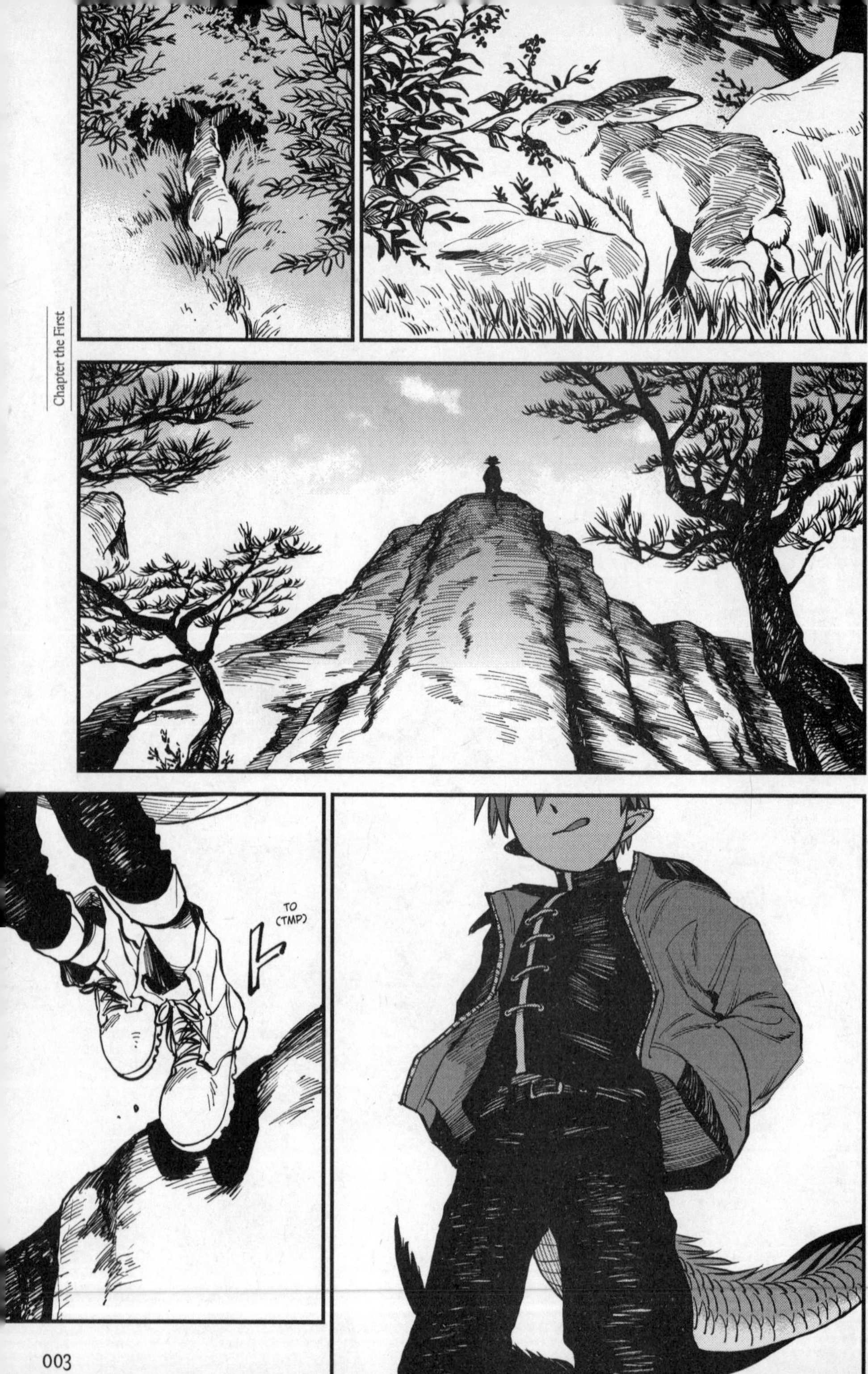
TO
(TMP)

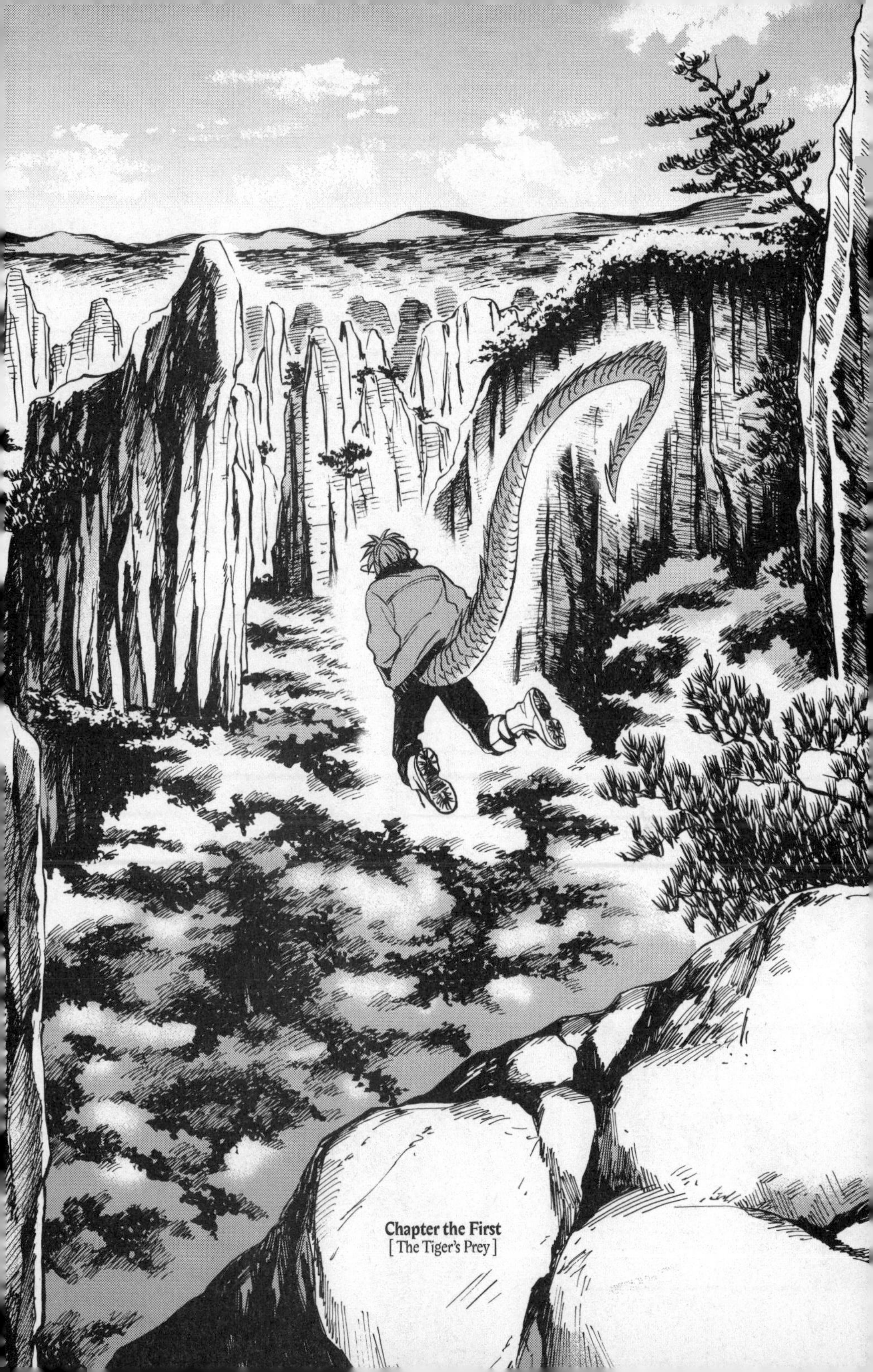
Chapter the First
[The Tiger's Prey]

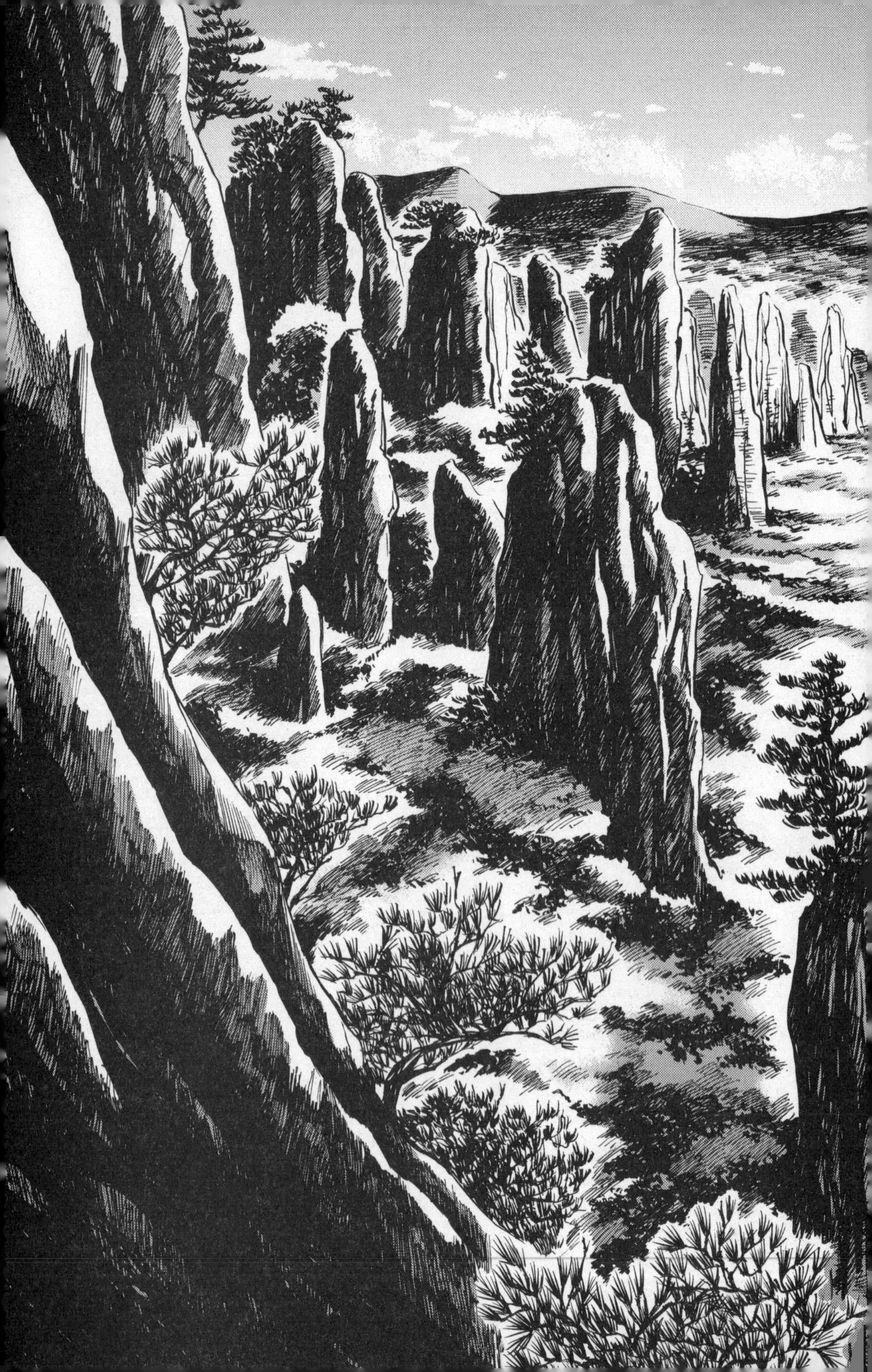

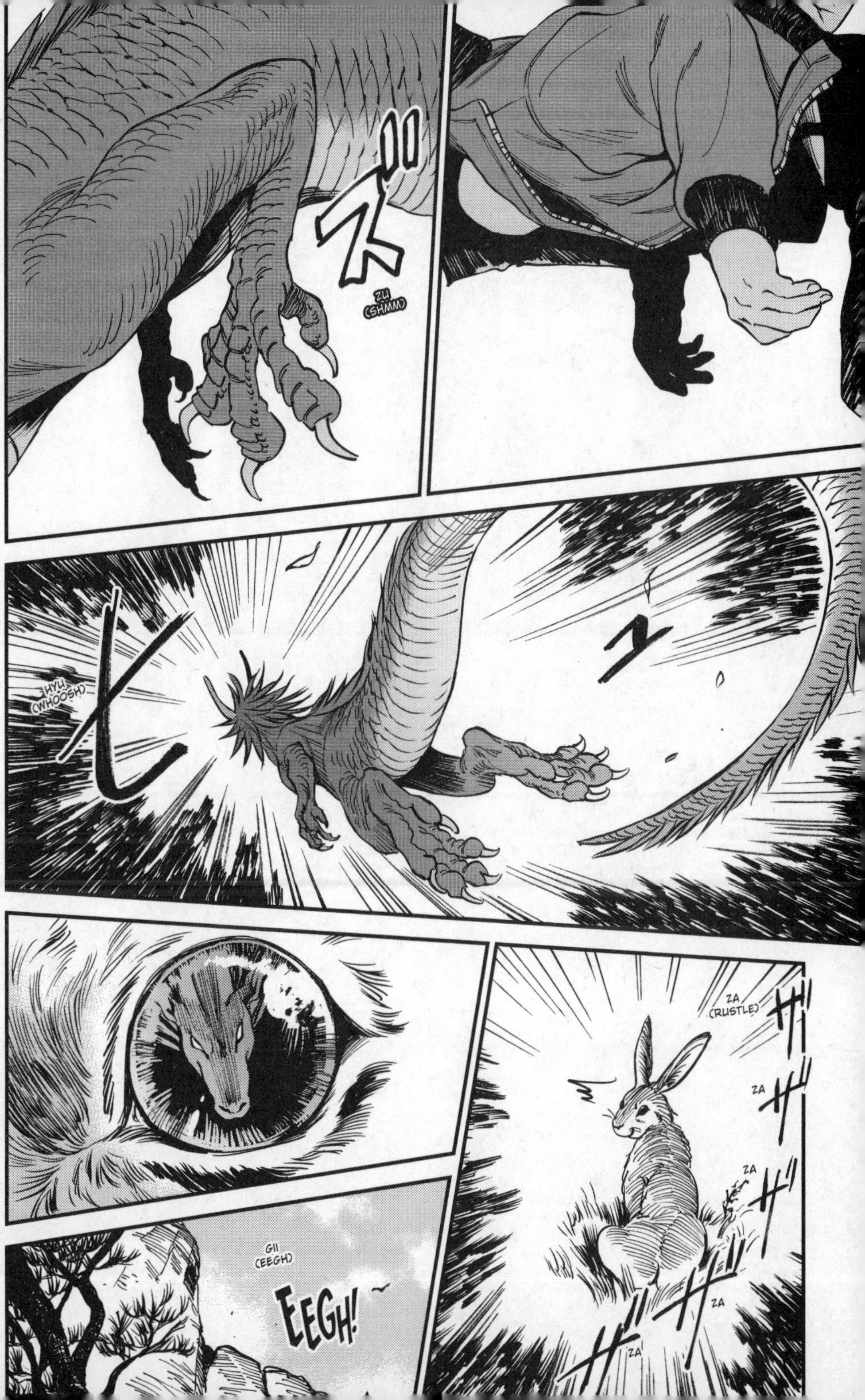
ZU
(SHMM)
HYU
(WHOOSH)
ZA
(RUSTLE)
ZA
ZA
ZA
ZA
GII
(EEGH)
EEGH!

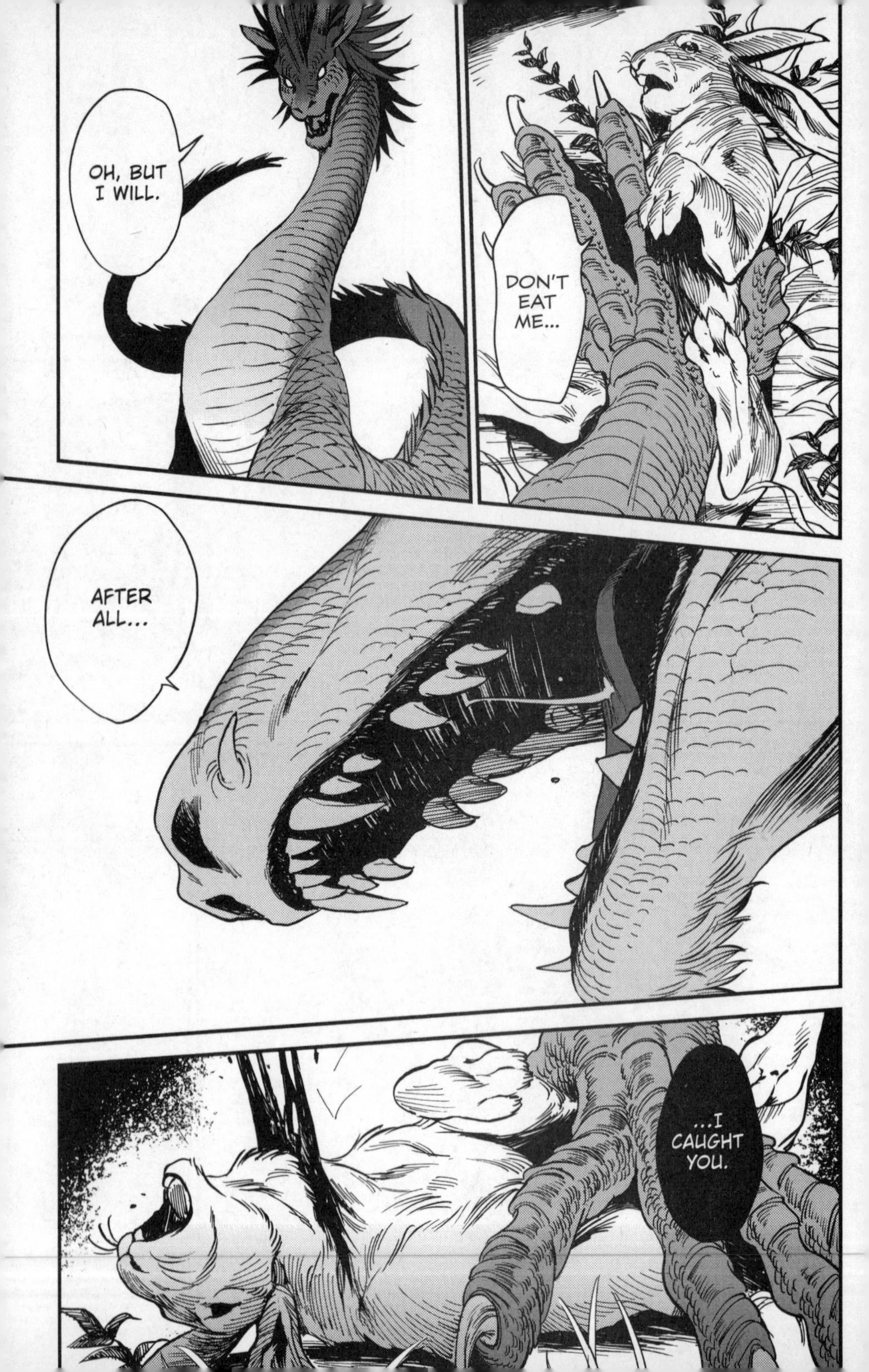
DON'T EAT ME...
OH, BUT I WILL.
AFTER ALL...
...I CAUGHT YOU.

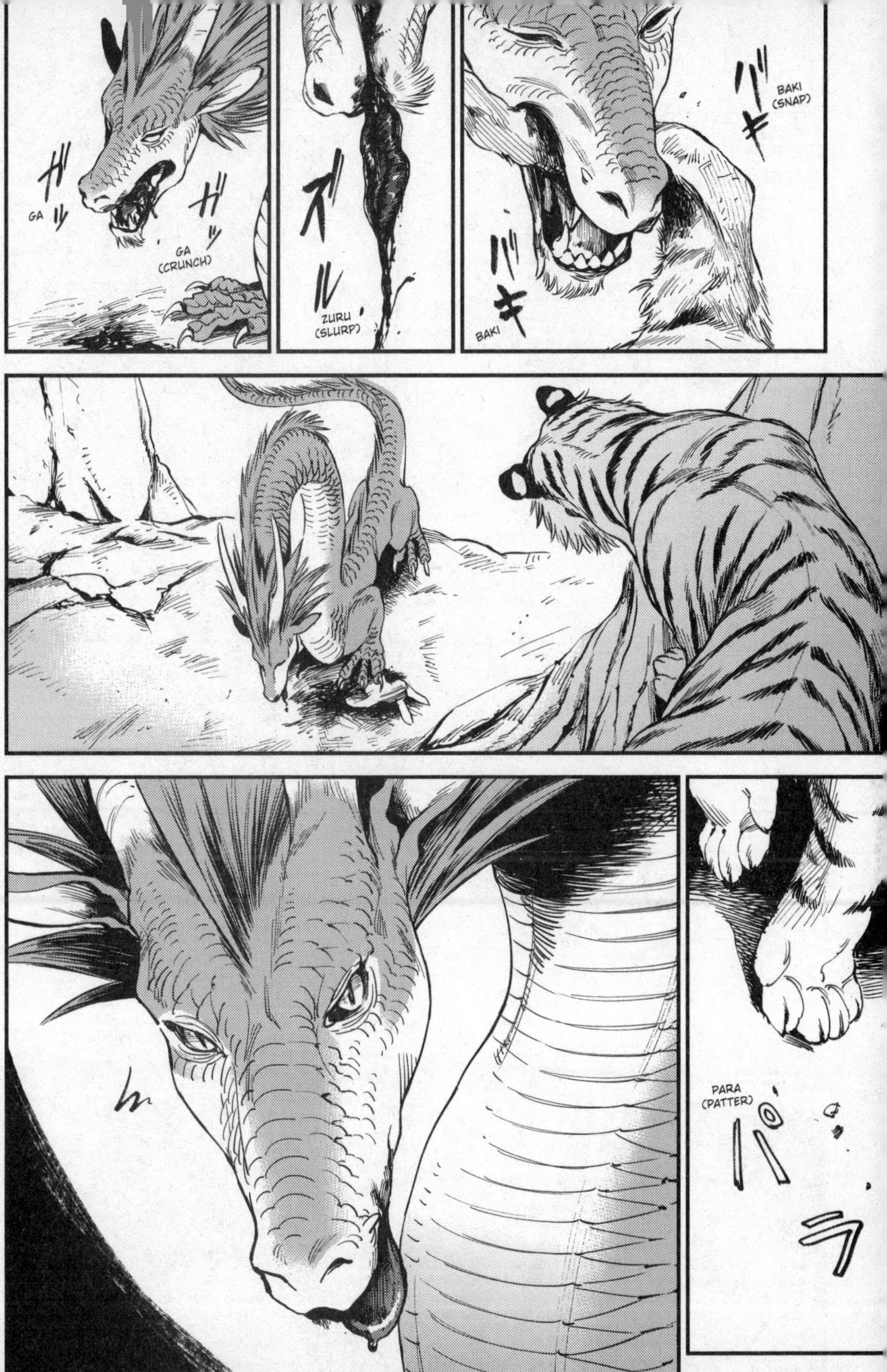
バキ
BAKI (SNAP)
バキ
BAKI
ズル
ZURU (SLURP)
ガッ
GA
ガッ
GA (CRUNCH)
パラ
PARA (PATTER)

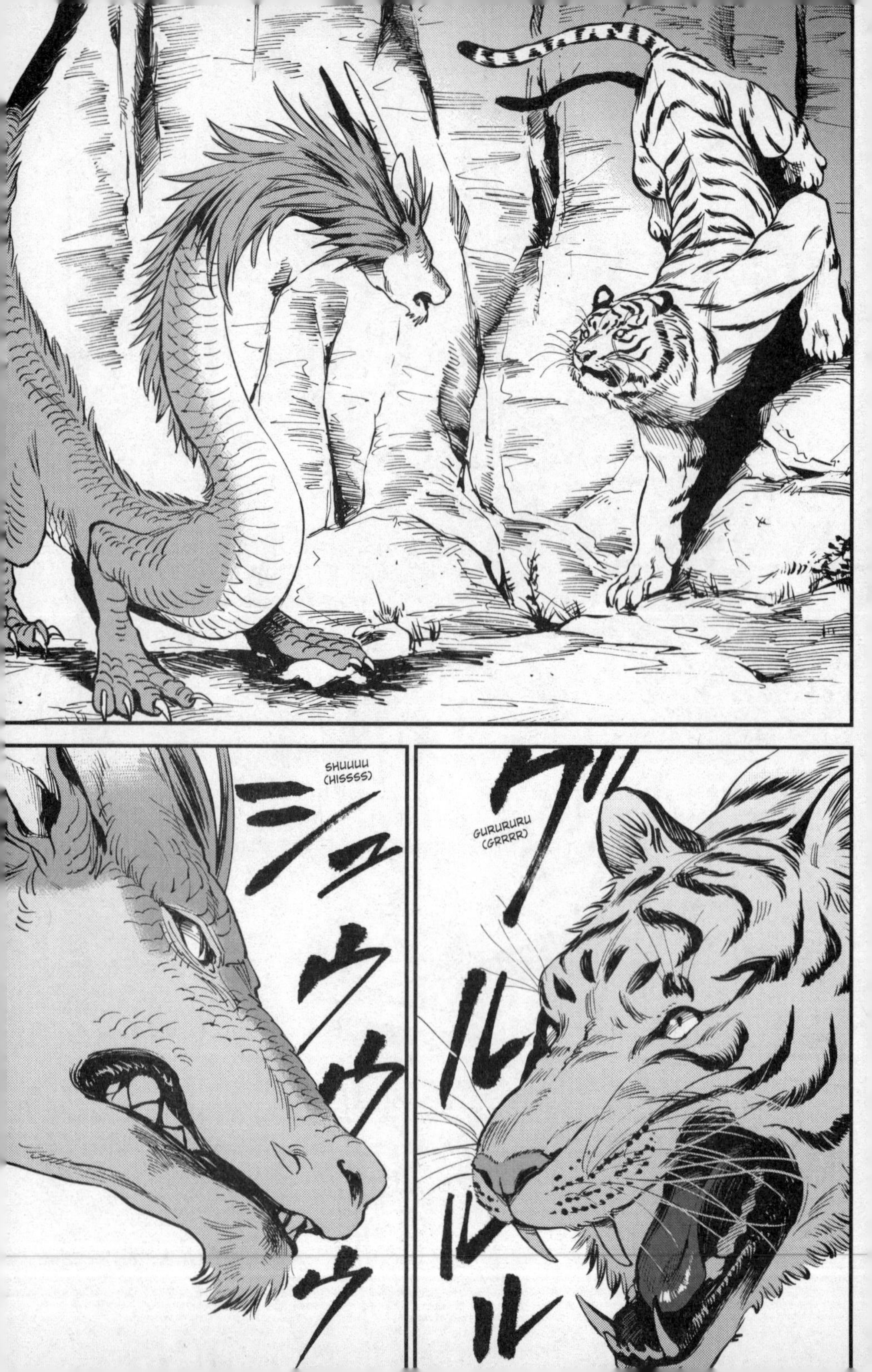
GURURURU
(GRRRR)
SHUUUU
(HISSSS)

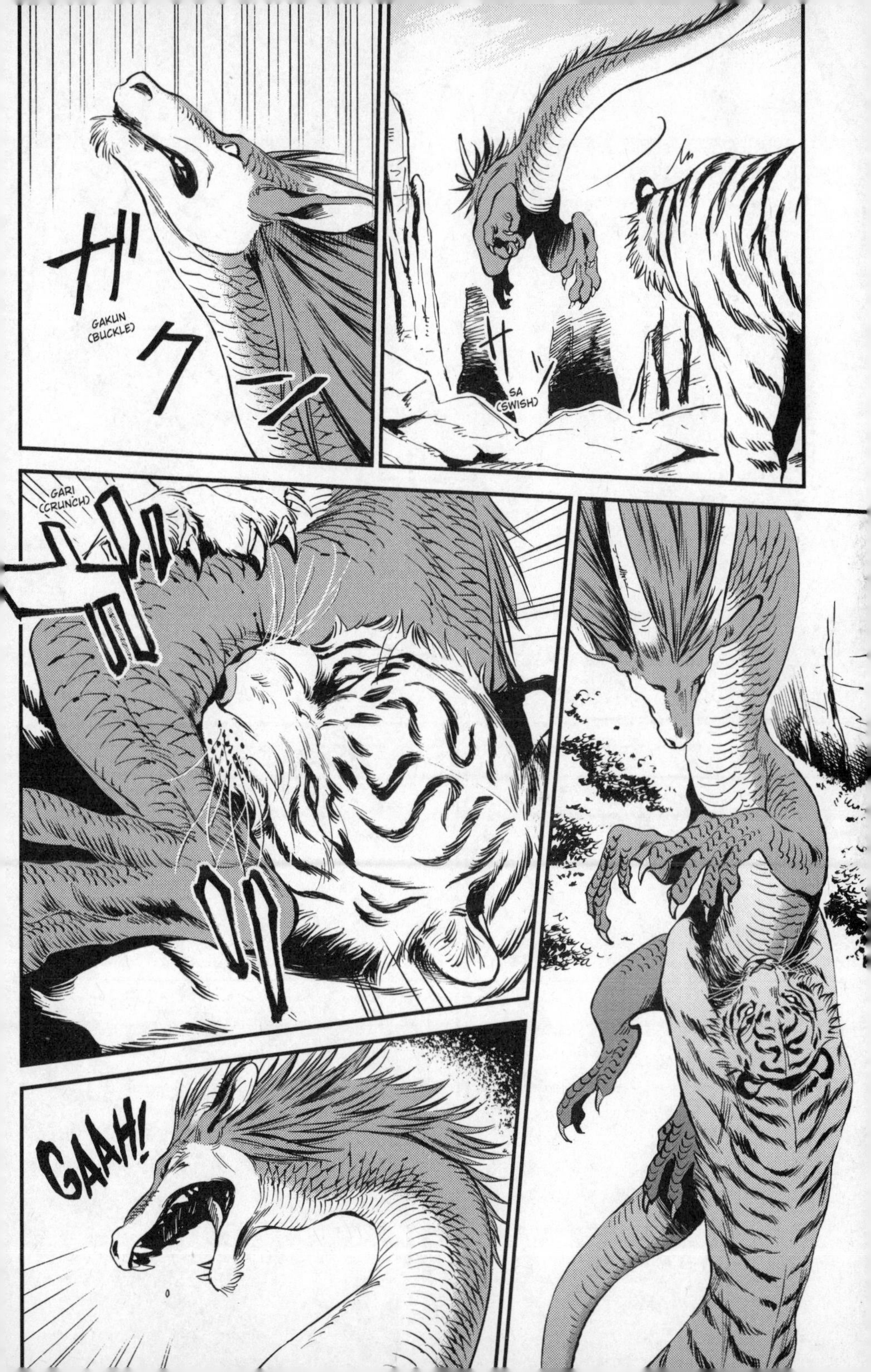
SA
(SWISH)
GAKUN
(BUCKLE)
GARI
(CRUNCH)
GAAH!

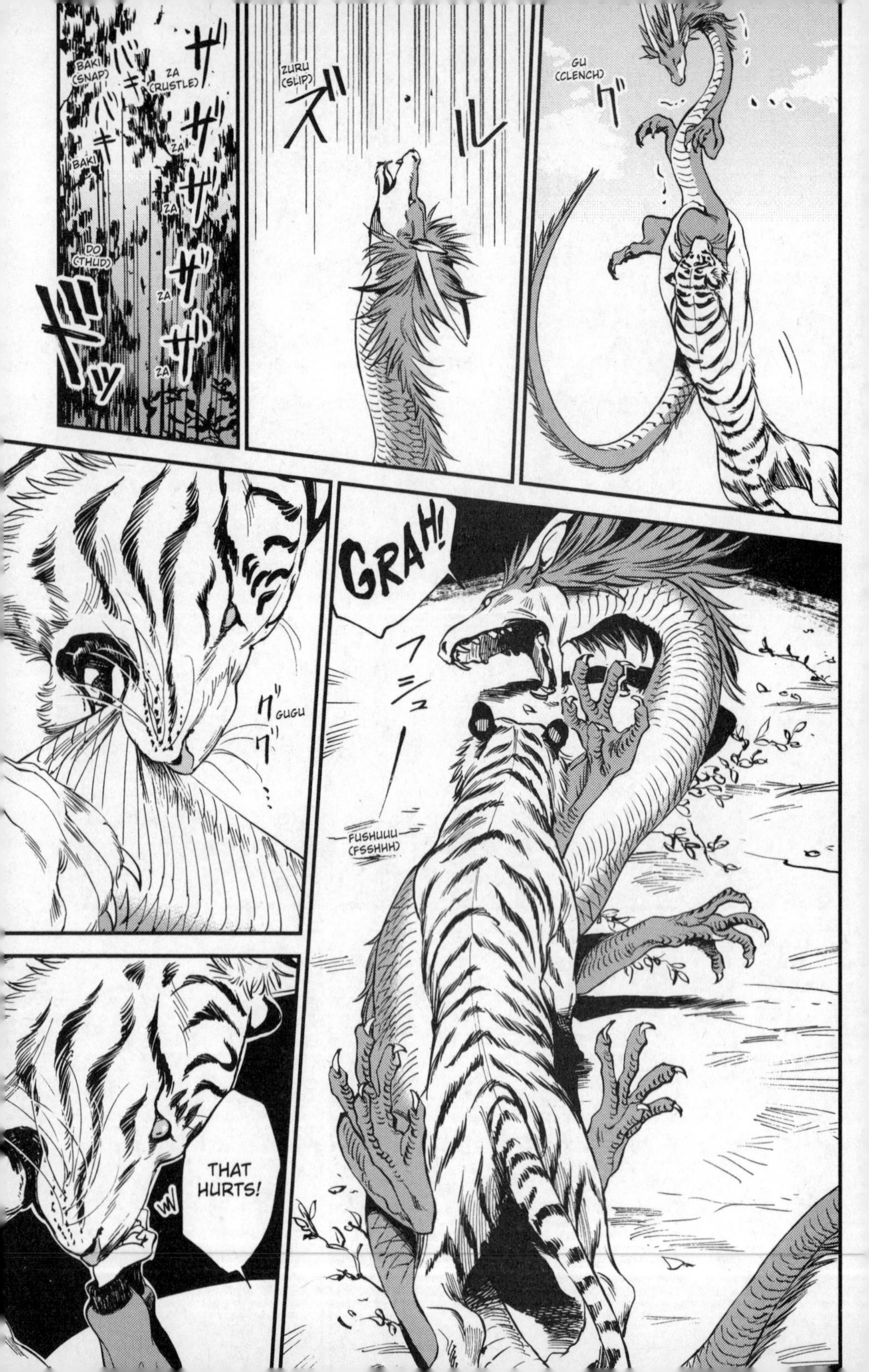

グ
GU (CLENCH)
...
ズル
ZURU (SLIP)
バキバキ
BAKI (SNAP)
BAKI
ザザザザザ
ZA (RUSTLE)
ZA
ZA
ZA
ZA
ドッ
DO (THUD)
GRAH!
フシュー
FUSHUUU (FSSHHH)
ググ
GUGU
THAT HURTS!

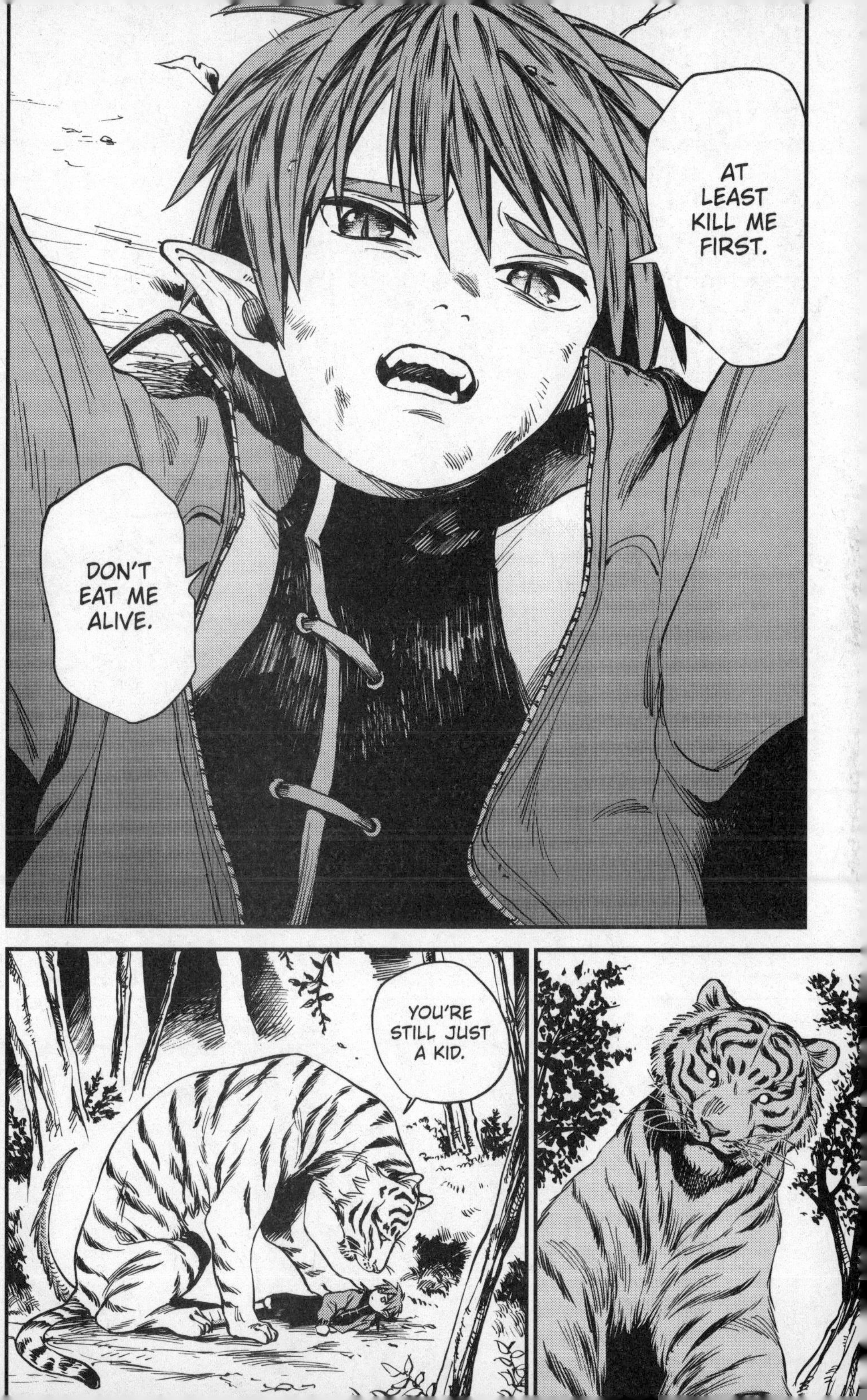
AT LEAST KILL ME FIRST.
DON'T EAT ME ALIVE.
YOU'RE STILL JUST A KID.

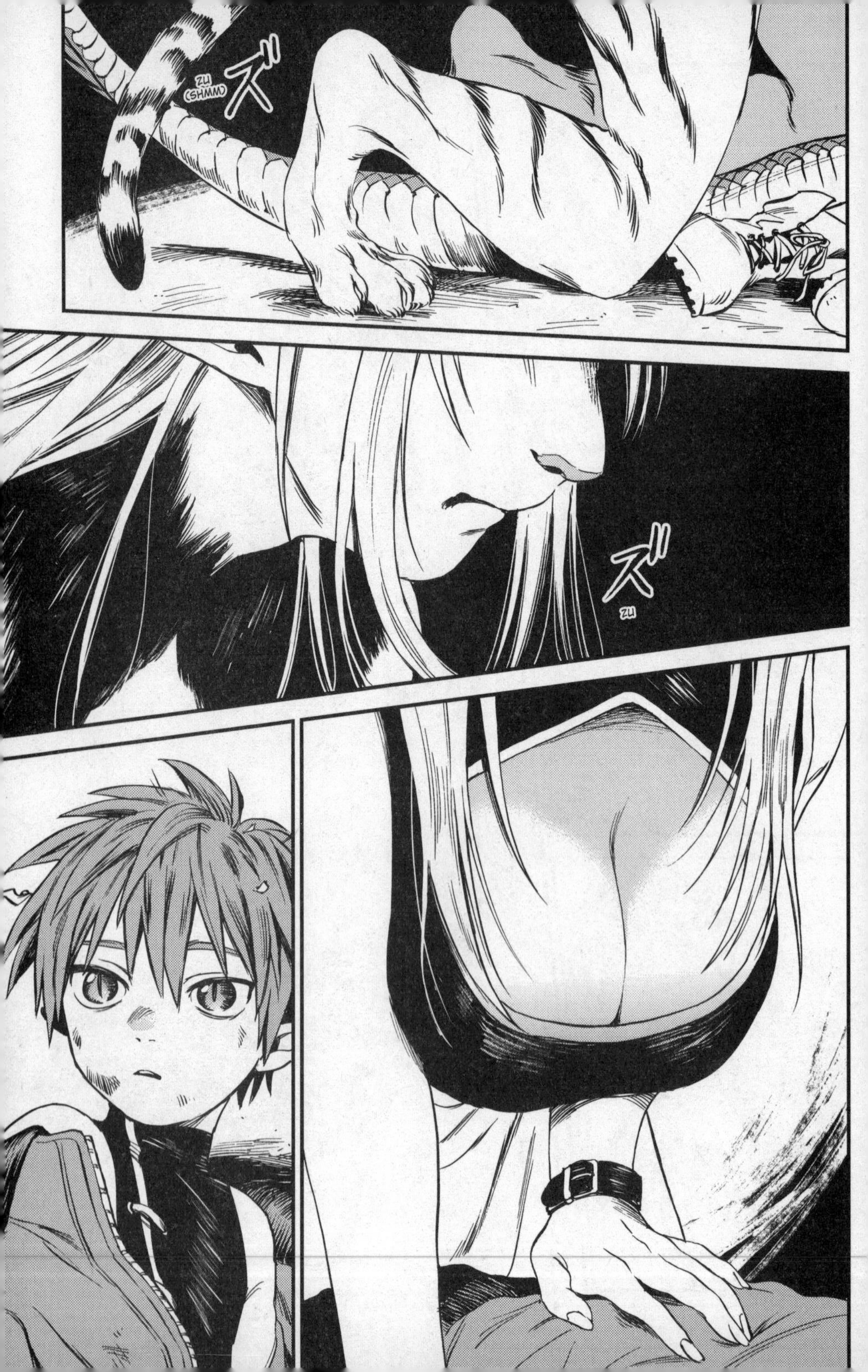
ズ
ZU (SHMM)
ズ
ZU

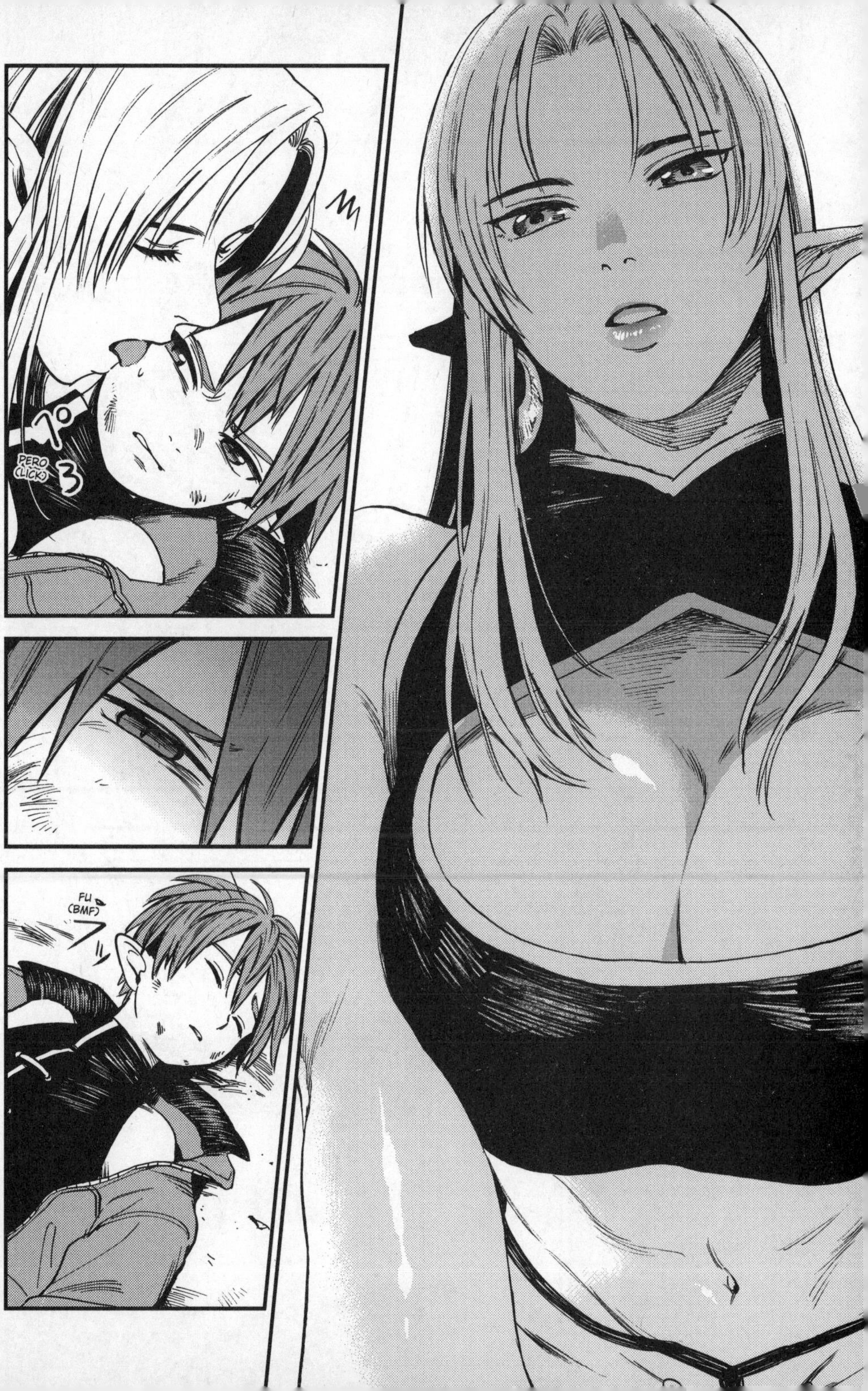
PERO (CLICK)
FU (BMF)

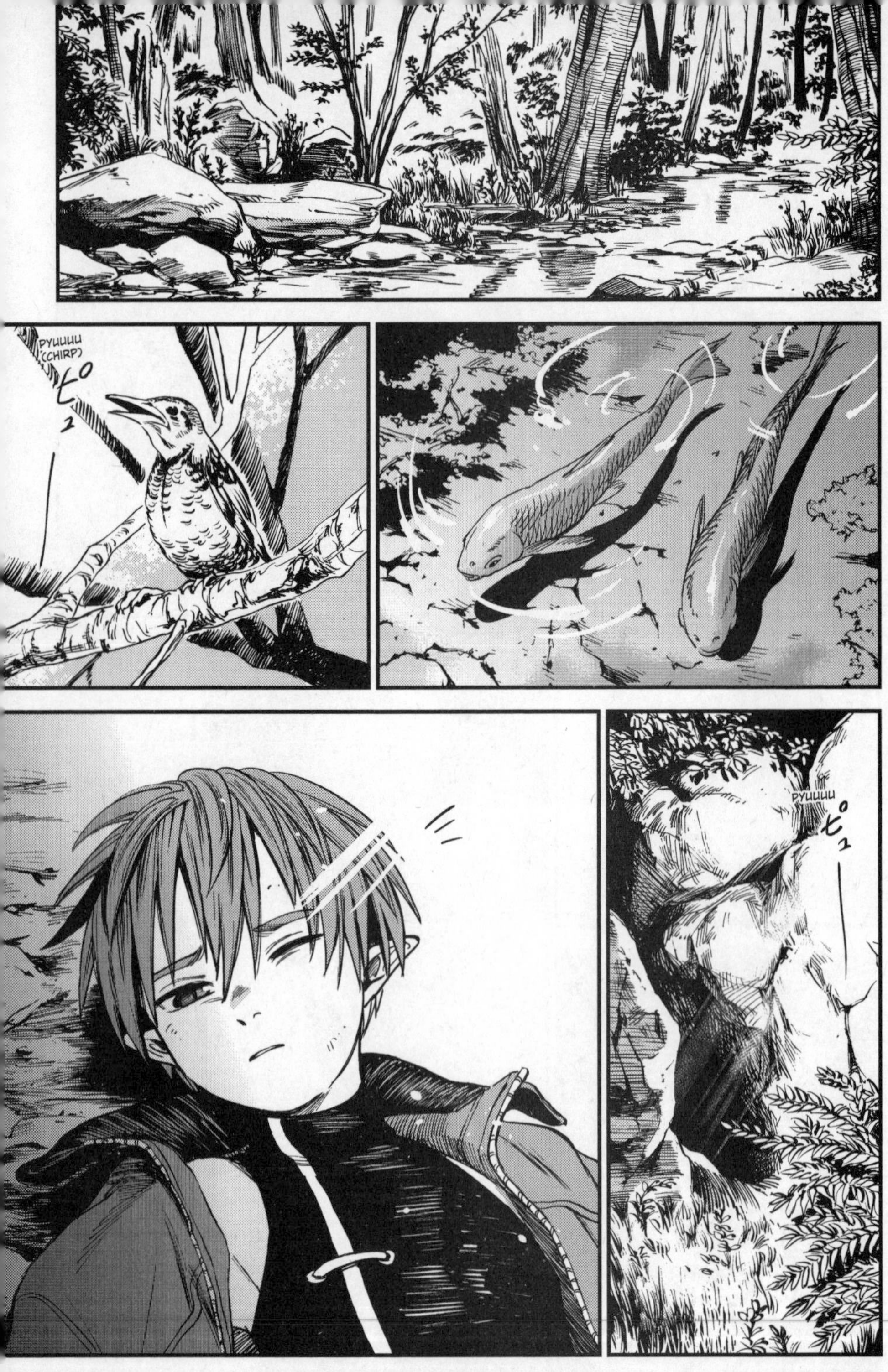
PYUUUU (CHIRP)
PYUUUU

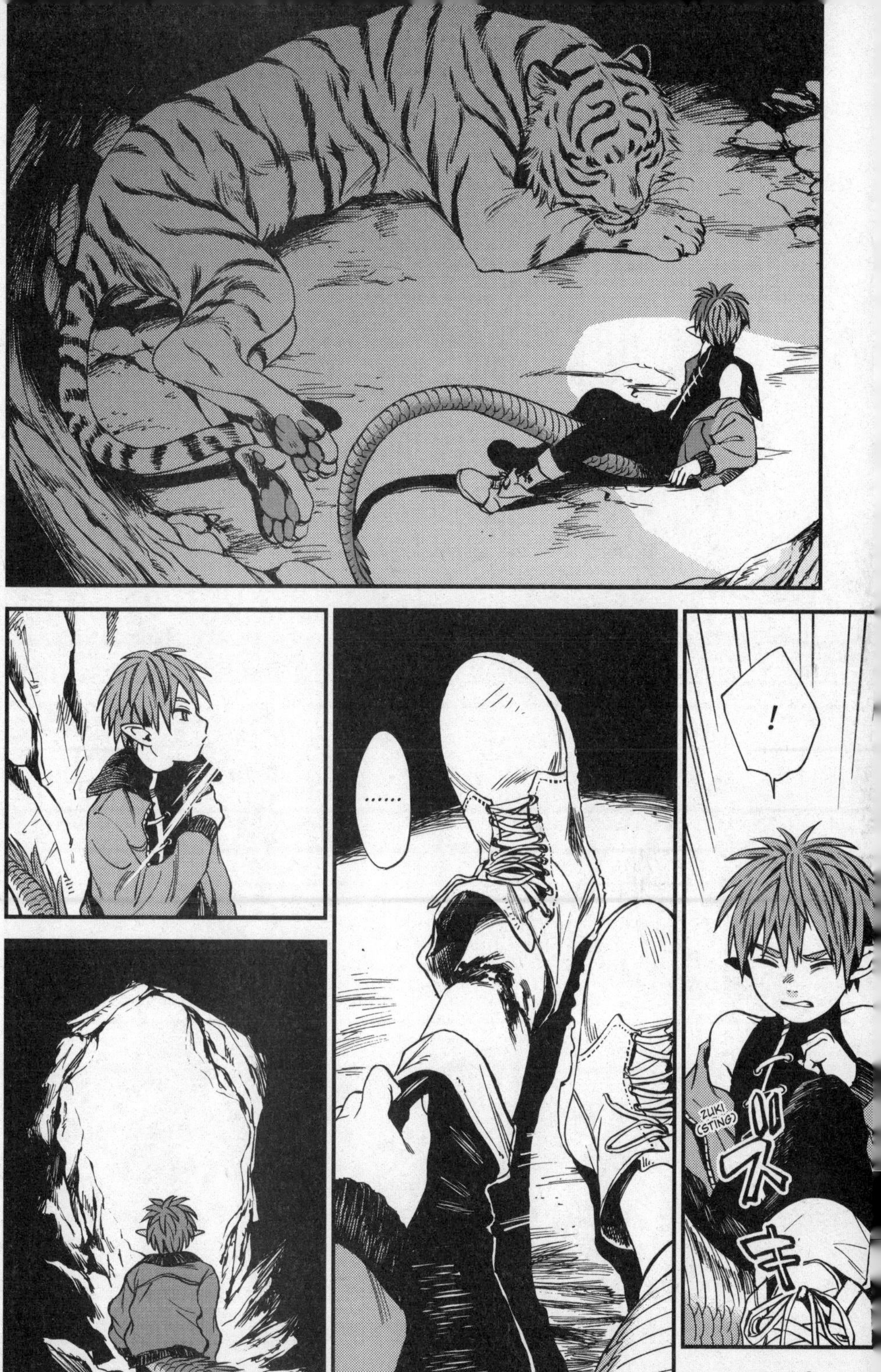
!
ZUKI (STING)
ズキ
......

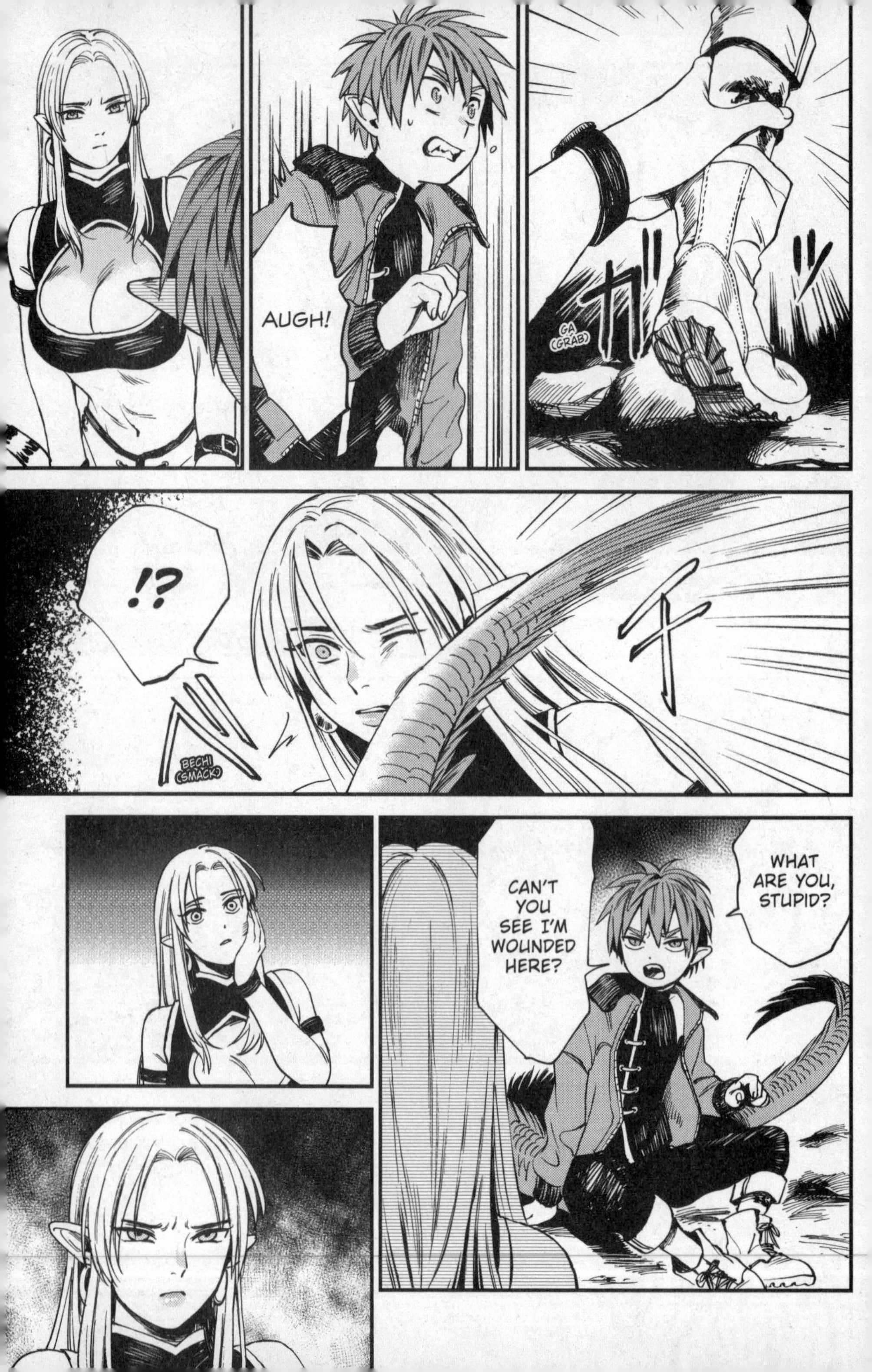
GA (GRAB)
AUGH!
!?
BECHI (SMACK)
WHAT ARE YOU, STUPID?
CAN'T YOU SEE I'M WOUNDED HERE?

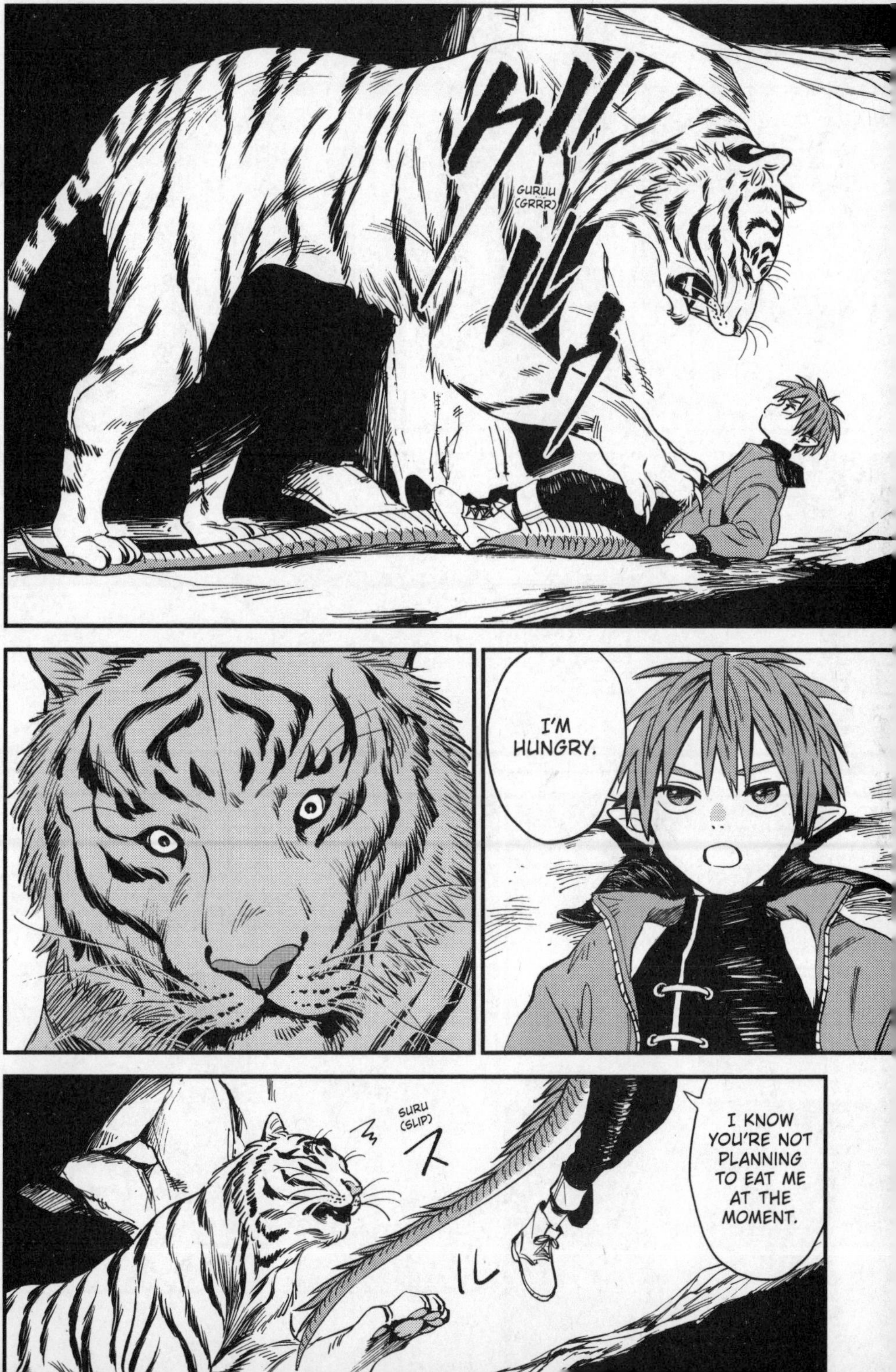
GURUU
(GRRR)
I'M HUNGRY.
I KNOW YOU'RE NOT PLANNING TO EAT ME AT THE MOMENT.
SURU
(SLIP)

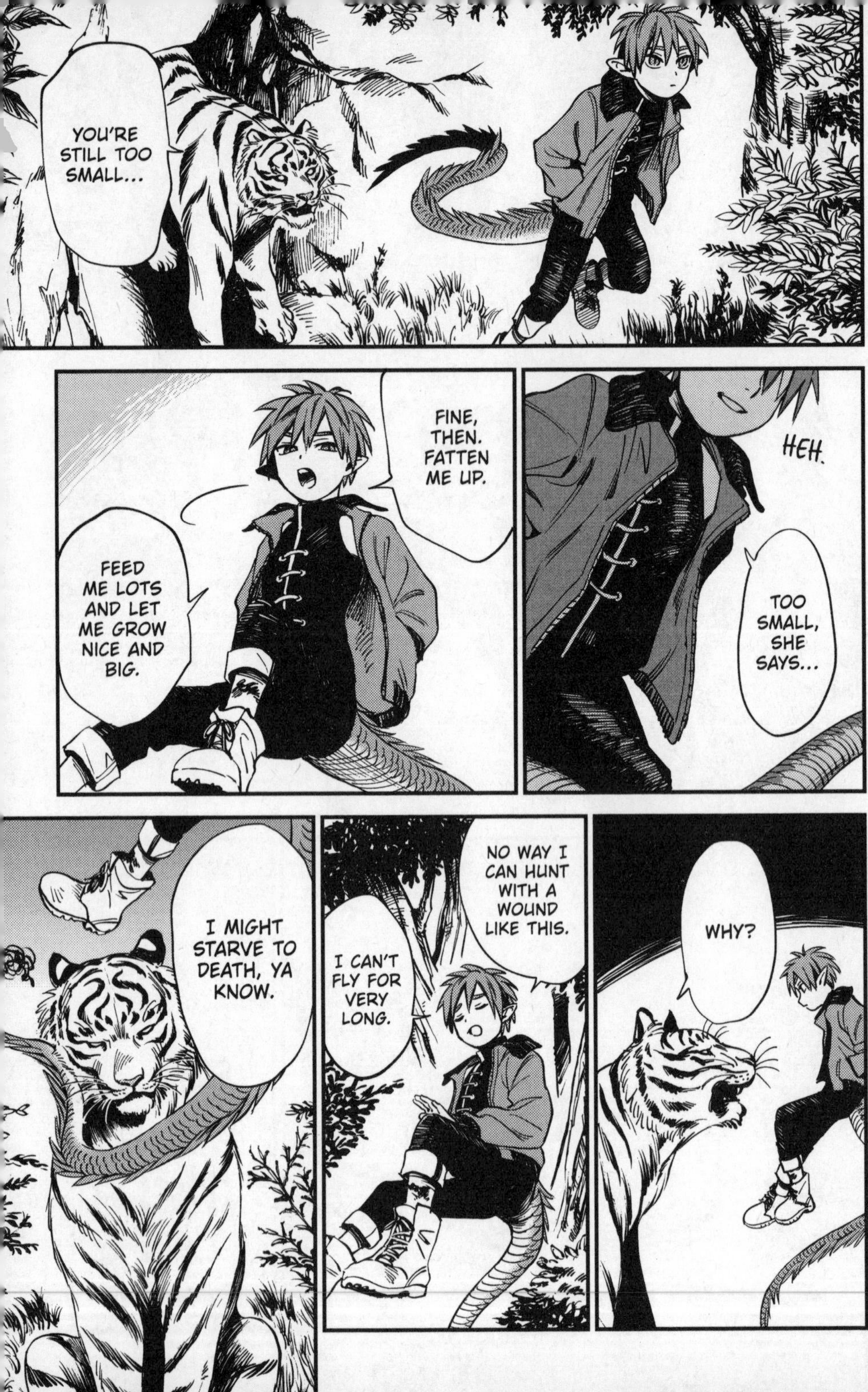
YOU'RE STILL TOO SMALL...
HEH.
TOO SMALL, SHE SAYS...
FINE, THEN. FATTEN ME UP.
FEED ME LOTS AND LET ME GROW NICE AND BIG.
WHY?
NO WAY I CAN HUNT WITH A WOUND LIKE THIS.
I CAN'T FLY FOR VERY LONG.
I MIGHT STARVE TO DEATH, YA KNOW.

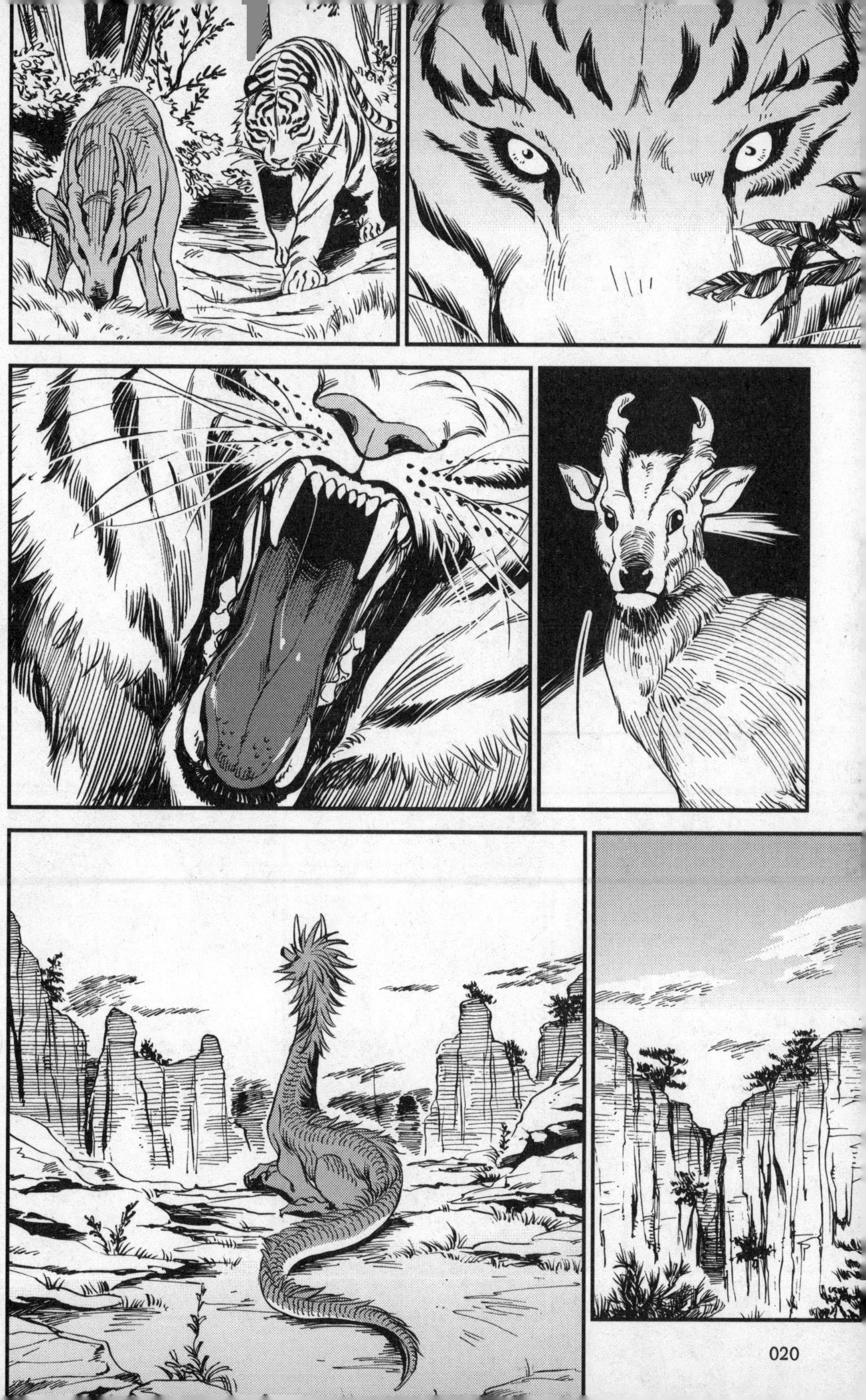

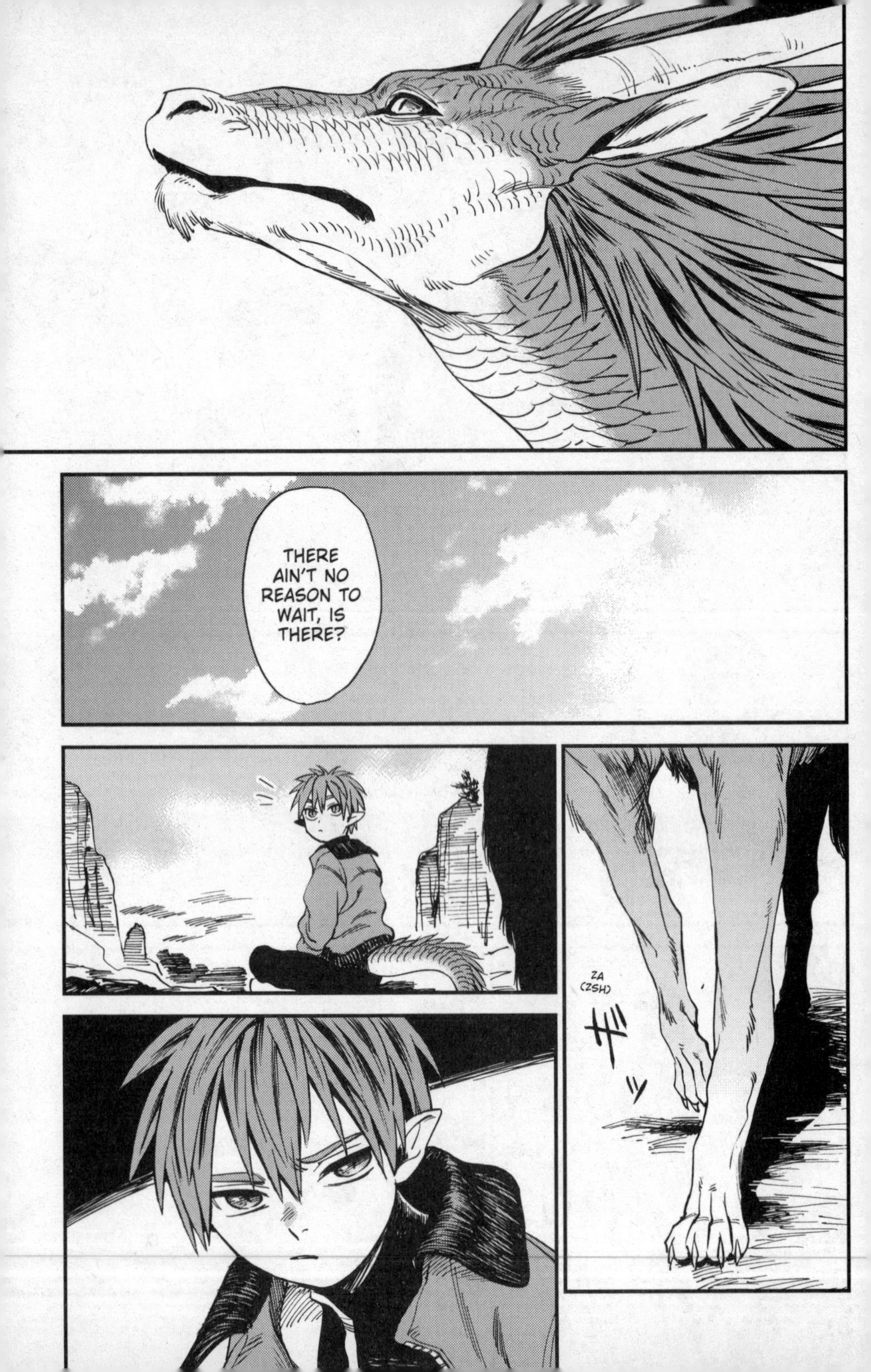
THERE AIN'T NO REASON TO WAIT, IS THERE?
ZA (ZSH)
ザッ

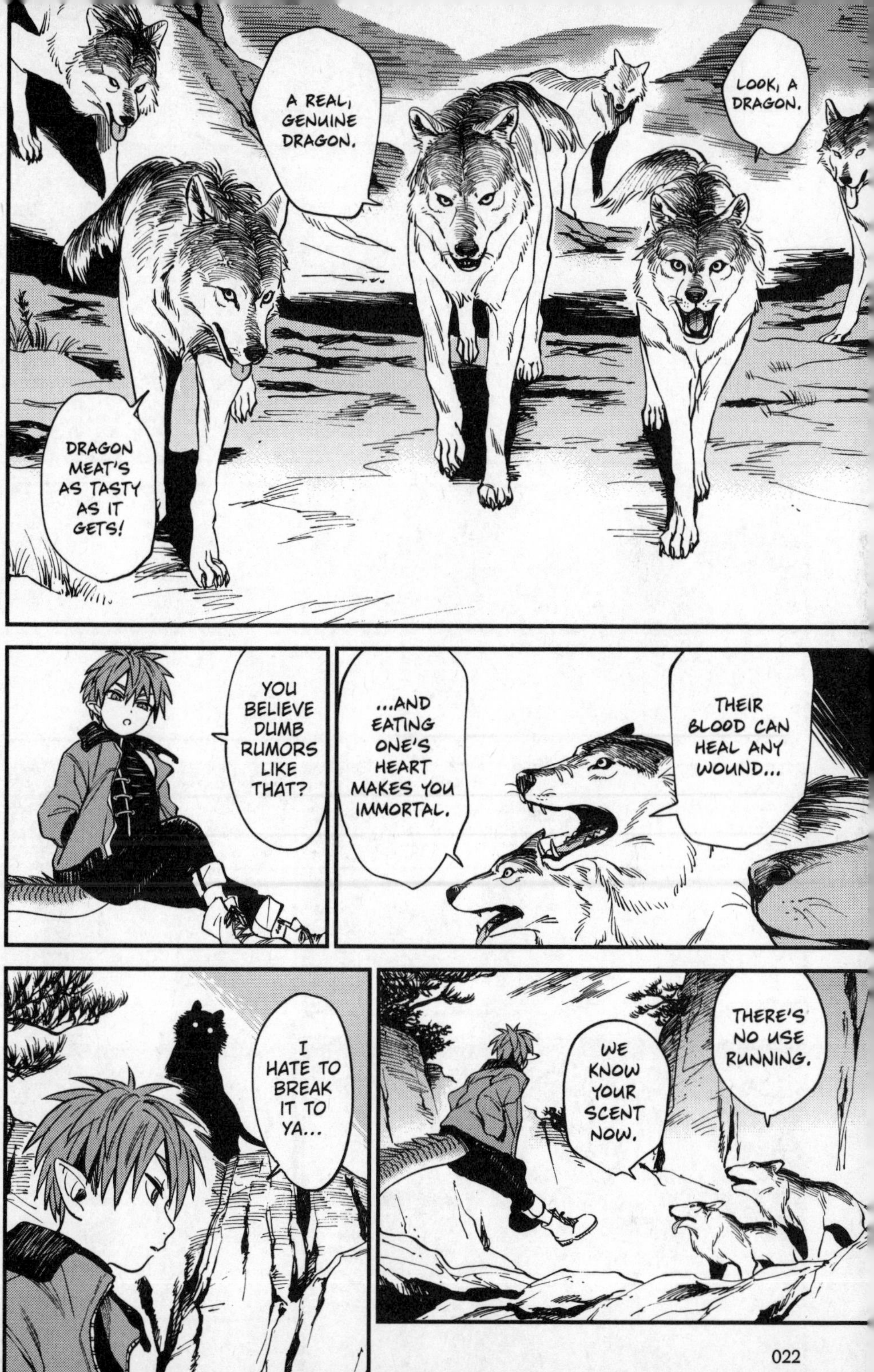
LOOK, A DRAGON.
A REAL, GENUINE DRAGON.
DRAGON MEAT'S AS TASTY AS IT GETS!
THEIR BLOOD CAN HEAL ANY WOUND...
...AND EATING ONE'S HEART MAKES YOU IMMORTAL.
YOU BELIEVE DUMB RUMORS LIKE THAT?
THERE'S NO USE RUNNING.
WE KNOW YOUR SCENT NOW.
I HATE TO BREAK IT TO YA...

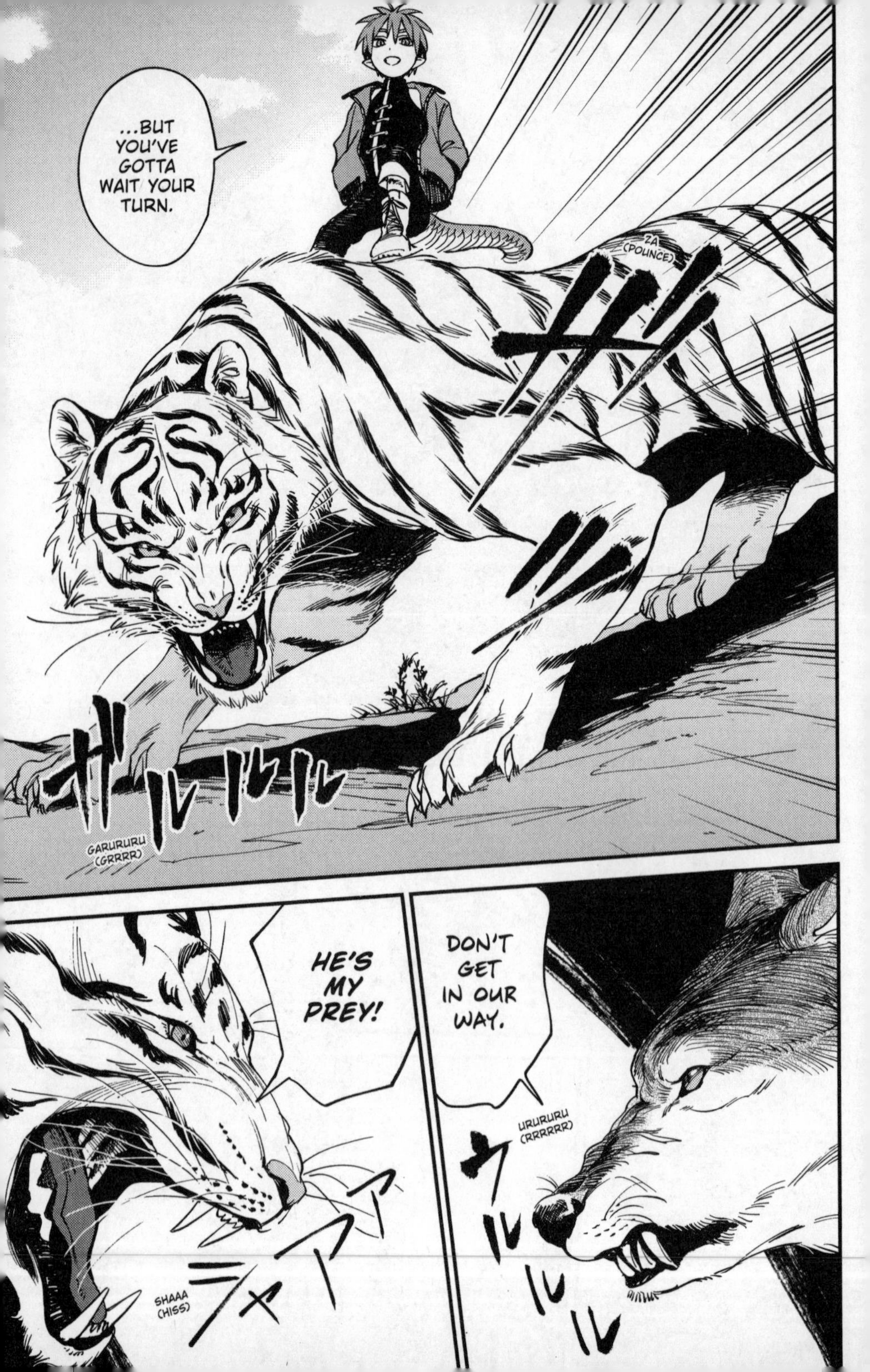

ZA (POUNCE)
...BUT YOU'VE GOTTA WAIT YOUR TURN.
GARURURU (GRRRR)
DON'T GET IN OUR WAY.
URURURU (RRRRRR)
HE'S MY PREY!
SHAAA (HISS)

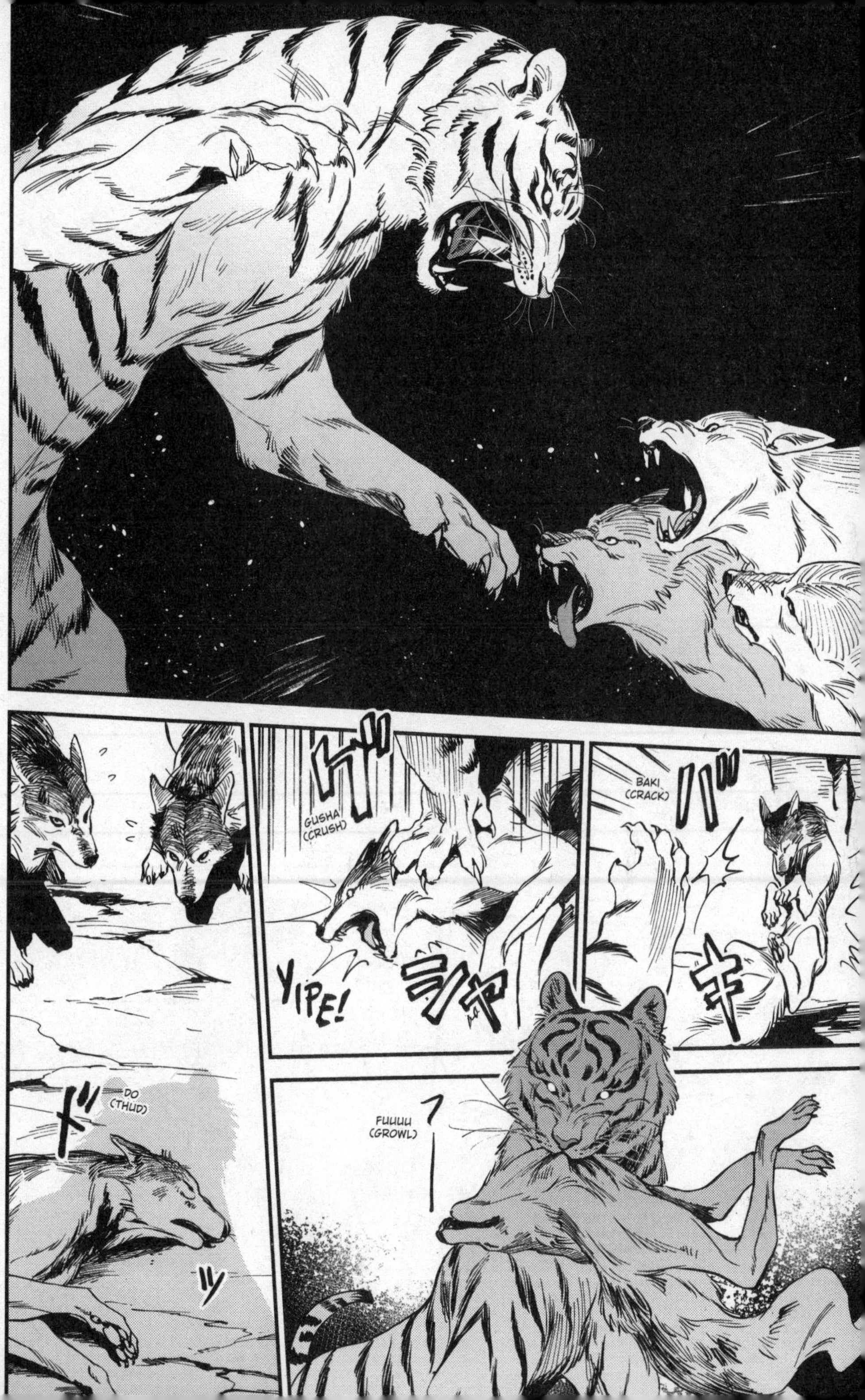
BAKI (CRACK)
バキ
GUSHA (CRUSH)
グシャ
YIPE!
FUUUU (GROWL)
DO (THUD)
ドッ

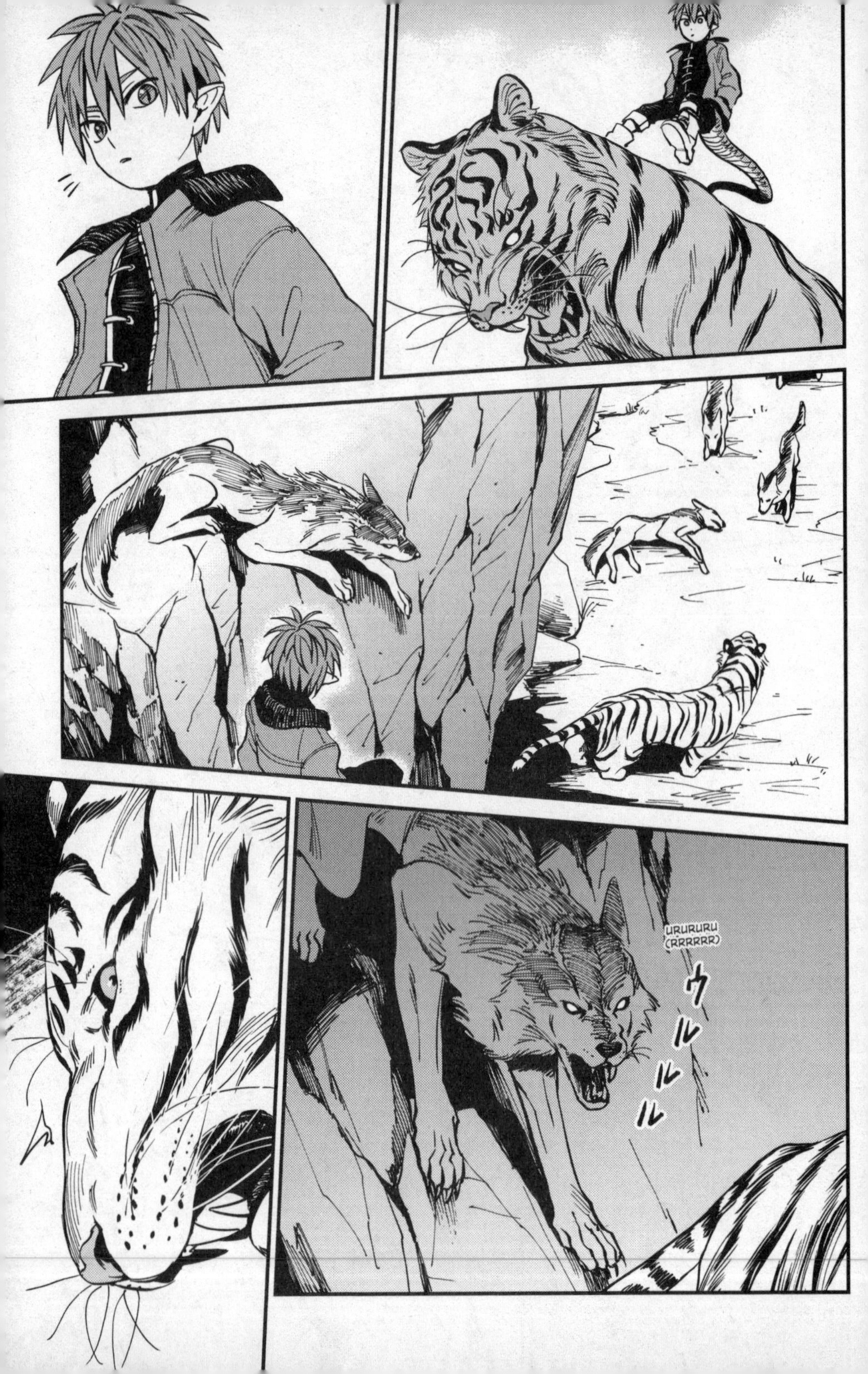
URURURU (RRRRRR)
ウルルル

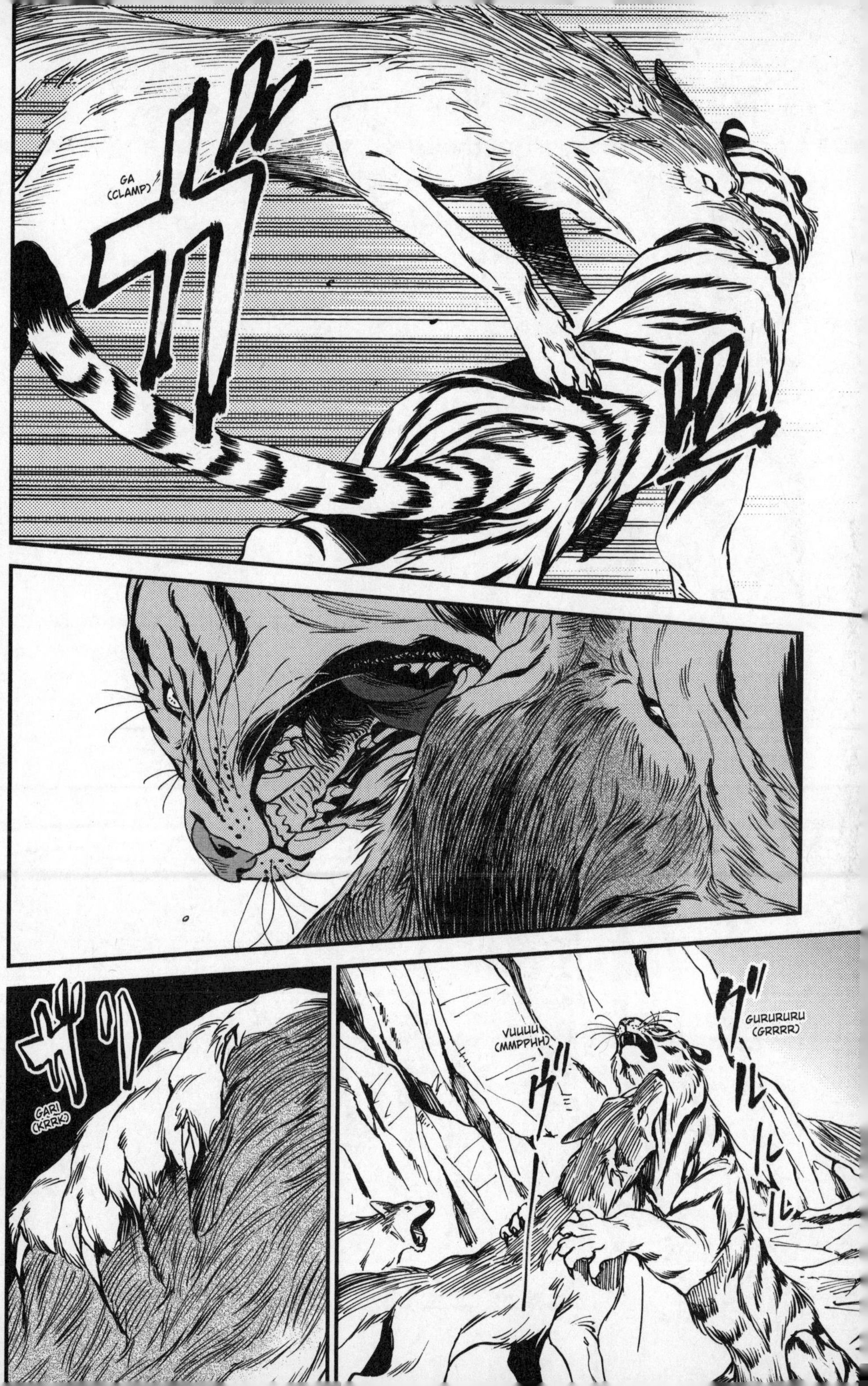
GA
(CLAMP)
GURURURU
(GRRRR)
VUUUU
(MMPPHH)
GARI
(KRRK)

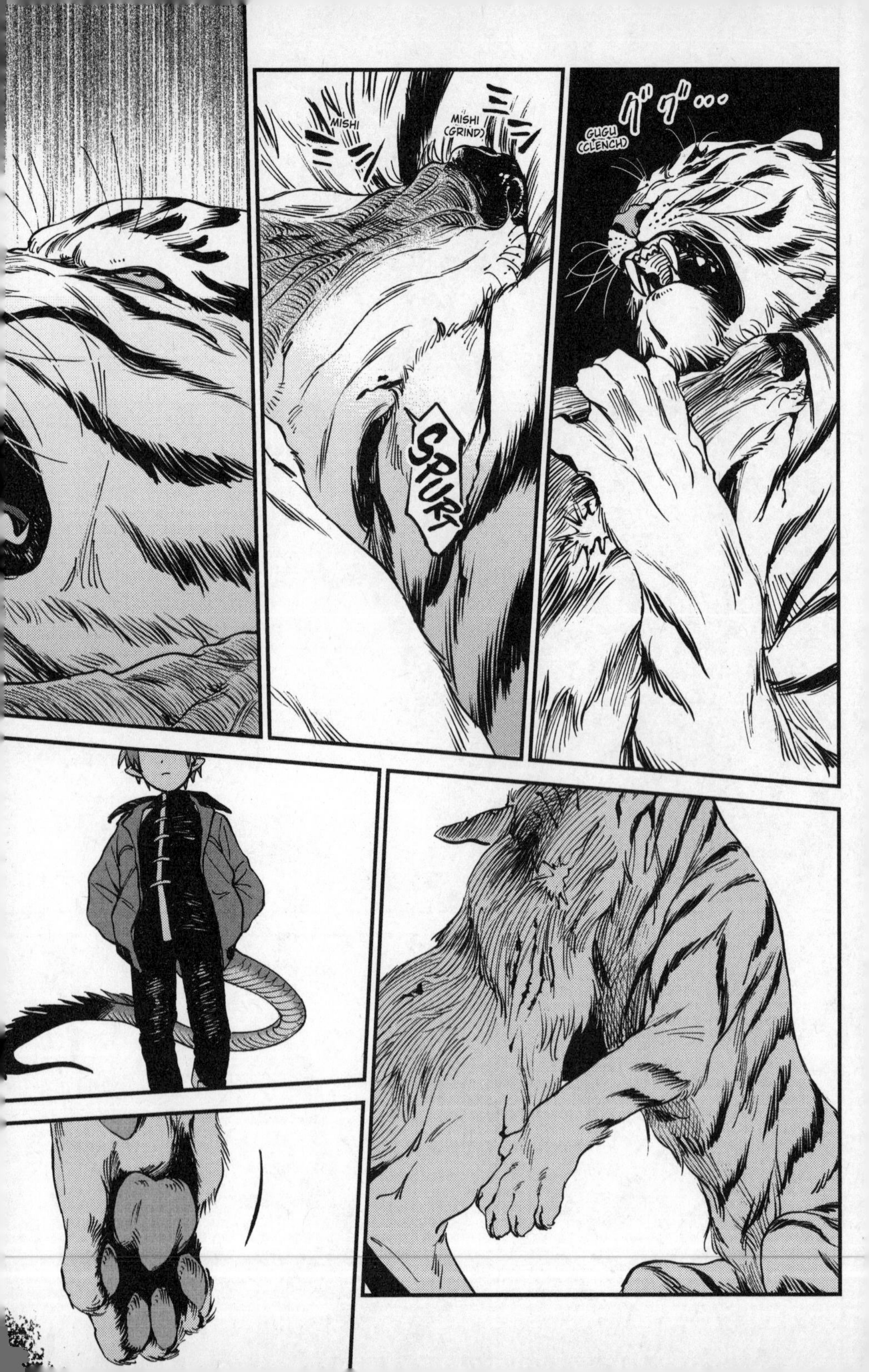
ググ…
GUGU (CLENCH)
MISHI (GRIND)
MISHI
SPURT

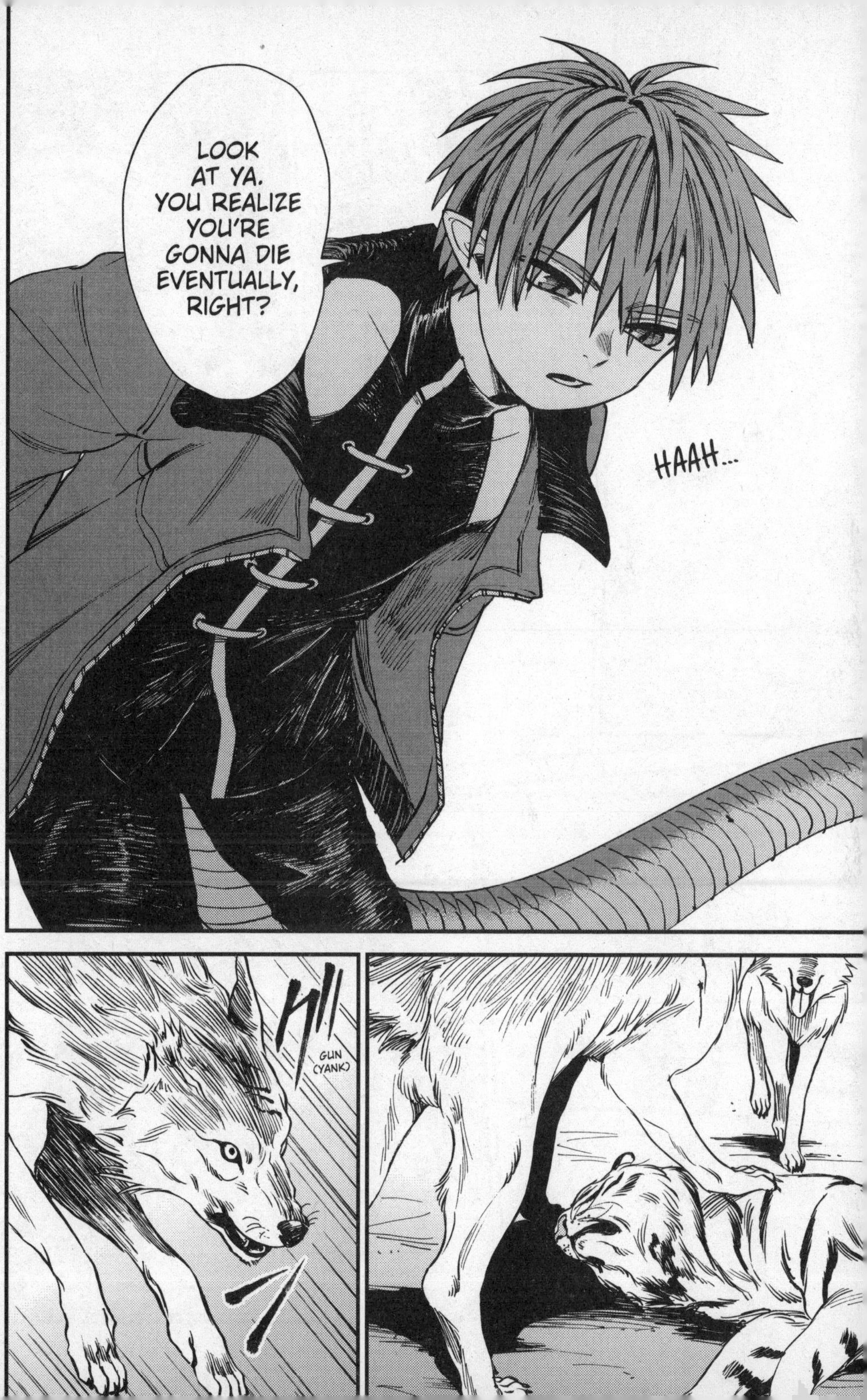
LOOK AT YA. YOU REALIZE YOU'RE GONNA DIE EVENTUALLY, RIGHT?
HAAH...
GUN (YANK)

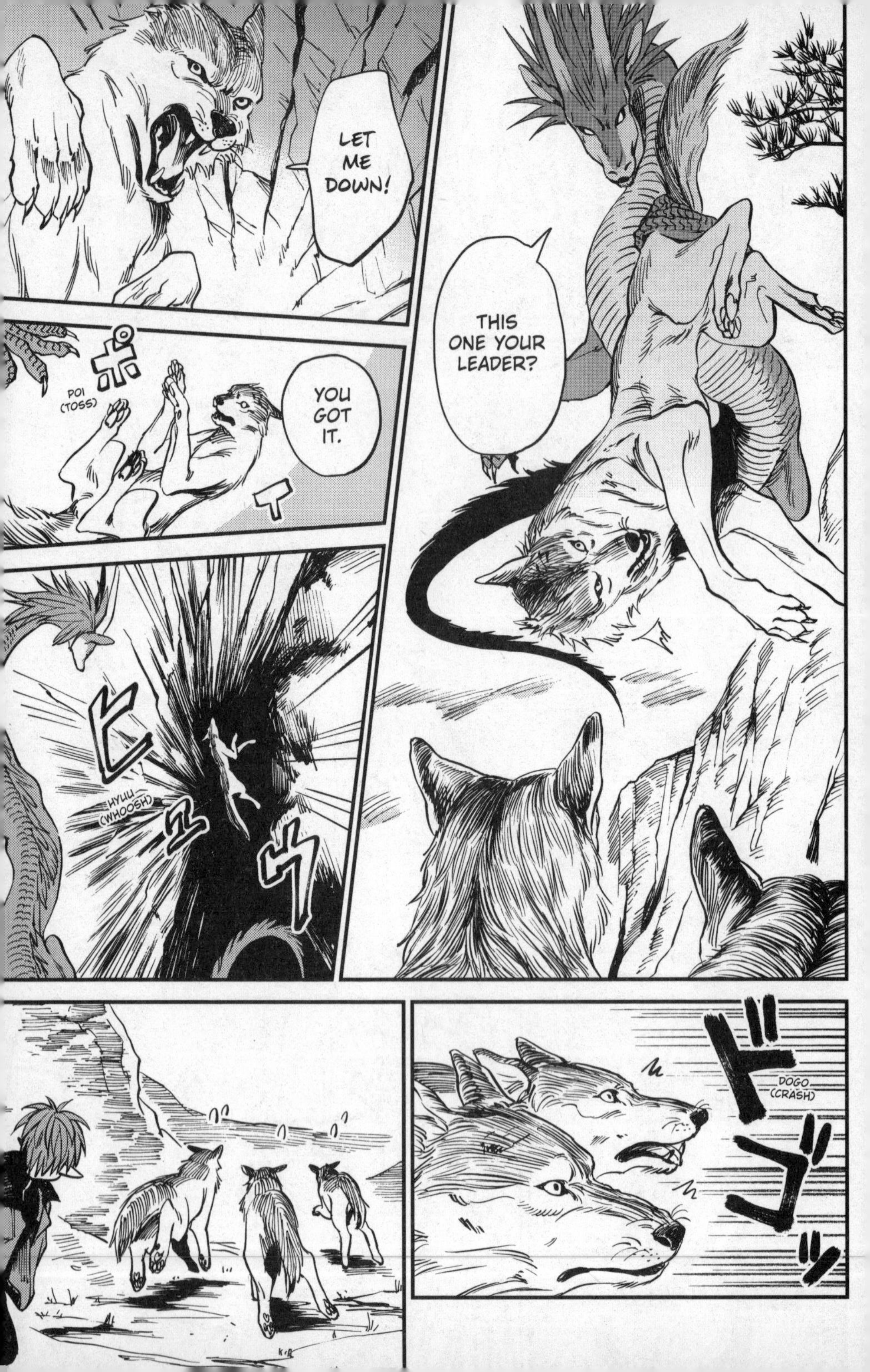
THIS ONE YOUR LEADER?
LET ME DOWN!
YOU GOT IT.
POI (TOSS)
HYUU (WHOOSH)
DOGO (CRASH)

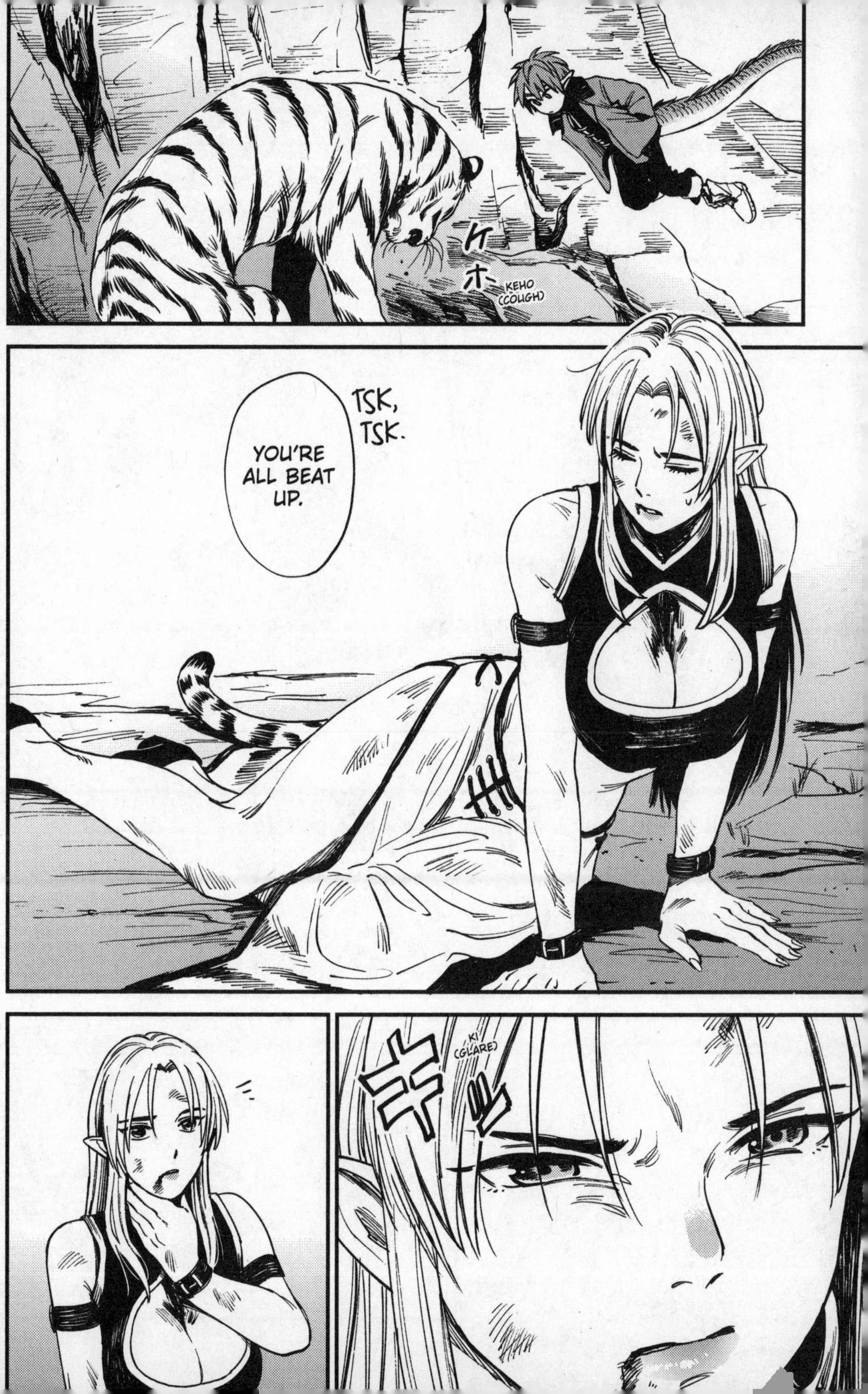
ケホー
KEHO (COUGH)
TSK, TSK.
YOU'RE ALL BEAT UP.
キッ
KI (GLARE)

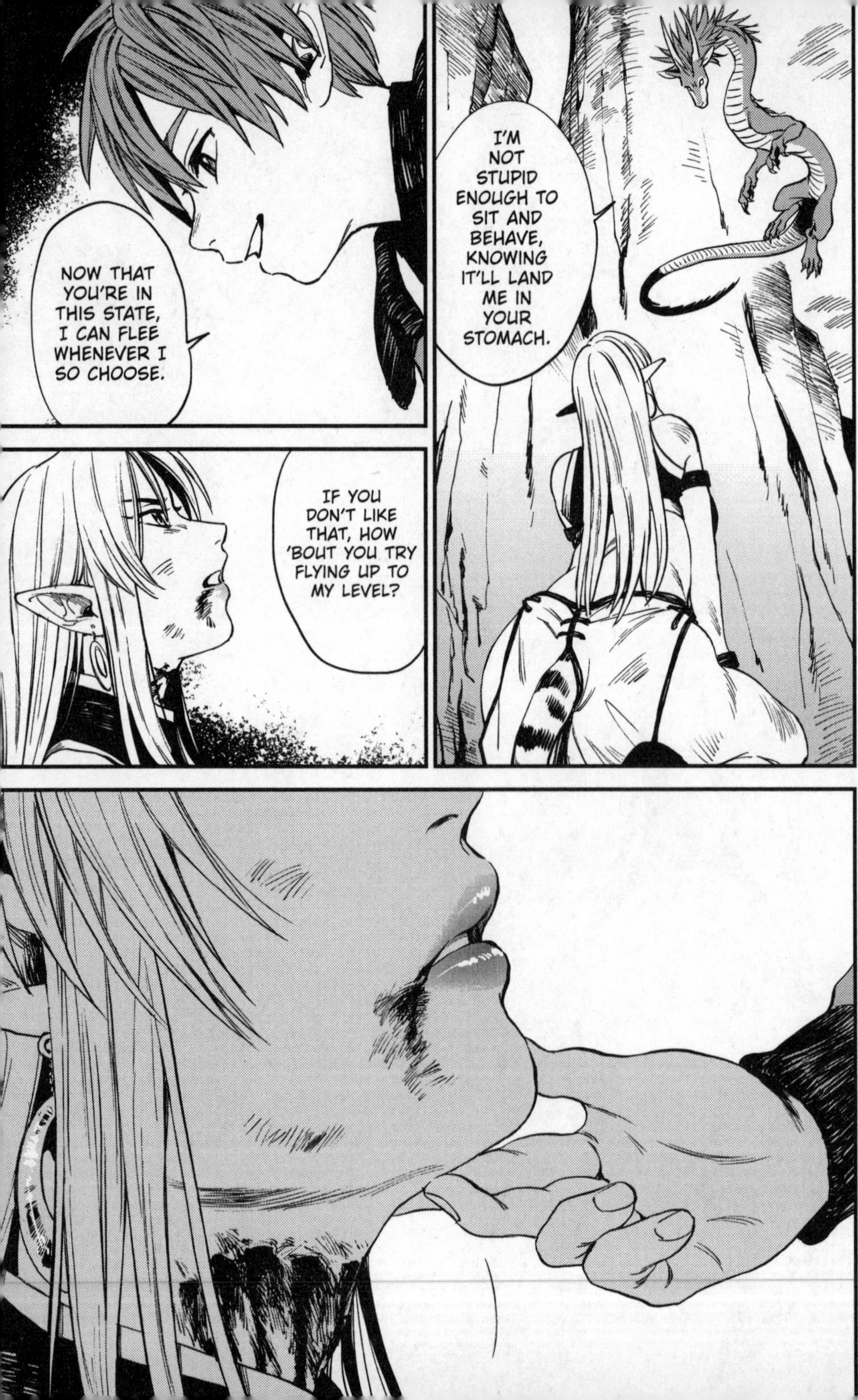
I'M NOT STUPID ENOUGH TO SIT AND BEHAVE, KNOWING IT'LL LAND ME IN YOUR STOMACH.
NOW THAT YOU'RE IN THIS STATE, I CAN FLEE WHENEVER I SO CHOOSE.
IF YOU DON'T LIKE THAT, HOW 'BOUT YOU TRY FLYING UP TO MY LEVEL?

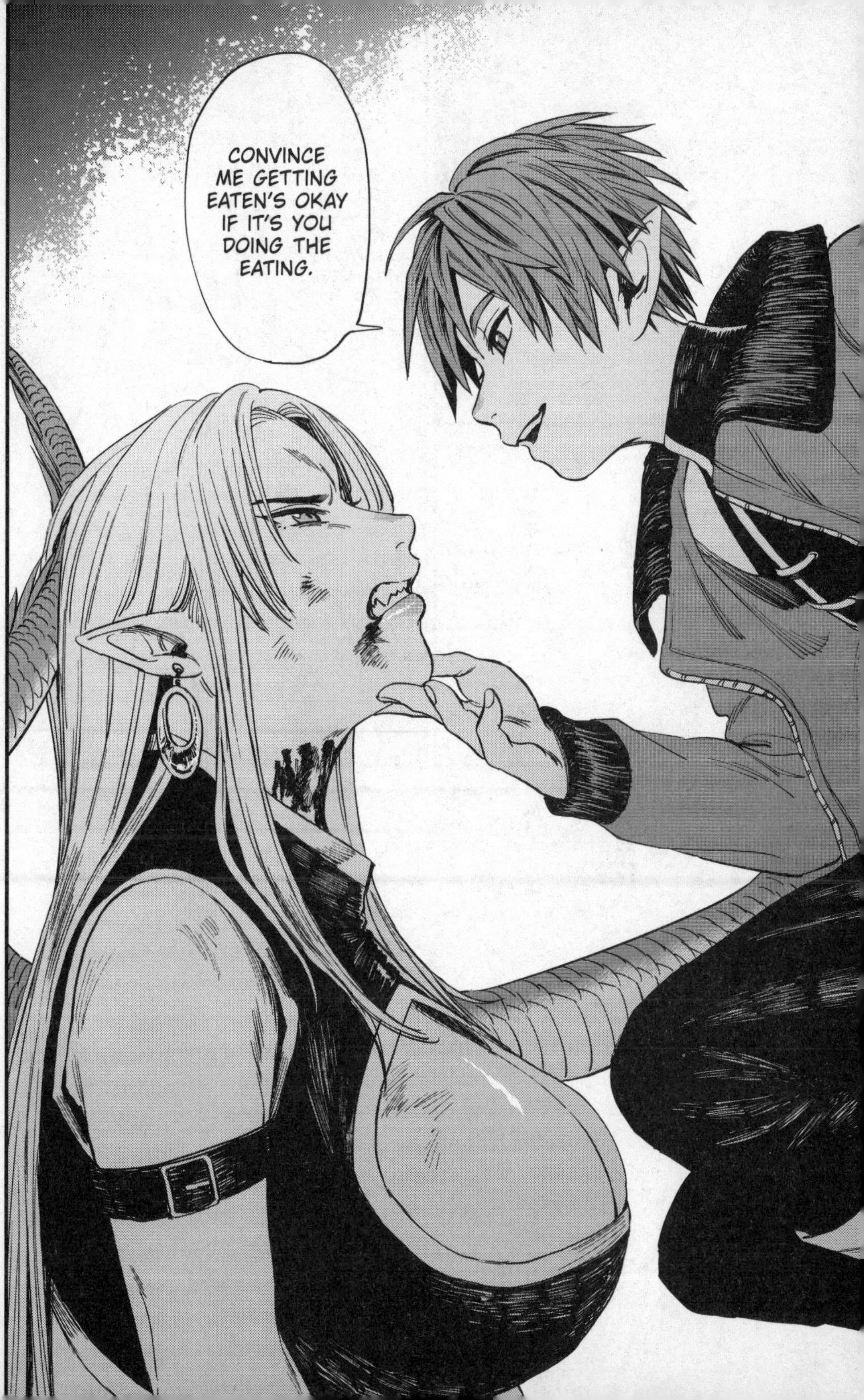
CONVINCE ME GETTING EATEN'S OKAY IF IT'S YOU DOING THE EATING.

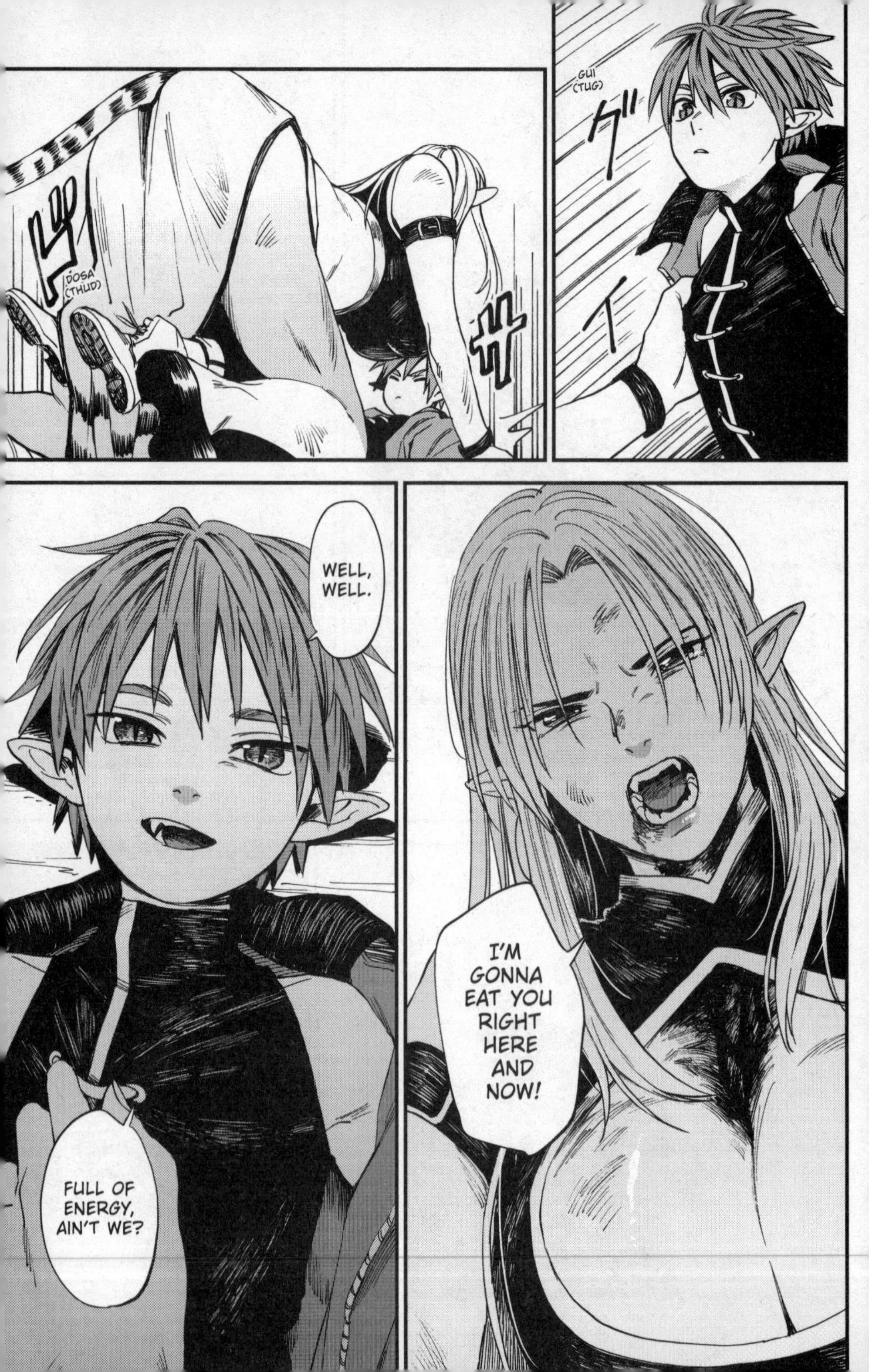
GUI
(TUG)
DOSA
(THUD)
I'M GONNA EAT YOU RIGHT HERE AND NOW!
WELL, WELL.
FULL OF ENERGY, AIN'T WE?

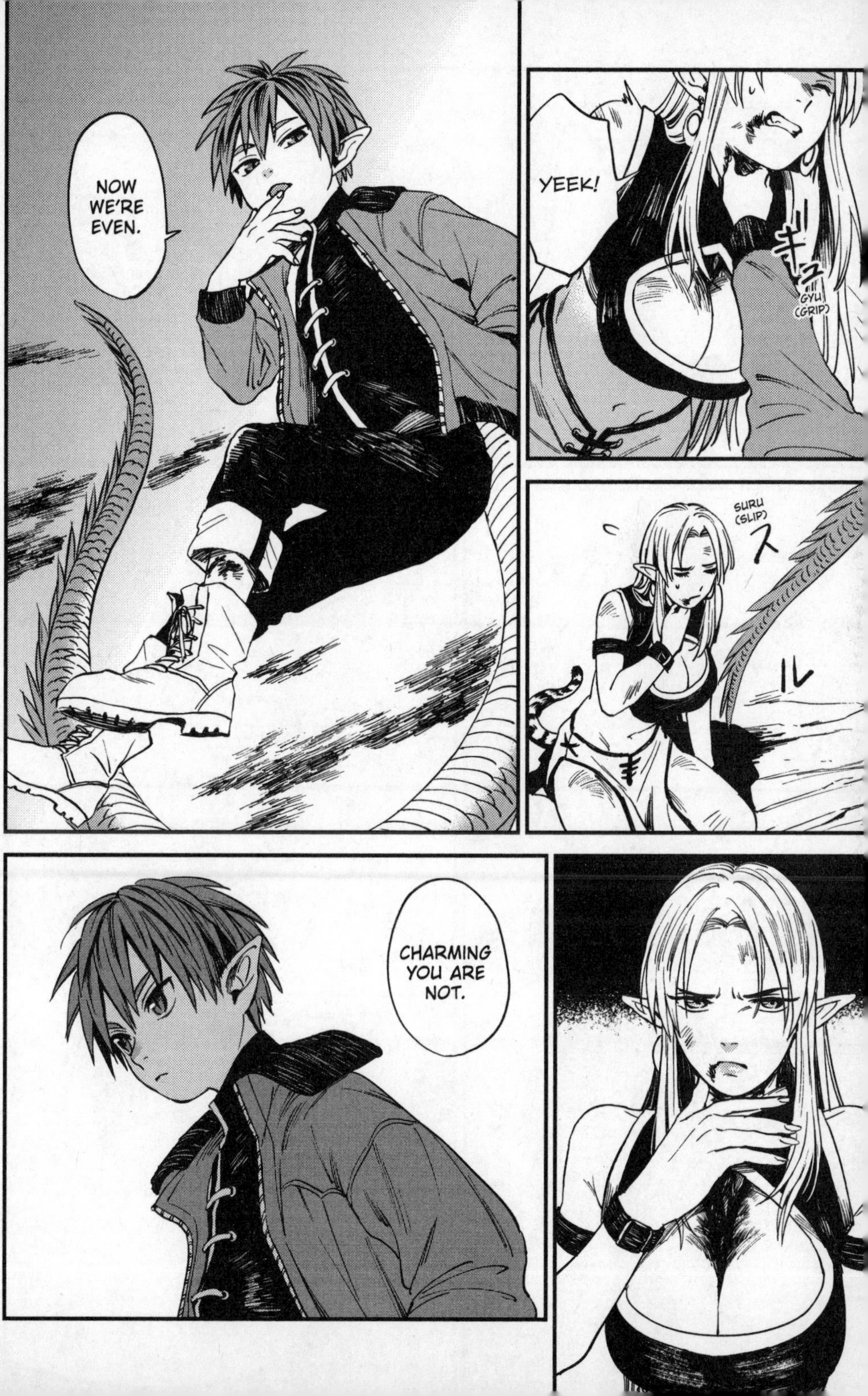
YEEK!
ギュ
GYU (GRIP)
SURU (SLIP)
スル
NOW WE'RE EVEN.
CHARMING YOU ARE NOT.

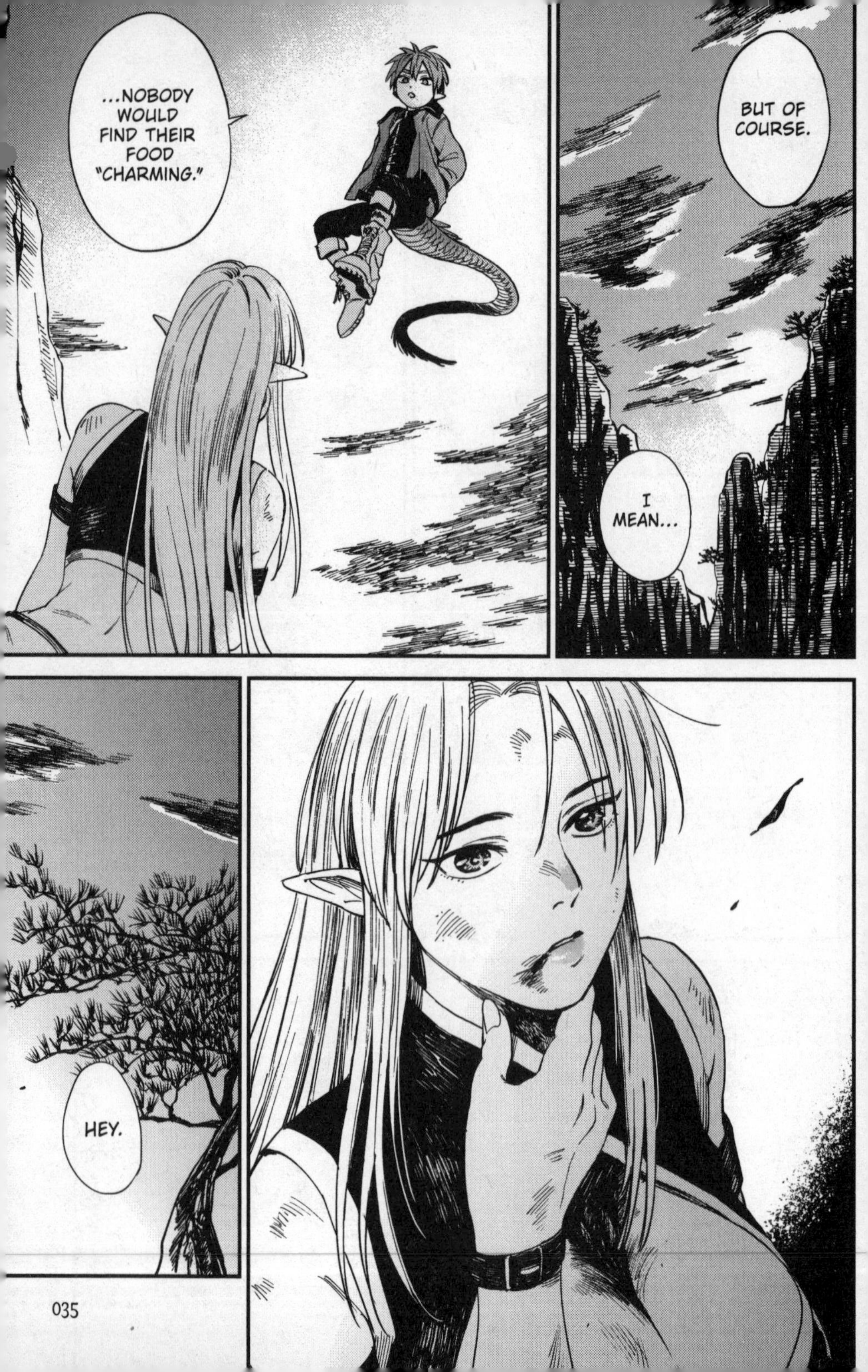
BUT OF COURSE.
I MEAN...
...NOBODY WOULD FIND THEIR FOOD "CHARMING."
HEY.

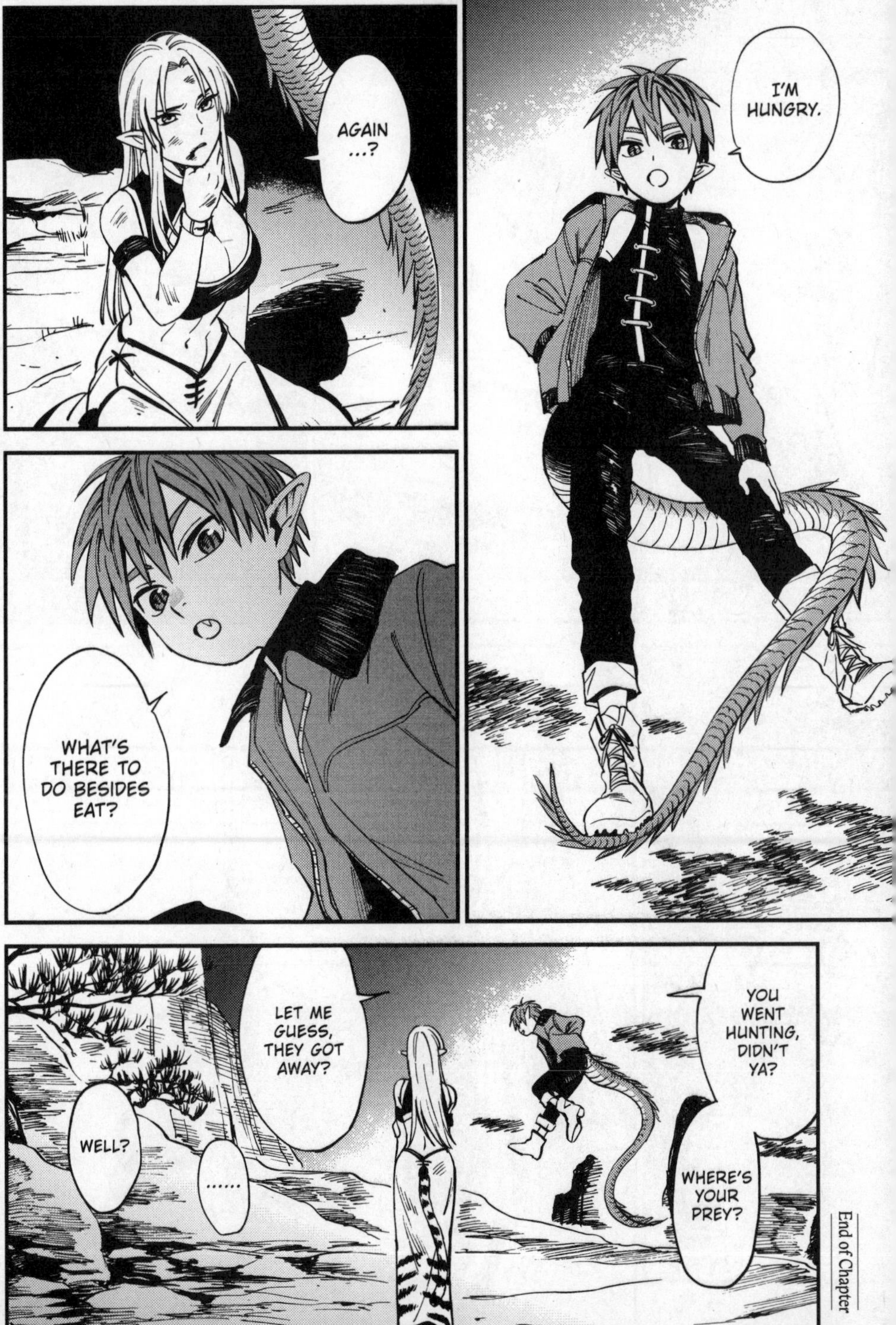
I'M HUNGRY.
AGAIN ...?
WHAT'S THERE TO DO BESIDES EAT?
YOU WENT HUNTING, DIDN'T YA?
WHERE'S YOUR PREY?
LET ME GUESS, THEY GOT AWAY?
......
WELL?

End of Chapter

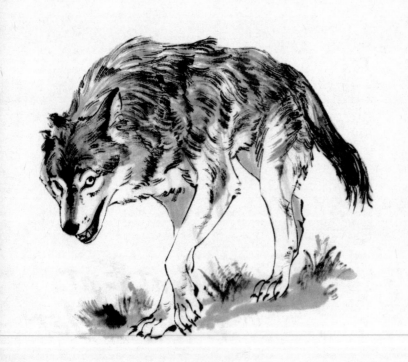

The **Tiger Won't Eat** *the* **Dragon Yet**

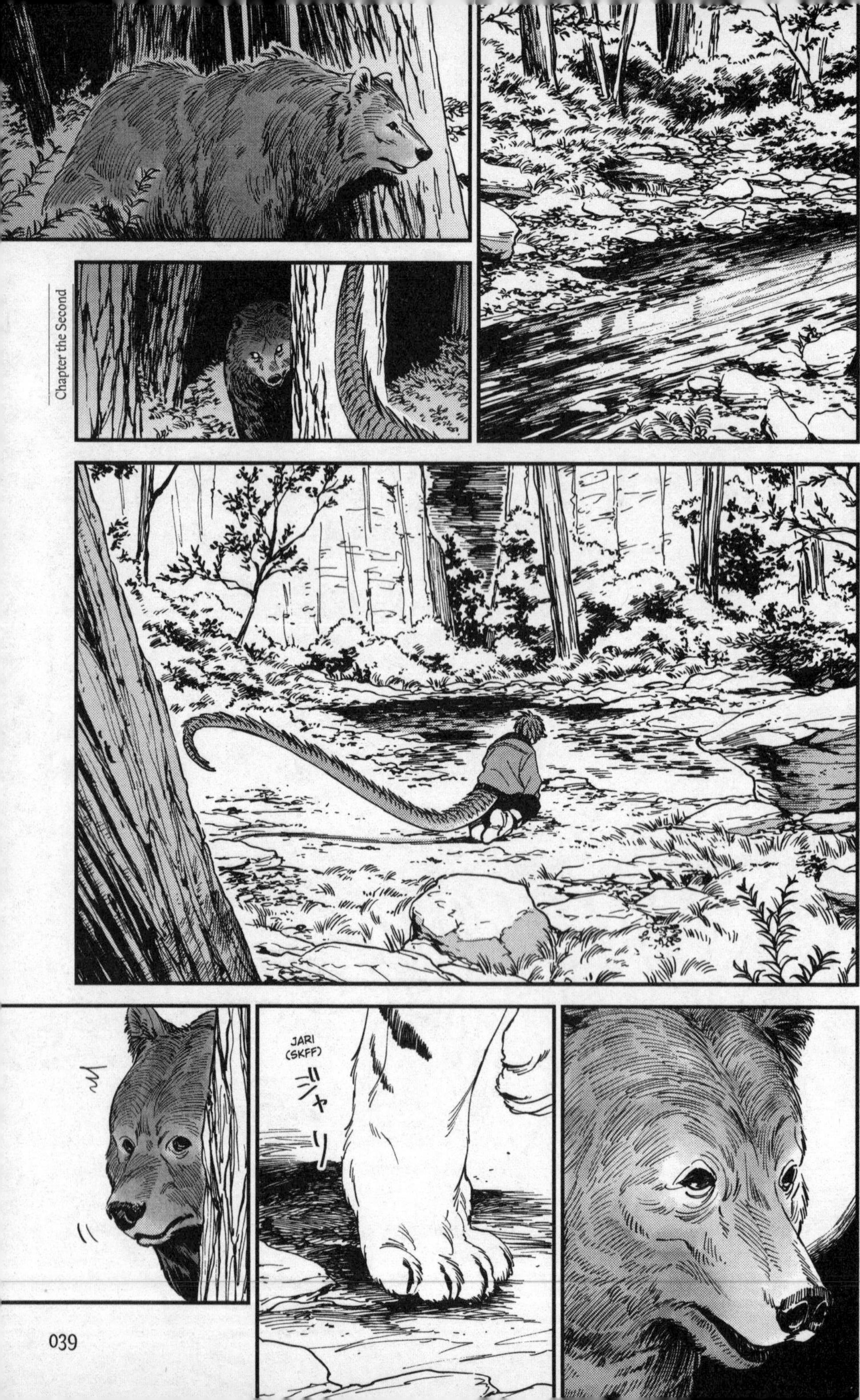
JARI
(SKFF)
ジャリ

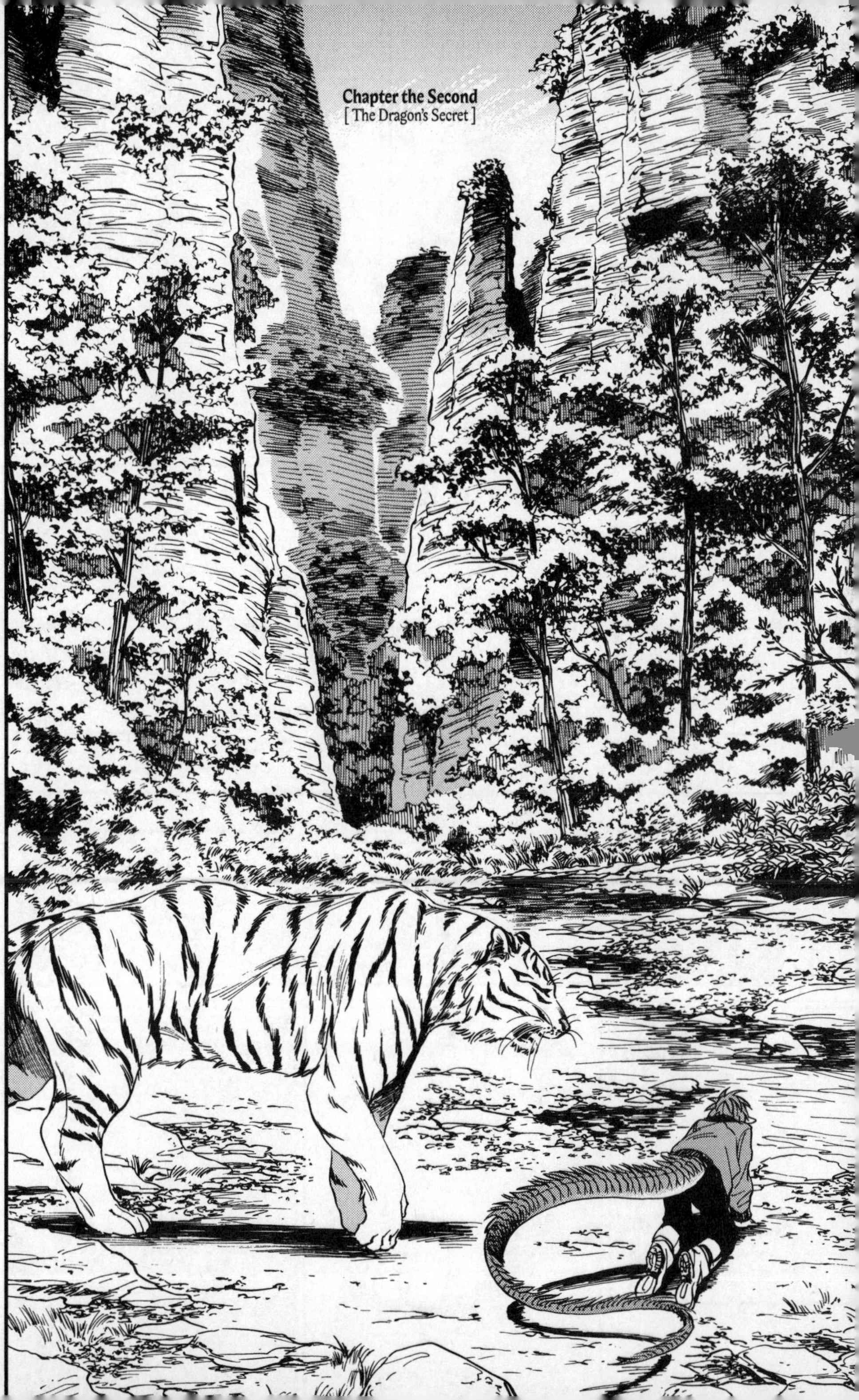
Chapter the Second
[The Dragon's Secret]

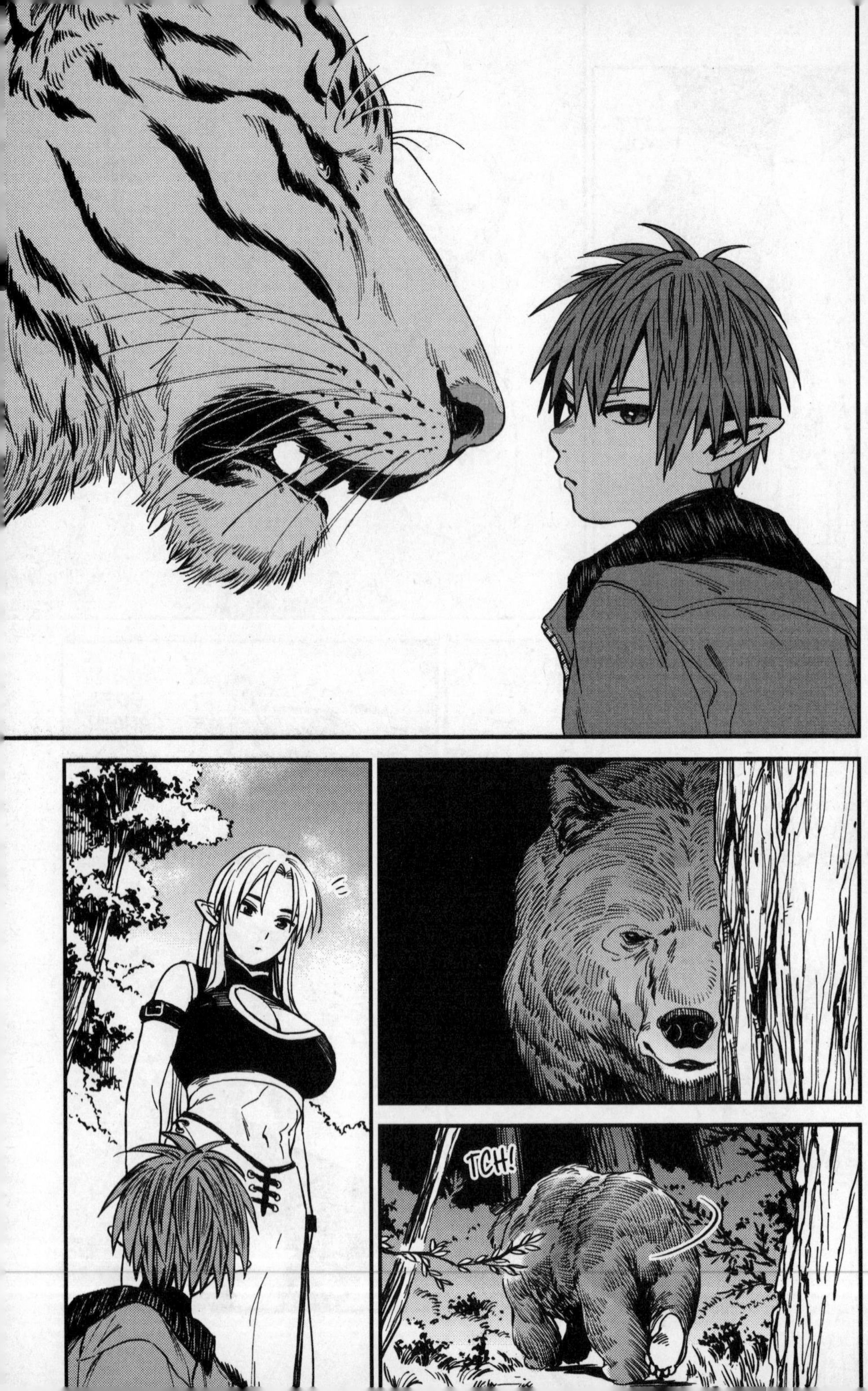
TCH!

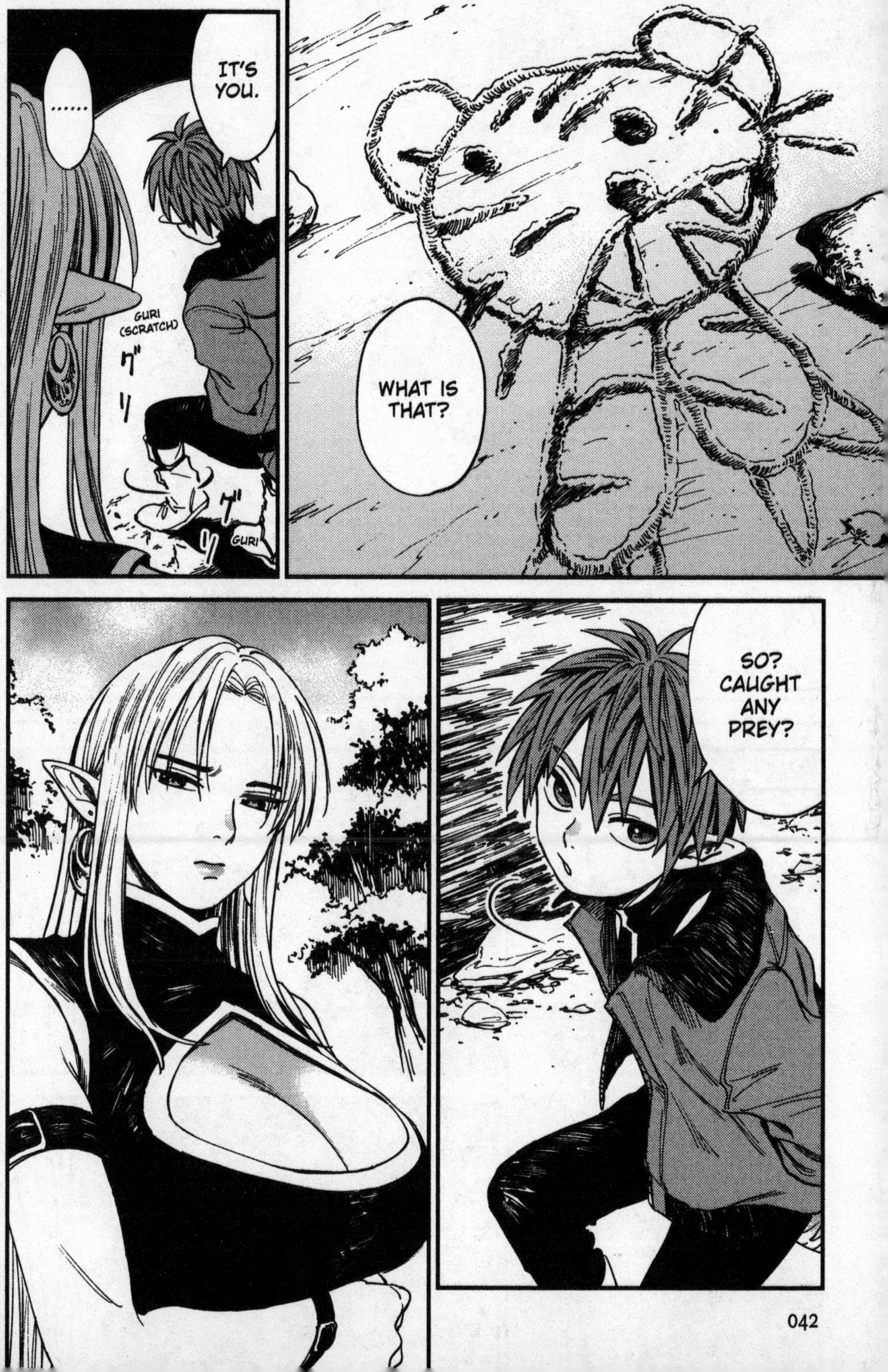
WHAT IS THAT?
IT'S YOU.
......
GURI (SCRATCH)
グリ
グリ
GURI
SO? CAUGHT ANY PREY?

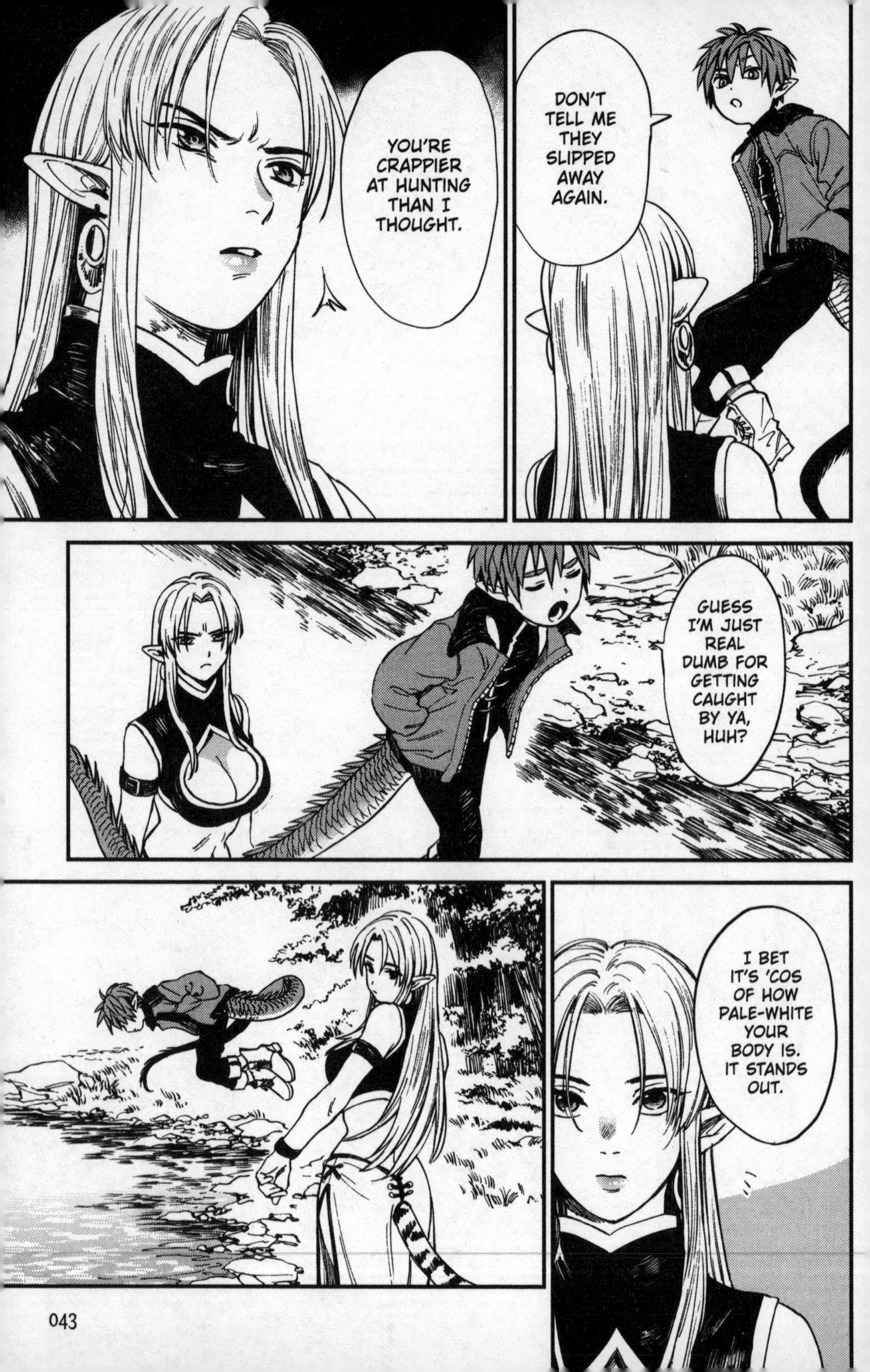
DON'T TELL ME THEY SLIPPED AWAY AGAIN.
YOU'RE CRAPPIER AT HUNTING THAN I THOUGHT.
GUESS I'M JUST REAL DUMB FOR GETTING CAUGHT BY YA, HUH?
I BET IT'S 'COS OF HOW PALE-WHITE YOUR BODY IS. IT STANDS OUT.

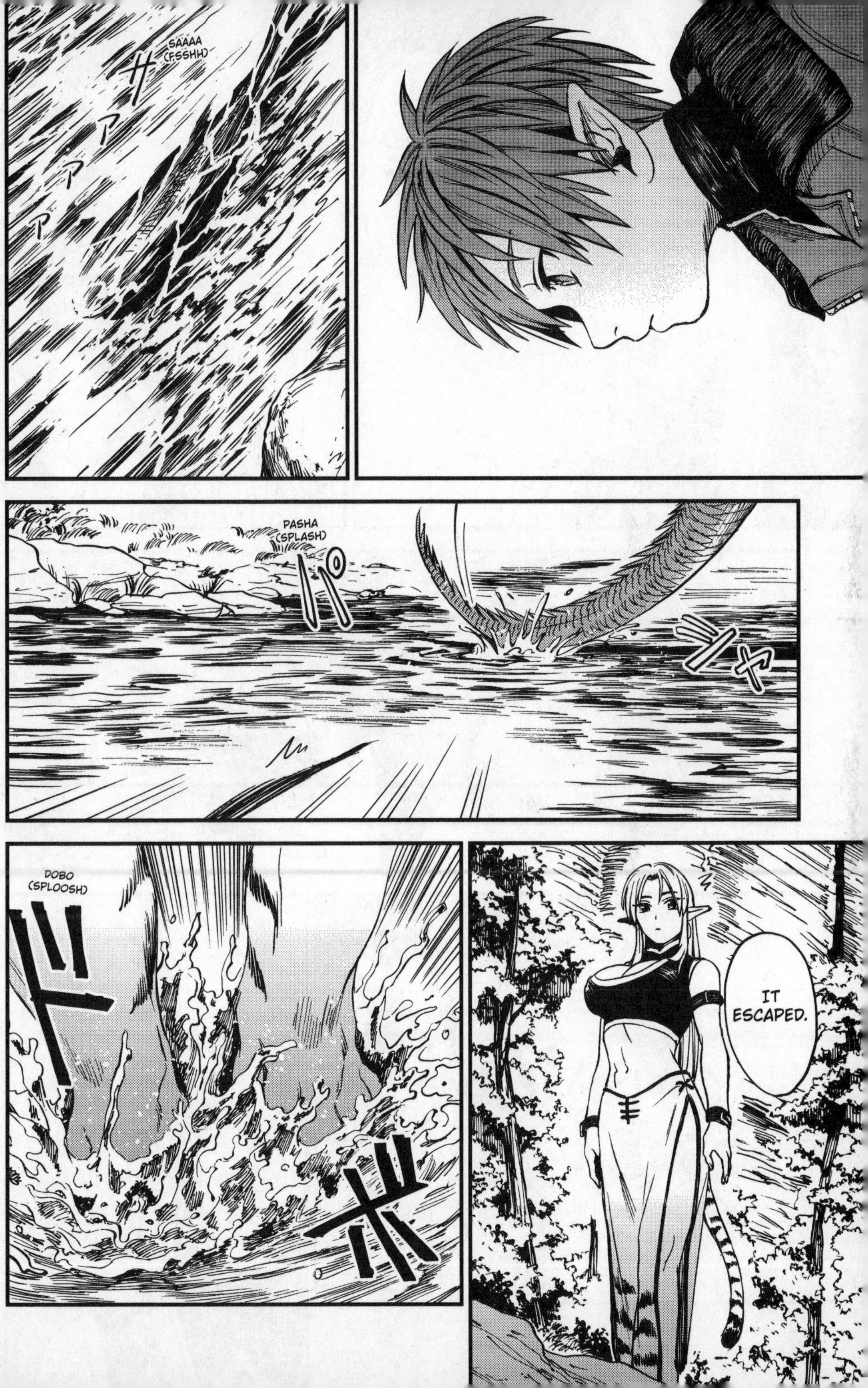
SAAAA (FSSHH)
PASHA (SPLASH)
IT ESCAPED.
DOBO (SPLOOSH)

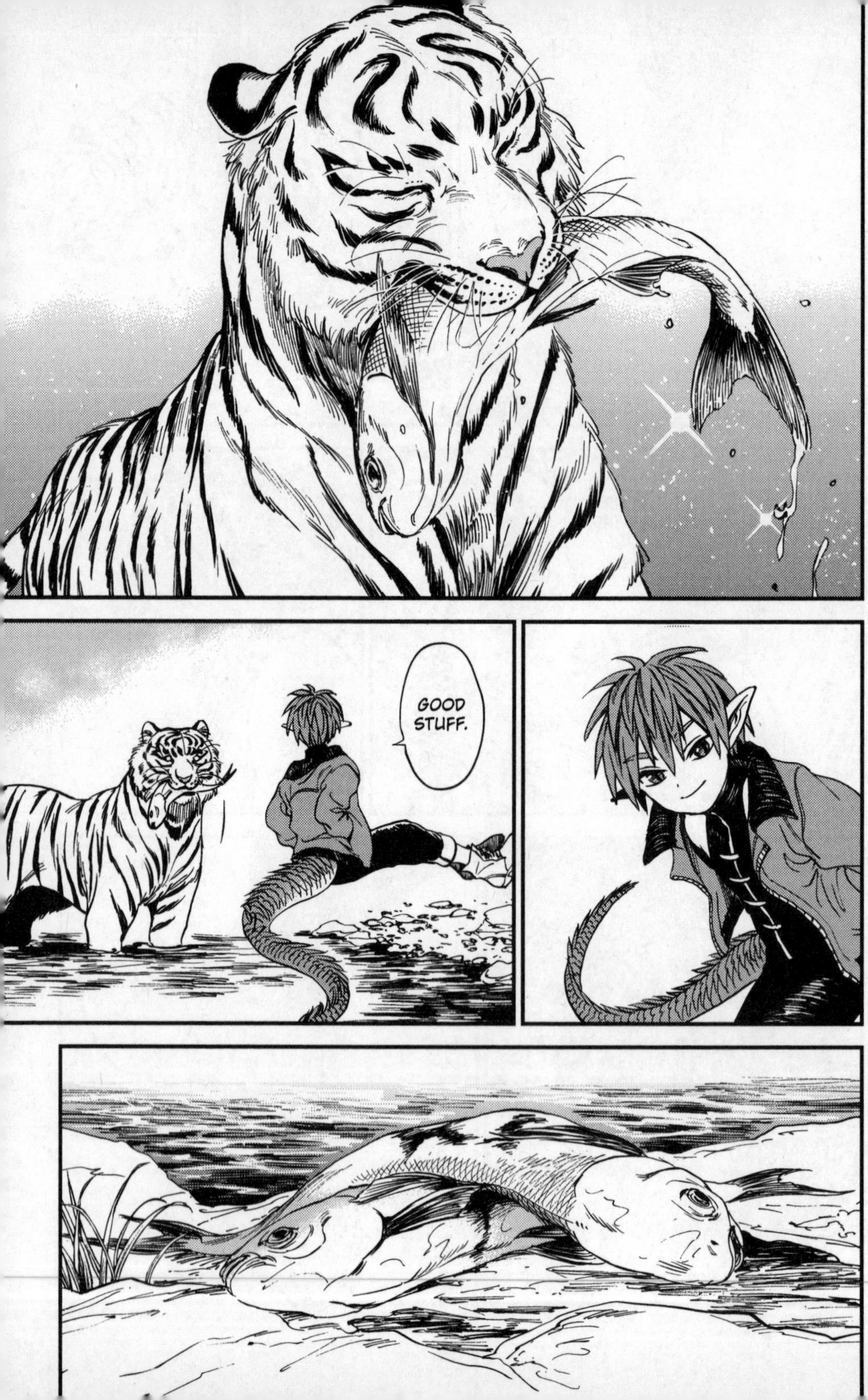
GOOD STUFF.

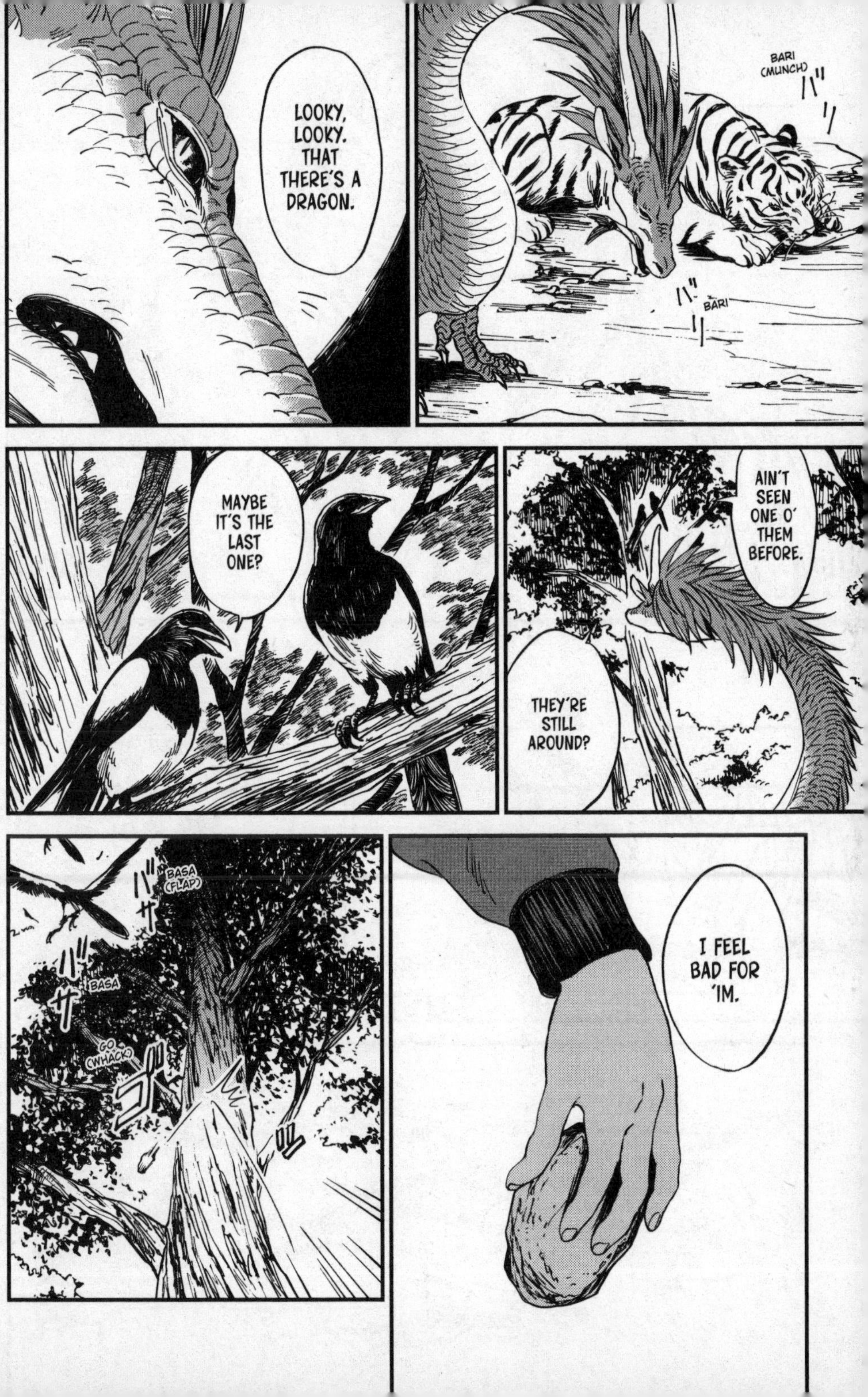
BARI (MUNCH)
バリ
バリ
BARI
LOOKY, LOOKY. THAT THERE'S A DRAGON.
AIN'T SEEN ONE O' THEM BEFORE.
THEY'RE STILL AROUND?
MAYBE IT'S THE LAST ONE?
I FEEL BAD FOR 'IM.
BASA (FLAP)
バサ
バサ
BASA
GO (WHACK)
ゴッ

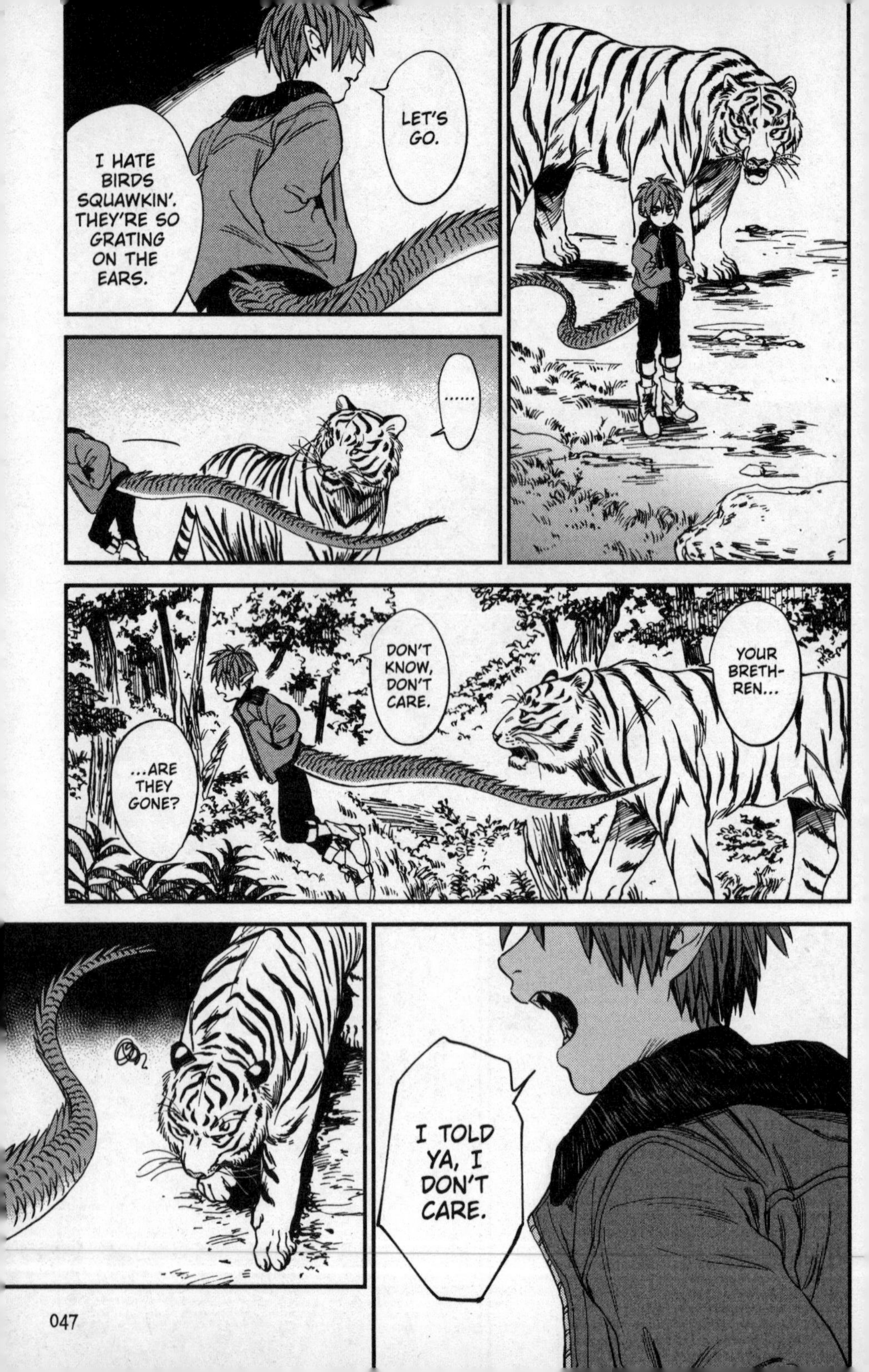
LET'S GO.
I HATE BIRDS SQUAWKIN'. THEY'RE SO GRATING ON THE EARS.
......
YOUR BRETH-REN...
...ARE THEY GONE?
DON'T KNOW, DON'T CARE.
I TOLD YA, I DON'T CARE.

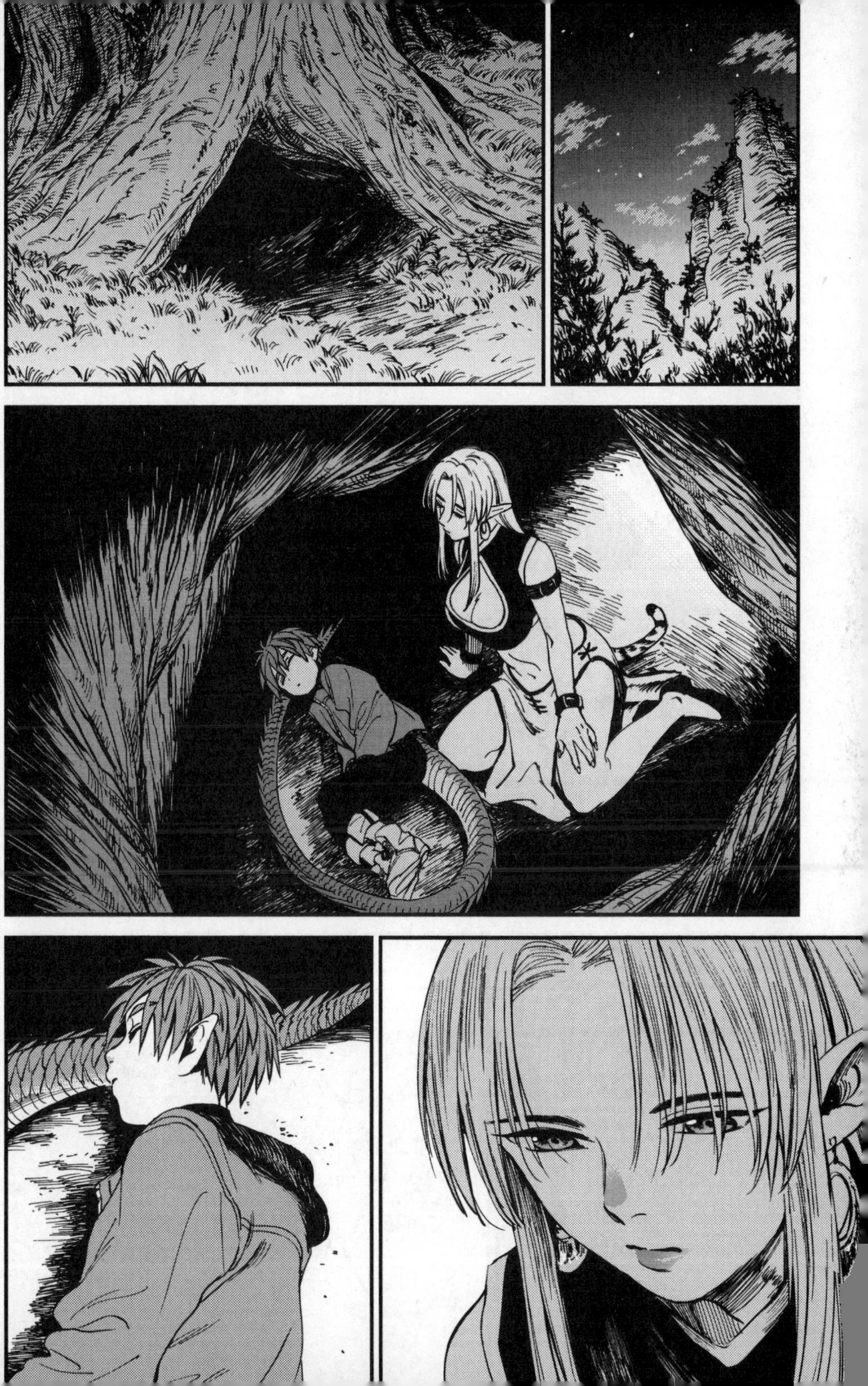

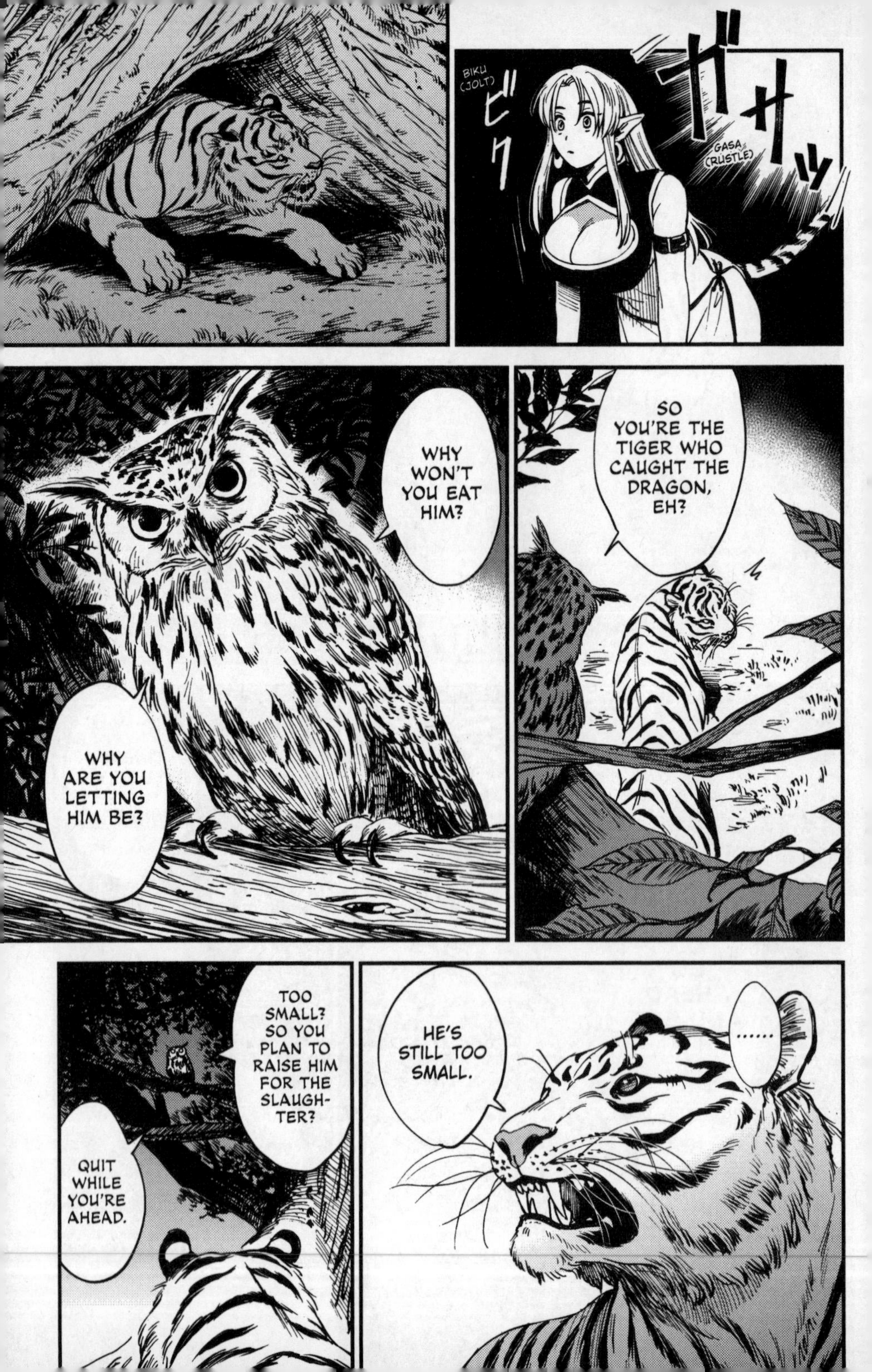
ガサッ
GASA (RUSTLE)
ビク
BIKU (JOLT)
SO YOU'RE THE TIGER WHO CAUGHT THE DRAGON, EH?
WHY WON'T YOU EAT HIM?
WHY ARE YOU LETTING HIM BE?
......
HE'S STILL TOO SMALL.
TOO SMALL? SO YOU PLAN TO RAISE HIM FOR THE SLAUGHTER?
QUIT WHILE YOU'RE AHEAD.

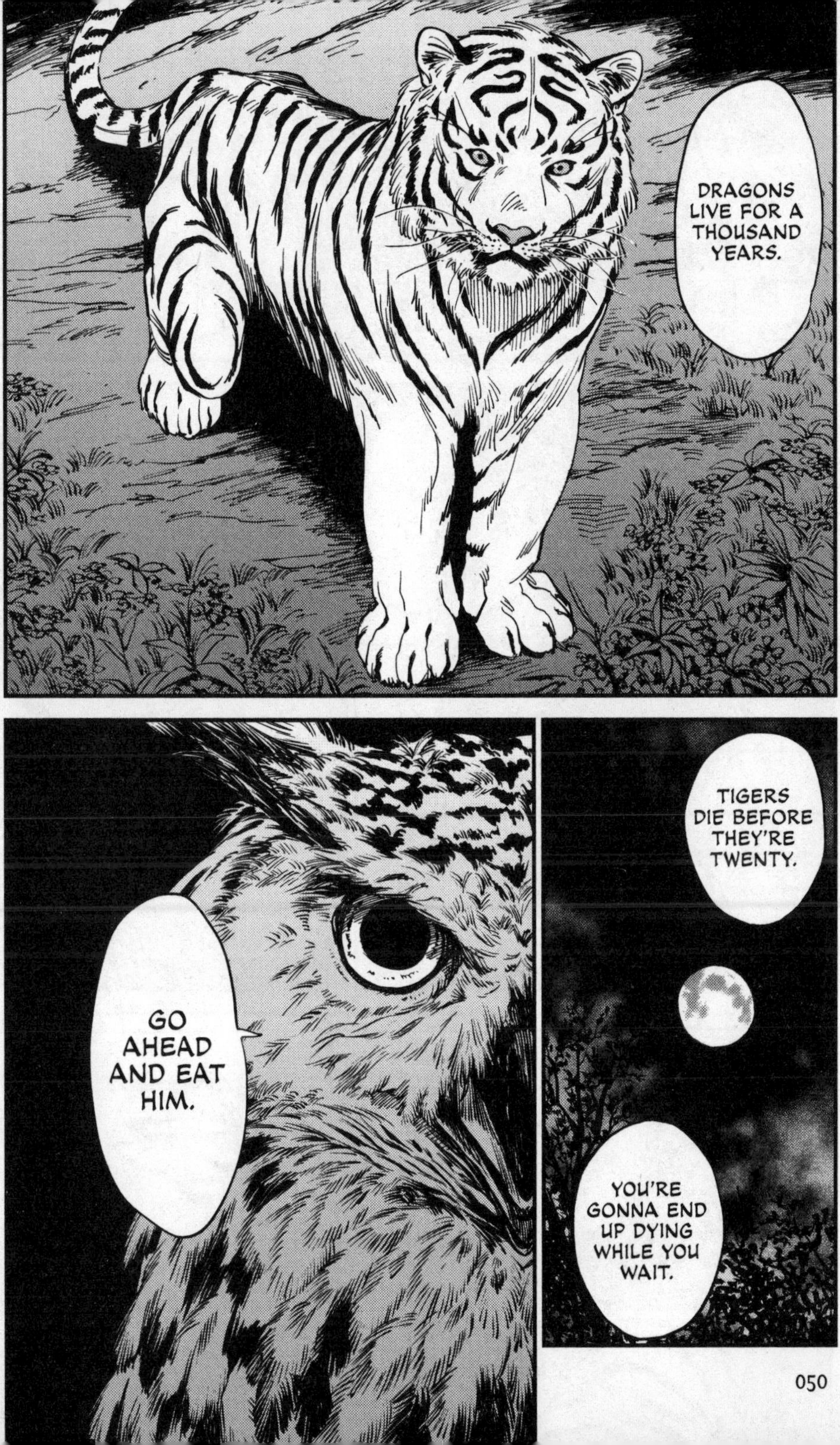
DRAGONS LIVE FOR A THOUSAND YEARS.
TIGERS DIE BEFORE THEY'RE TWENTY.
YOU'RE GONNA END UP DYING WHILE YOU WAIT.
GO AHEAD AND EAT HIM.

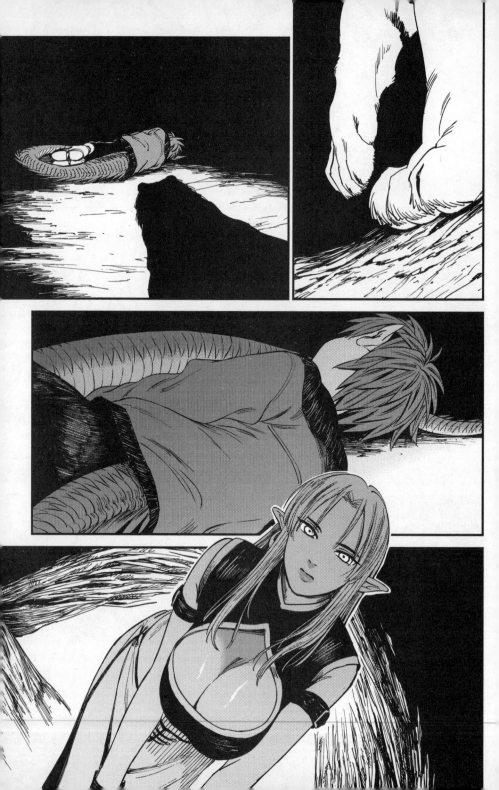

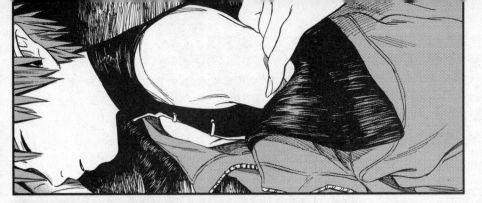

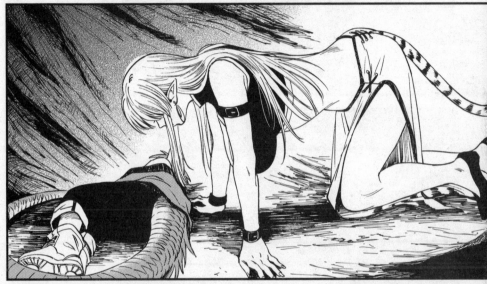

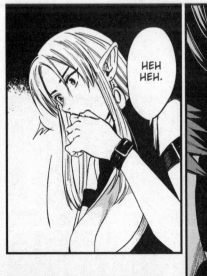

HEH
HEH.

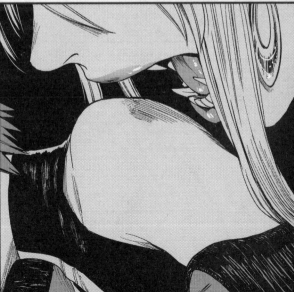

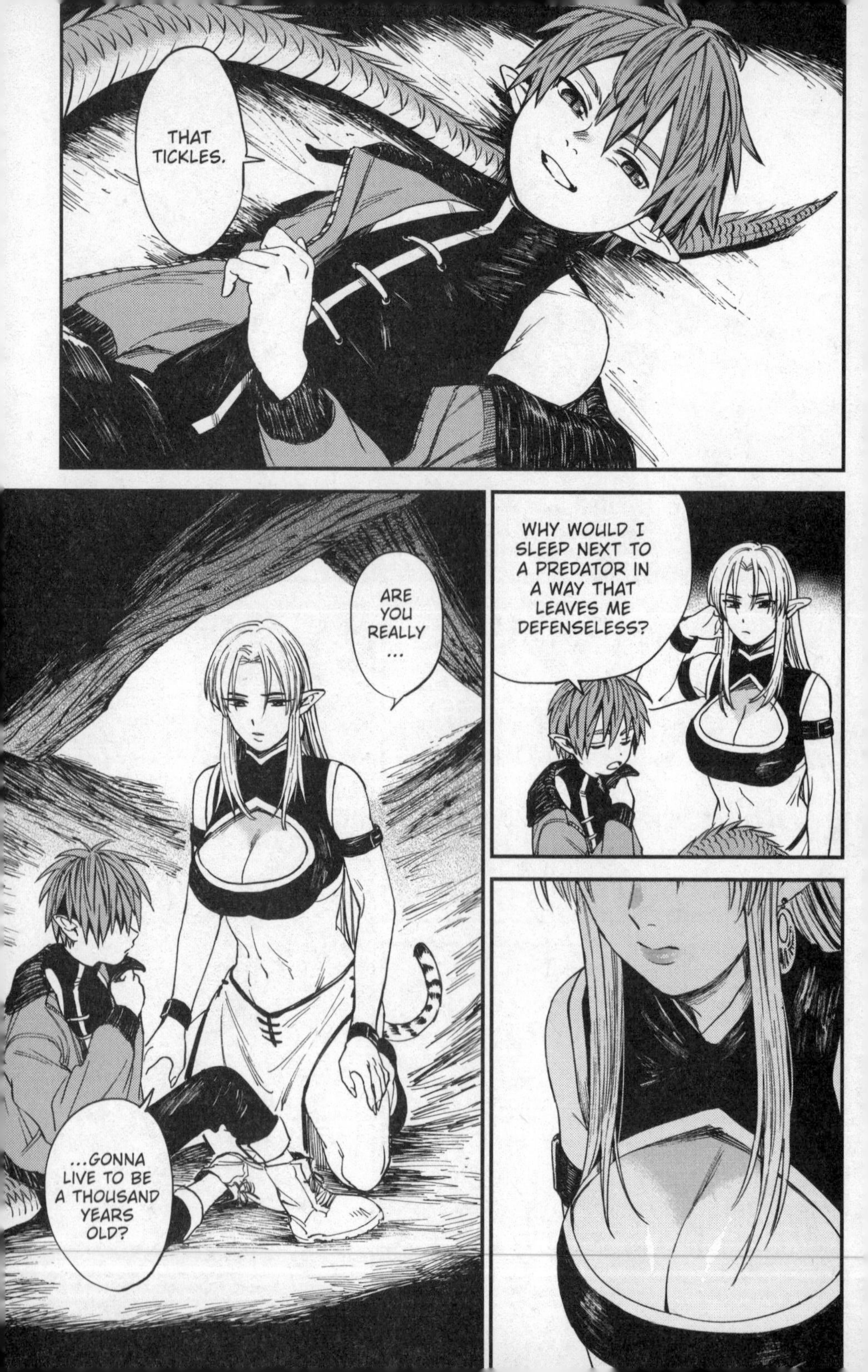
THAT TICKLES.
WHY WOULD I SLEEP NEXT TO A PREDATOR IN A WAY THAT LEAVES ME DEFENSELESS?
ARE YOU REALLY ...
...GONNA LIVE TO BE A THOUSAND YEARS OLD?

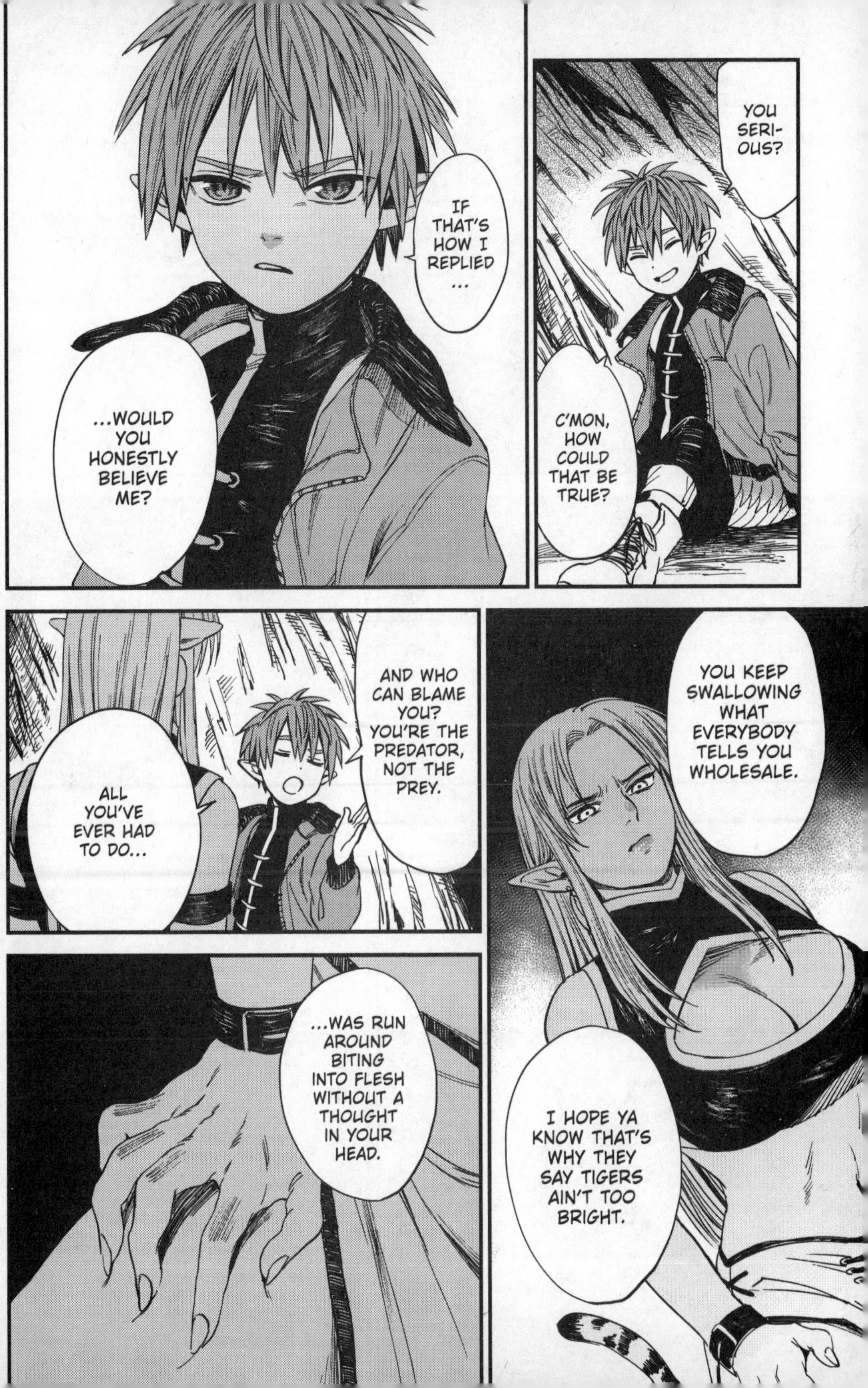
YOU SERI-OUS?
C'MON, HOW COULD THAT BE TRUE?
IF THAT'S HOW I REPLIED ...
...WOULD YOU HONESTLY BELIEVE ME?
YOU KEEP SWALLOWING WHAT EVERYBODY TELLS YOU WHOLESALE.
I HOPE YA KNOW THAT'S WHY THEY SAY TIGERS AIN'T TOO BRIGHT.
AND WHO CAN BLAME YOU? YOU'RE THE PREDATOR, NOT THE PREY.
ALL YOU'VE EVER HAD TO DO...
...WAS RUN AROUND BITING INTO FLESH WITHOUT A THOUGHT IN YOUR HEAD.

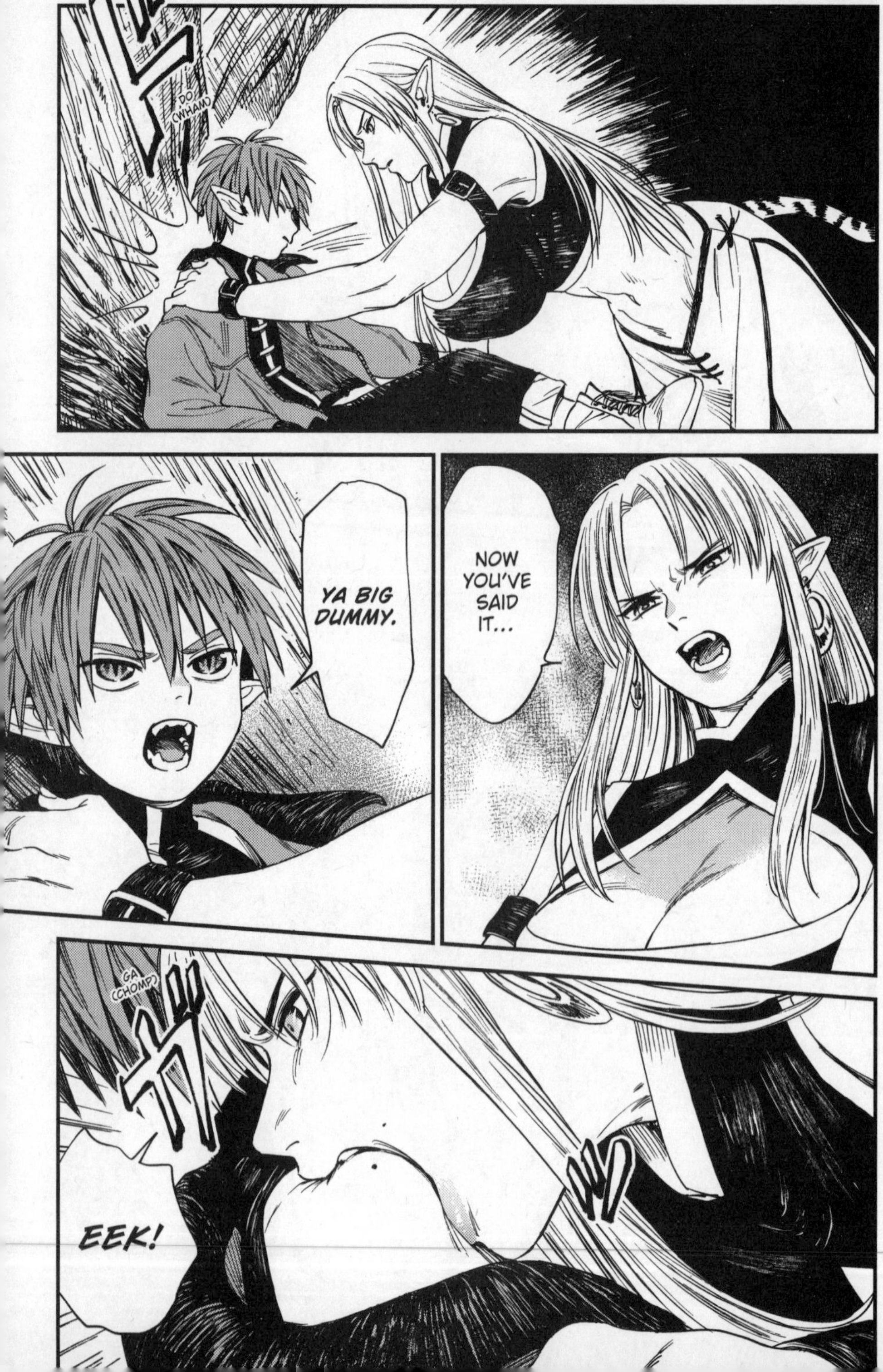

DO (WHAM)
NOW YOU'VE SAID IT...
YA BIG DUMMY.
GA (CHOMP)
EEK!

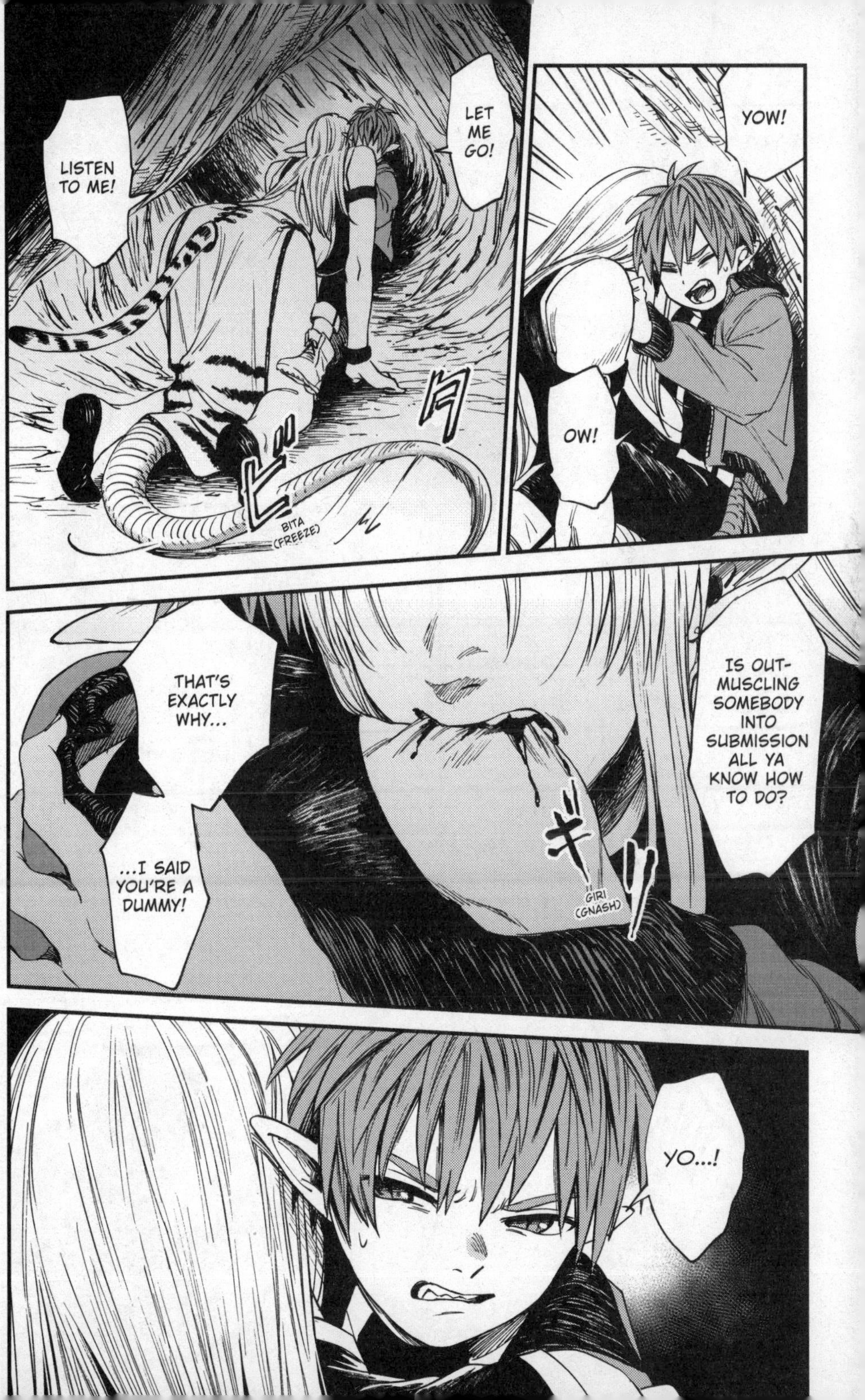
YOW!
OW!
LET ME GO!
LISTEN TO ME!
BITA (FREEZE)
IS OUT-MUSCLING SOMEBODY INTO SUBMISSION ALL YA KNOW HOW TO DO?
GIRI (GNASH)
THAT'S EXACTLY WHY...
...I SAID YOU'RE A DUMMY!
YO...!

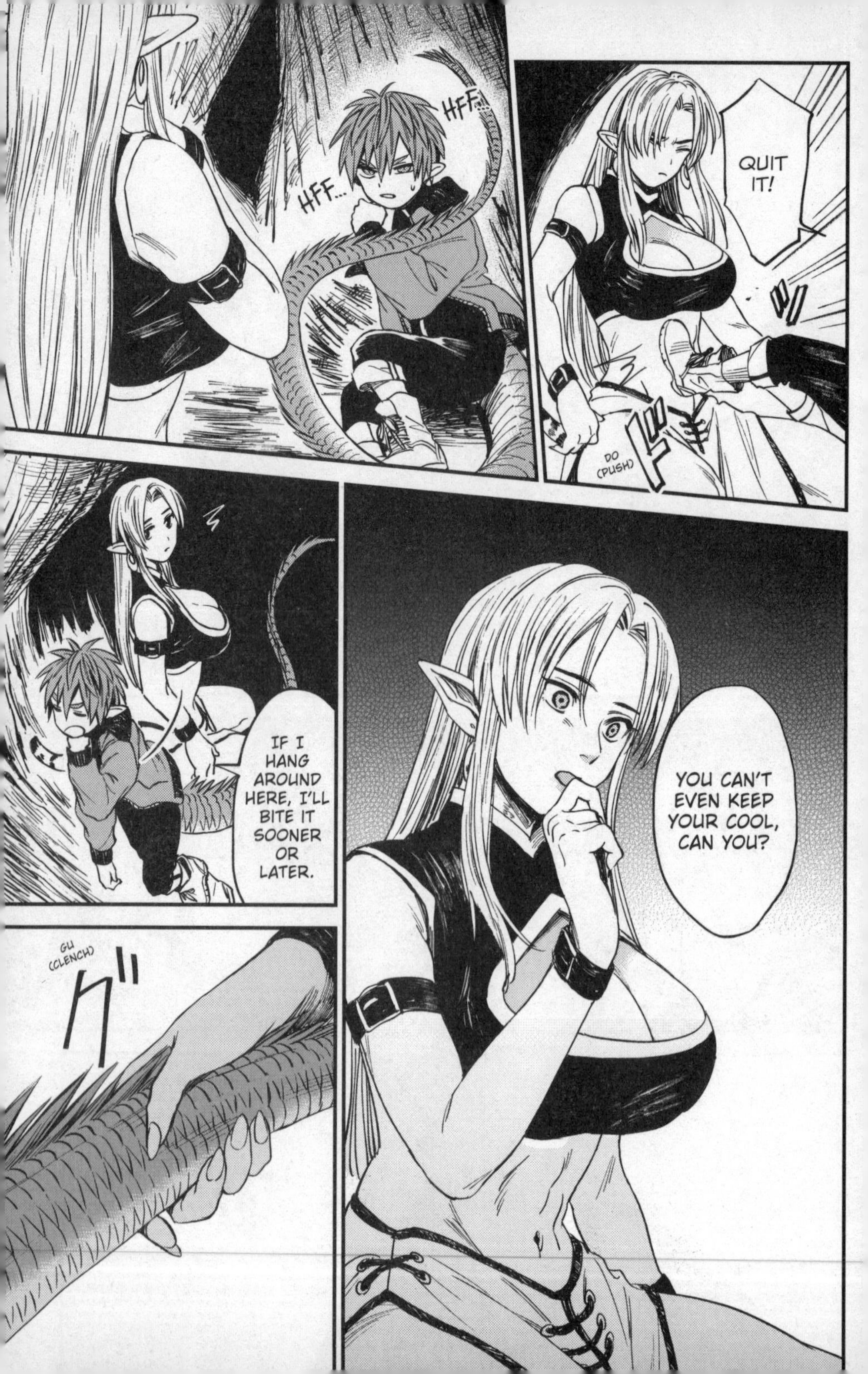
QUIT IT!
DO (PUSH)
HFF...
HFF...
YOU CAN'T EVEN KEEP YOUR COOL, CAN YOU?
IF I HANG AROUND HERE, I'LL BITE IT SOONER OR LATER.
GU (CLENCH)

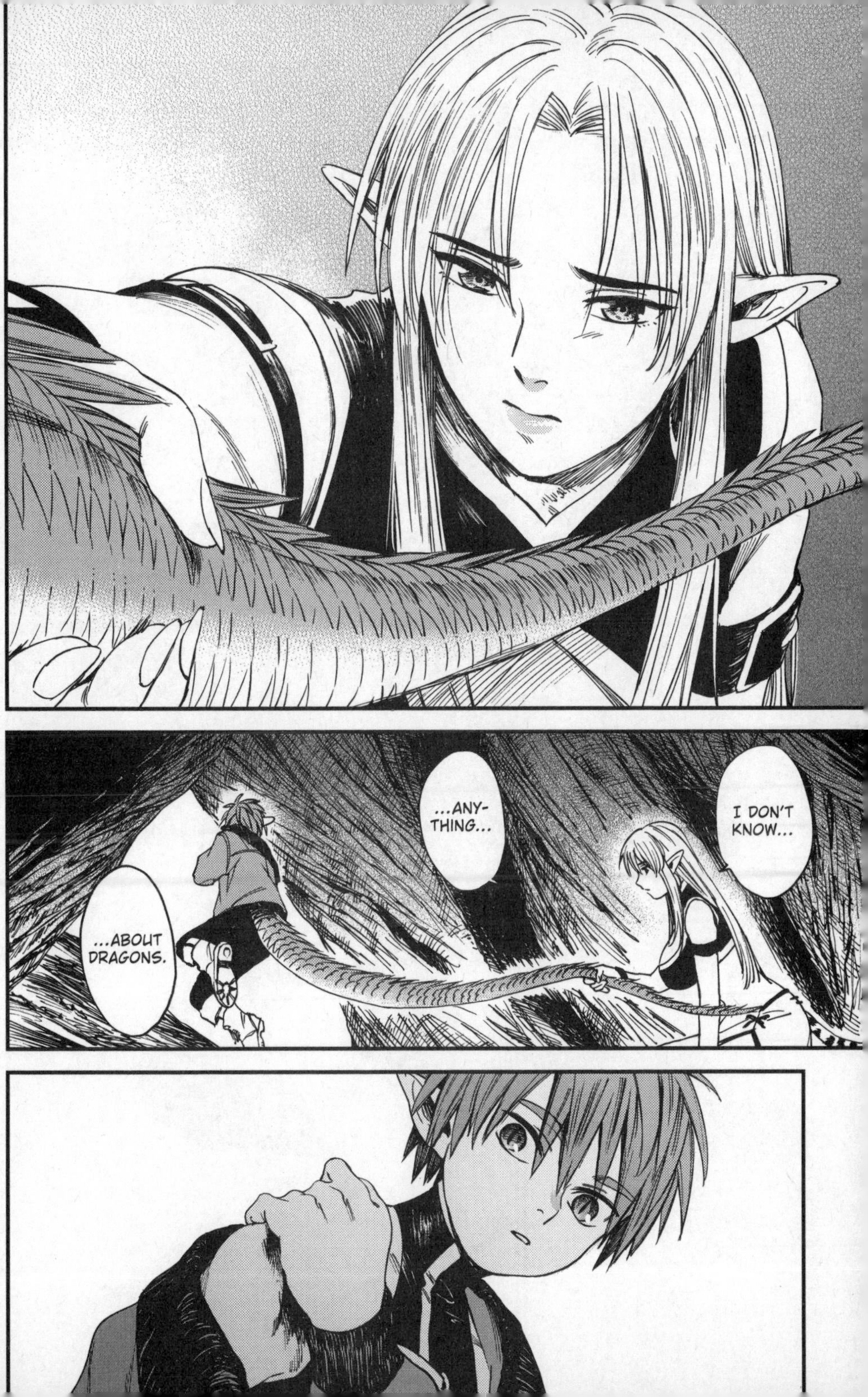
I DON'T KNOW...
...ANY-THING...
...ABOUT DRAGONS.

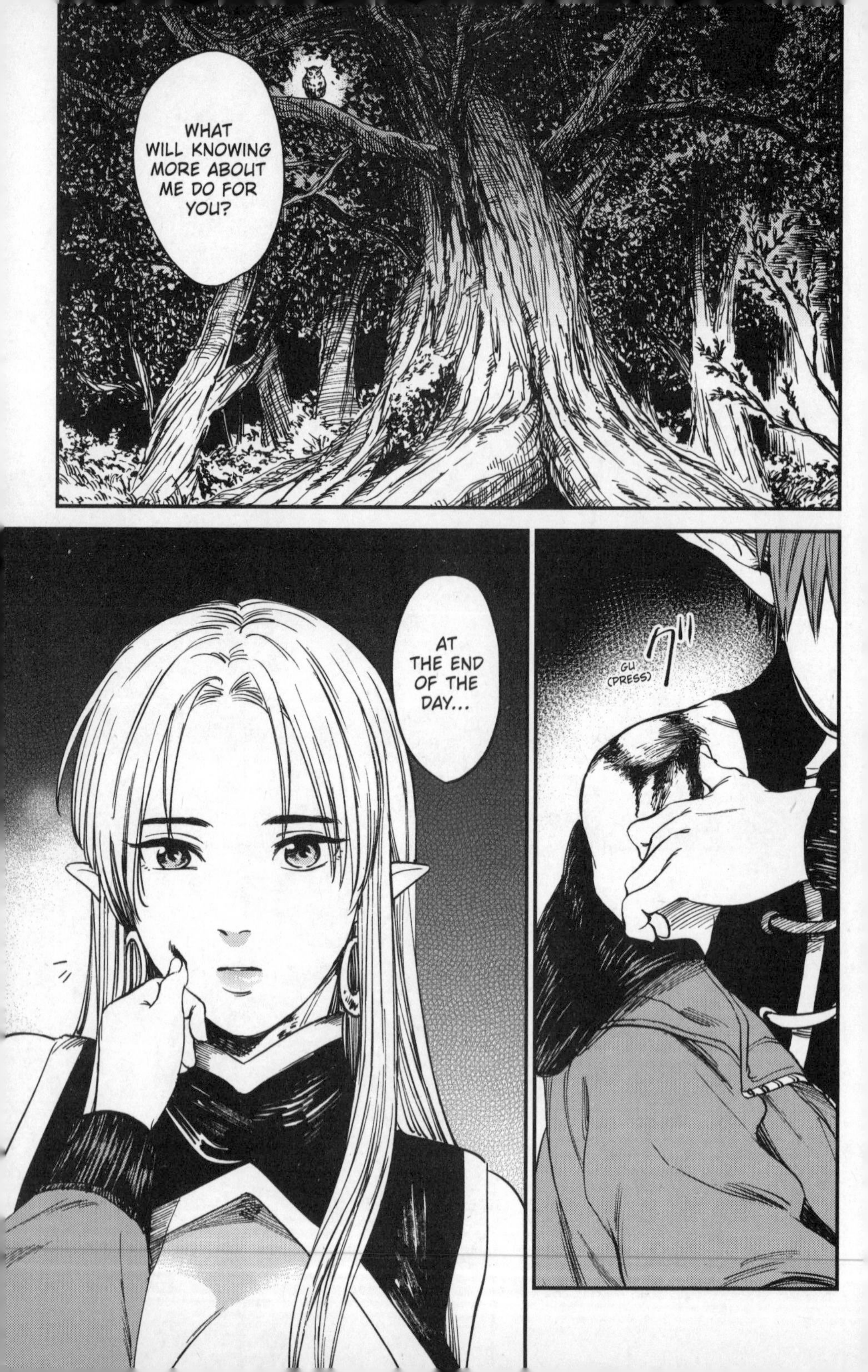
WHAT WILL KNOWING MORE ABOUT ME DO FOR YOU?
GU (PRESS)
AT THE END OF THE DAY...

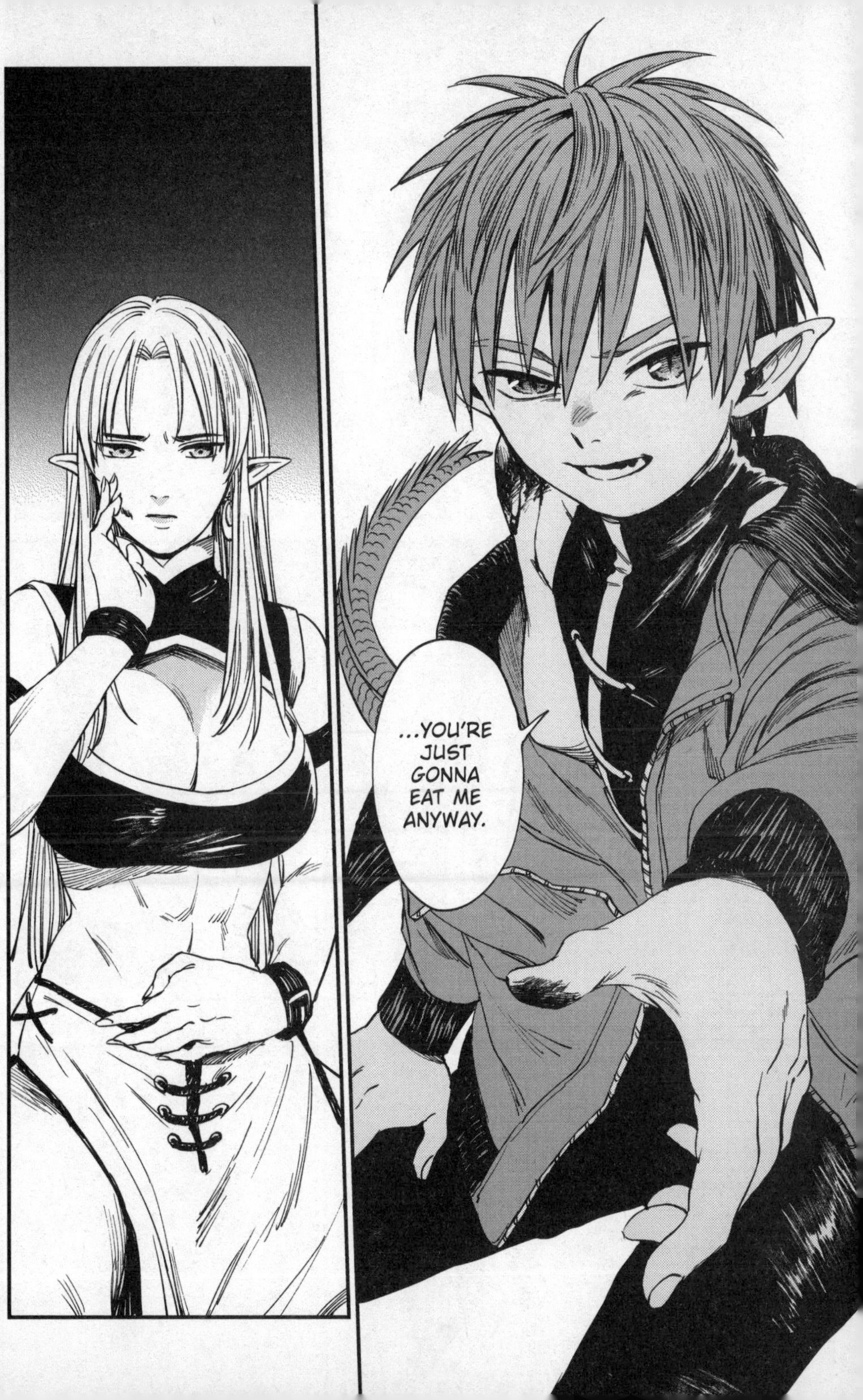
...YOU'RE JUST GONNA EAT ME ANYWAY.

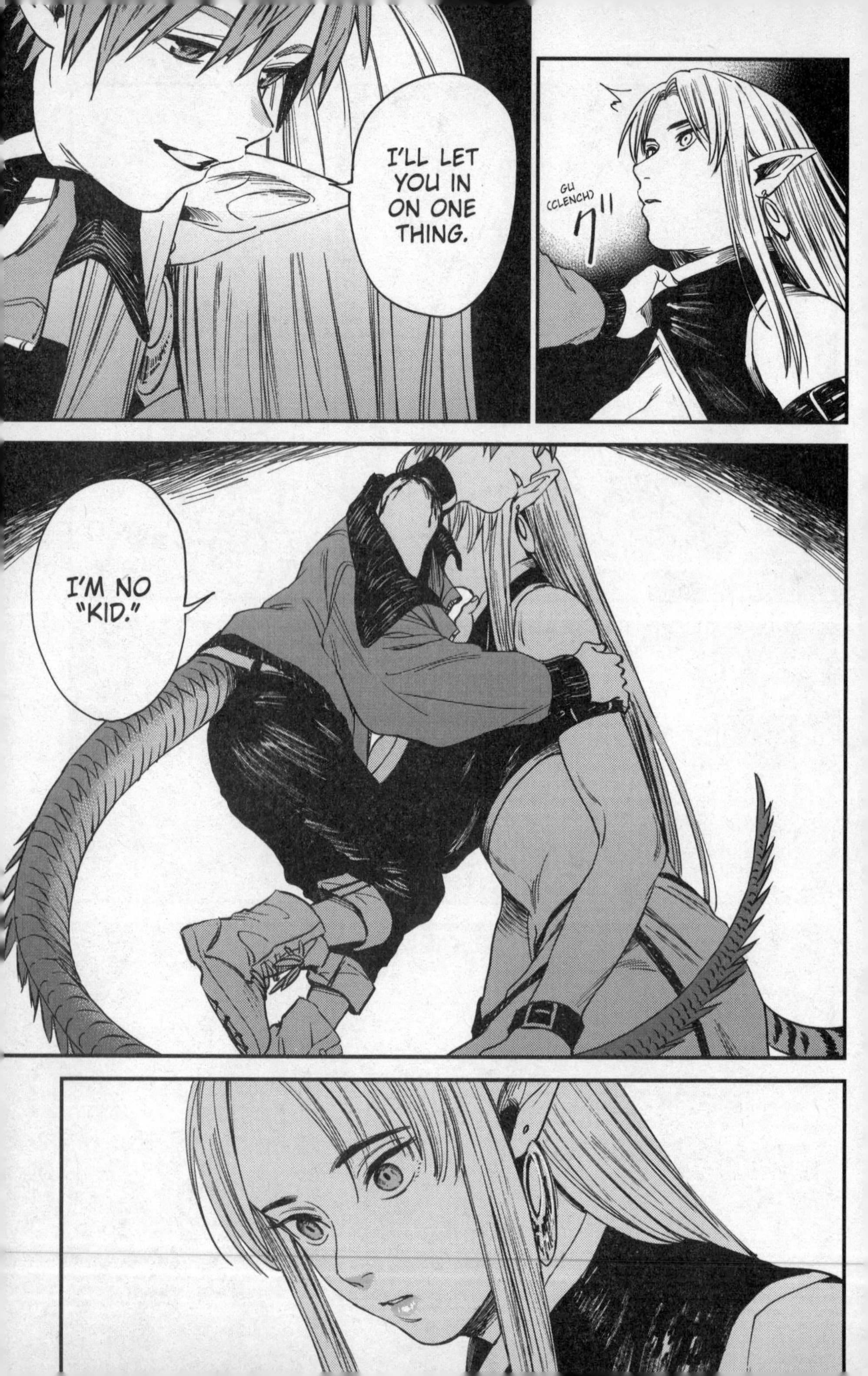
GU (CLENCH)
グッ
I'LL LET YOU IN ON ONE THING.
I'M NO "KID."

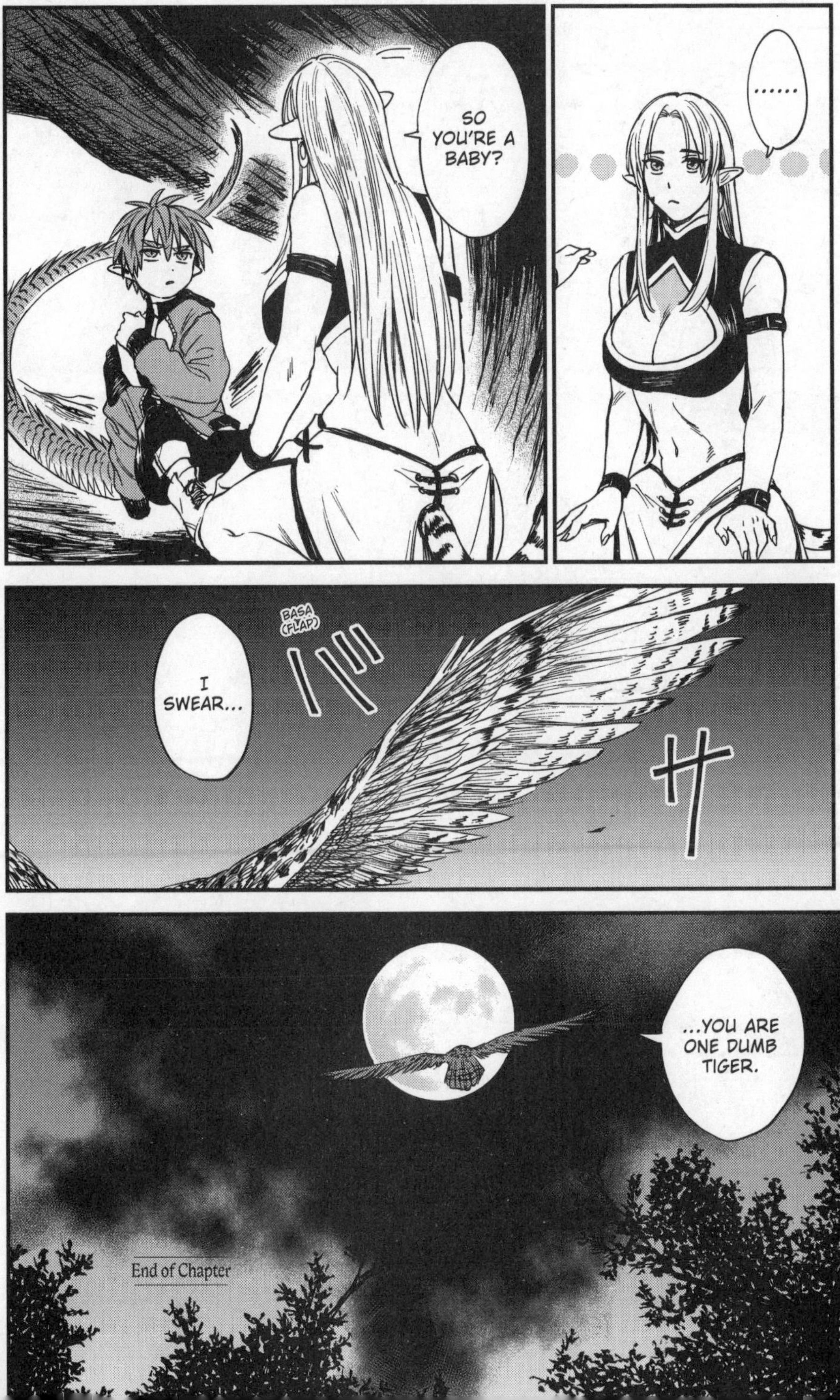
......
SO YOU'RE A BABY?
BASA (FLAP)
I SWEAR...
...YOU ARE ONE DUMB TIGER.
End of Chapter

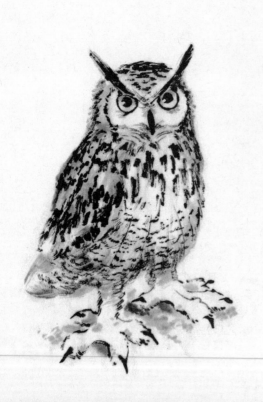

The Tiger Won't Eat the Dragon Yet

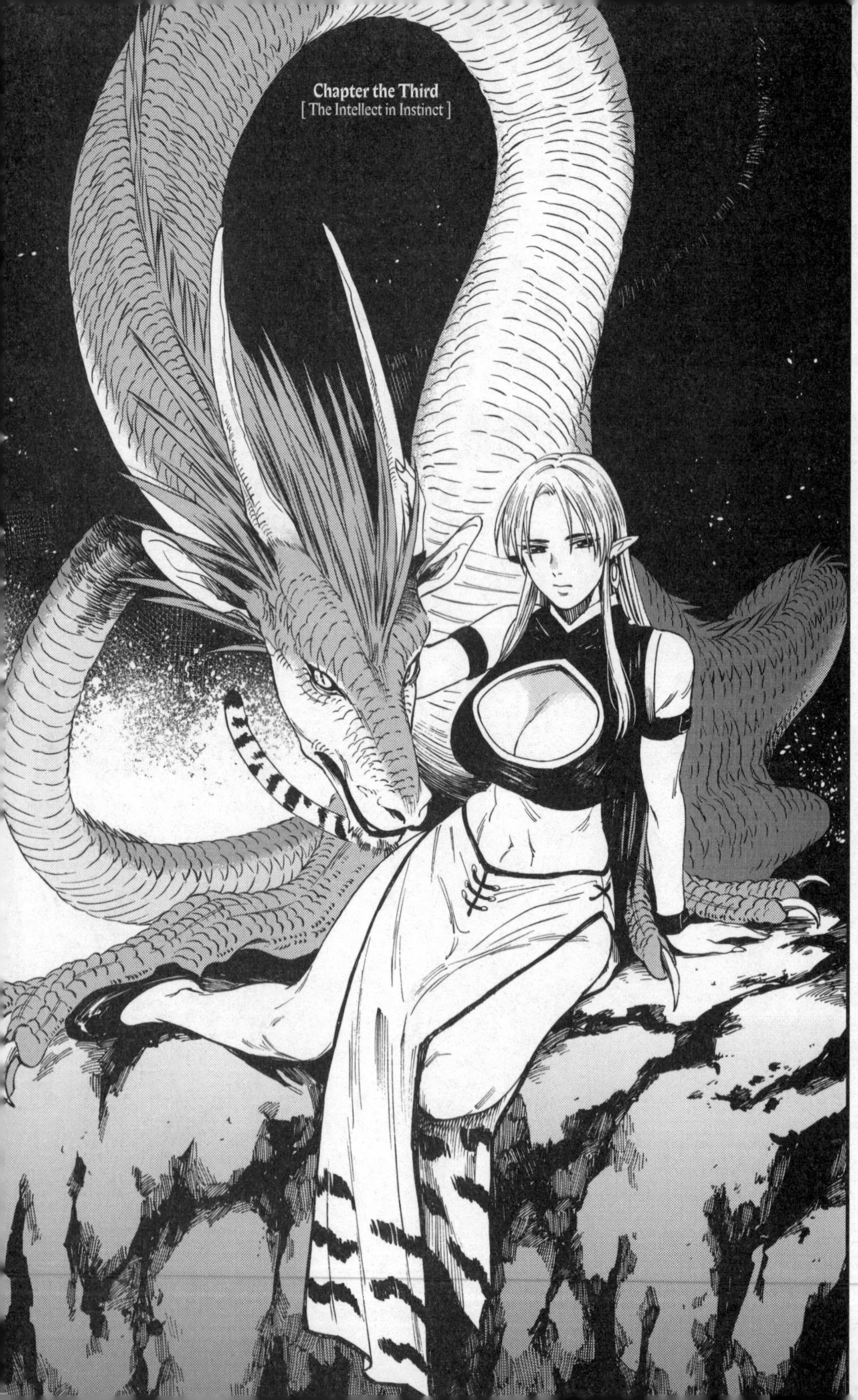
Chapter the Third
[The Intellect in Instinct]

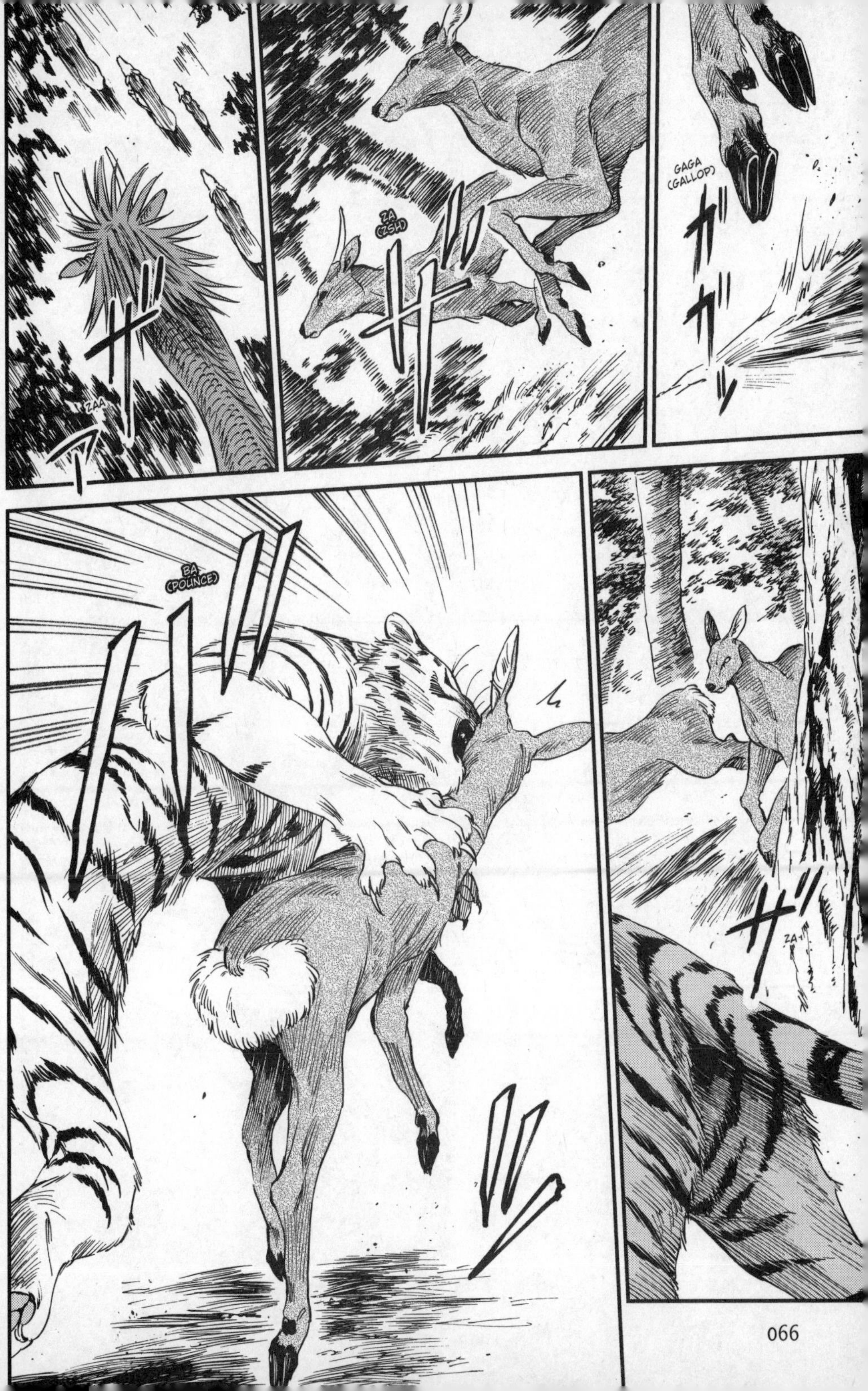
GAGA (GALLOP)
ZA (ZSH)
ZAA
ZA
BA (POUNCE)

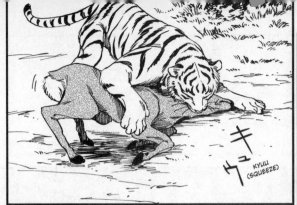

キュ
ゥ
KYUU
(SQUEEZE)

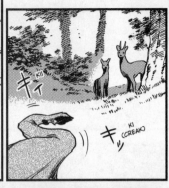

キィ
KII

キッ
KI
(CREAK)

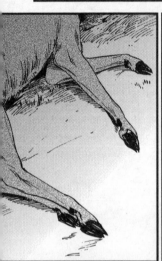

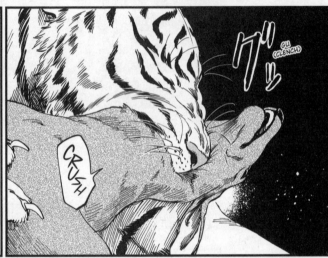

グ
ッ
GU
(CLENCH)

CRUSH

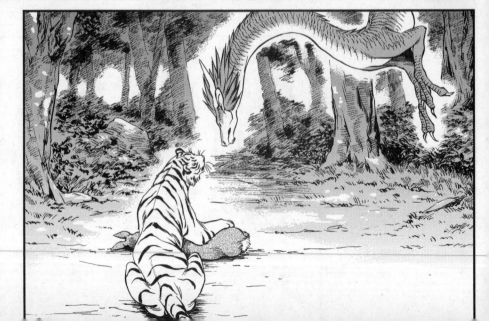

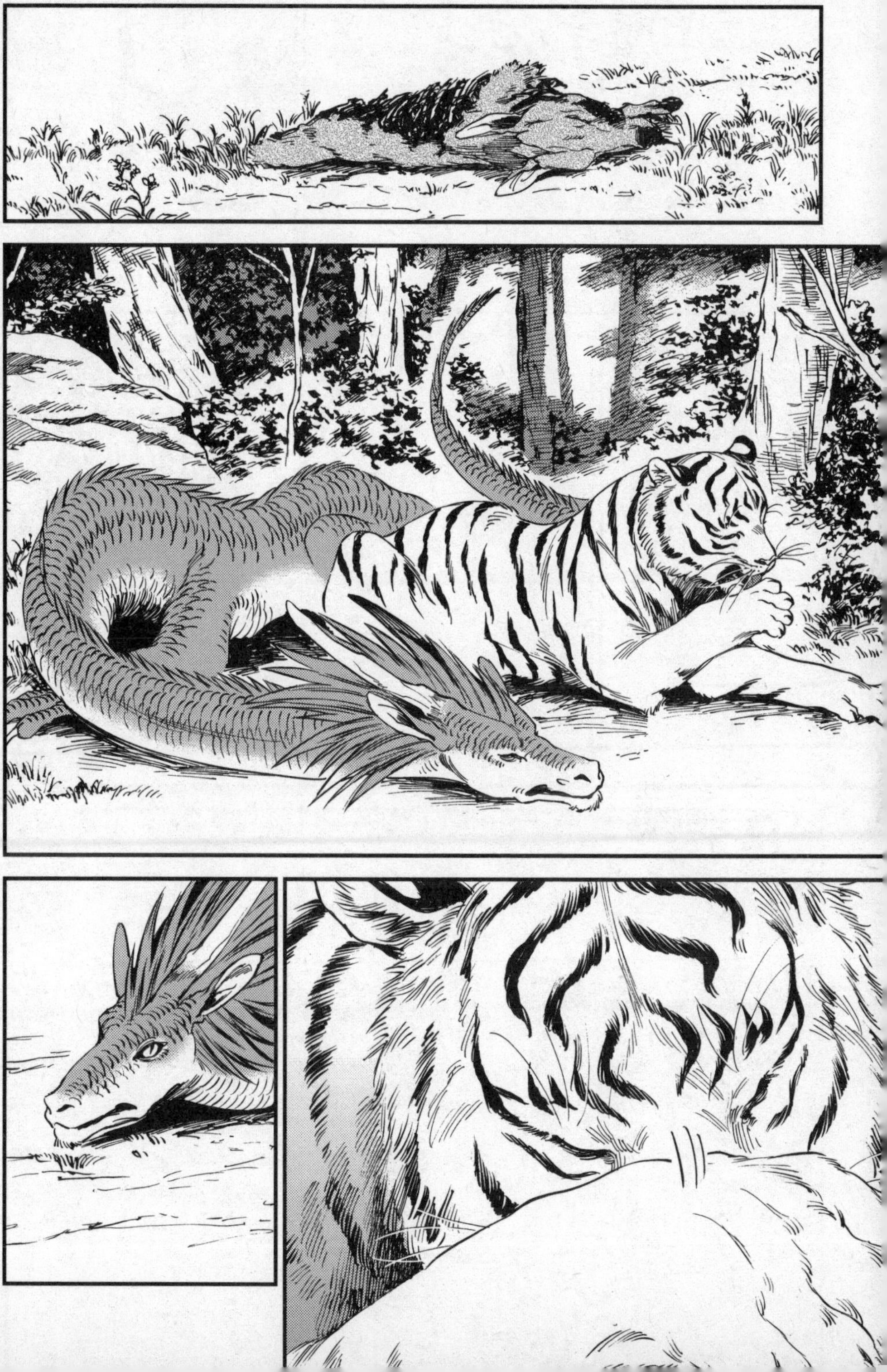

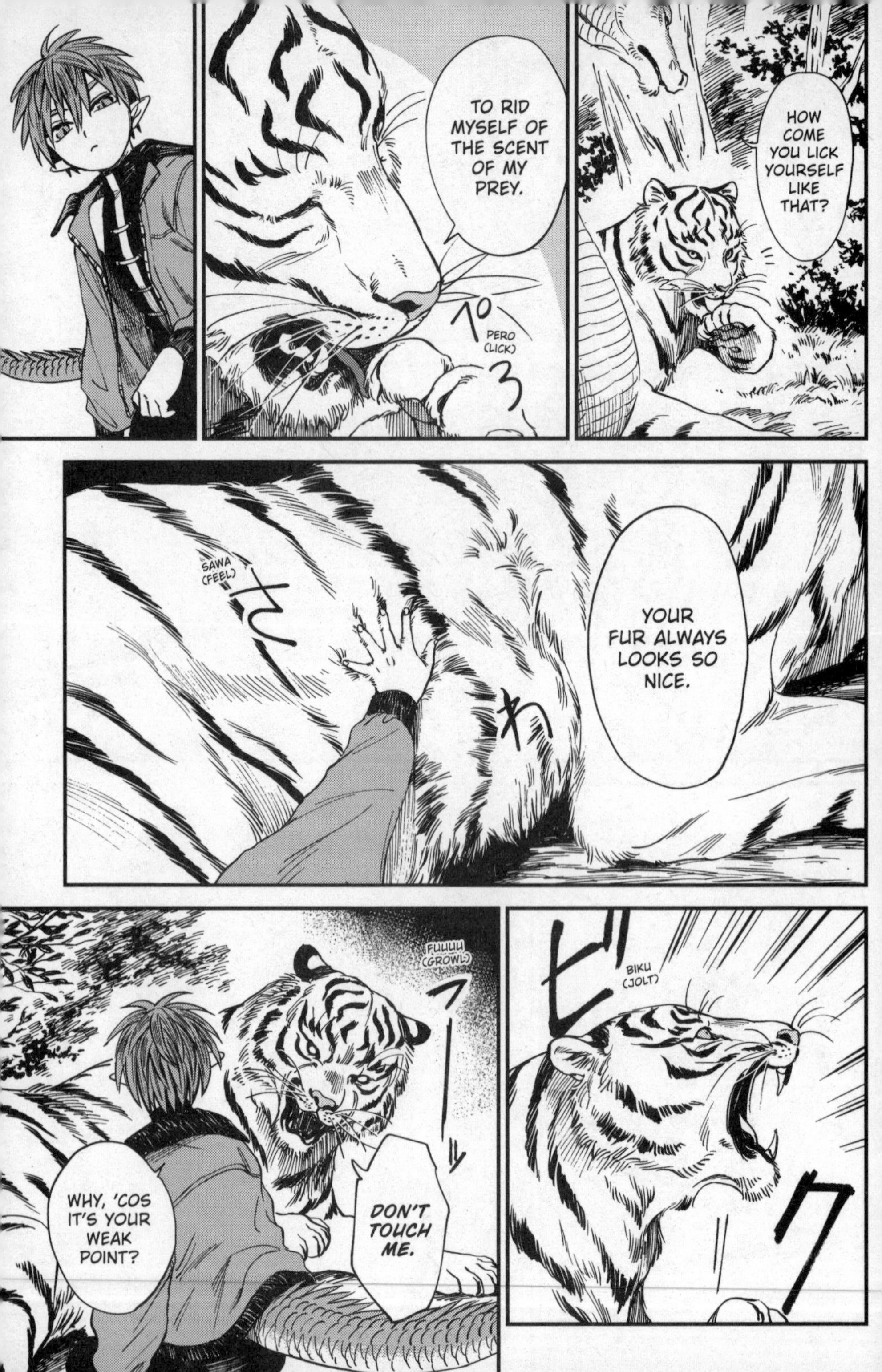
HOW COME YOU LICK YOURSELF LIKE THAT?
TO RID MYSELF OF THE SCENT OF MY PREY.
PERO (LICK)
YOUR FUR ALWAYS LOOKS SO NICE.
SAWA (FEEL)
BIKU (JOLT)
FUUUU (GROWL)
DON'T TOUCH ME.
WHY, 'COS IT'S YOUR WEAK POINT?

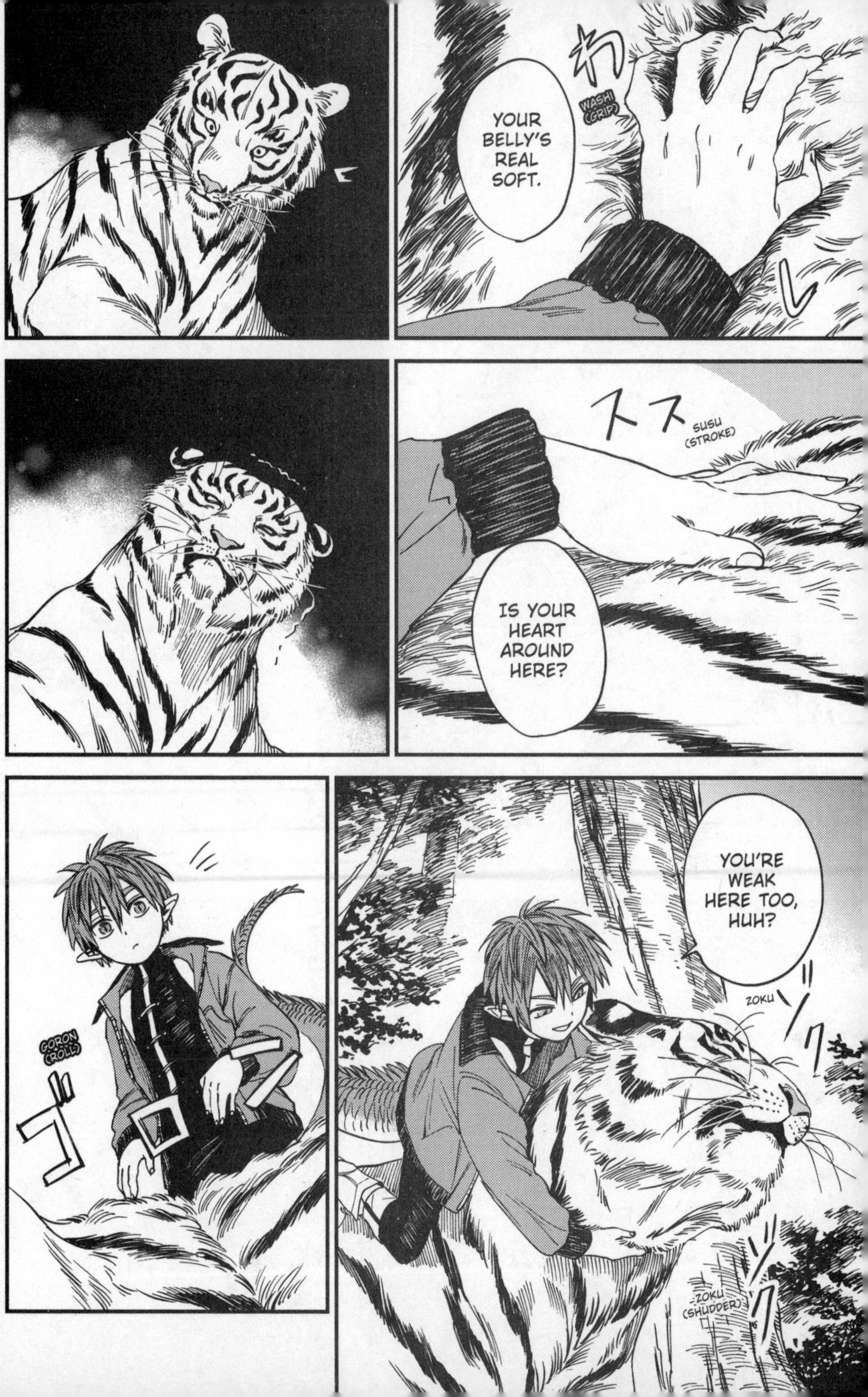
WASHI (GRIP)
YOUR BELLY'S REAL SOFT.
スス
SUSU (STROKE)
IS YOUR HEART AROUND HERE?
YOU'RE WEAK HERE TOO, HUH?
ZOKU
ZOKU (SHUDDER)
GORON (ROLL)

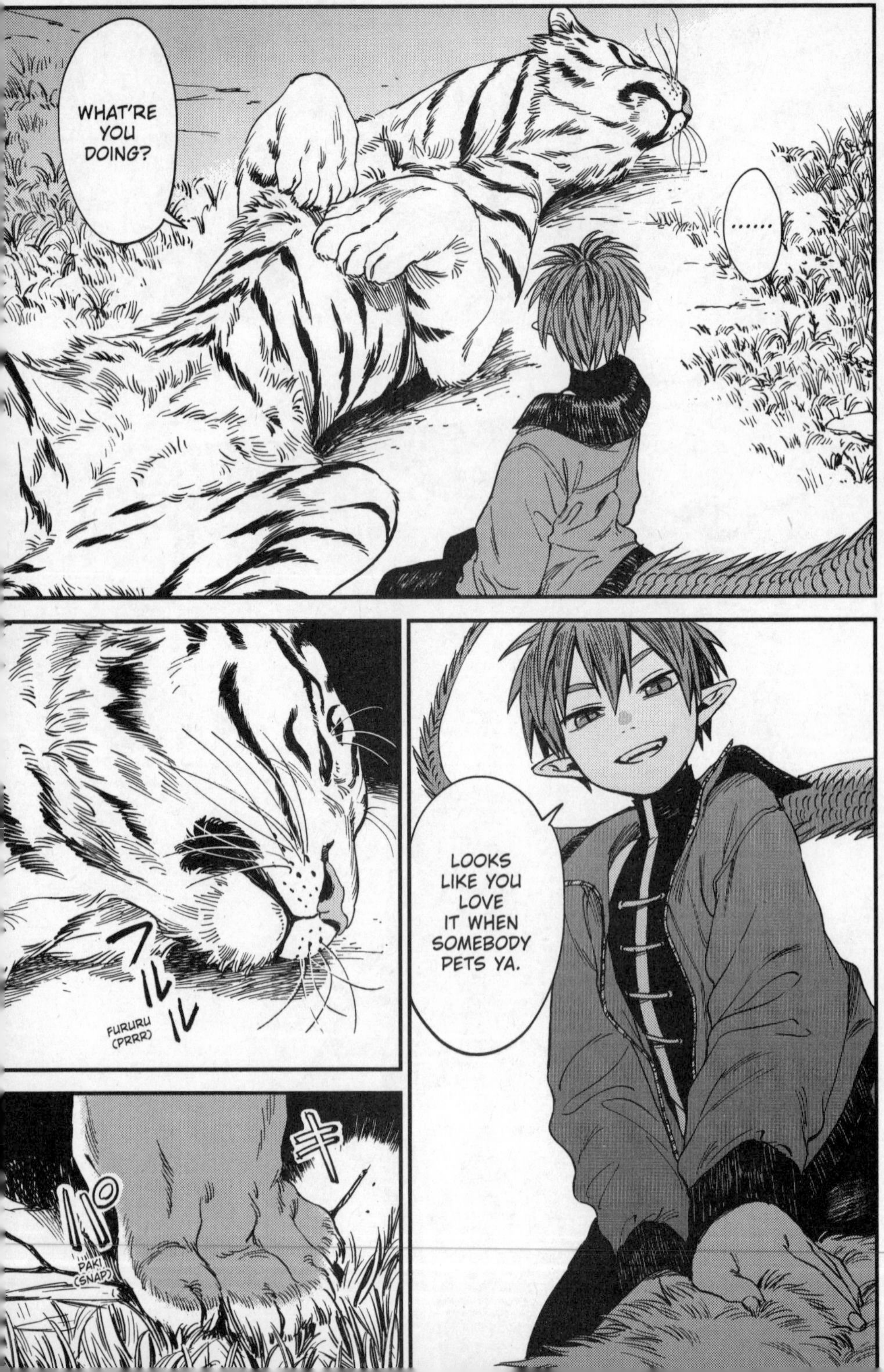
WHAT'RE YOU DOING?
......
LOOKS LIKE YOU LOVE IT WHEN SOMEBODY PETS YA.
フルル
FURURU (PRRR)
パキ
PAKI (SNAP)

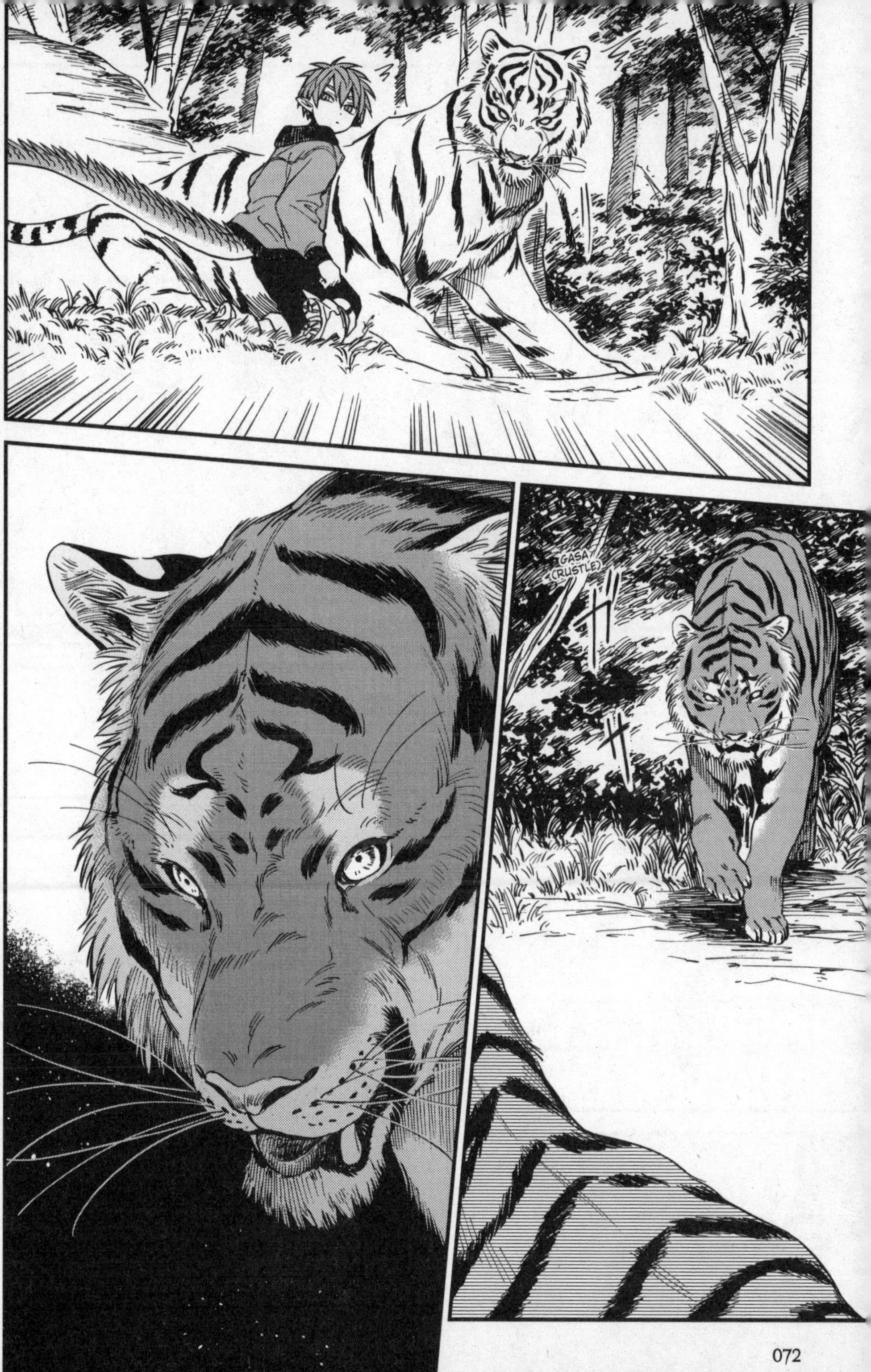
GASA (RUSTLE)

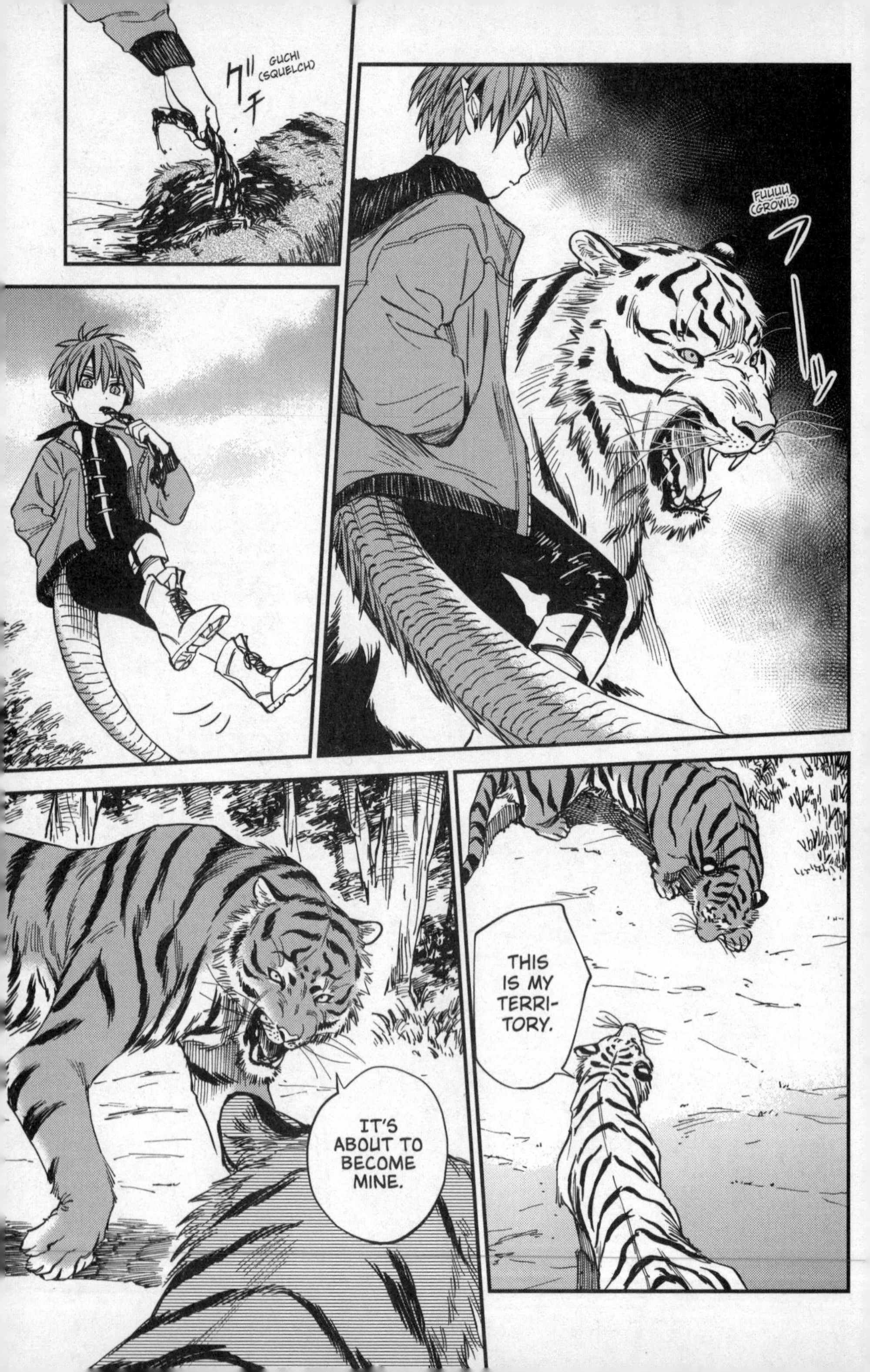
FUUUU (GROWL)
フーッ
GUCHI (SQUELCH)
グチ
THIS IS MY TERRI- TORY.
IT'S ABOUT TO BECOME MINE.

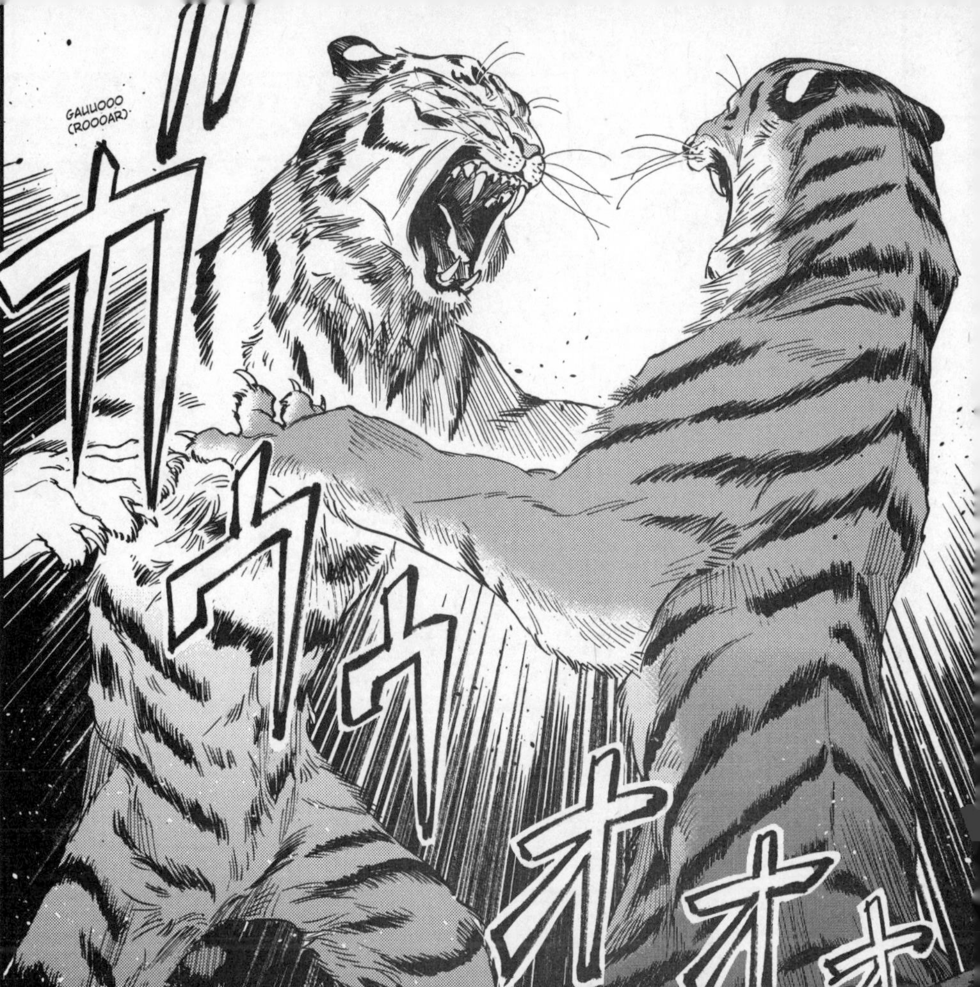
GAUUOOO
(ROOOAR)
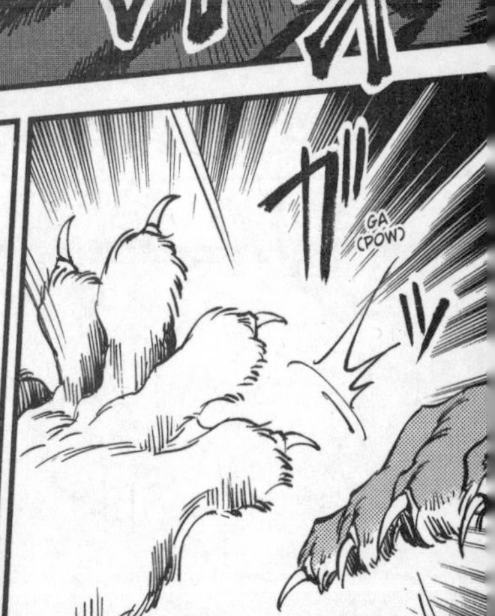
GA
(POW)
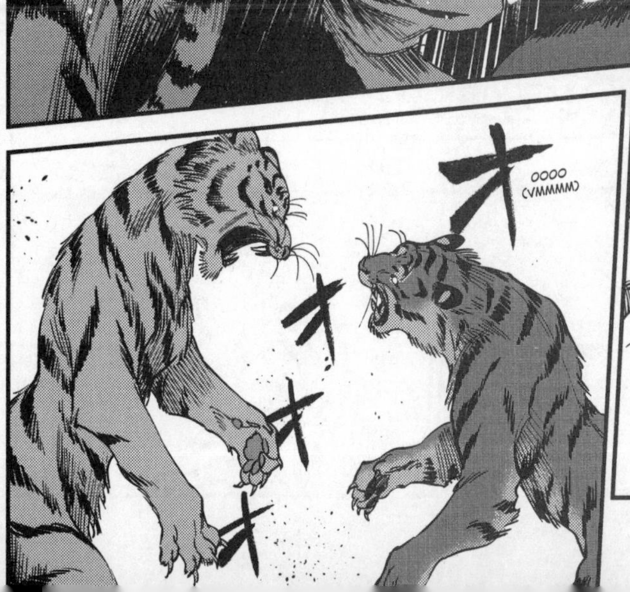
OOOO
(VMMMM)

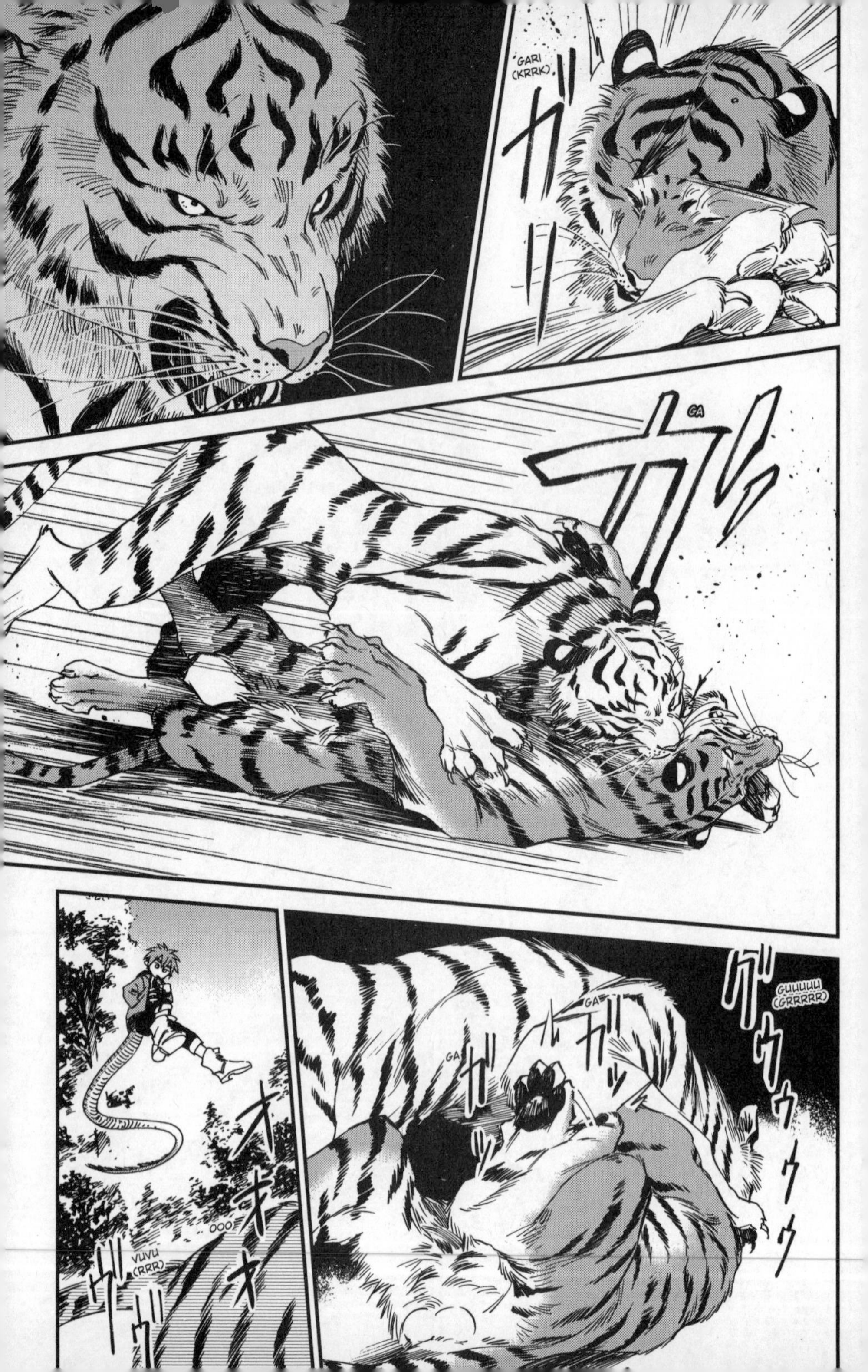
GARI (KRRK)
GA
GUUUUU (GRRRRR)
GA
GA
OOO
VUVU (RRR)

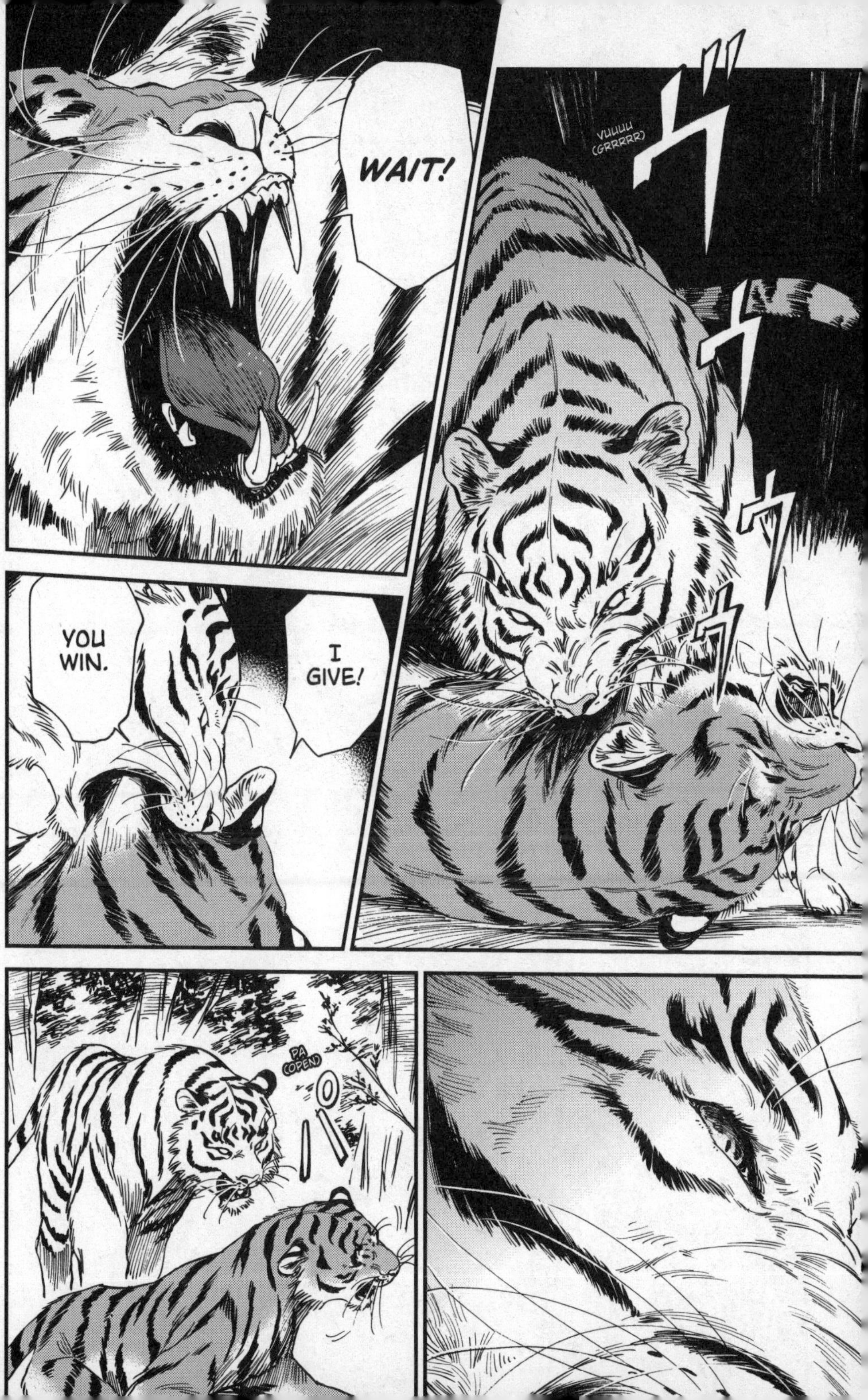
VUUUU
(GRRRRR)
WAIT!
I GIVE!
YOU WIN.
PA
(OPEN)

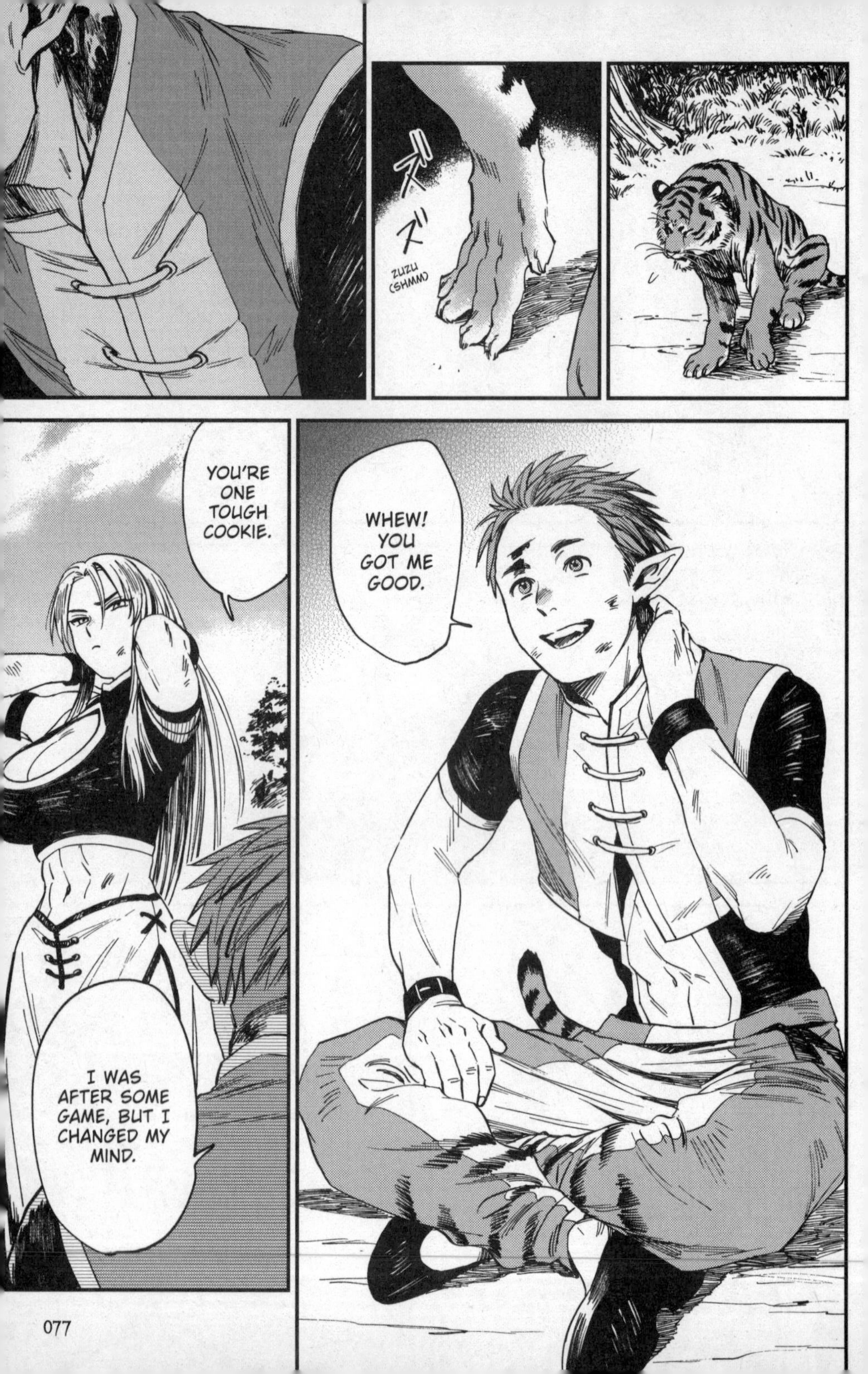
ズズ
ZUZU (SHMMM)
WHEW! YOU GOT ME GOOD.
YOU'RE ONE TOUGH COOKIE.
I WAS AFTER SOME GAME, BUT I CHANGED MY MIND.

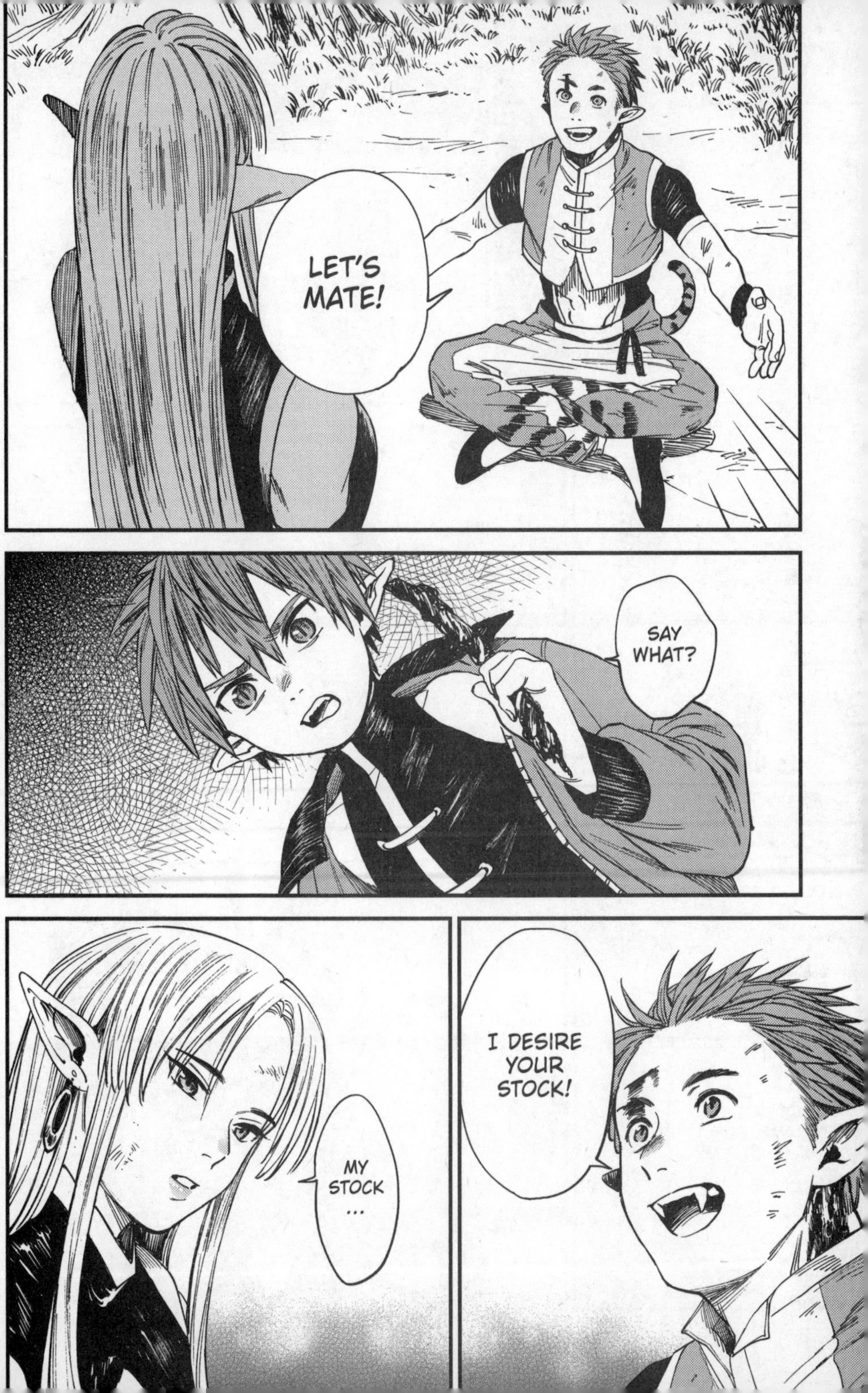
LET'S MATE!
SAY WHAT?
I DESIRE YOUR STOCK!
MY STOCK ...

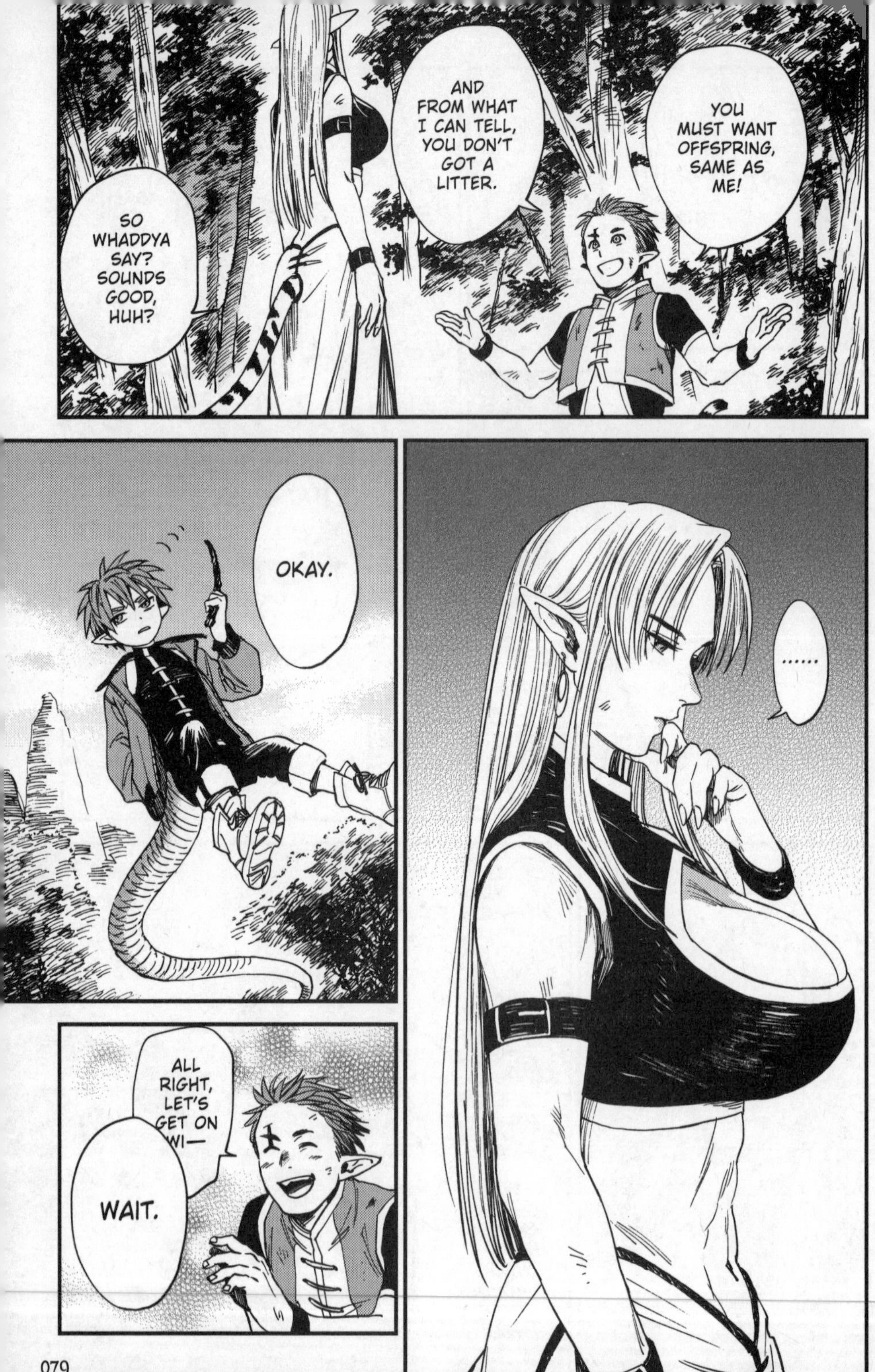
YOU MUST WANT OFFSPRING, SAME AS ME!
AND FROM WHAT I CAN TELL, YOU DON'T GOT A LITTER.
SO WHADDYA SAY? SOUNDS GOOD, HUH?
......
OKAY.
ALL RIGHT, LET'S GET ON WI—
WAIT.

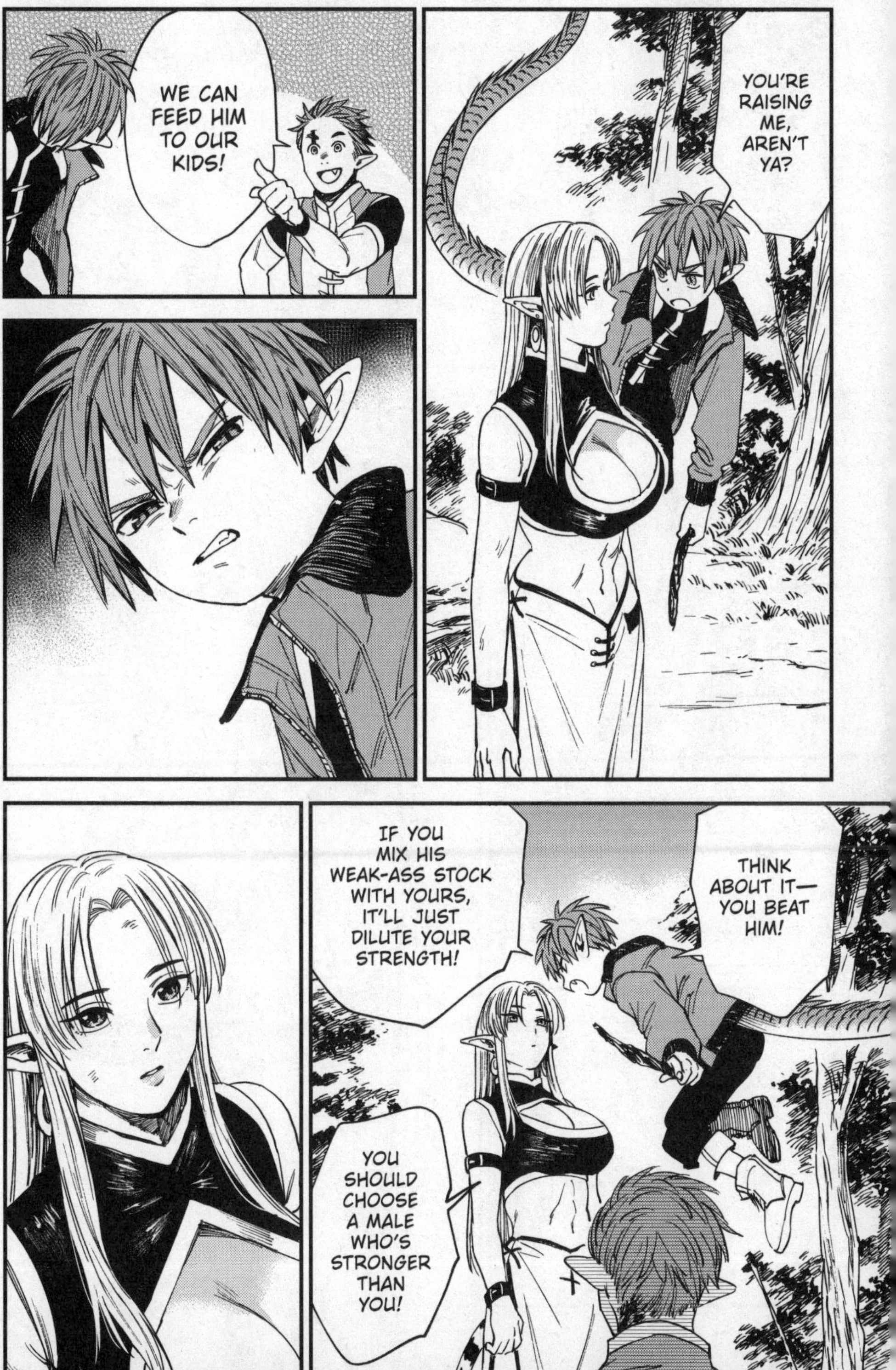
YOU'RE RAISING ME, AREN'T YA?
WE CAN FEED HIM TO OUR KIDS!
THINK ABOUT IT— YOU BEAT HIM!
IF YOU MIX HIS WEAK-ASS STOCK WITH YOURS, IT'LL JUST DILUTE YOUR STRENGTH!
YOU SHOULD CHOOSE A MALE WHO'S STRONGER THAN YOU!

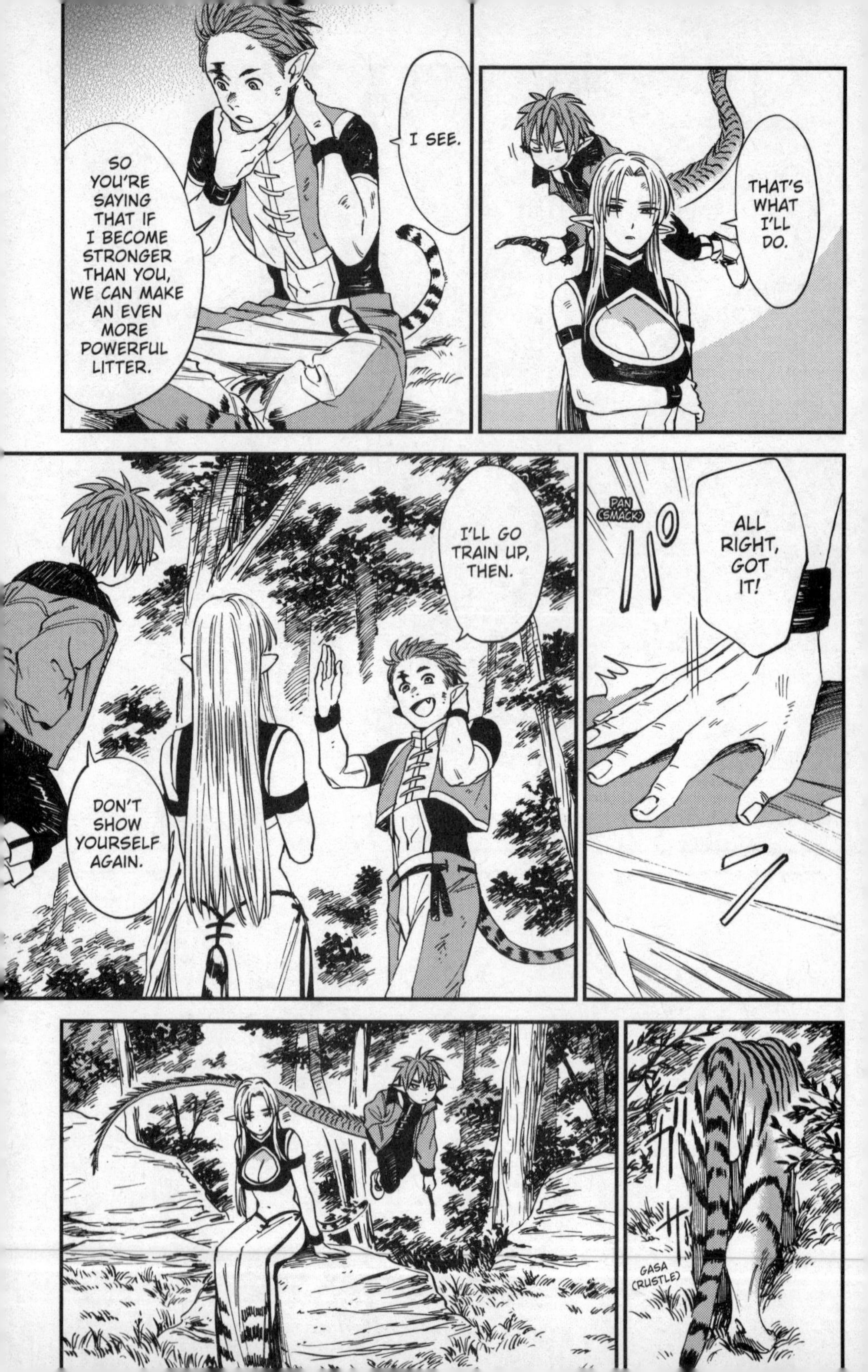
THAT'S WHAT I'LL DO.
I SEE.
SO YOU'RE SAYING THAT IF I BECOME STRONGER THAN YOU, WE CAN MAKE AN EVEN MORE POWERFUL LITTER.
ALL RIGHT, GOT IT!
PAN (SMACK)
I'LL GO TRAIN UP, THEN.
DON'T SHOW YOURSELF AGAIN.
GASA (RUSTLE)

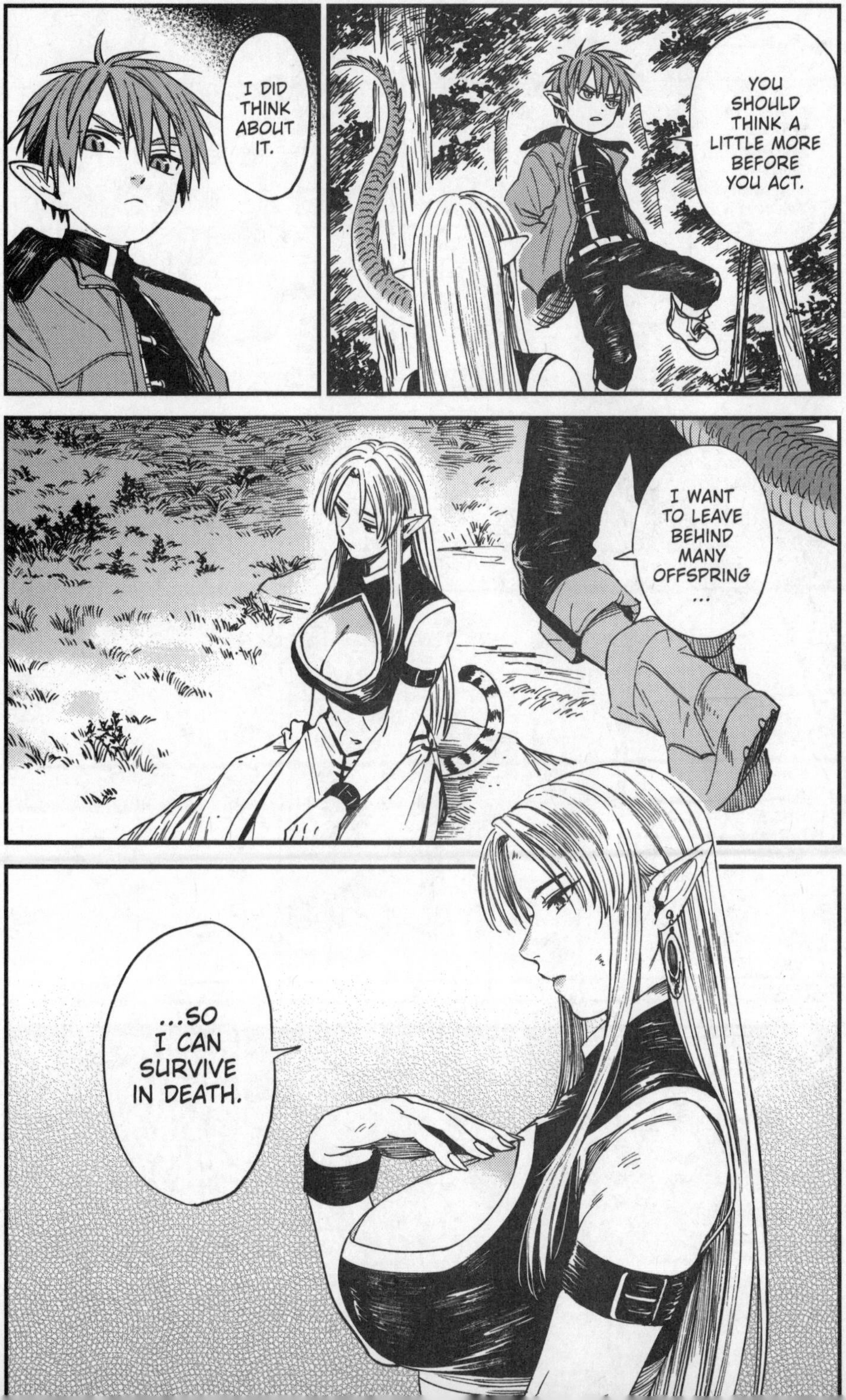
YOU SHOULD THINK A LITTLE MORE BEFORE YOU ACT.
I DID THINK ABOUT IT.
I WANT TO LEAVE BEHIND MANY OFFSPRING ...
...SO I CAN SURVIVE IN DEATH.

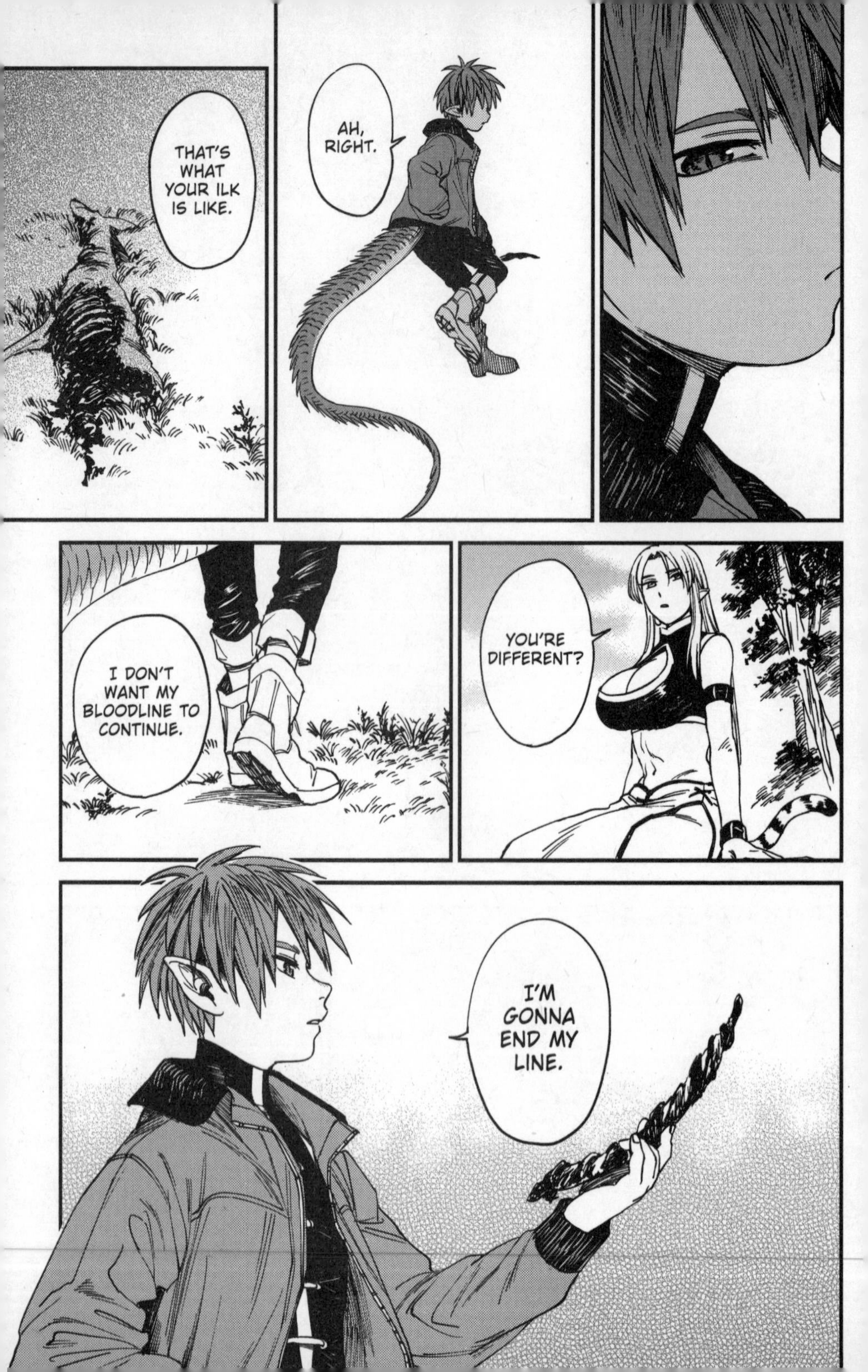
AH, RIGHT.
THAT'S WHAT YOUR ILK IS LIKE.
YOU'RE DIFFERENT?
I DON'T WANT MY BLOODLINE TO CONTINUE.
I'M GONNA END MY LINE.

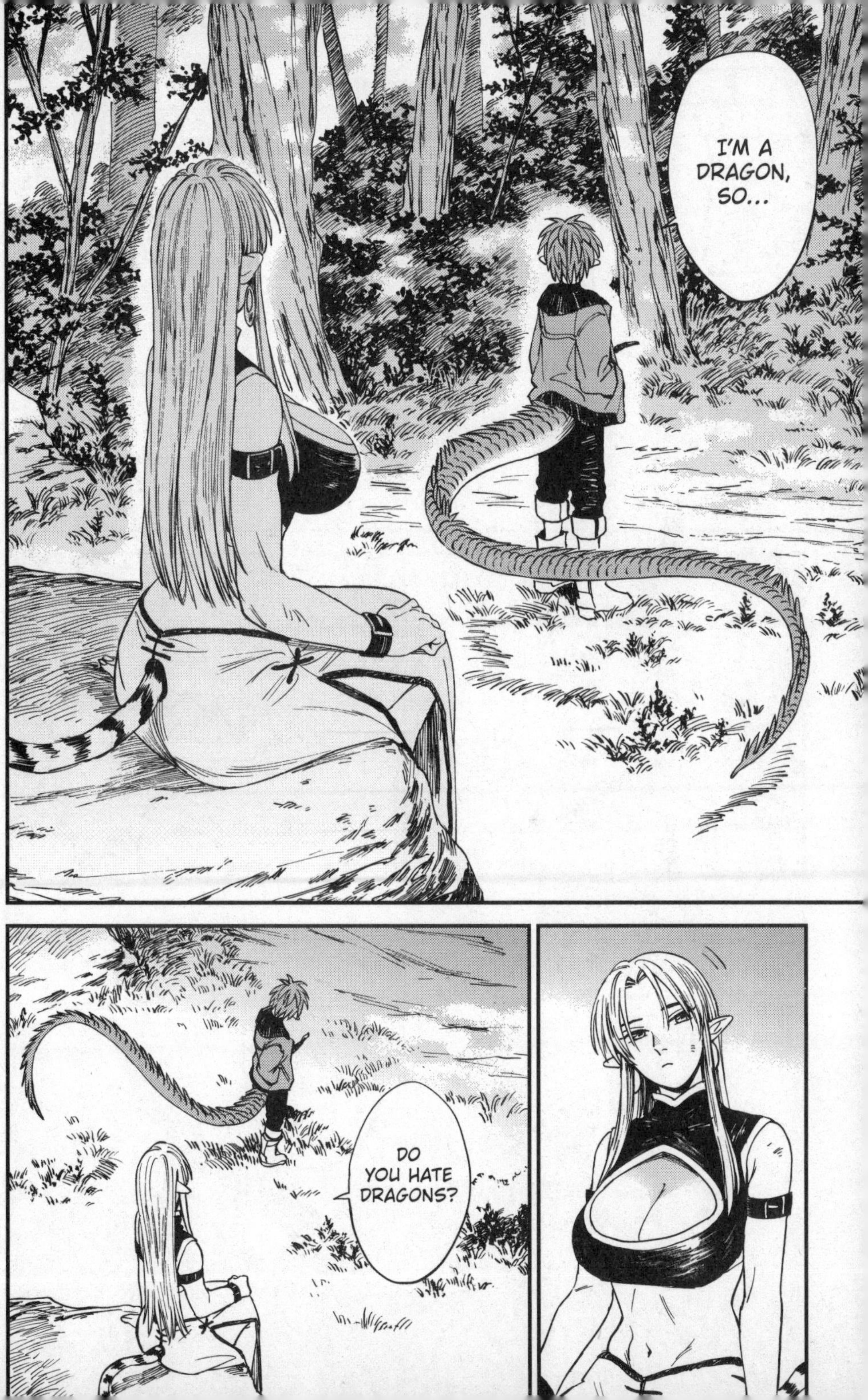
I'M A DRAGON, SO...
DO YOU HATE DRAGONS?

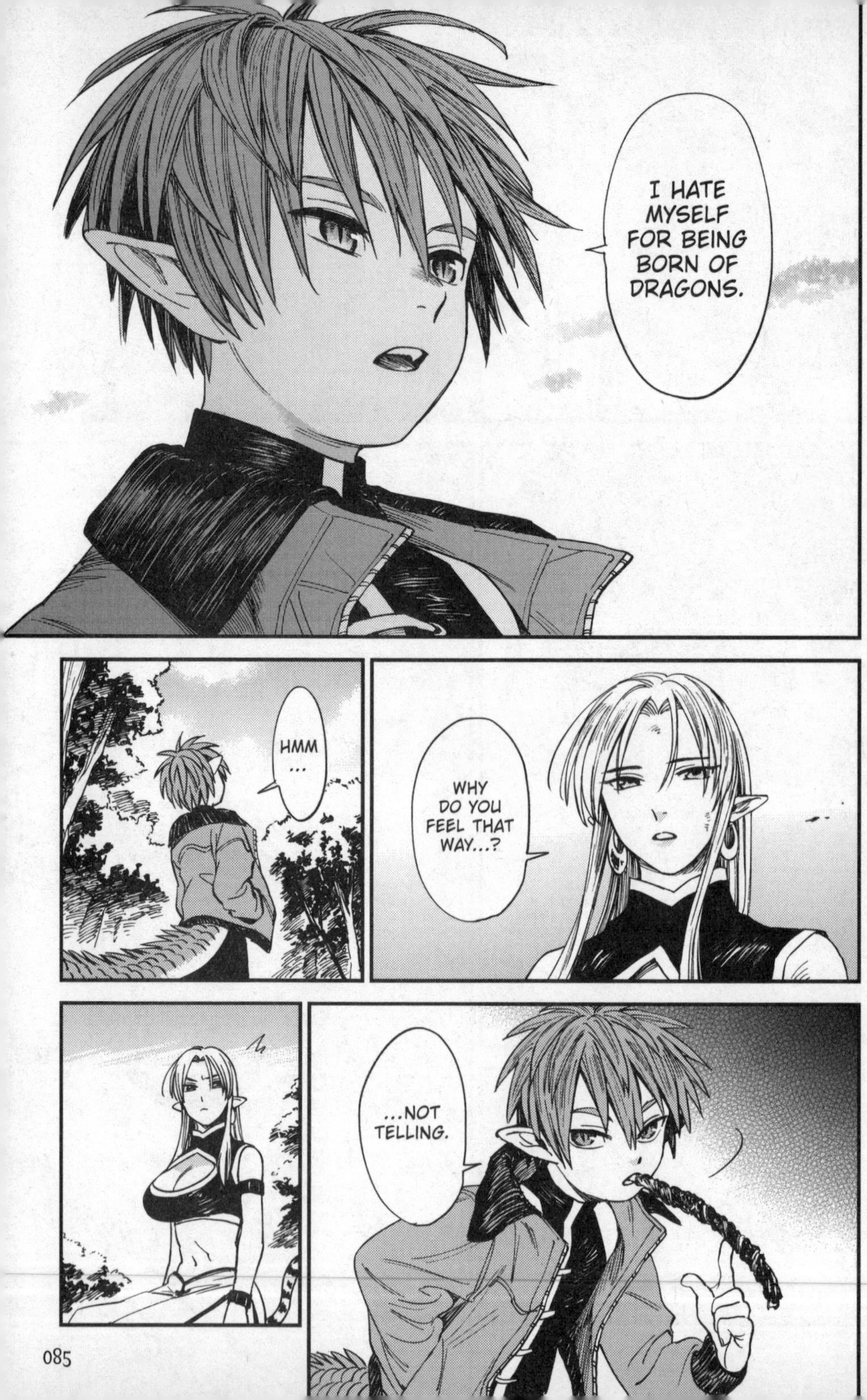
I HATE MYSELF FOR BEING BORN OF DRAGONS.
WHY DO YOU FEEL THAT WAY...?
HMM ...
...NOT TELLING.

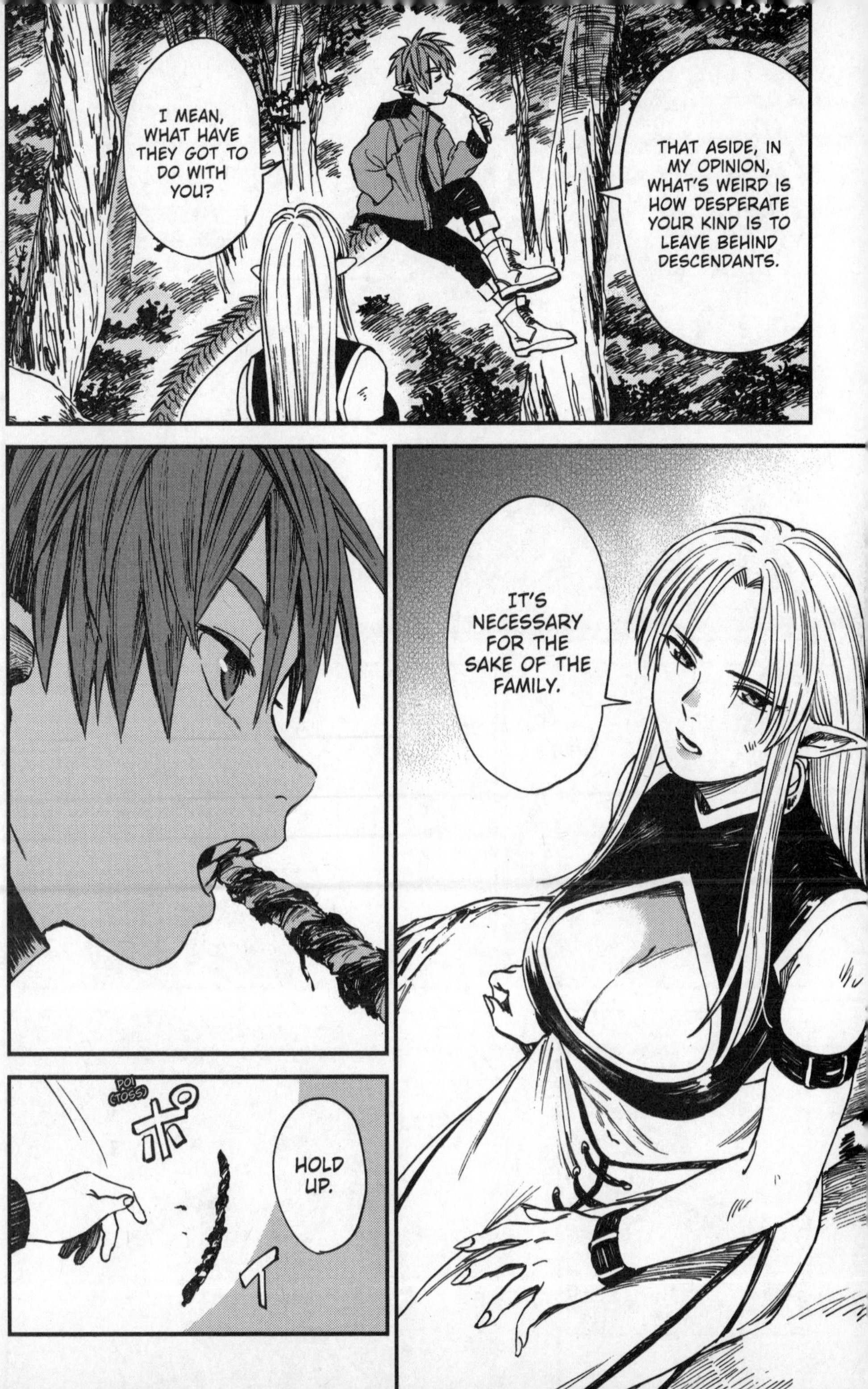
THAT ASIDE, IN MY OPINION, WHAT'S WEIRD IS HOW DESPERATE YOUR KIND IS TO LEAVE BEHIND DESCENDANTS.
I MEAN, WHAT HAVE THEY GOT TO DO WITH YOU?
IT'S NECESSARY FOR THE SAKE OF THE FAMILY.
ポイ
POI (TOSS)
HOLD UP.

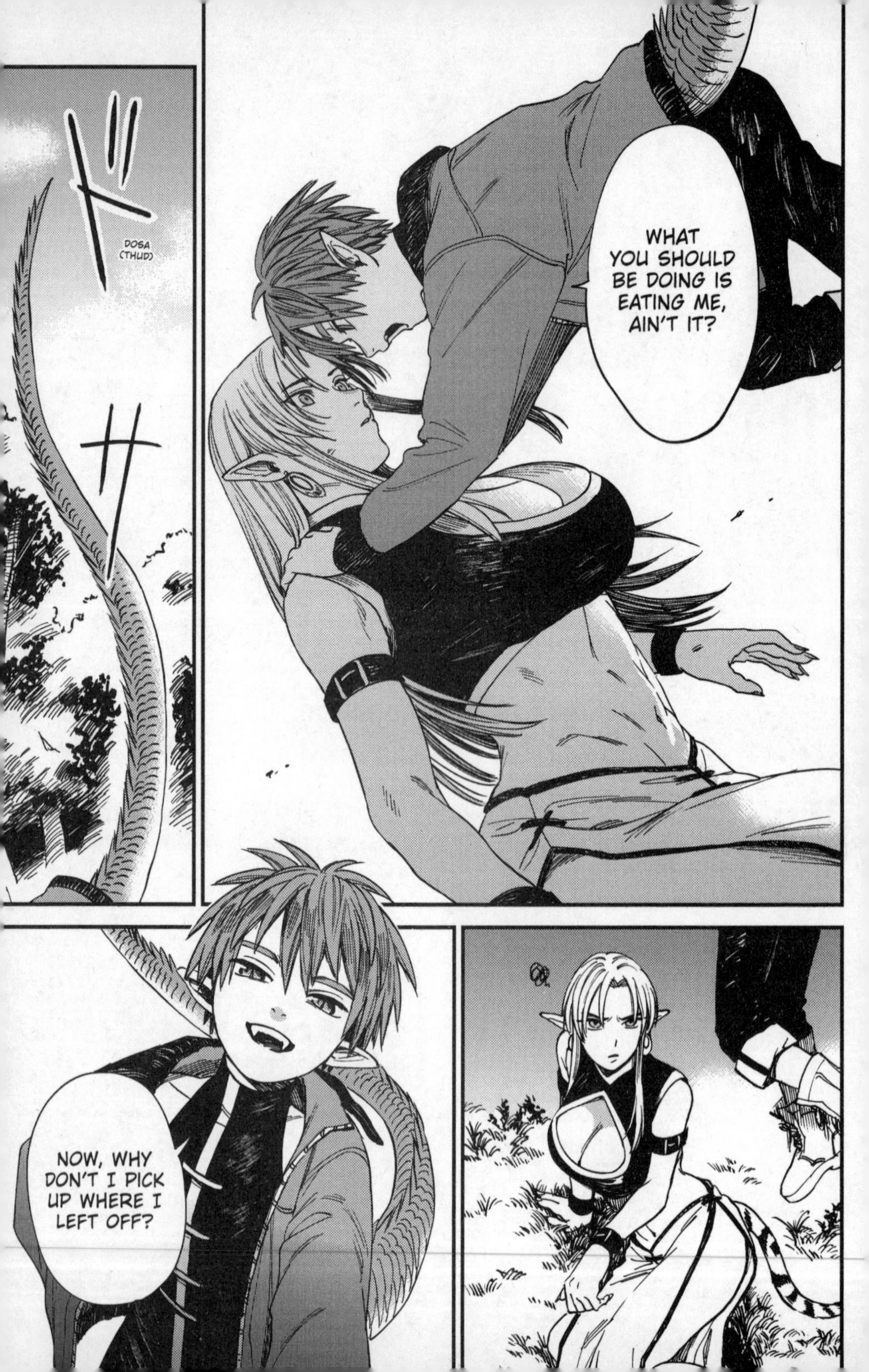
WHAT YOU SHOULD BE DOING IS EATING ME, AIN'T IT?
ドサ
DOSA (THUD)
NOW, WHY DON'T I PICK UP WHERE I LEFT OFF?

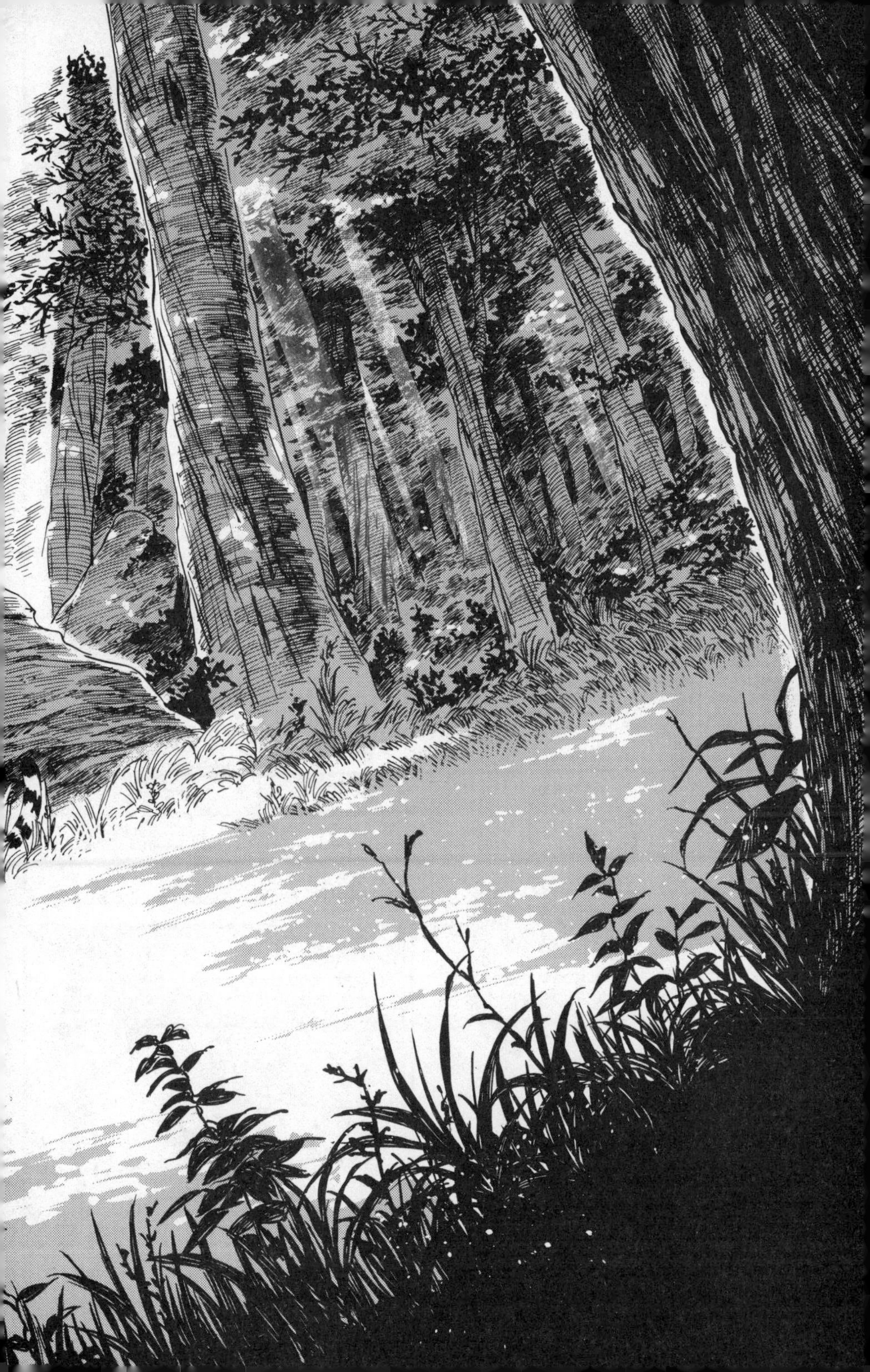

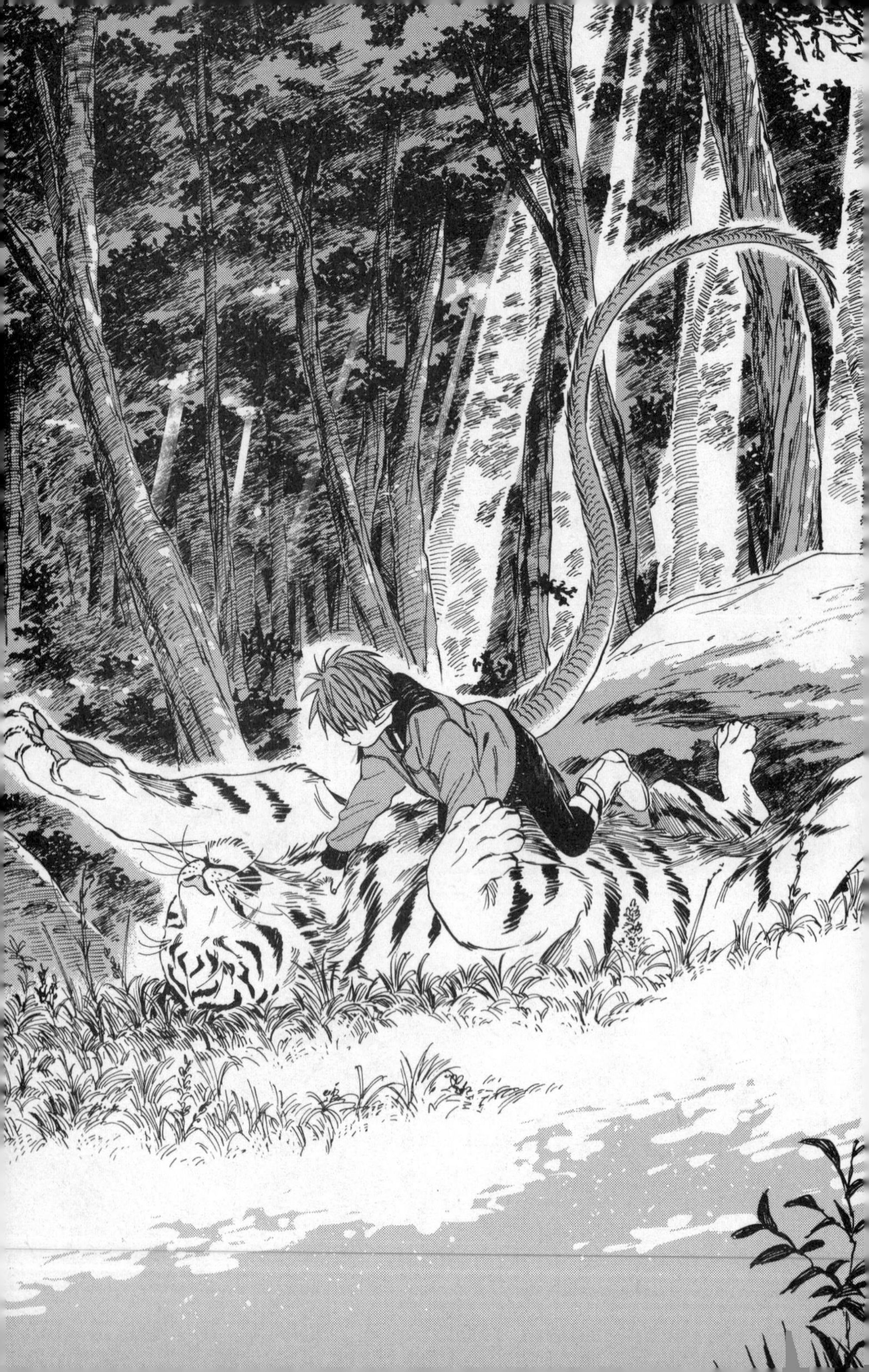

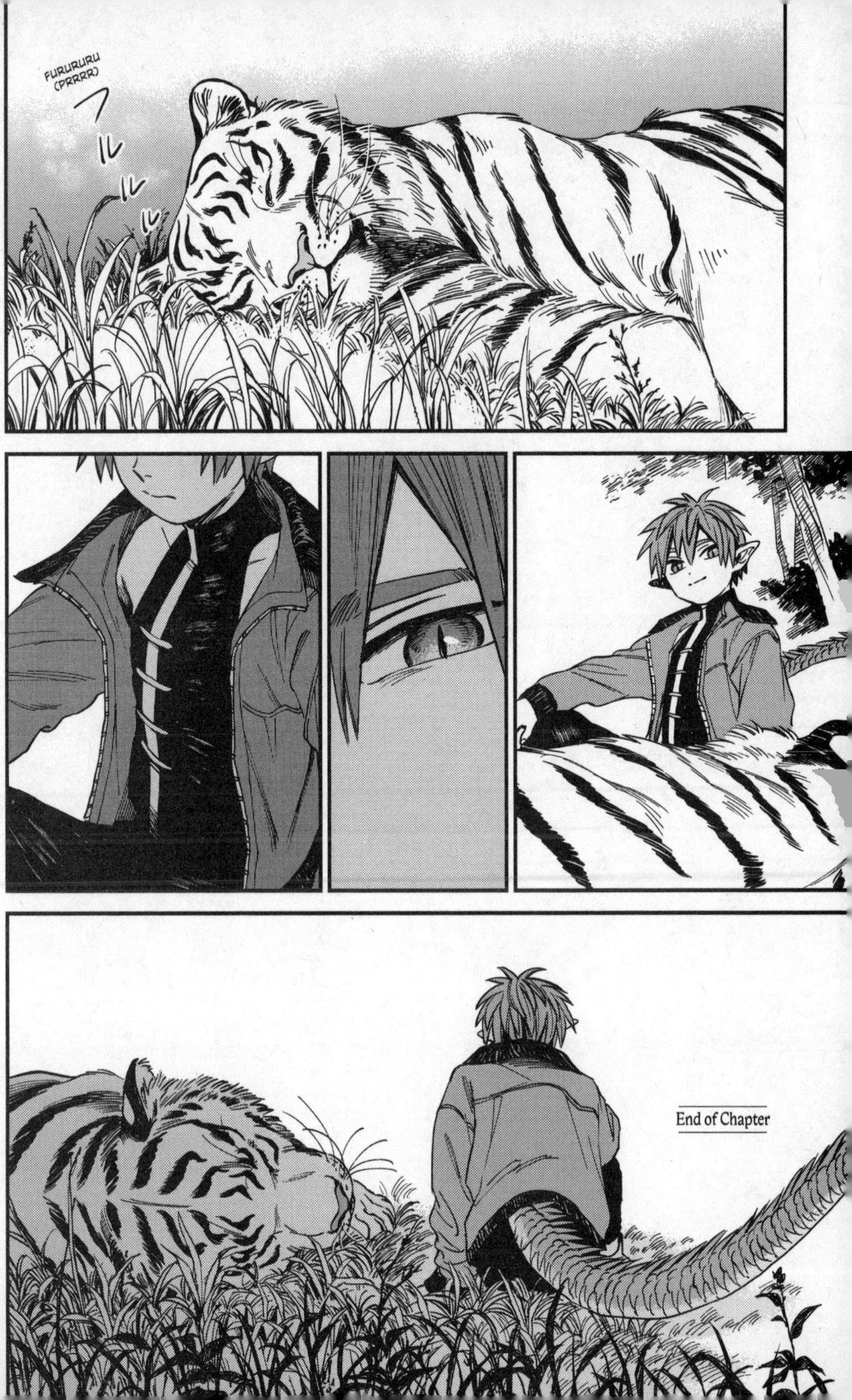
FURURURU (PRRRR)
フルルル
End of Chapter

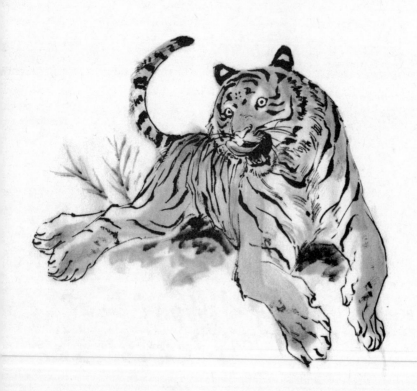

The Tiger Won't Eat the Dragon Yet

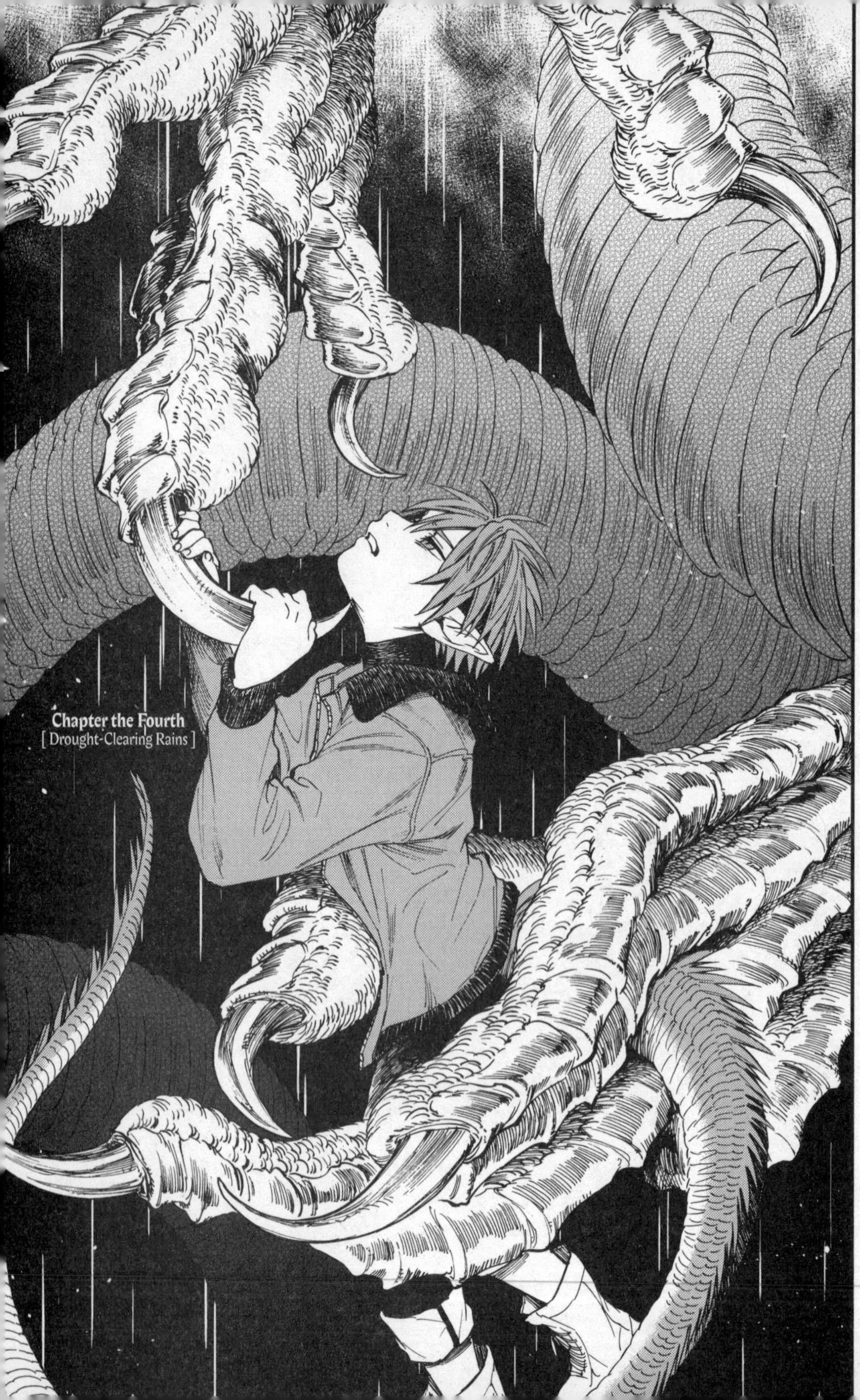
Chapter the Fourth
[Drought-Clearing Rains]

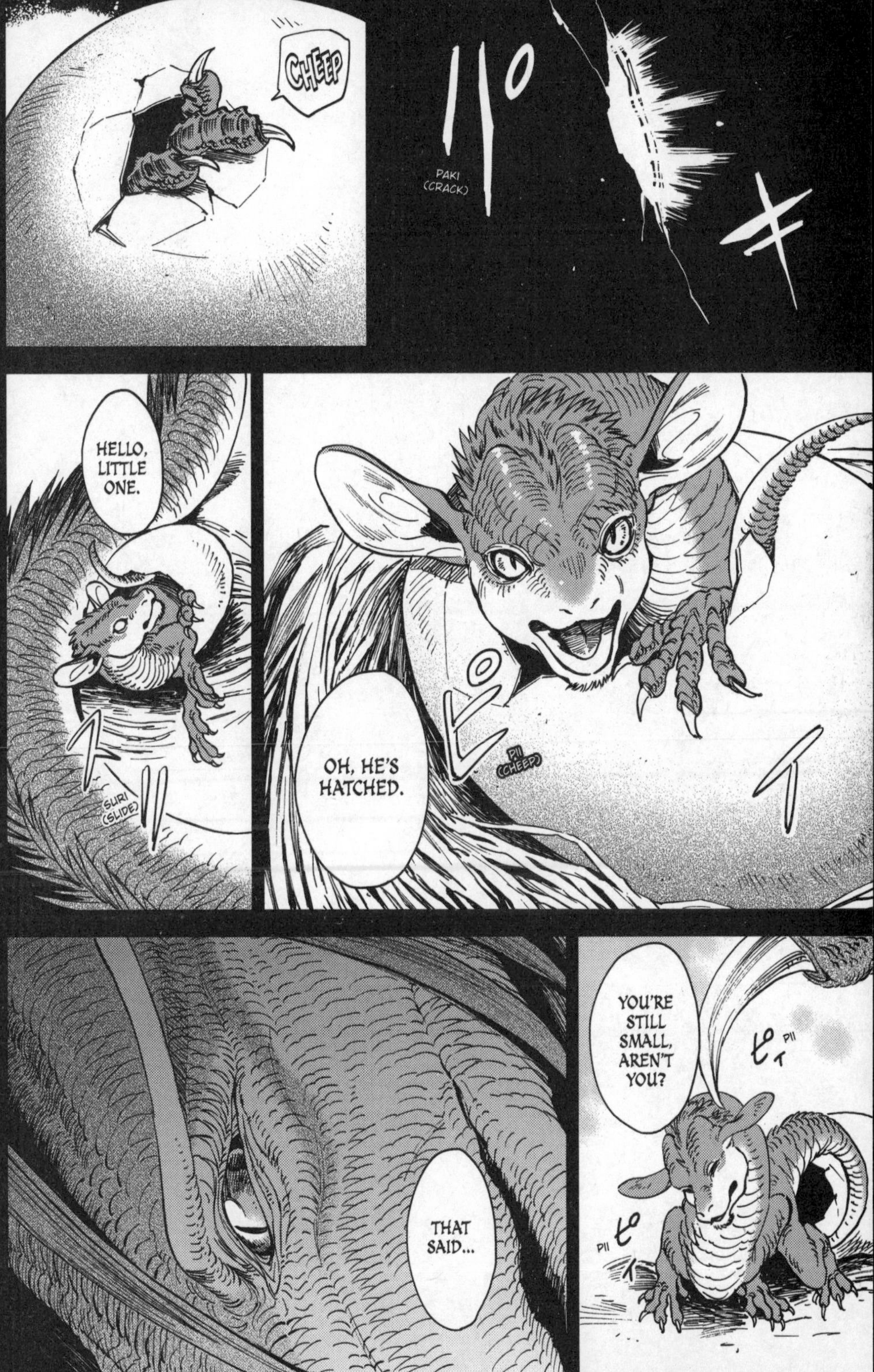
PAKI (CRACK)
CHEEP
PII (CHEEP)
OH, HE'S HATCHED.
HELLO, LITTLE ONE.
SURI (SLIDE)
YOU'RE STILL SMALL, AREN'T YOU?
PII
PII
THAT SAID...

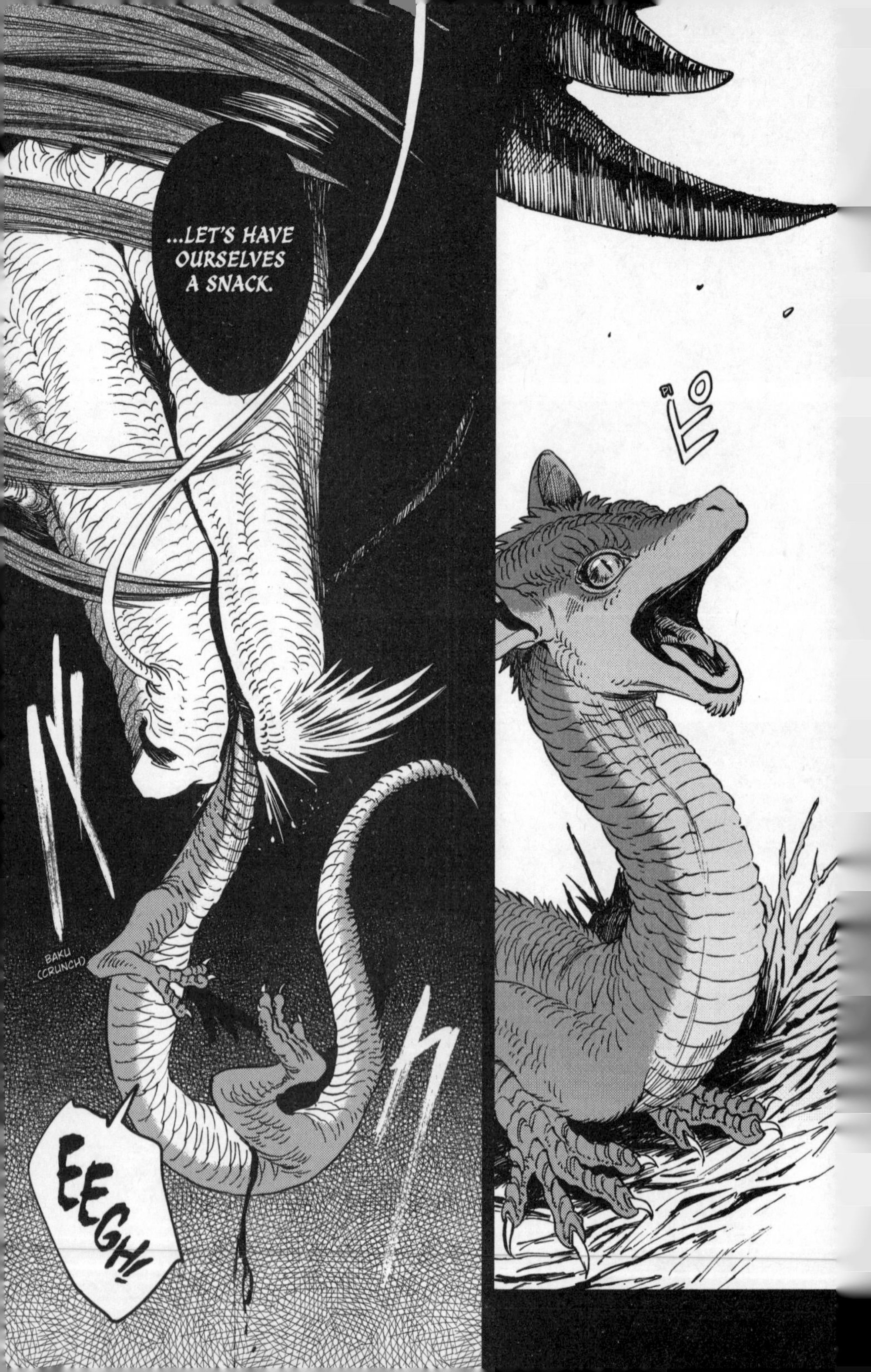
PI
...LET'S HAVE OURSELVES A SNACK.
BAKU (CRUNCH)
EEGH!

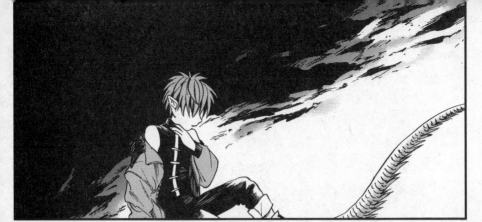

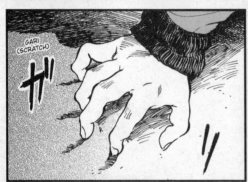

GARI
(SCRATCH)

ザ"

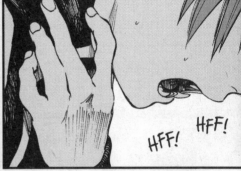

HFF! HFF!

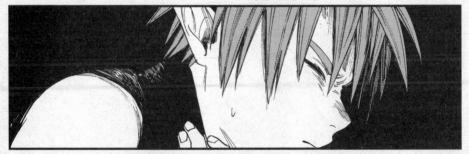

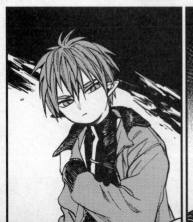

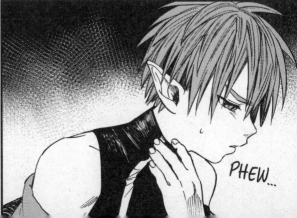

PHEW...

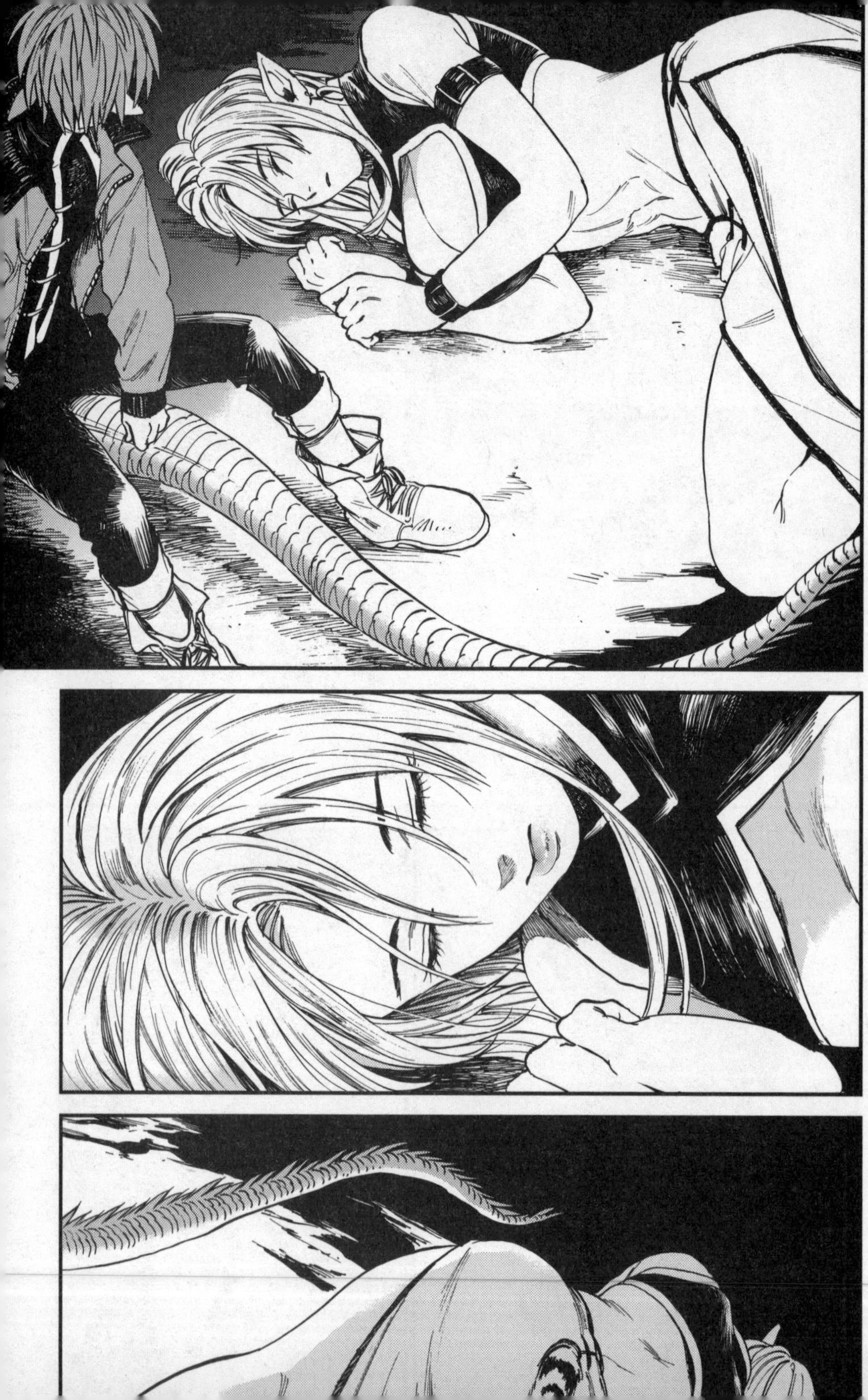

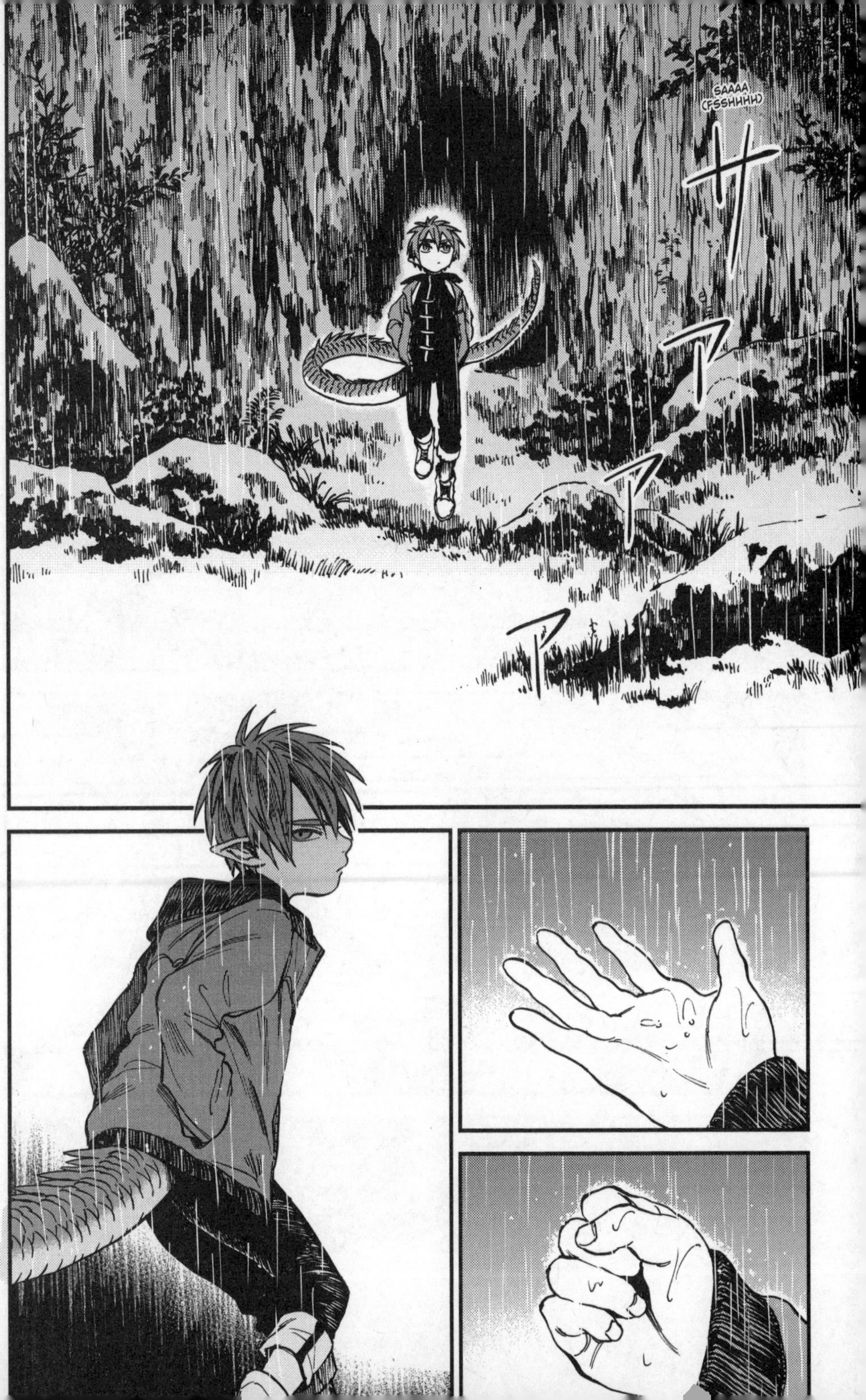
SAAAA
(FSSHHHH)
サアアア

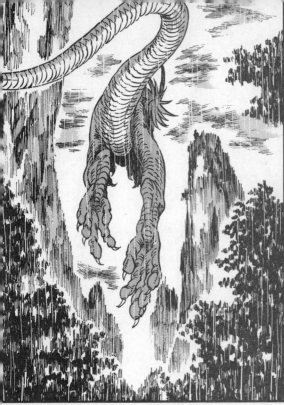
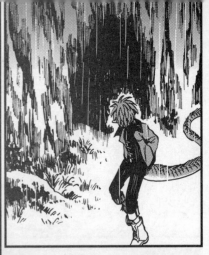
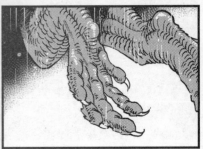

PII
(CHEEP)
ピィ

PII
ピィ

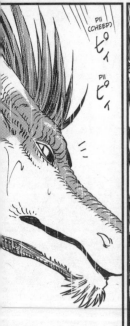
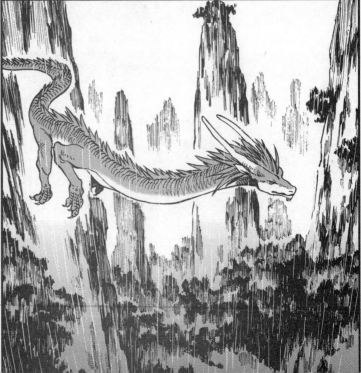

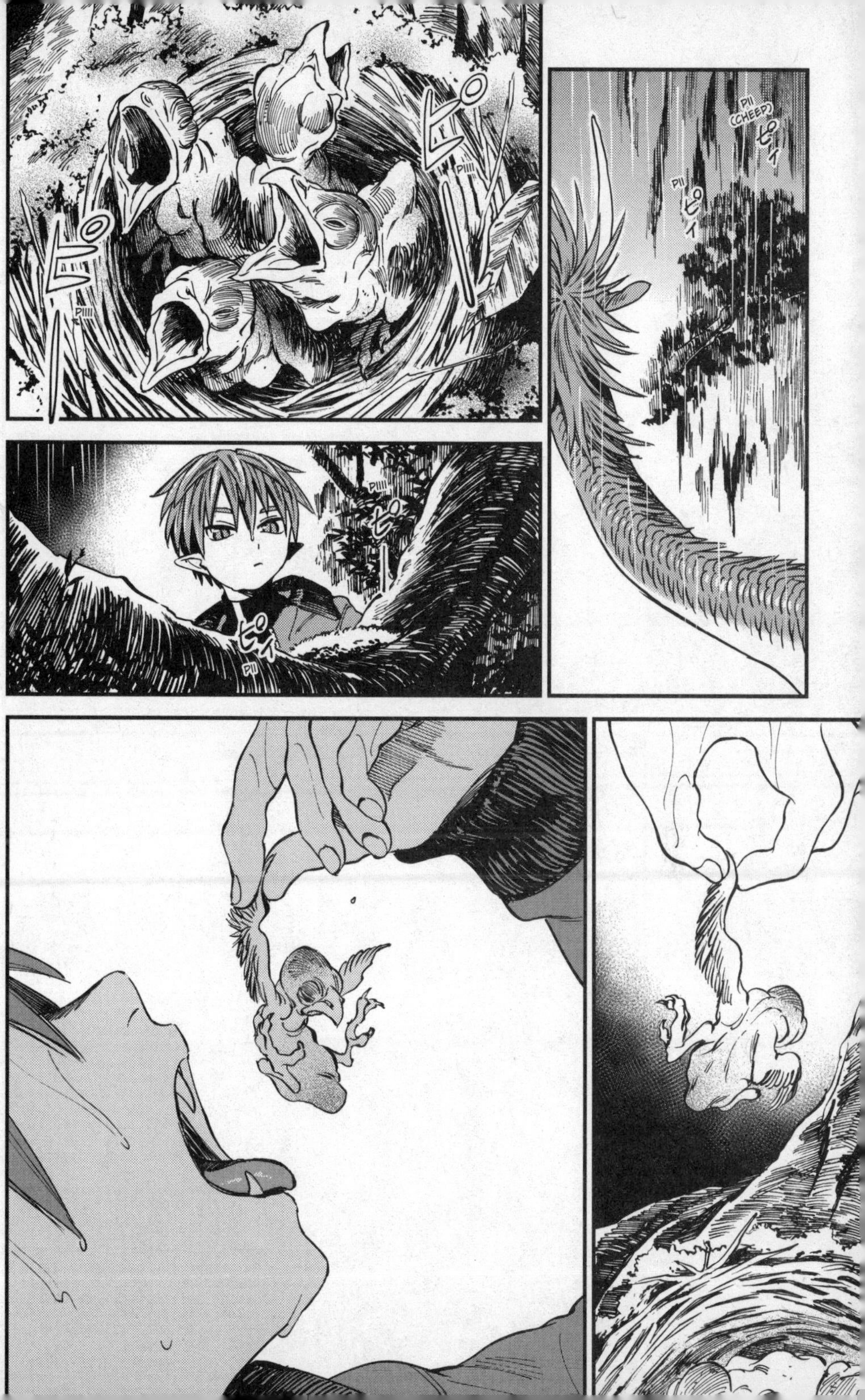
PII (CHEEP)
ピィ
PII
ピィ
ピィ
PIIII
ピィ
PIIII
PIIII
ピィ
ピィ
PII

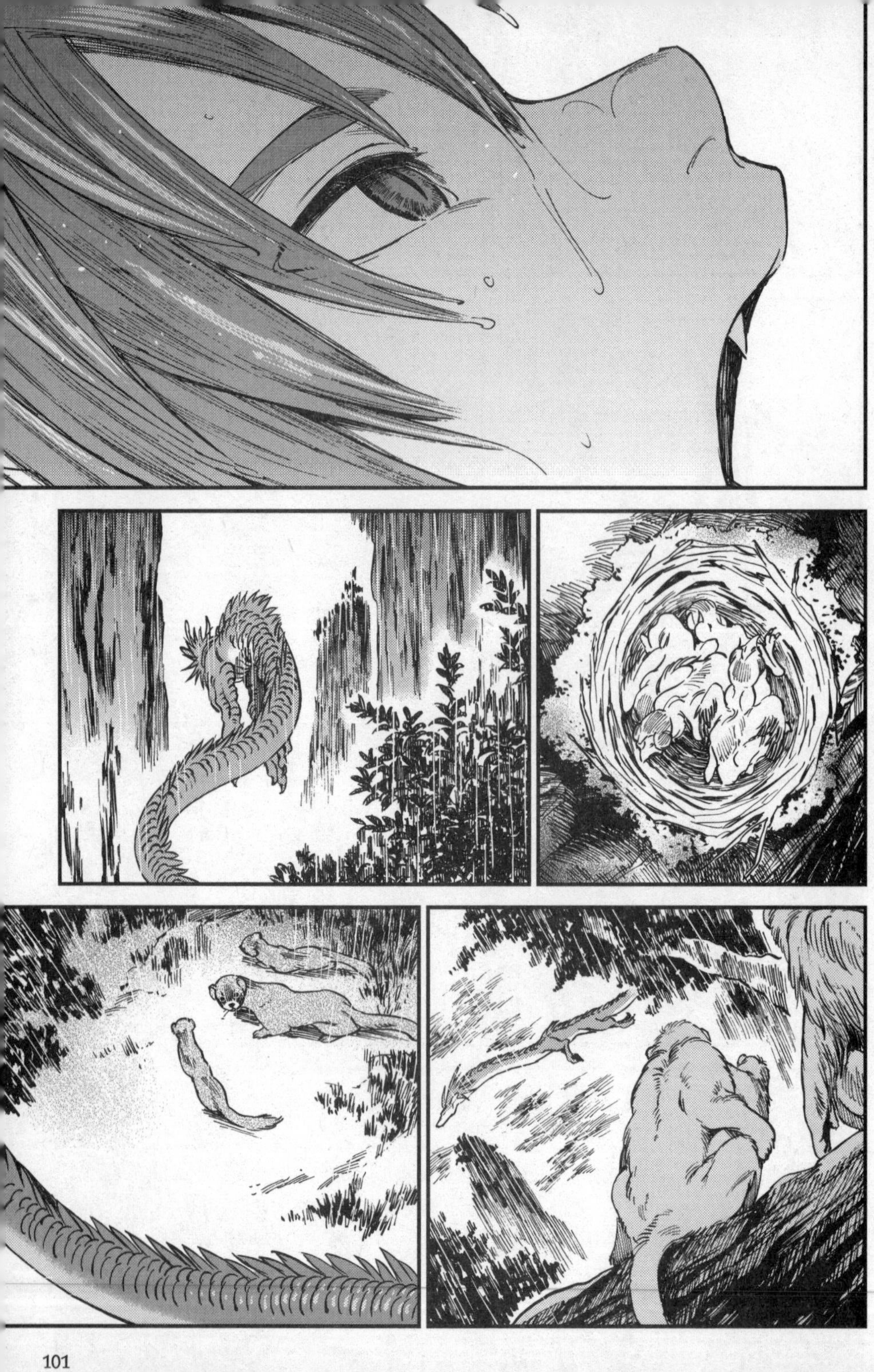

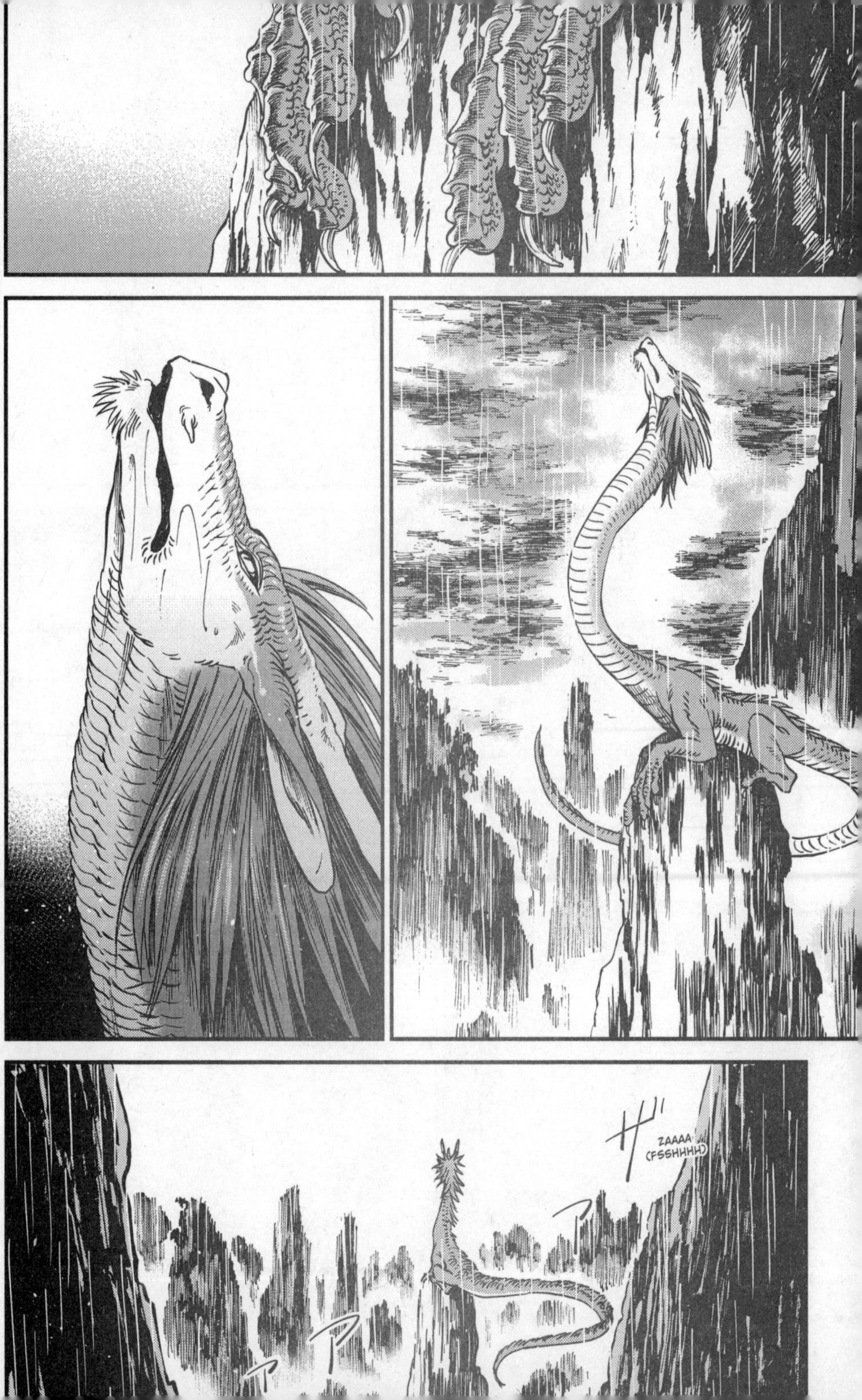
ZAAAA
(FSSHHHH)

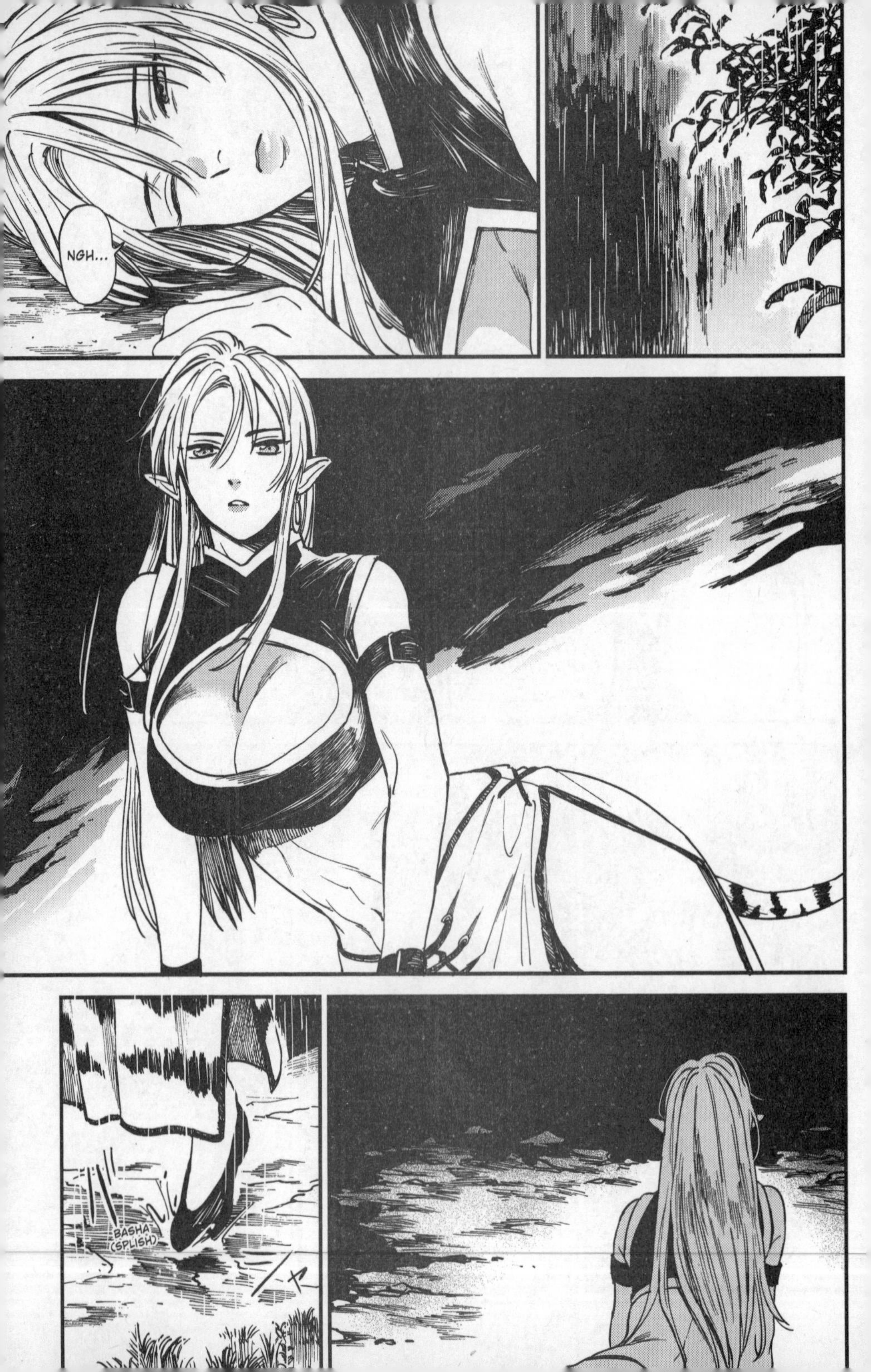
NGH...
BASHA
(SPLISH)

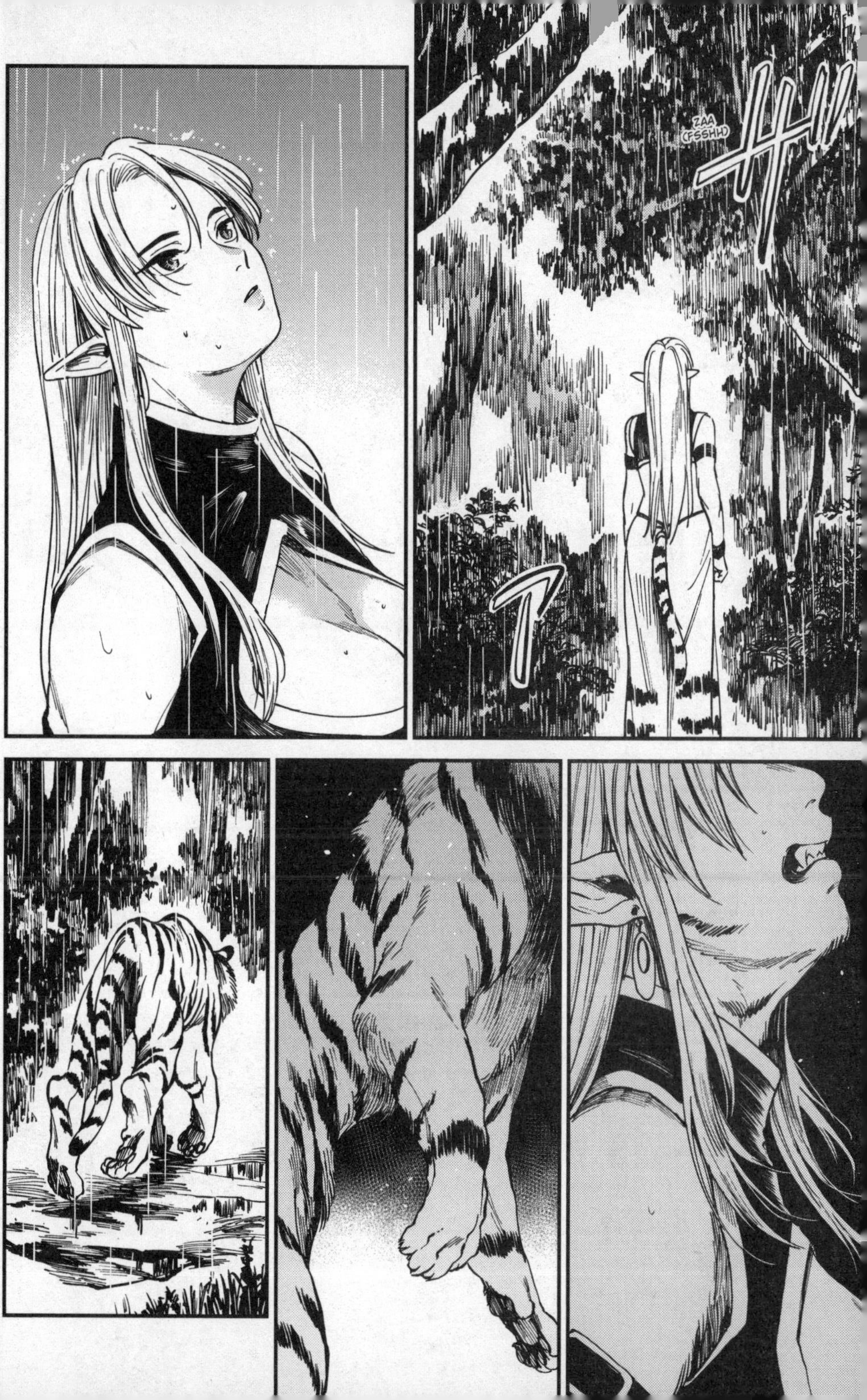
ZAA
(FSSHH)

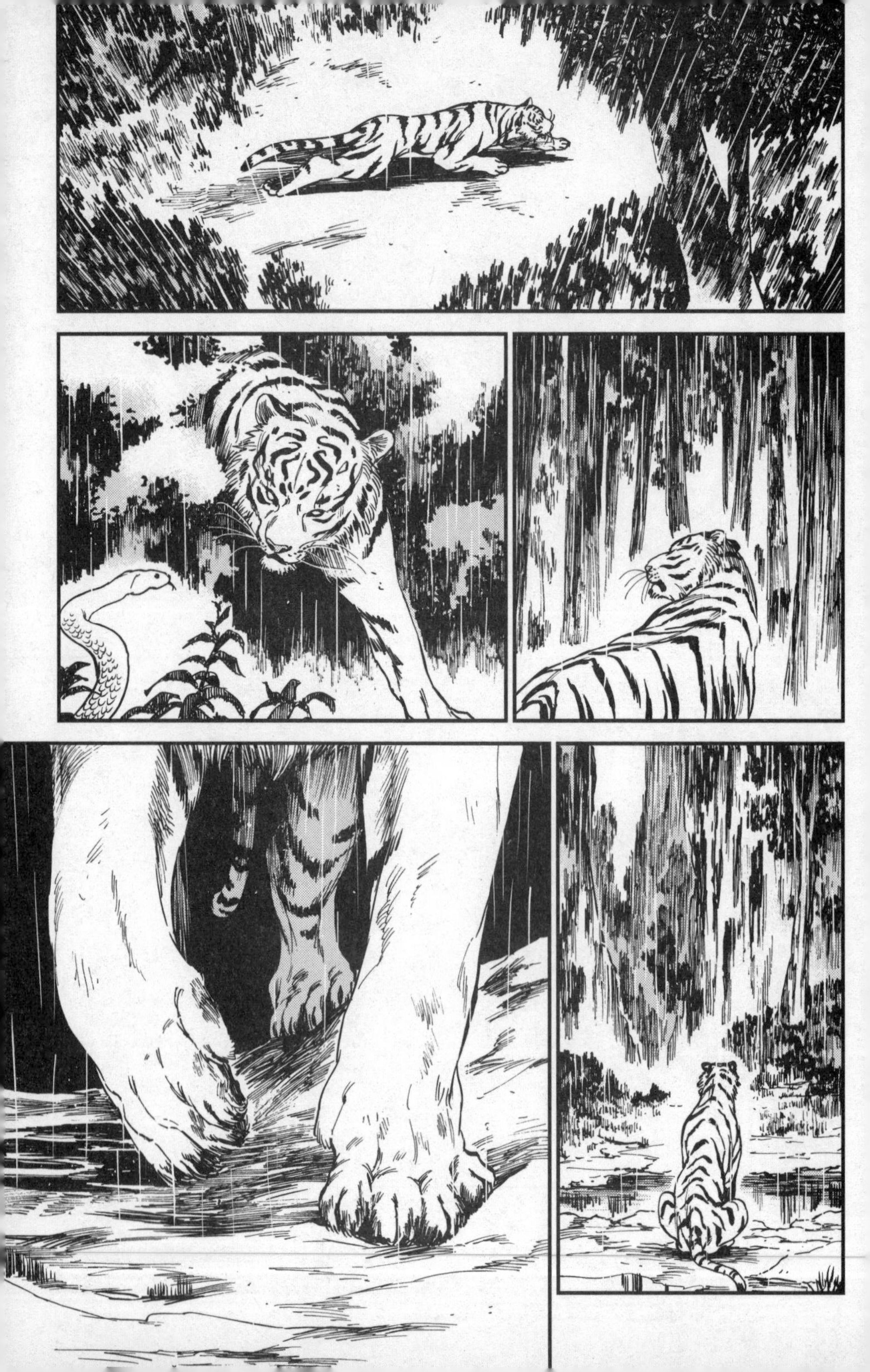

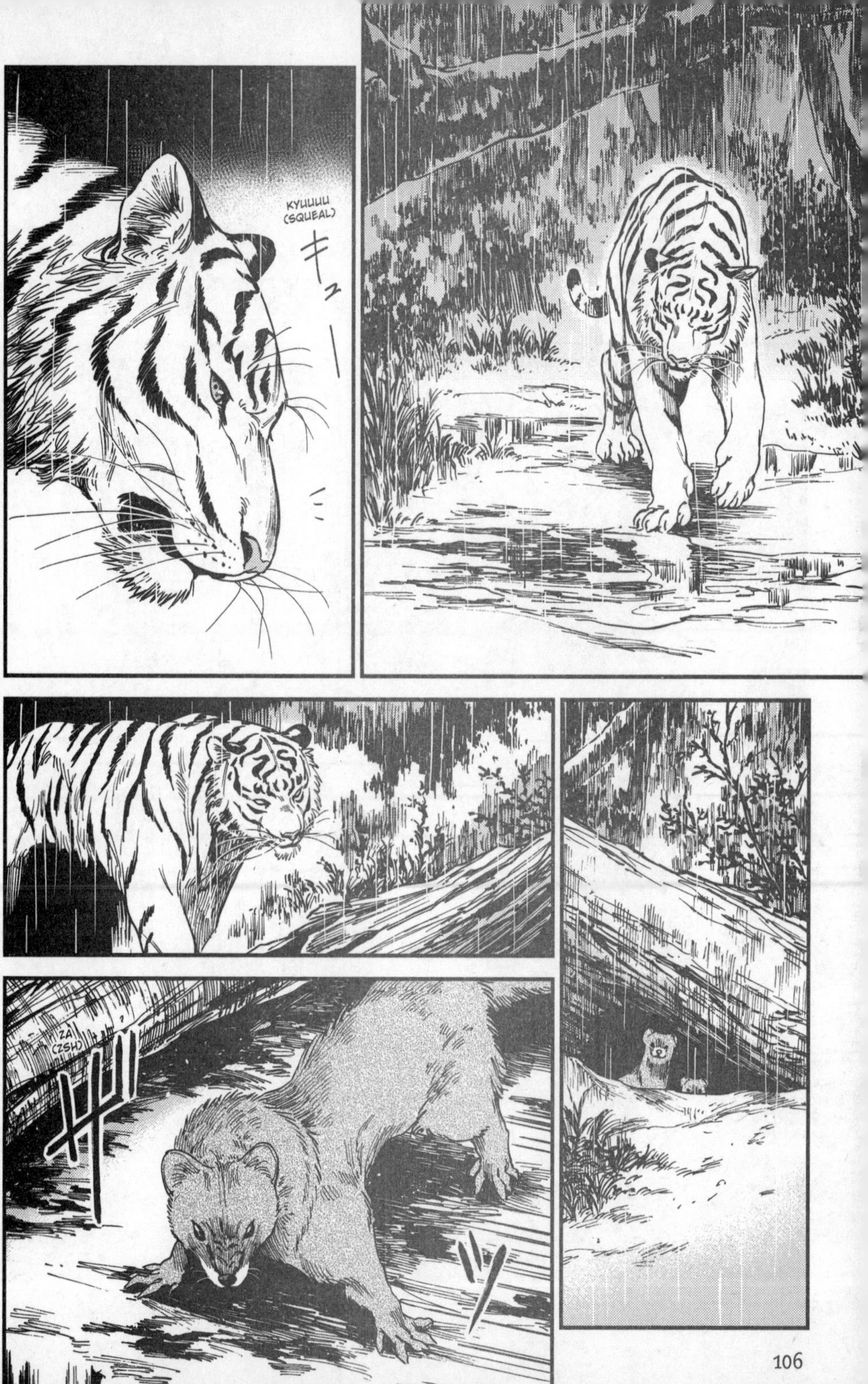
KYUUUU (SQUEAL)
キュー
ZA (CZSH)
ザッ

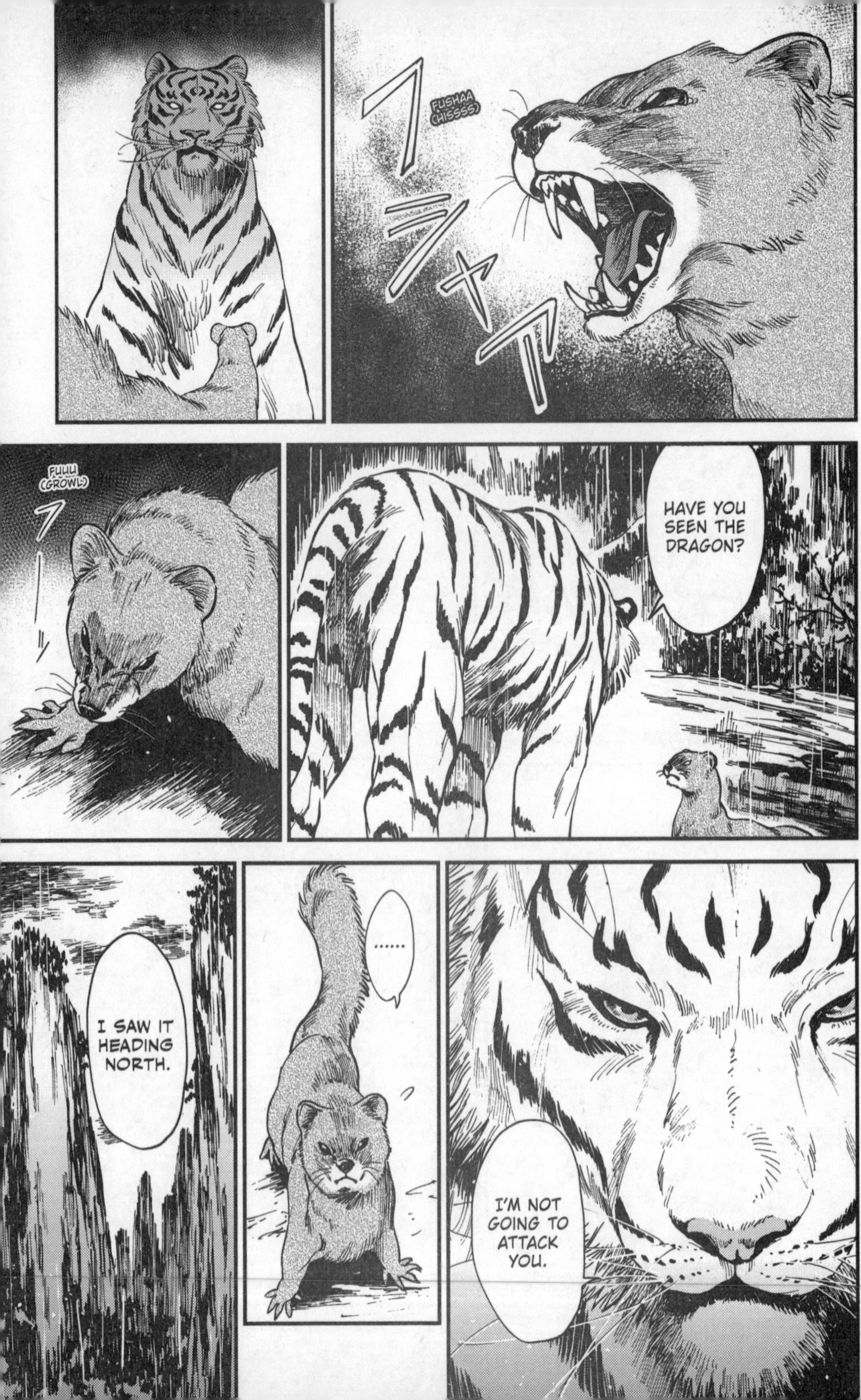
FUSHAA (HISSSS)
HAVE YOU SEEN THE DRAGON?
FUUU (GROWL)
I'M NOT GOING TO ATTACK YOU.
......
I SAW IT HEADING NORTH.

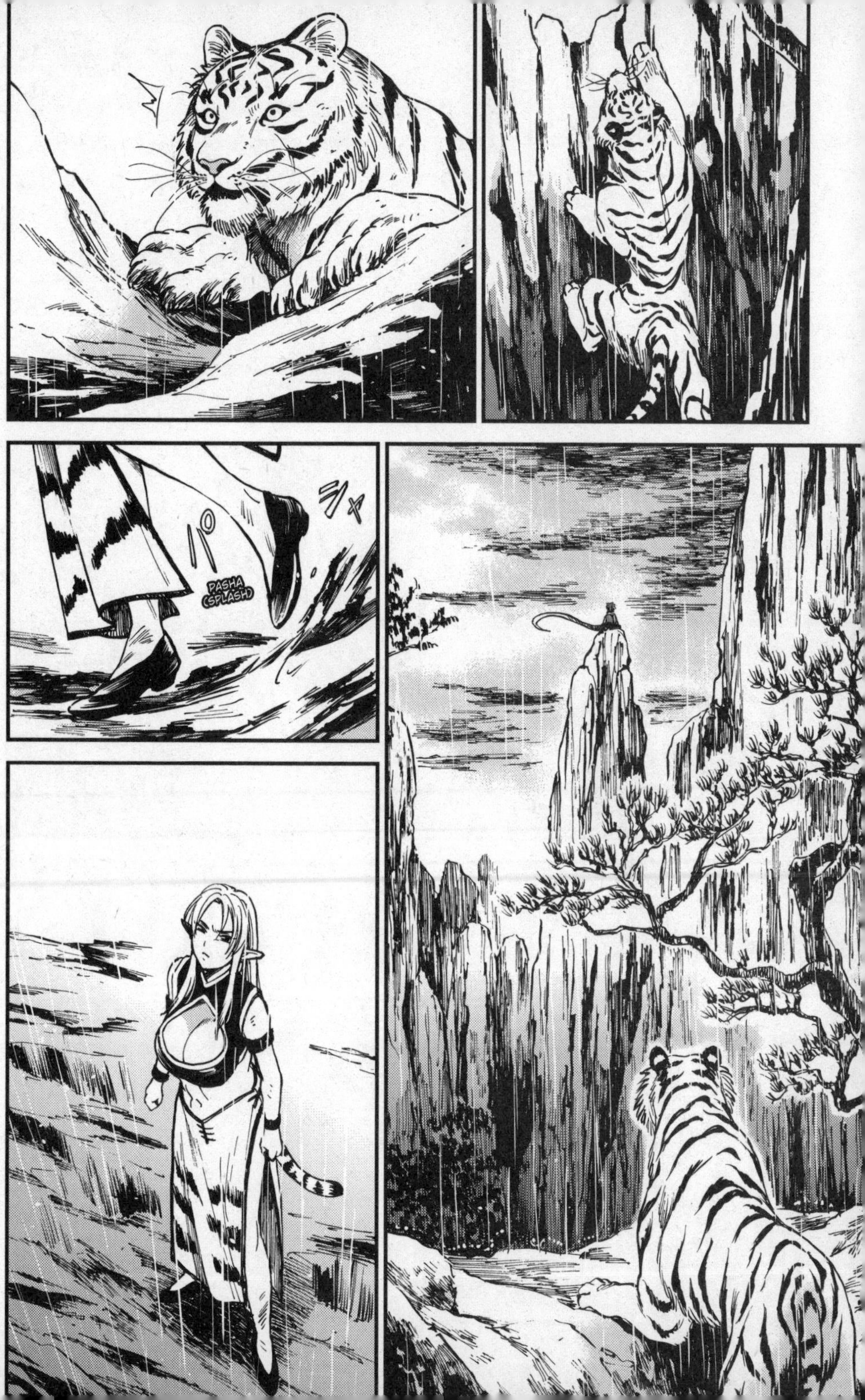
パ
シャ
PASHA (SPLASH)

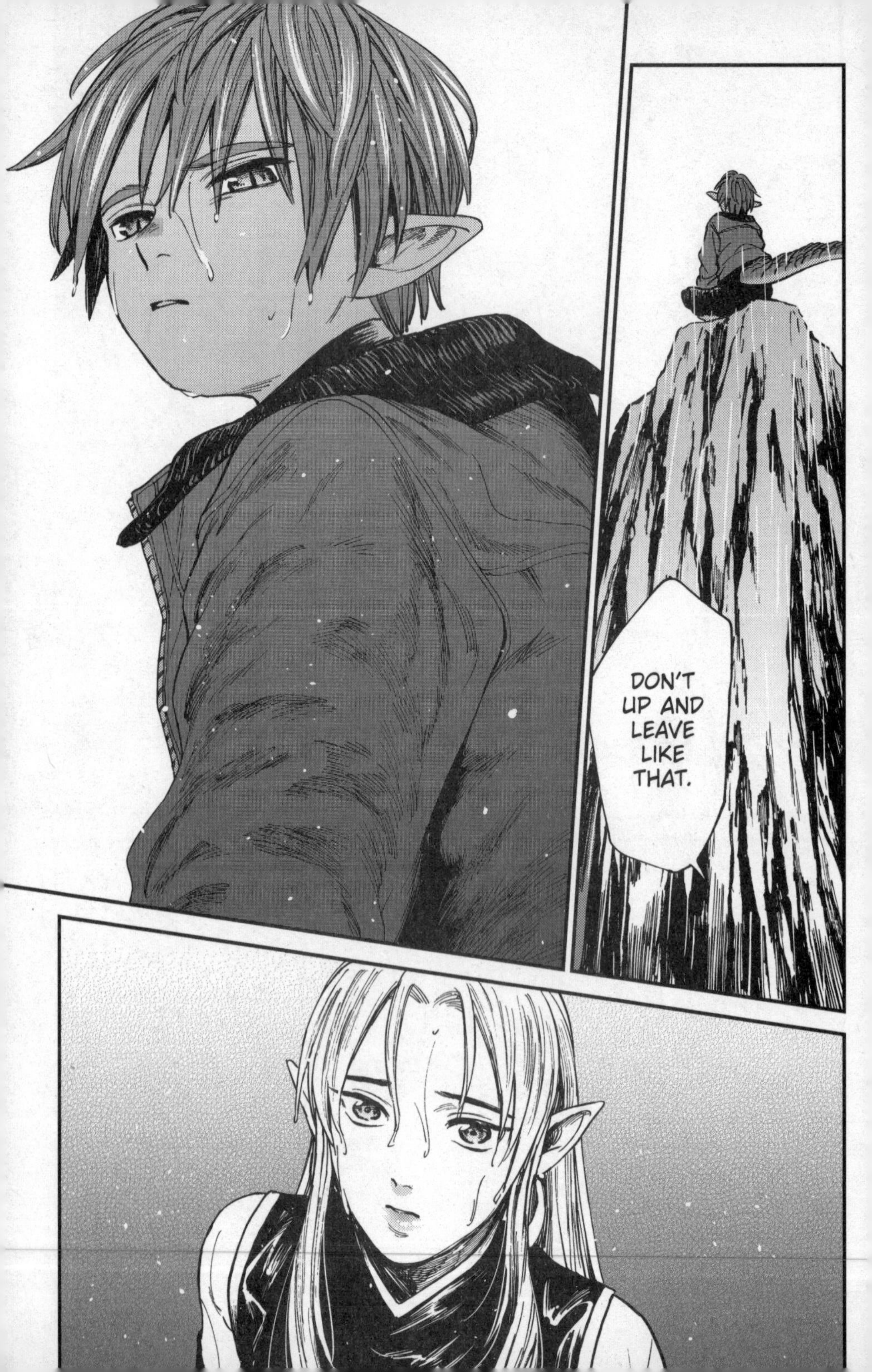
DON'T UP AND LEAVE LIKE THAT.

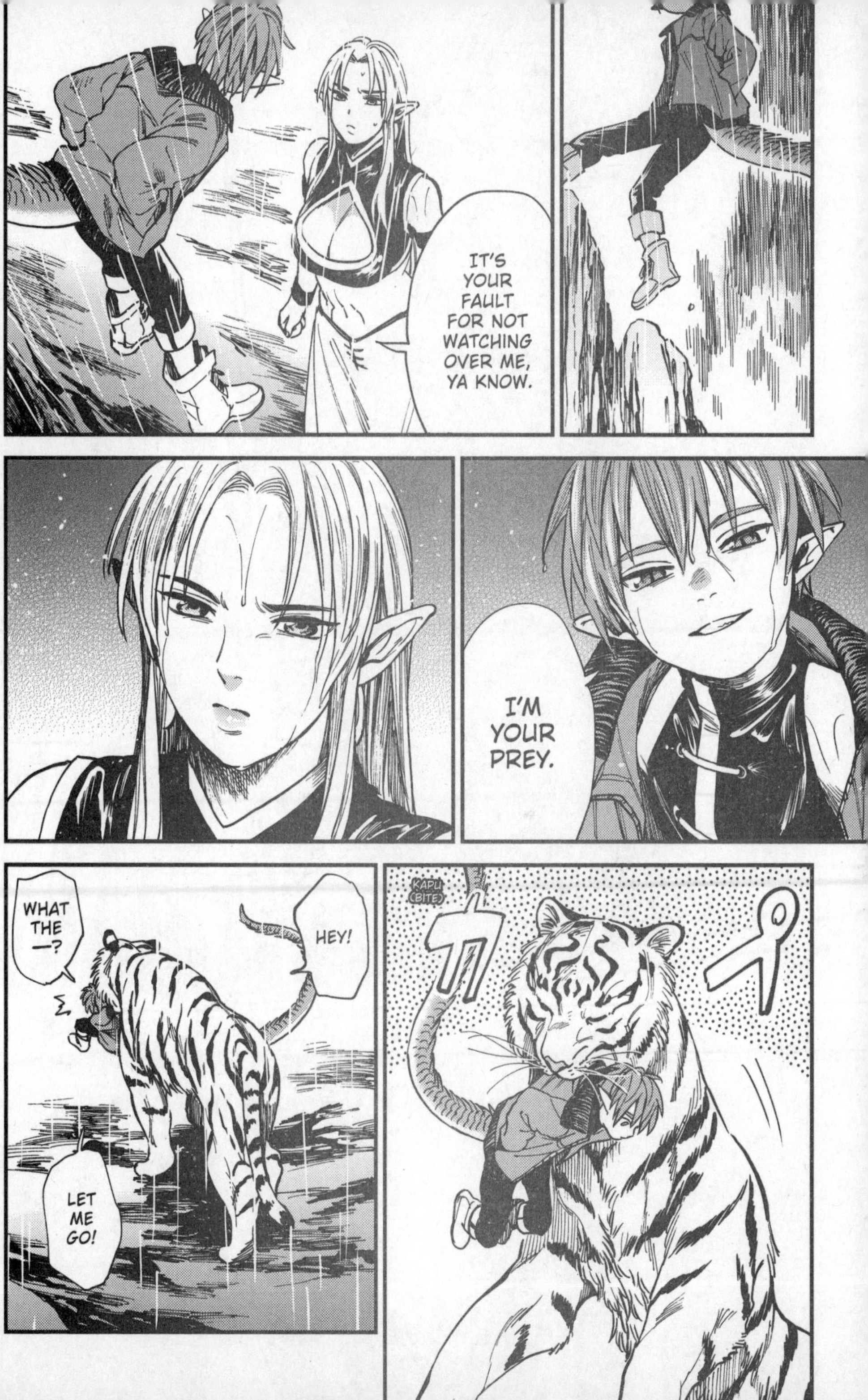
IT'S YOUR FAULT FOR NOT WATCHING OVER ME, YA KNOW.
I'M YOUR PREY.
KAPU (BITE)
HEY!
WHAT THE—?
LET ME GO!

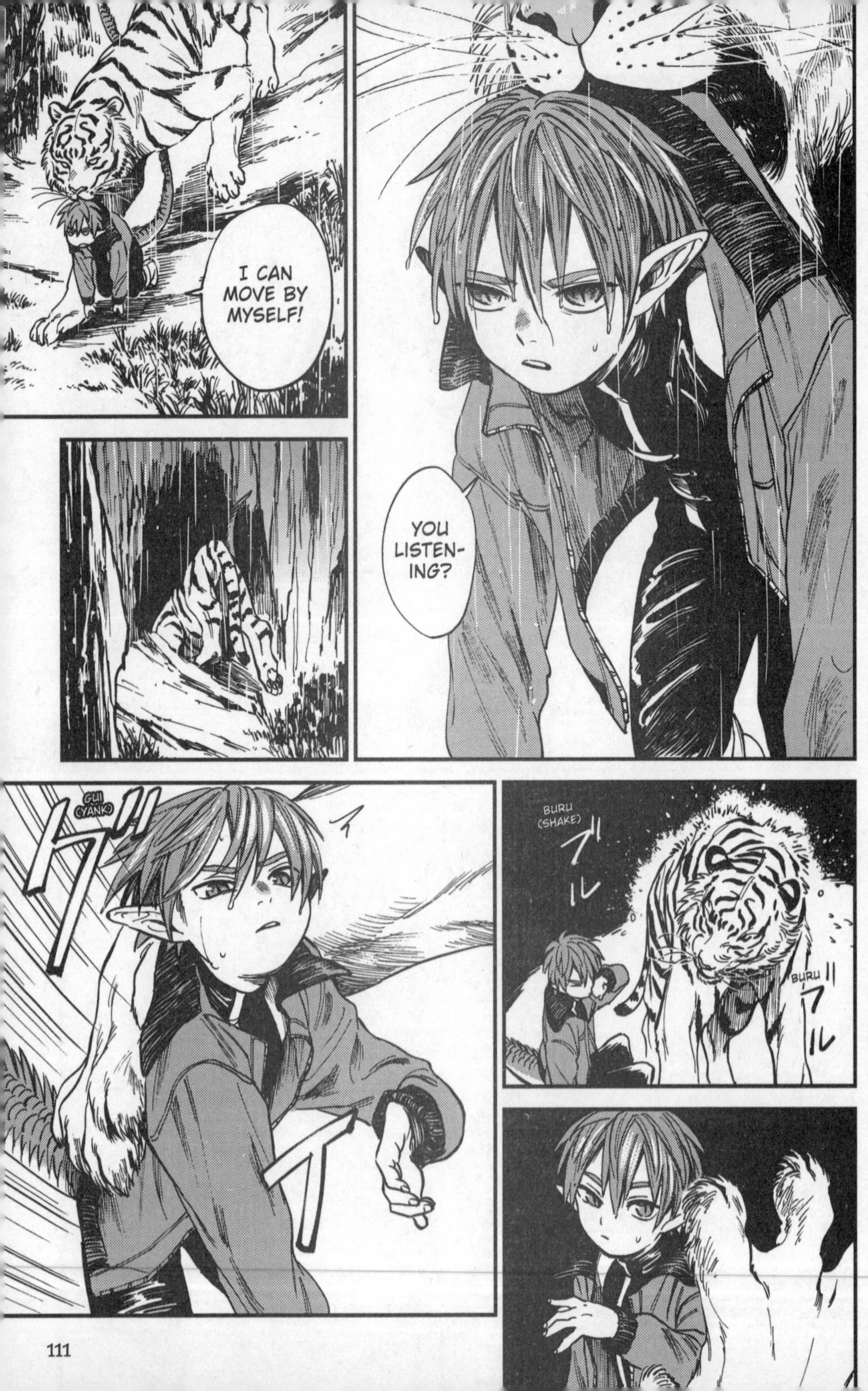

YOU LISTENING?
I CAN MOVE BY MYSELF!
BURU (SHAKE)
BURU
GUI (YANK)

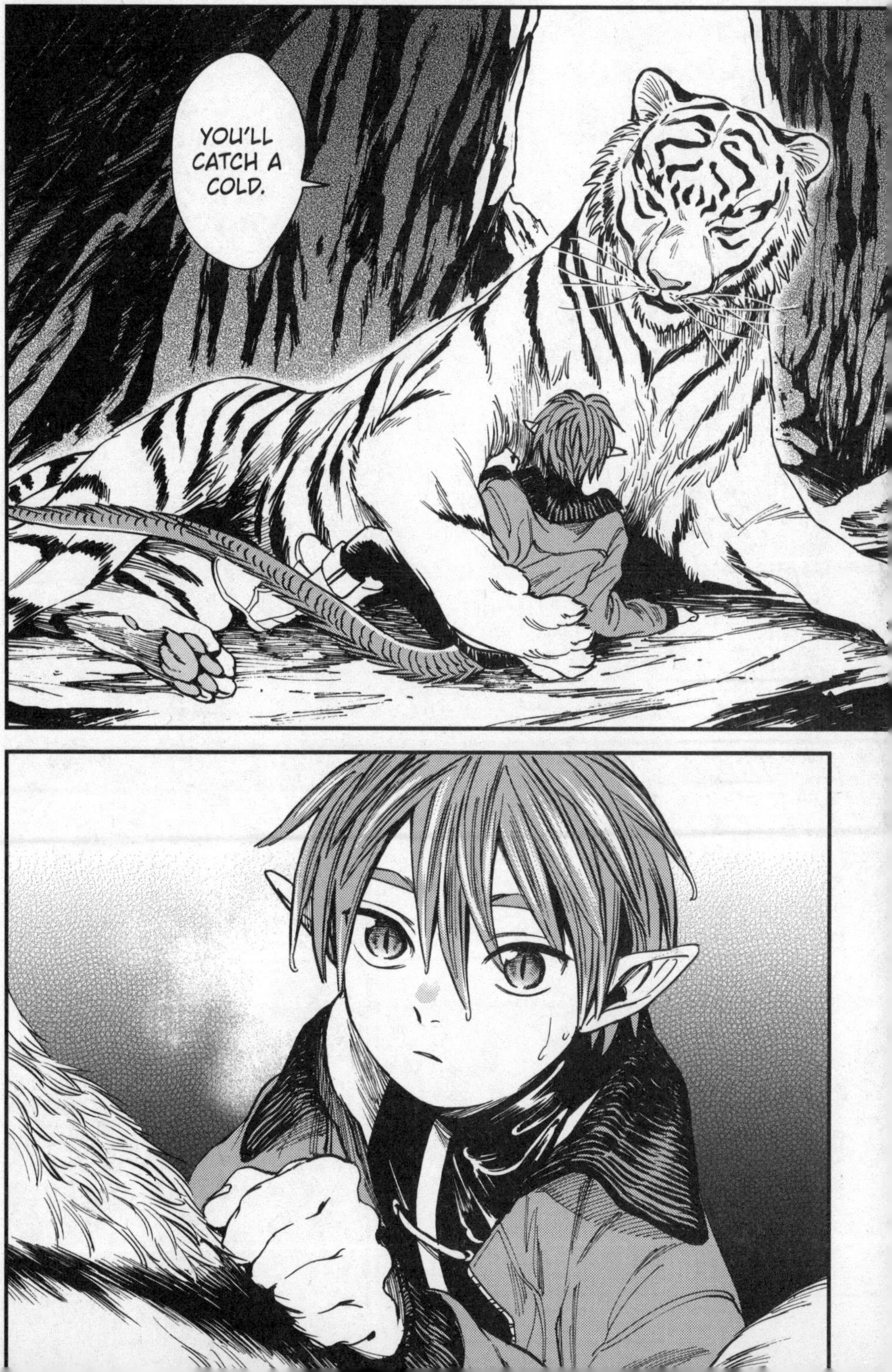
YOU'LL CATCH A COLD.

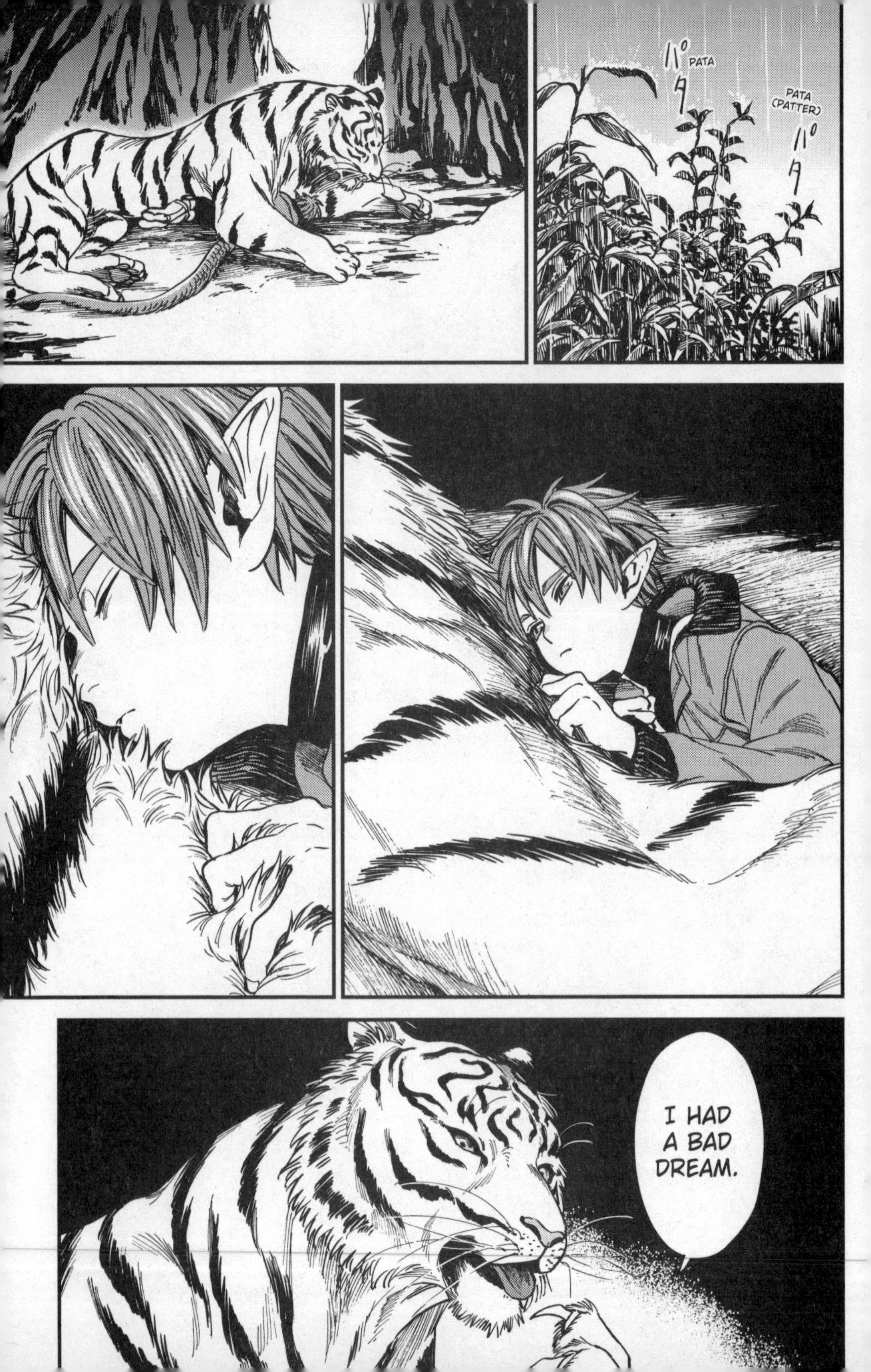
パ PATA
タ
PATA (PATTER)
パ
タ
I HAD A BAD DREAM.

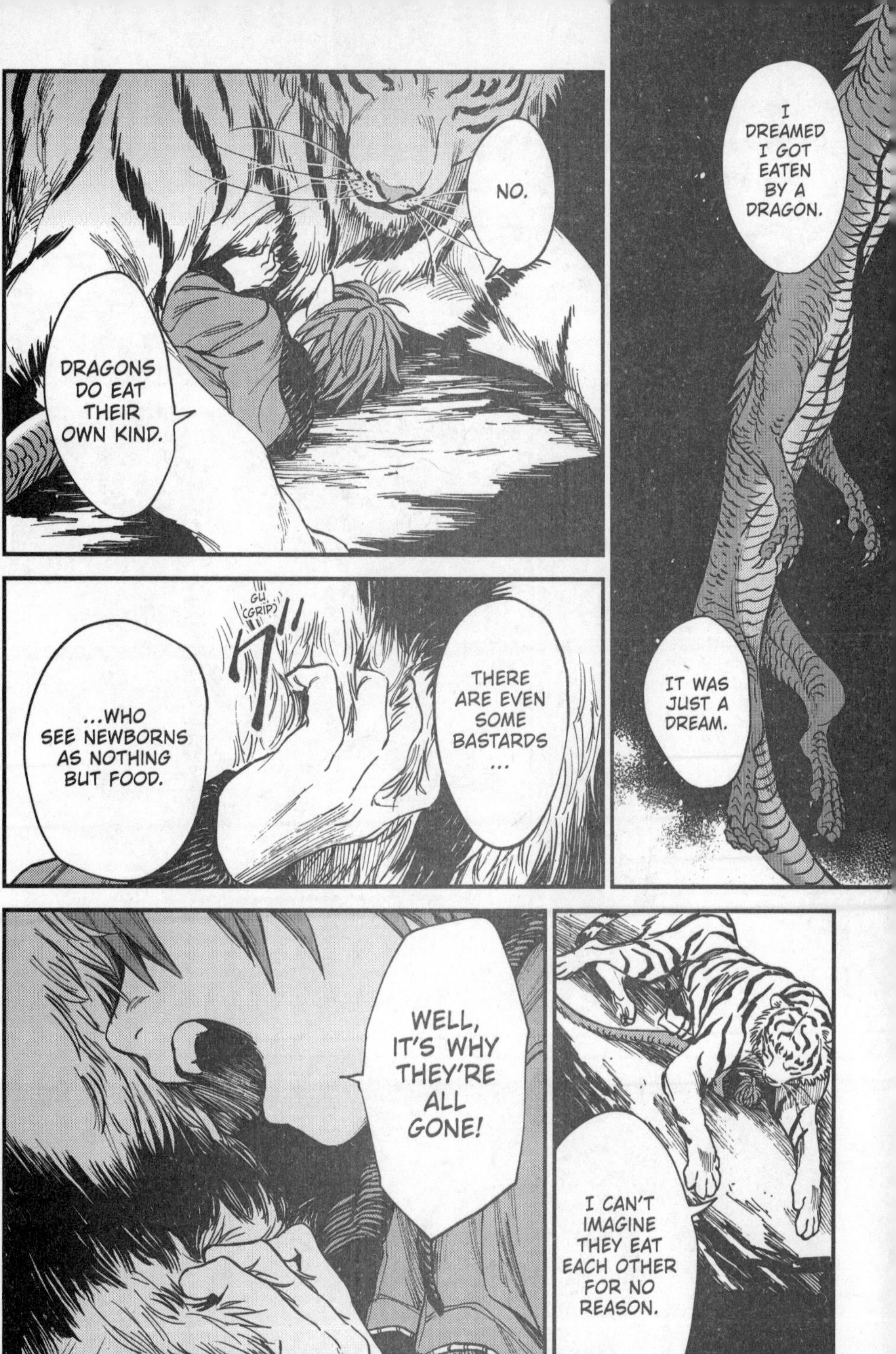
I DREAMED I GOT EATEN BY A DRAGON.
IT WAS JUST A DREAM.
NO.
DRAGONS DO EAT THEIR OWN KIND.
GU (GRIP)
THERE ARE EVEN SOME BASTARDS ...
...WHO SEE NEWBORNS AS NOTHING BUT FOOD.
I CAN'T IMAGINE THEY EAT EACH OTHER FOR NO REASON.
WELL, IT'S WHY THEY'RE ALL GONE!

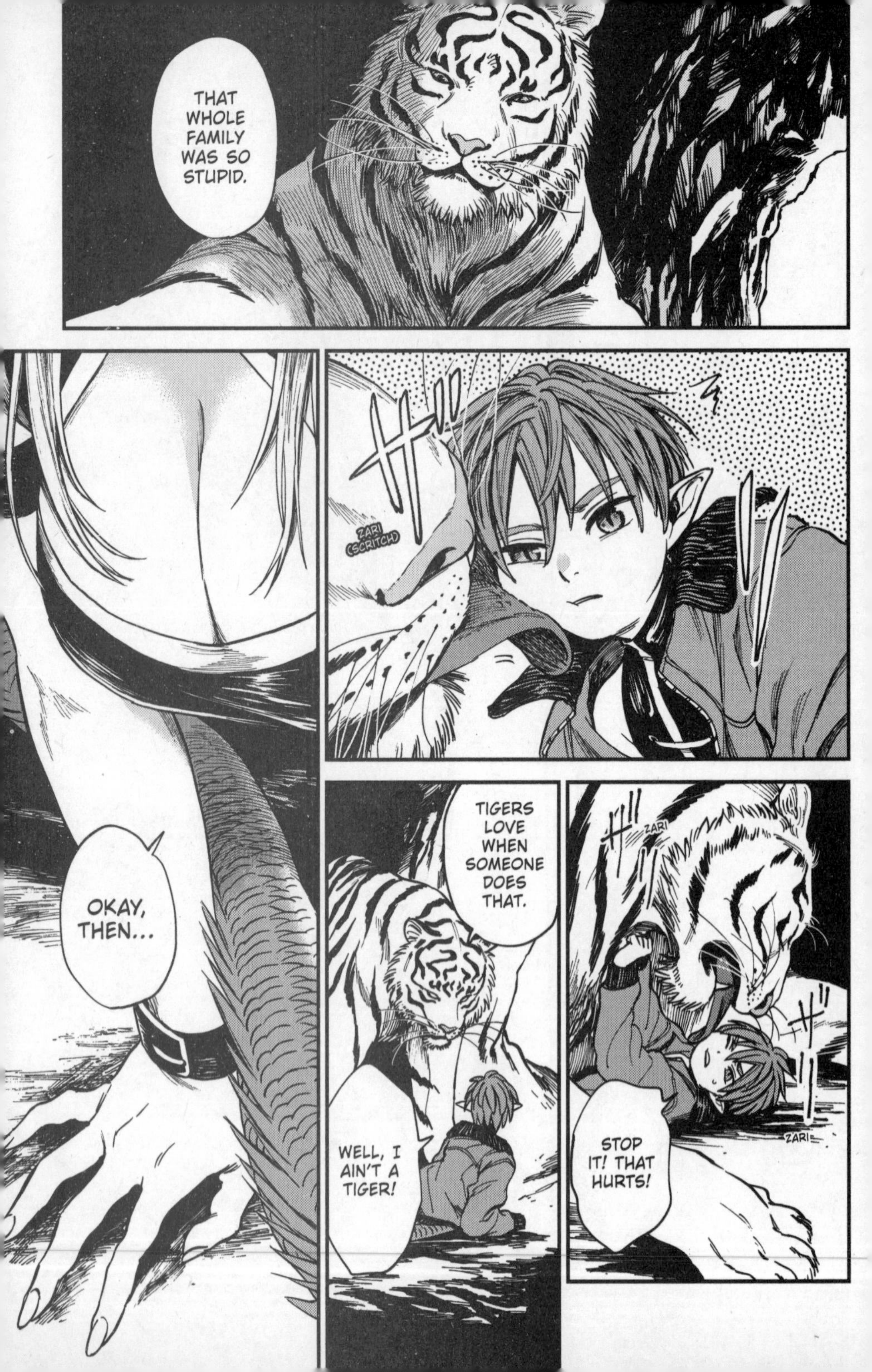
THAT WHOLE FAMILY WAS SO STUPID.
ZARI (SCRITCH)
ZARI
STOP IT! THAT HURTS!
ZARI
TIGERS LOVE WHEN SOMEONE DOES THAT.
WELL, I AIN'T A TIGER!
OKAY, THEN...

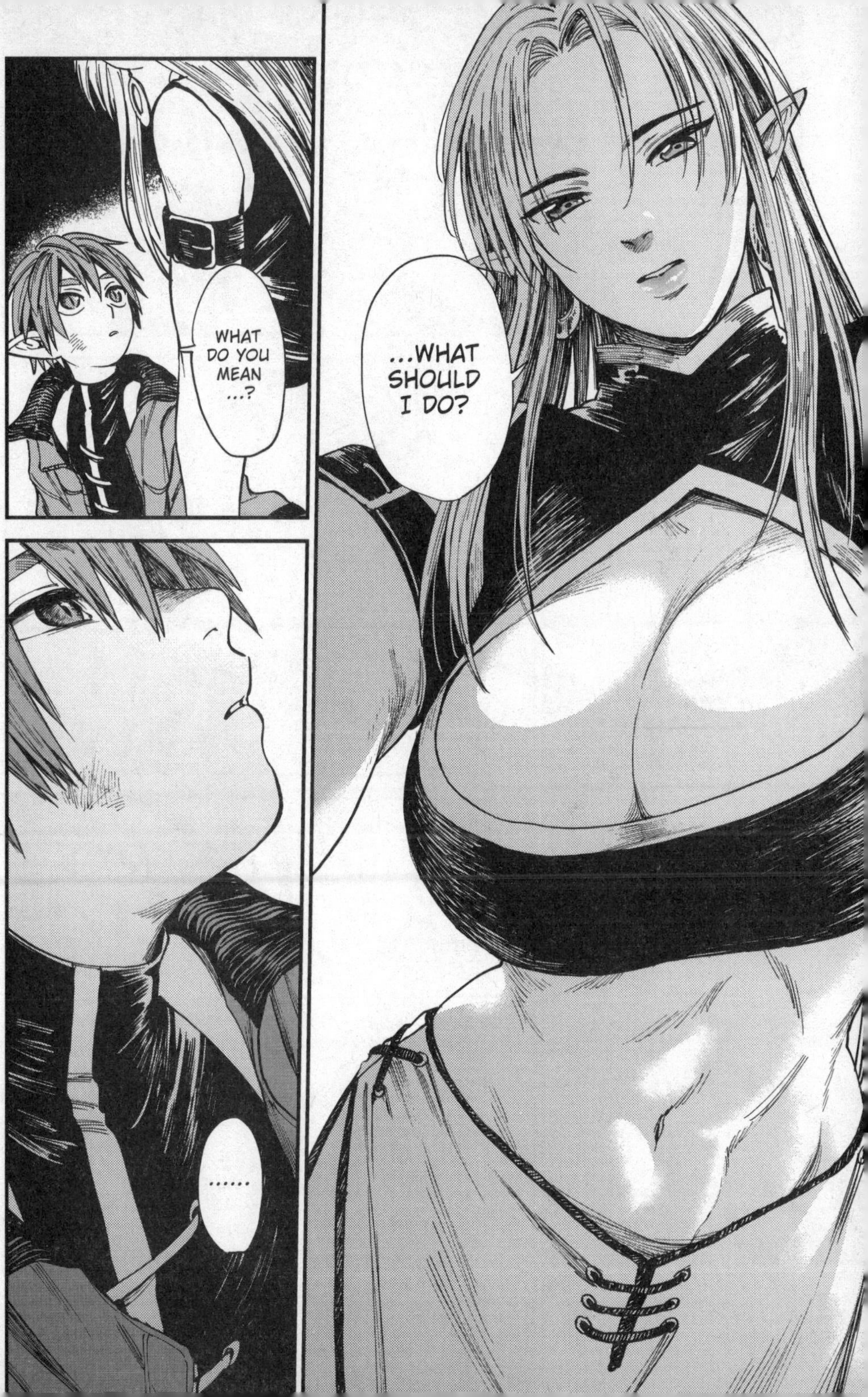
...WHAT SHOULD I DO?
WHAT DO YOU MEAN ...?
......

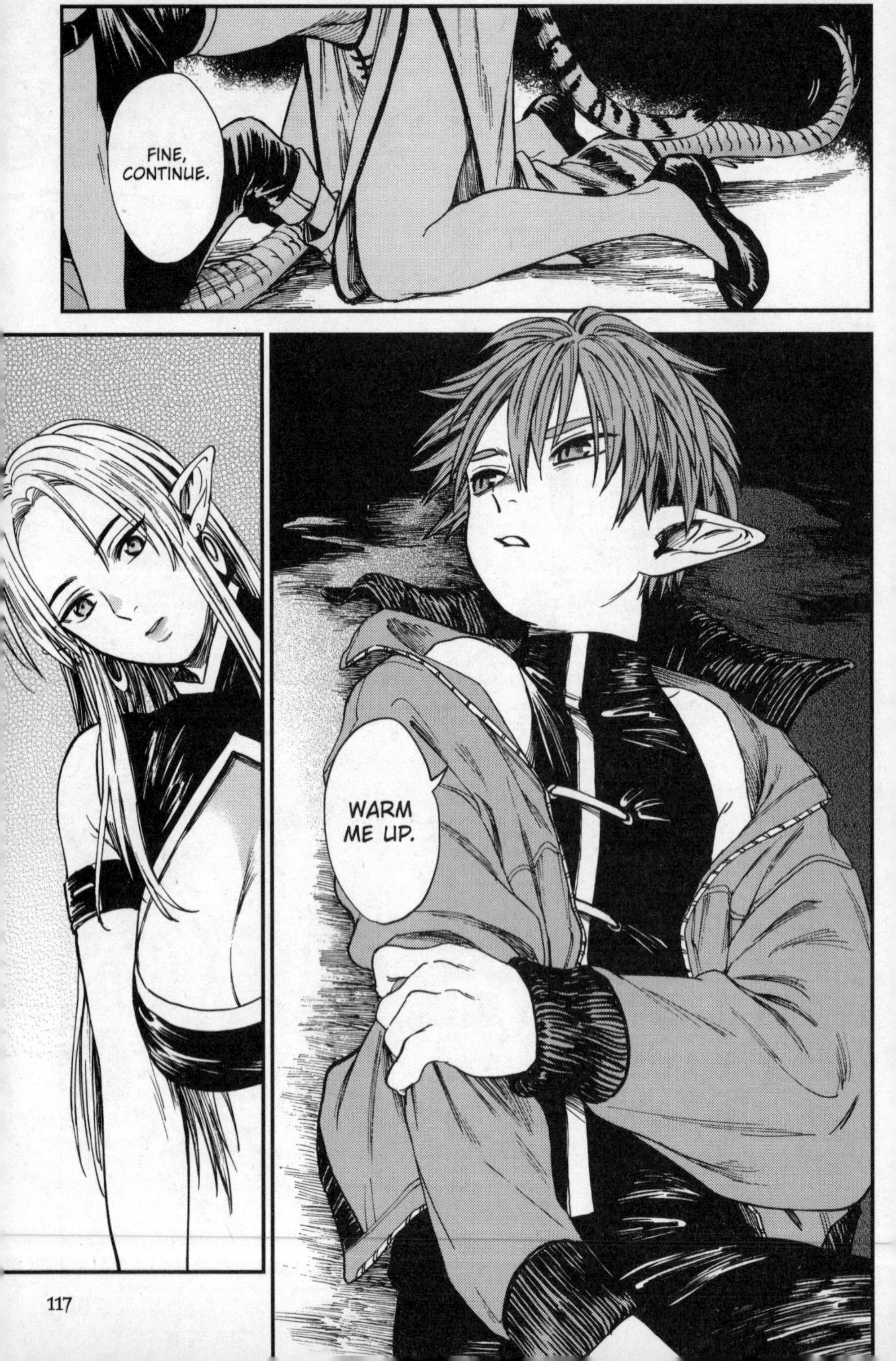
FINE, CONTINUE.
WARM ME UP.

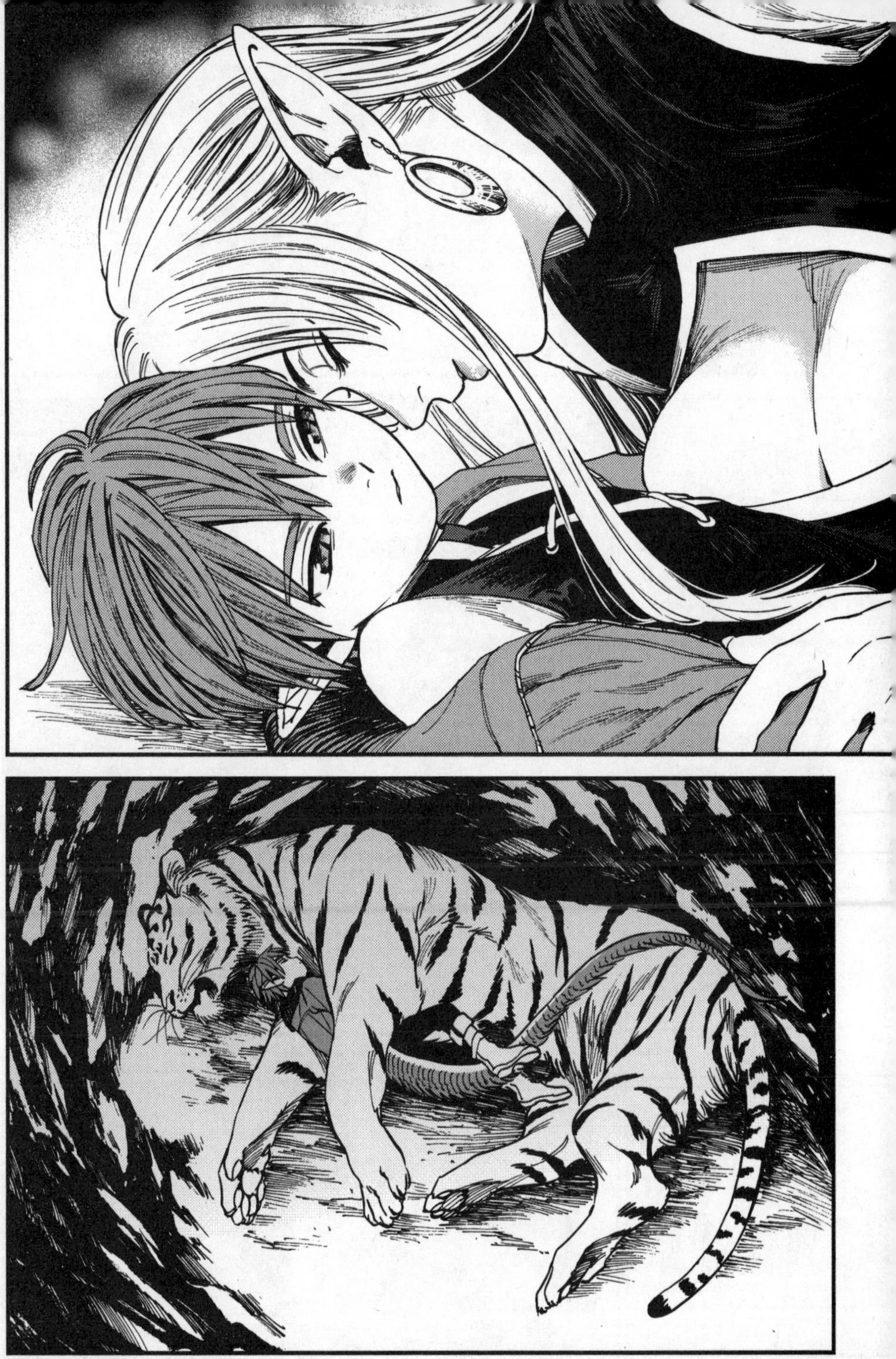

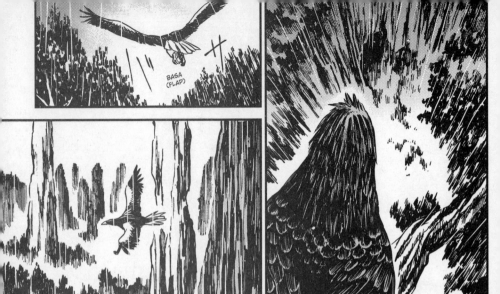

BASA
(FLAP)

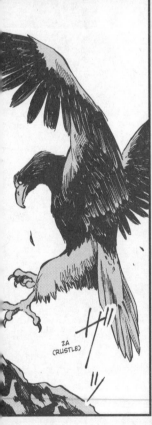

ZA
(RUSTLE)

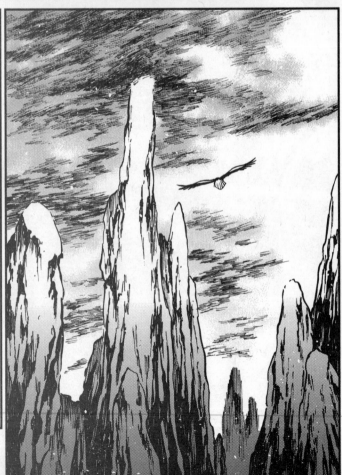

119

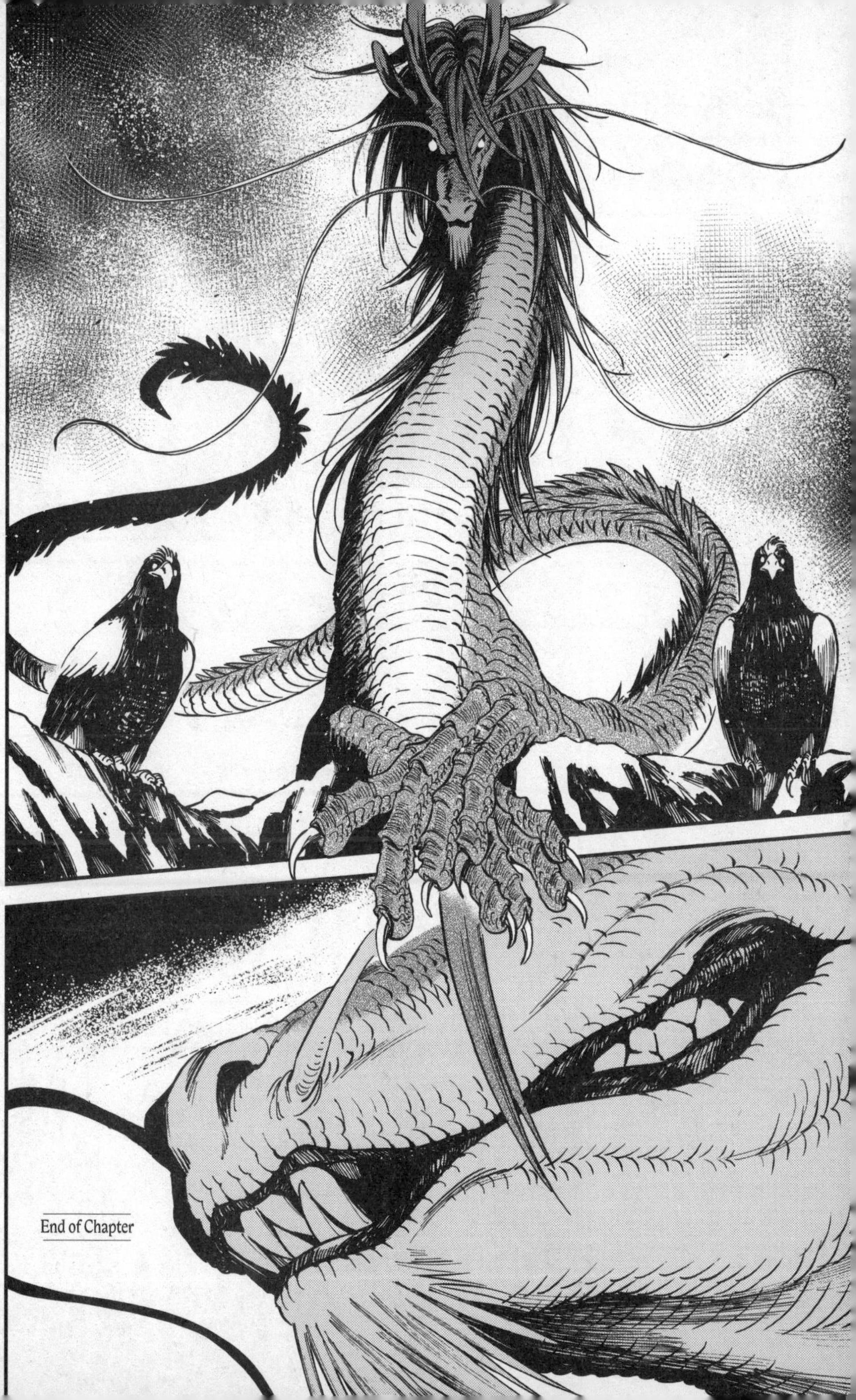
End of Chapter

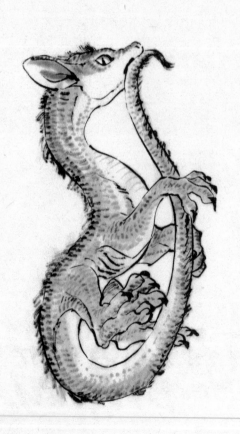

The Tiger Won't Eat the Dragon Yet

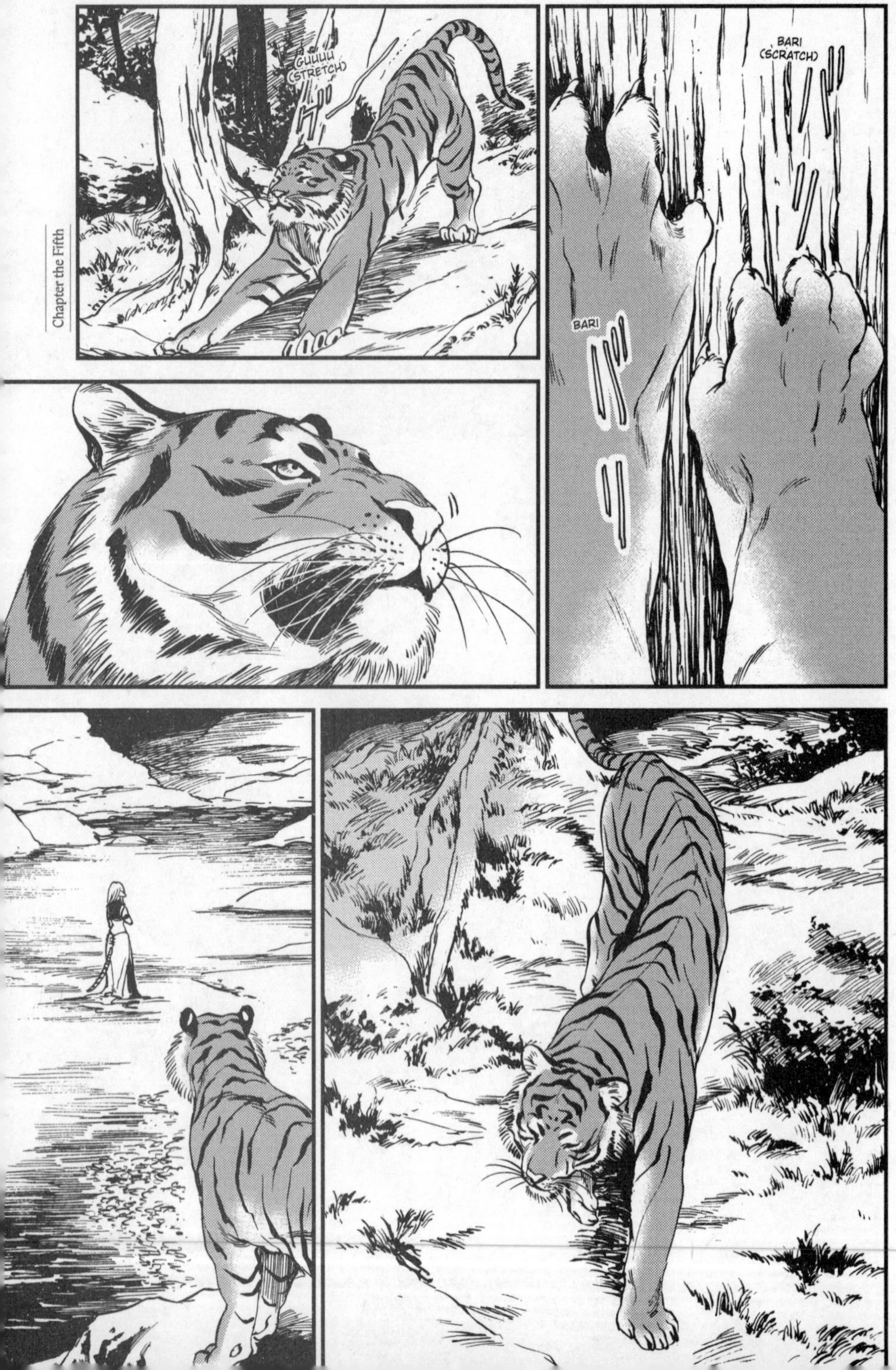
BARI (SCRATCH)
BARI
GUUUU (STRETCH)

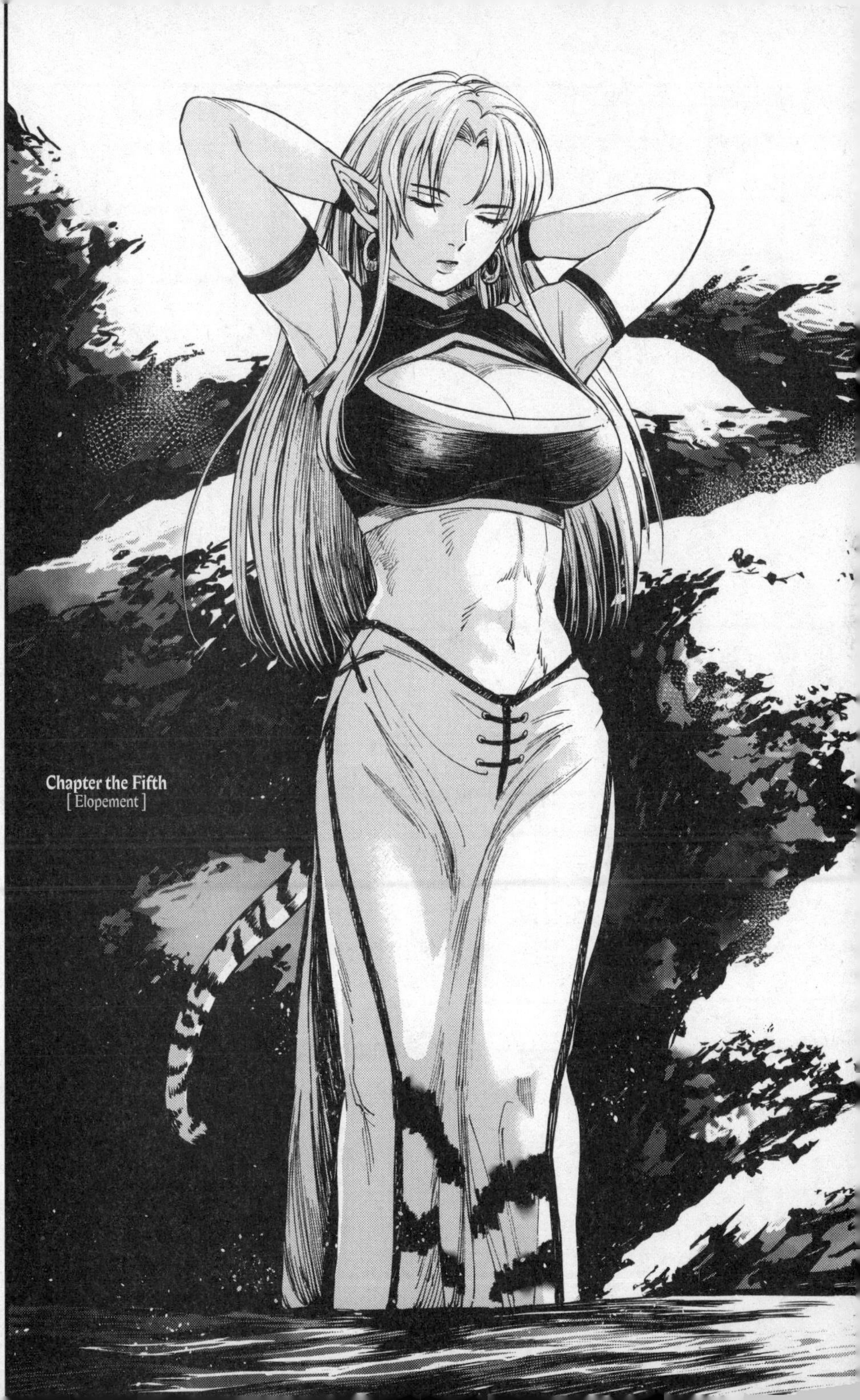

Chapter the Fifth
[Elopement]

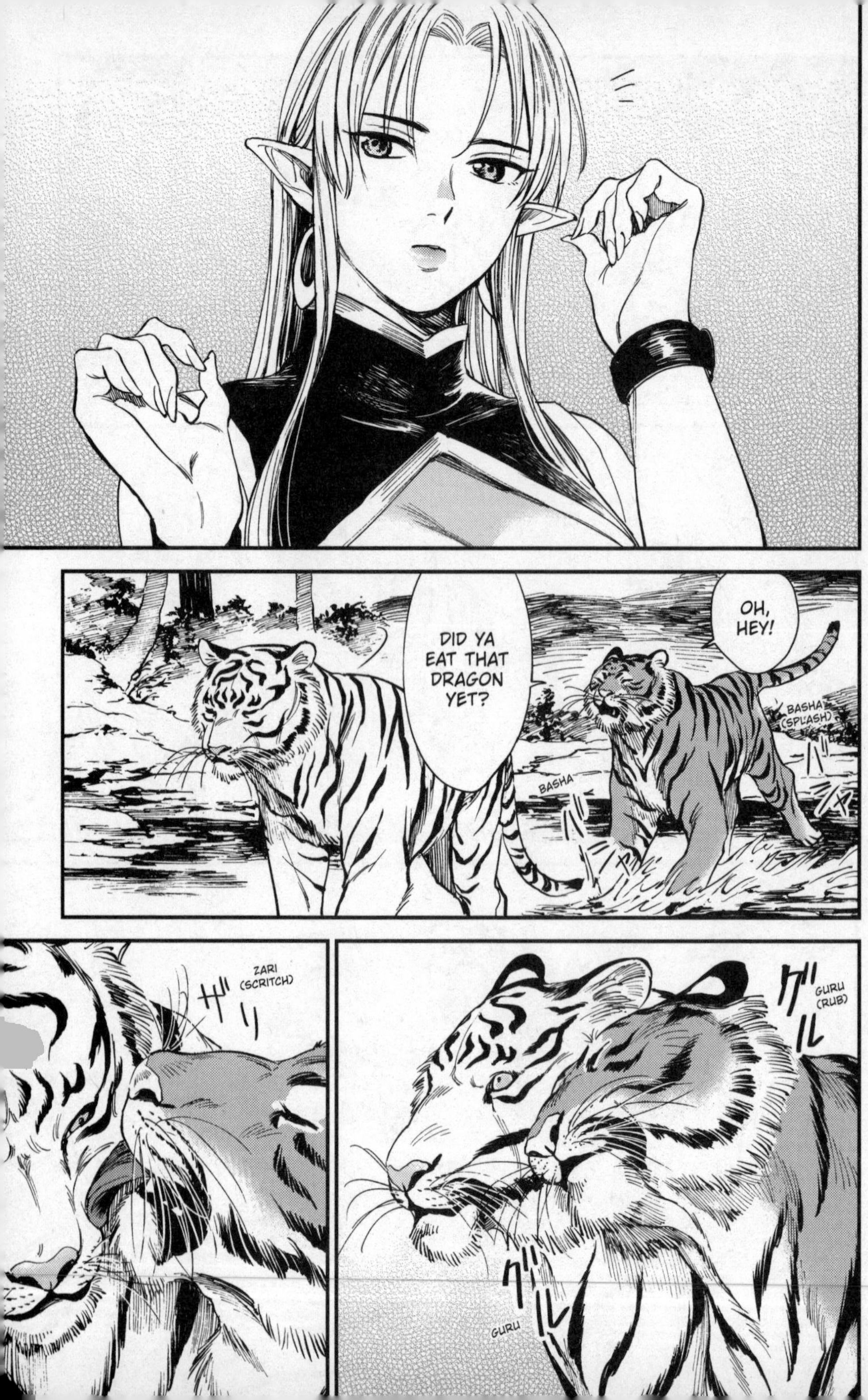
OH, HEY!
BASHA (SPLASH)
DID YA EAT THAT DRAGON YET?
BASHA
GURU (RUB)
GURU
ZARI (SCRITCH)

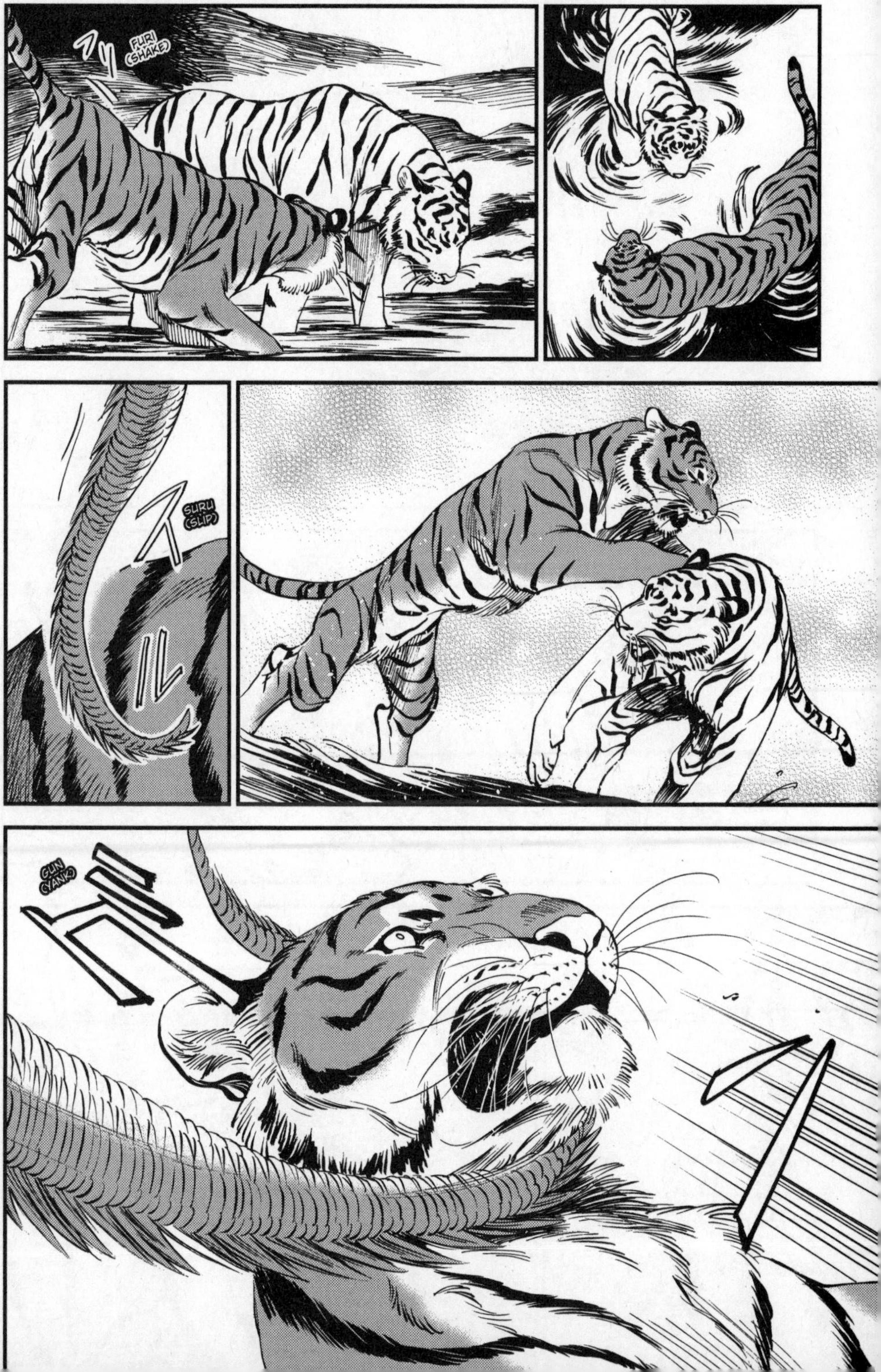
フリ
FURI (SHAKE)
スル
SURU (SLIP)
グン
GUN (YANK)

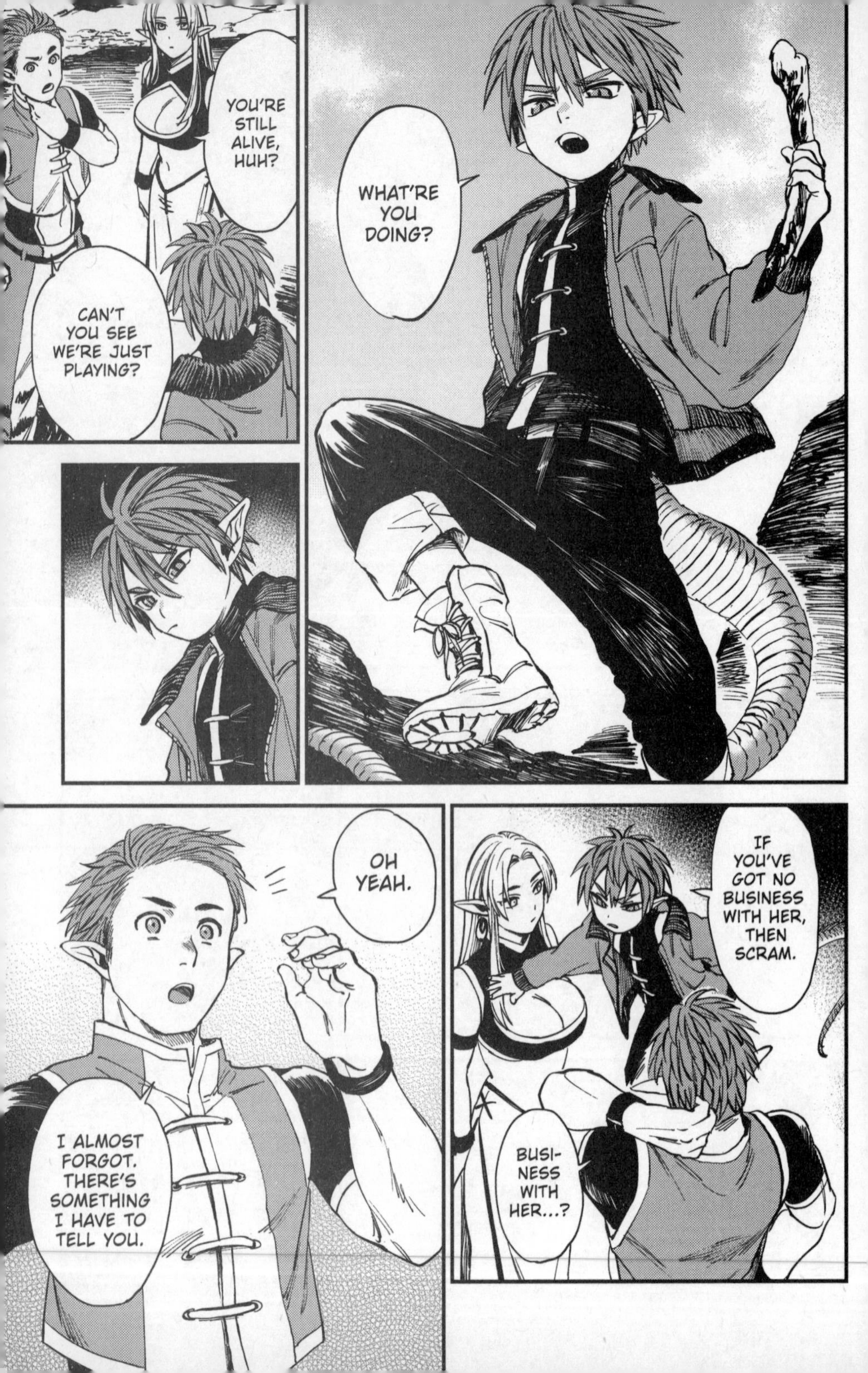
WHAT'RE YOU DOING?
YOU'RE STILL ALIVE, HUH?
CAN'T YOU SEE WE'RE JUST PLAYING?
IF YOU'VE GOT NO BUSINESS WITH HER, THEN SCRAM.
BUSI-NESS WITH HER...?
OH YEAH.
I ALMOST FORGOT. THERE'S SOMETHING I HAVE TO TELL YOU.

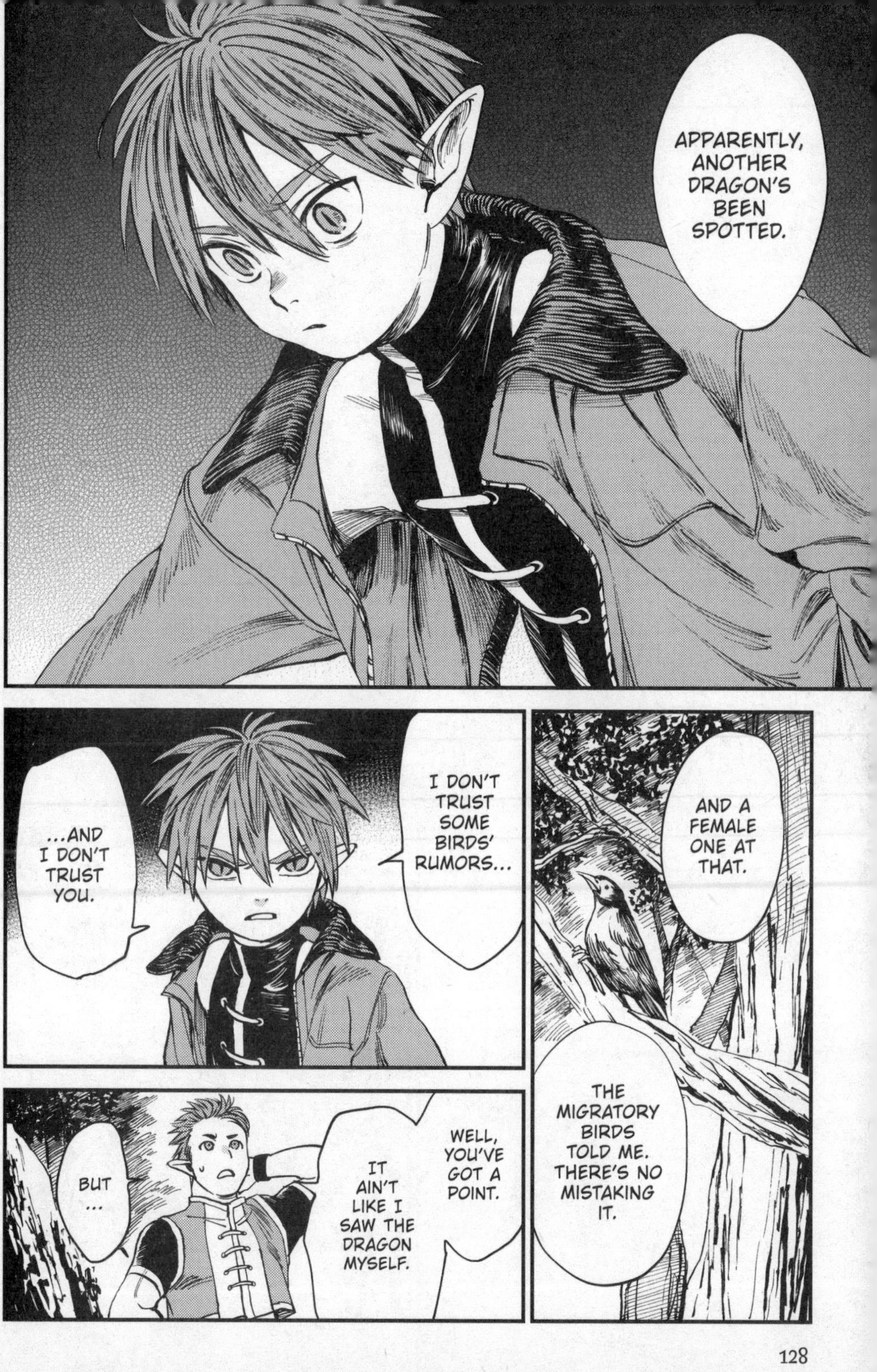
APPARENTLY, ANOTHER DRAGON'S BEEN SPOTTED.
AND A FEMALE ONE AT THAT.
THE MIGRATORY BIRDS TOLD ME. THERE'S NO MISTAKING IT.
I DON'T TRUST SOME BIRDS' RUMORS...
...AND I DON'T TRUST YOU.
WELL, YOU'VE GOT A POINT.
IT AIN'T LIKE I SAW THE DRAGON MYSELF.
BUT ...

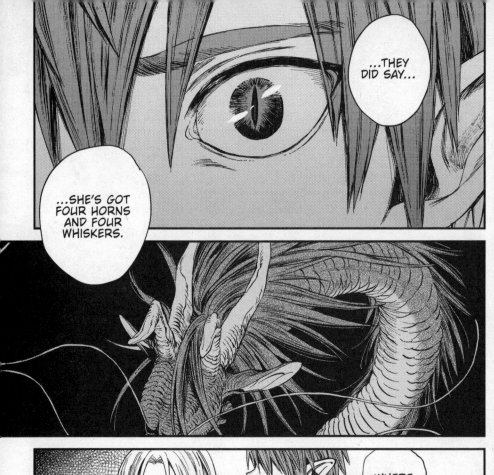

...THEY DID SAY...

...SHE'S GOT FOUR HORNS AND FOUR WHISKERS.

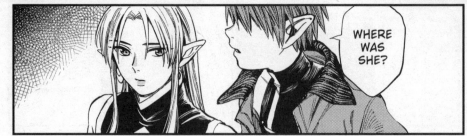

WHERE WAS SHE?

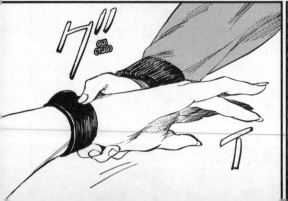

GUI (TUG)

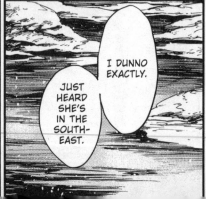

I DUNNO EXACTLY.

JUST HEARD SHE'S IN THE SOUTH-EAST.

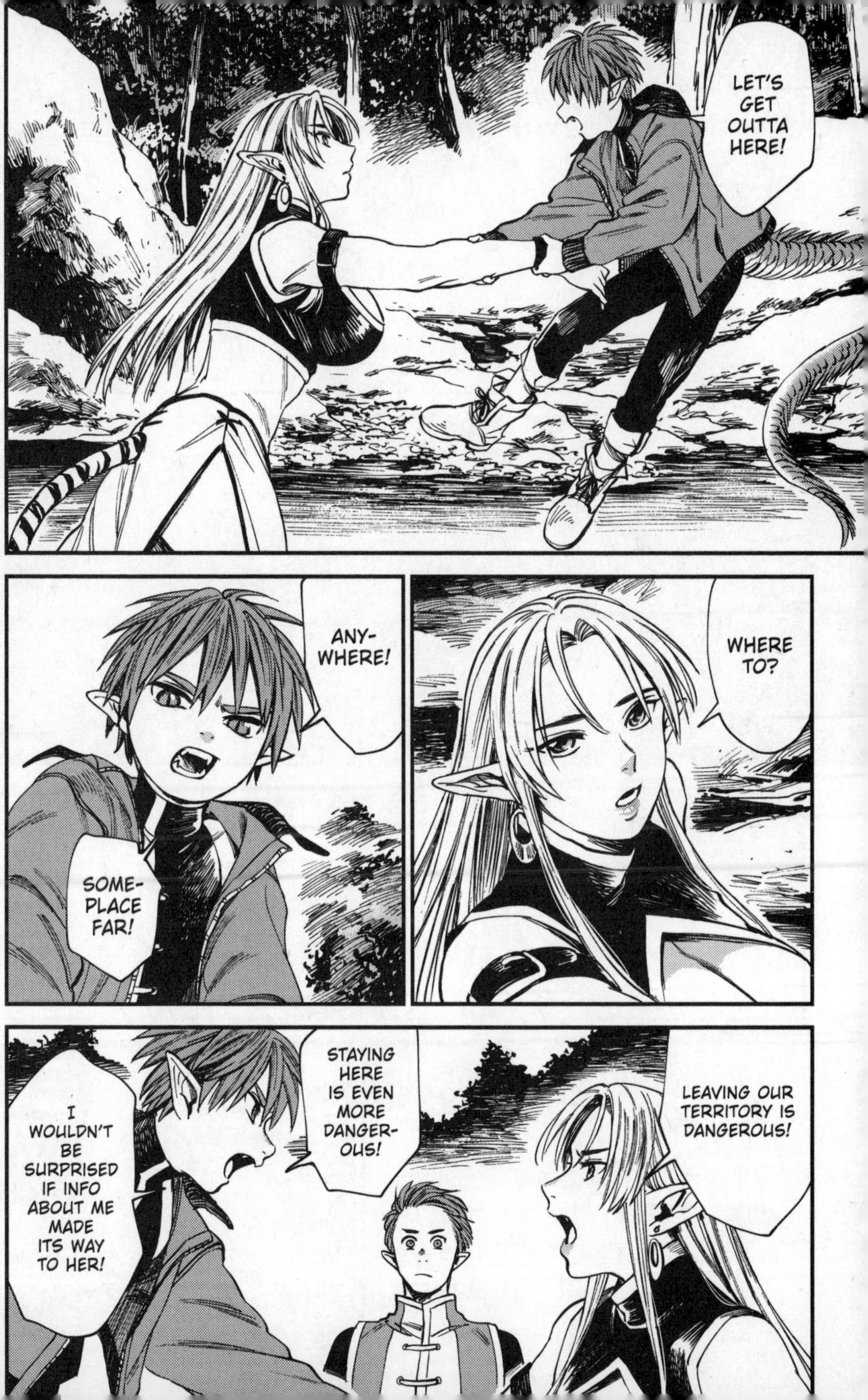
LET'S GET OUTTA HERE!
WHERE TO?
ANY-WHERE!
SOME-PLACE FAR!
LEAVING OUR TERRITORY IS DANGEROUS!
STAYING HERE IS EVEN MORE DANGER-OUS!
I WOULDN'T BE SURPRISED IF INFO ABOUT ME MADE ITS WAY TO HER!

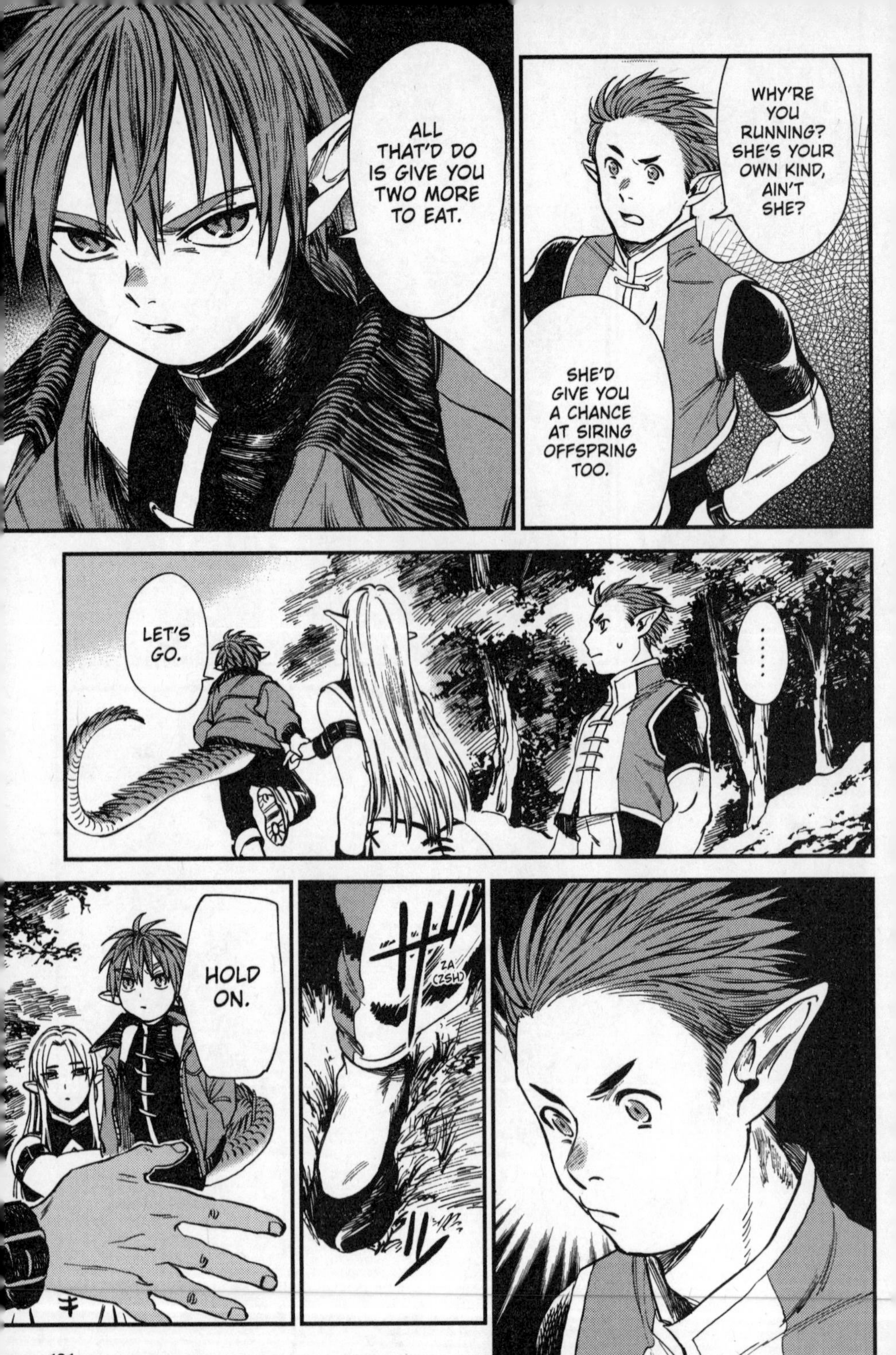
WHY'RE YOU RUNNING? SHE'S YOUR OWN KIND, AIN'T SHE?
SHE'D GIVE YOU A CHANCE AT SIRING OFFSPRING TOO.
ALL THAT'D DO IS GIVE YOU TWO MORE TO EAT.
.....
LET'S GO.
ZA (ZSH)
HOLD ON.
キ

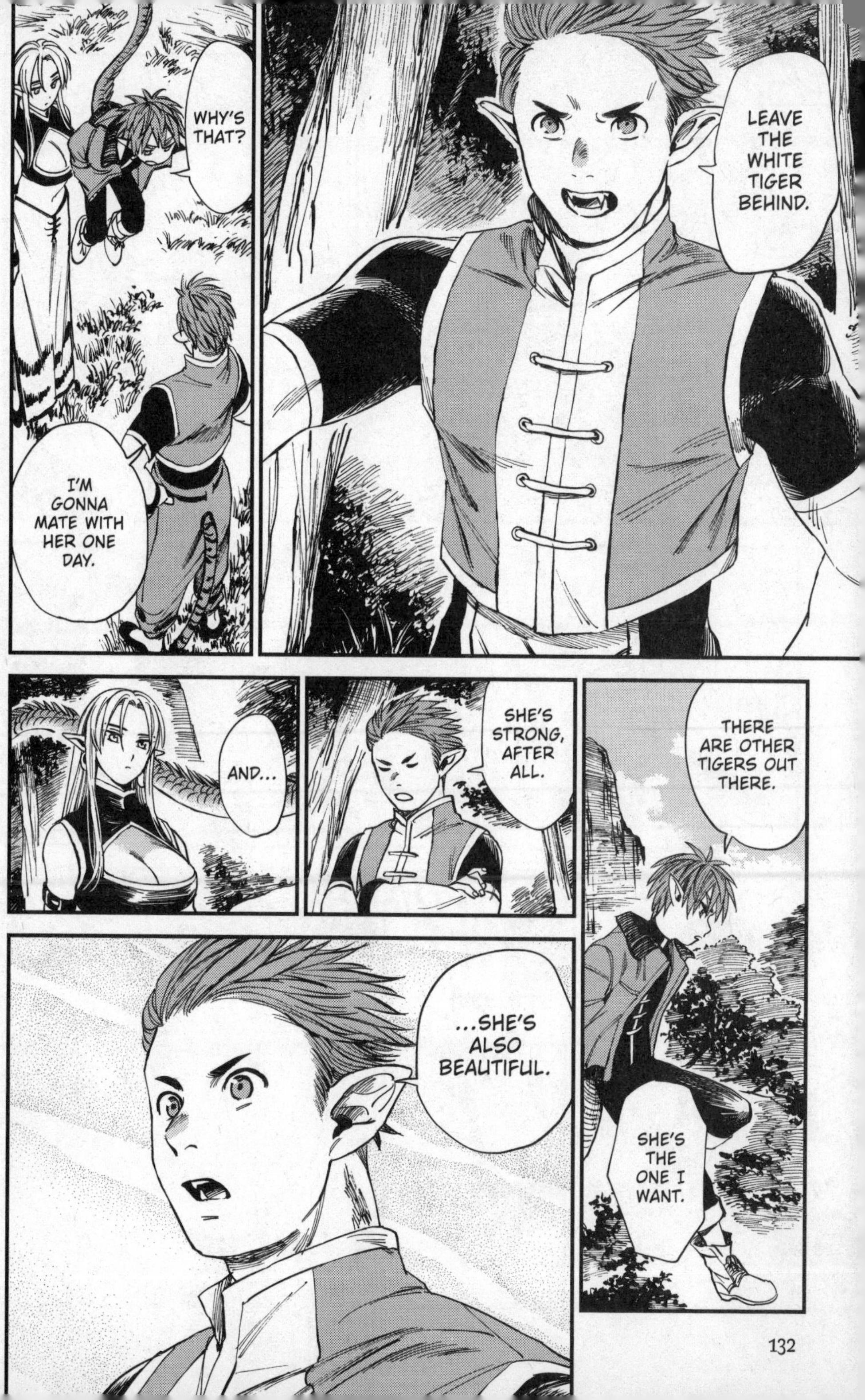
LEAVE THE WHITE TIGER BEHIND.
WHY'S THAT?
I'M GONNA MATE WITH HER ONE DAY.
THERE ARE OTHER TIGERS OUT THERE.
SHE'S THE ONE I WANT.
SHE'S STRONG, AFTER ALL.
AND...
...SHE'S ALSO BEAUTIFUL.

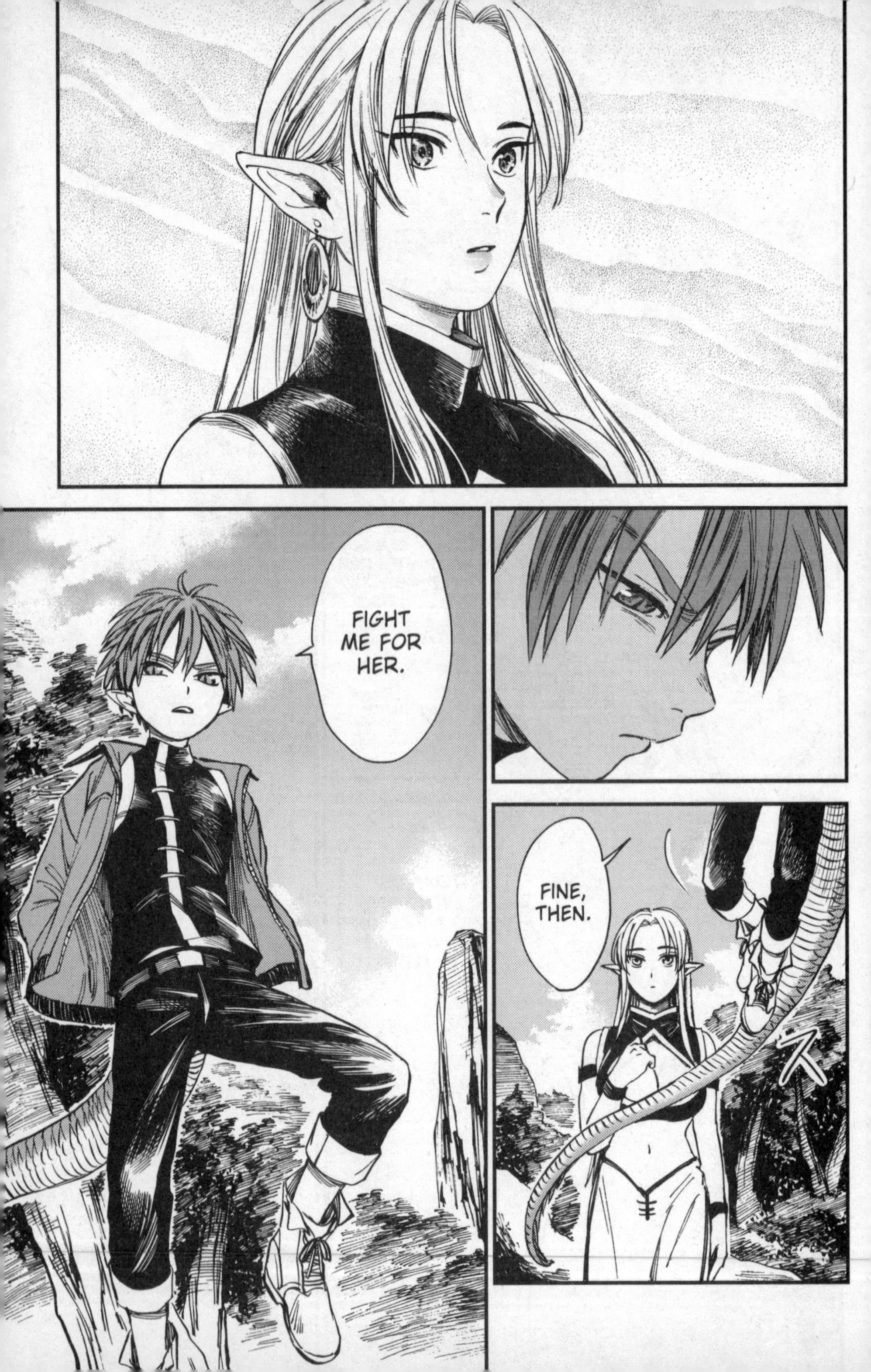
FINE, THEN.
FIGHT ME FOR HER.

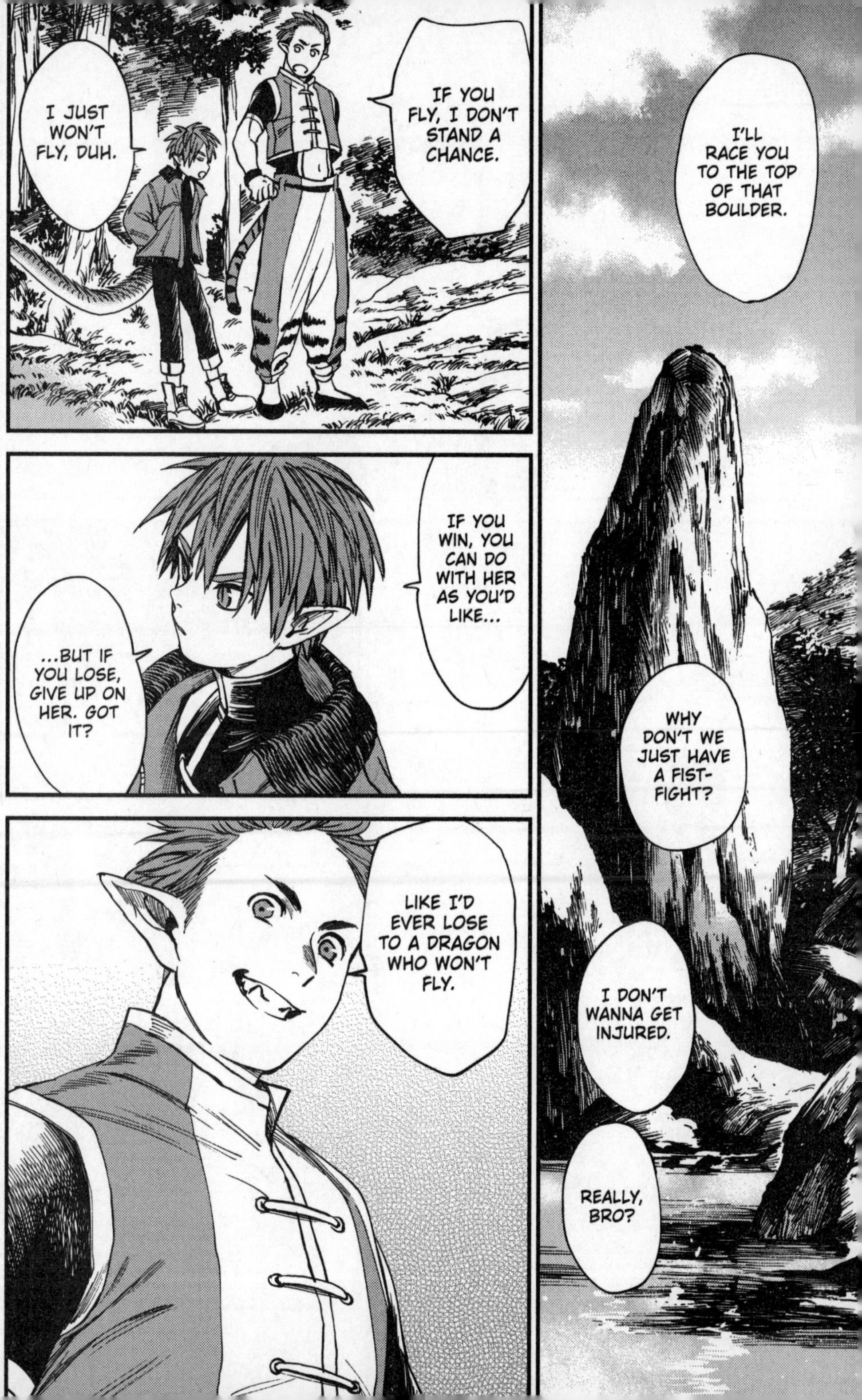
I'LL RACE YOU TO THE TOP OF THAT BOULDER.
WHY DON'T WE JUST HAVE A FIST-FIGHT?
I DON'T WANNA GET INJURED.
REALLY, BRO?
IF YOU FLY, I DON'T STAND A CHANCE.
I JUST WON'T FLY, DUH.
IF YOU WIN, YOU CAN DO WITH HER AS YOU'D LIKE...
...BUT IF YOU LOSE, GIVE UP ON HER. GOT IT?
LIKE I'D EVER LOSE TO A DRAGON WHO WON'T FLY.

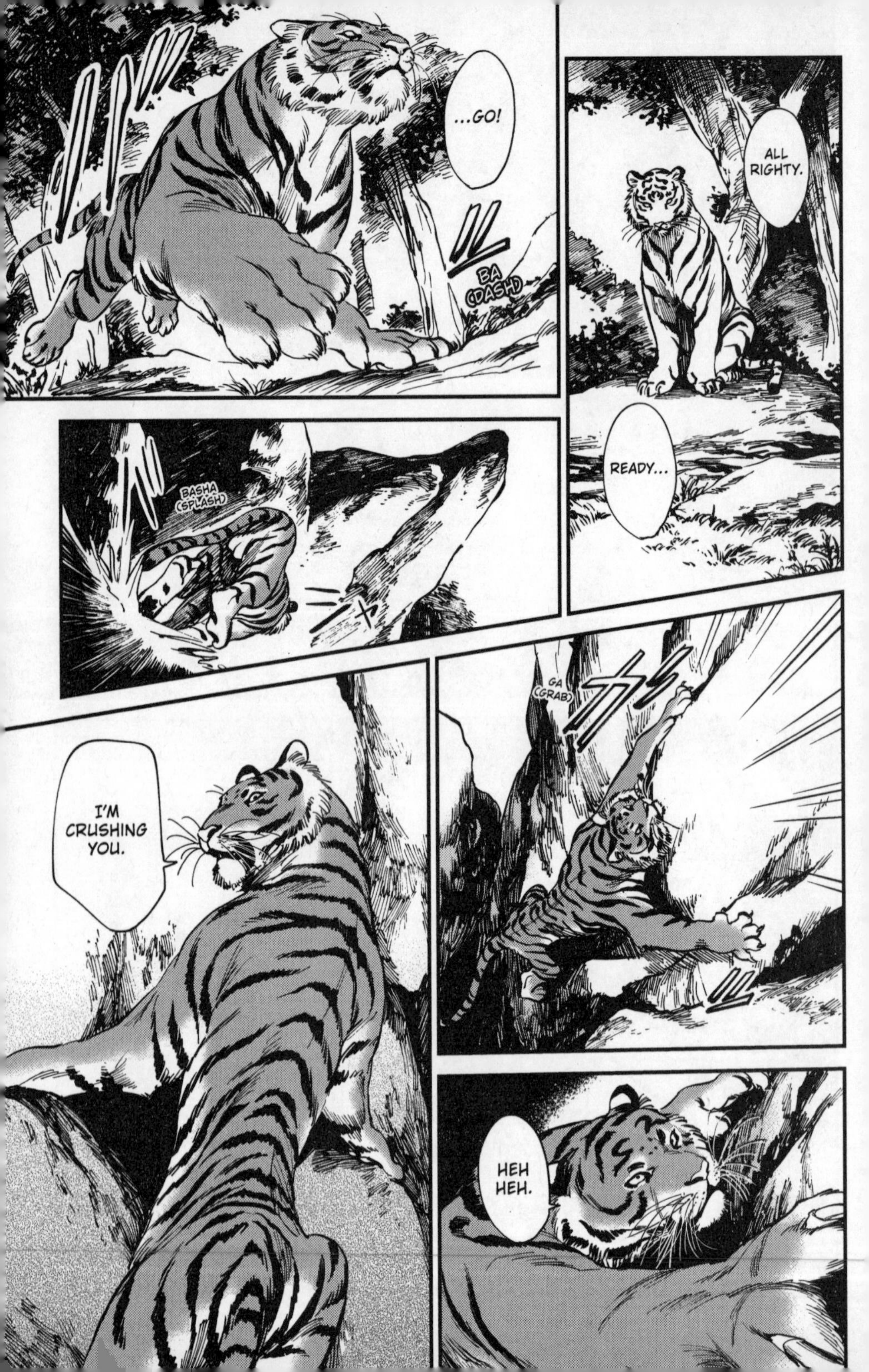
ALL RIGHTY.
READY...
...GO!
BA (DASH)
BASHA (SPLASH)
GA (GRAB)
HEH HEH.
I'M CRUSHING YOU.

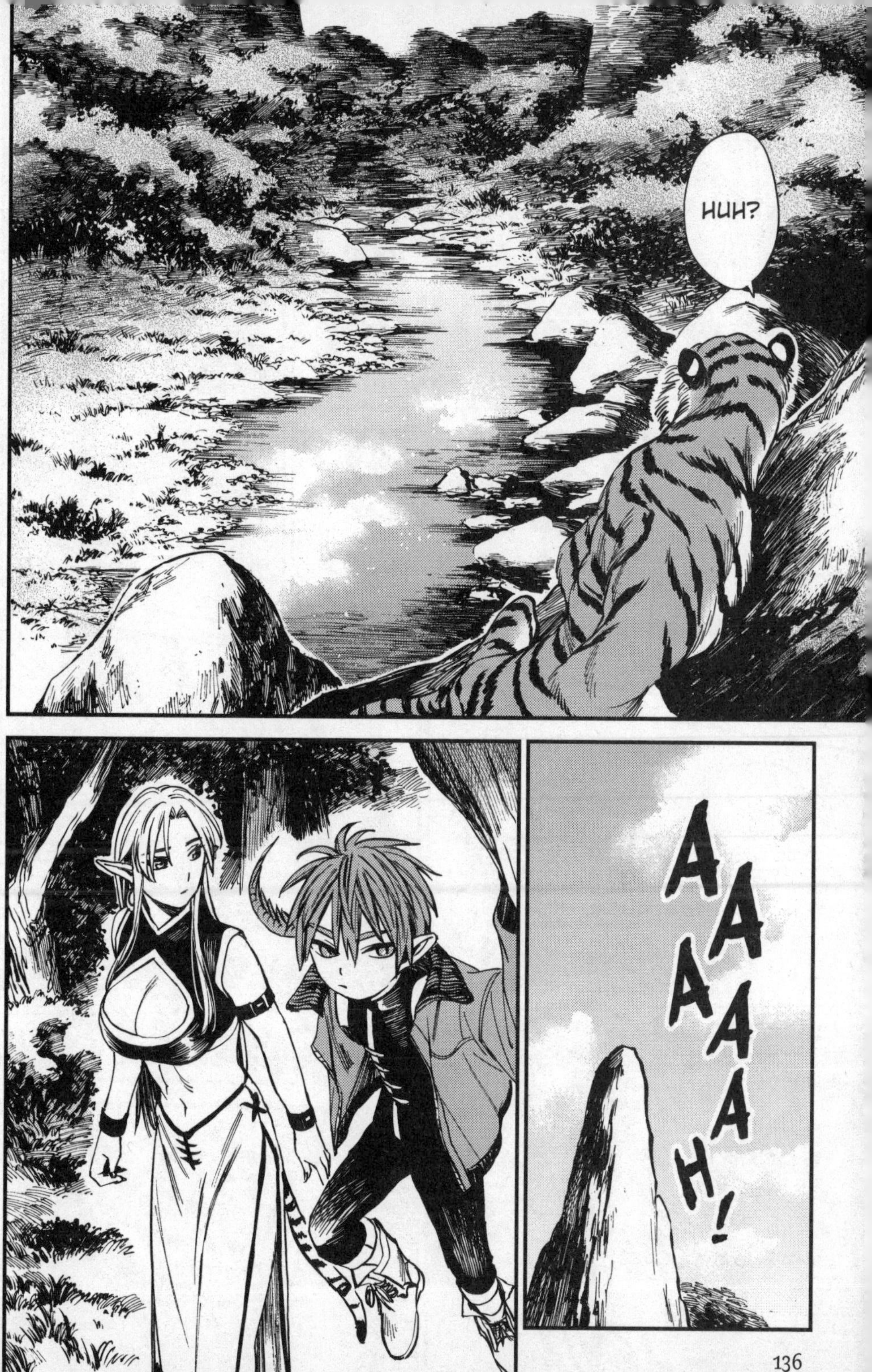
HUH?
AAAAAAAH!

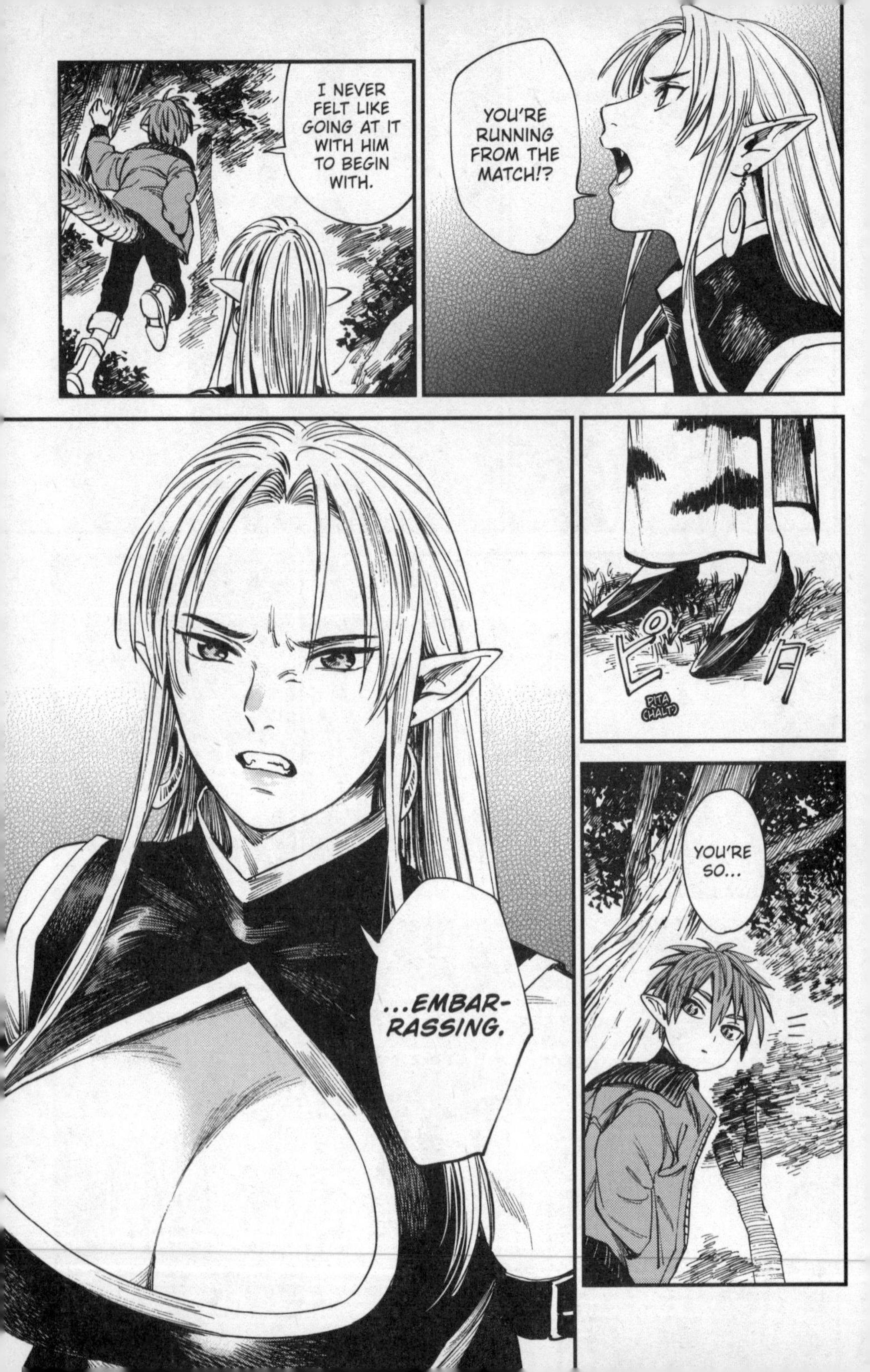

YOU'RE RUNNING FROM THE MATCH!?
I NEVER FELT LIKE GOING AT IT WITH HIM TO BEGIN WITH.
ピタ
PITA (HALT)
YOU'RE SO...
...EMBARRASSING.

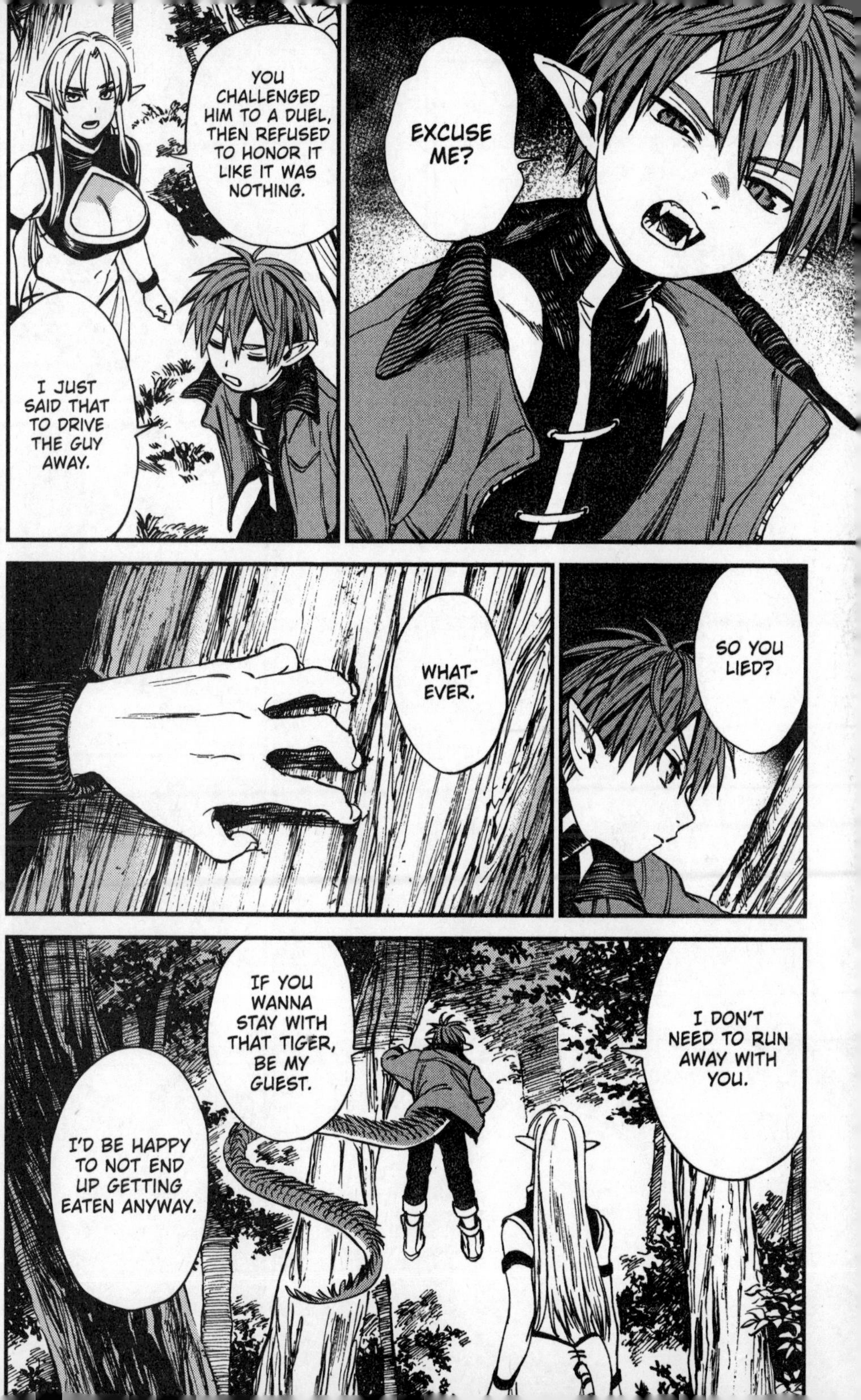
EXCUSE ME?
YOU CHALLENGED HIM TO A DUEL, THEN REFUSED TO HONOR IT LIKE IT WAS NOTHING.
I JUST SAID THAT TO DRIVE THE GUY AWAY.
SO YOU LIED?
WHAT-EVER.
I DON'T NEED TO RUN AWAY WITH YOU.
IF YOU WANNA STAY WITH THAT TIGER, BE MY GUEST.
I'D BE HAPPY TO NOT END UP GETTING EATEN ANYWAY.

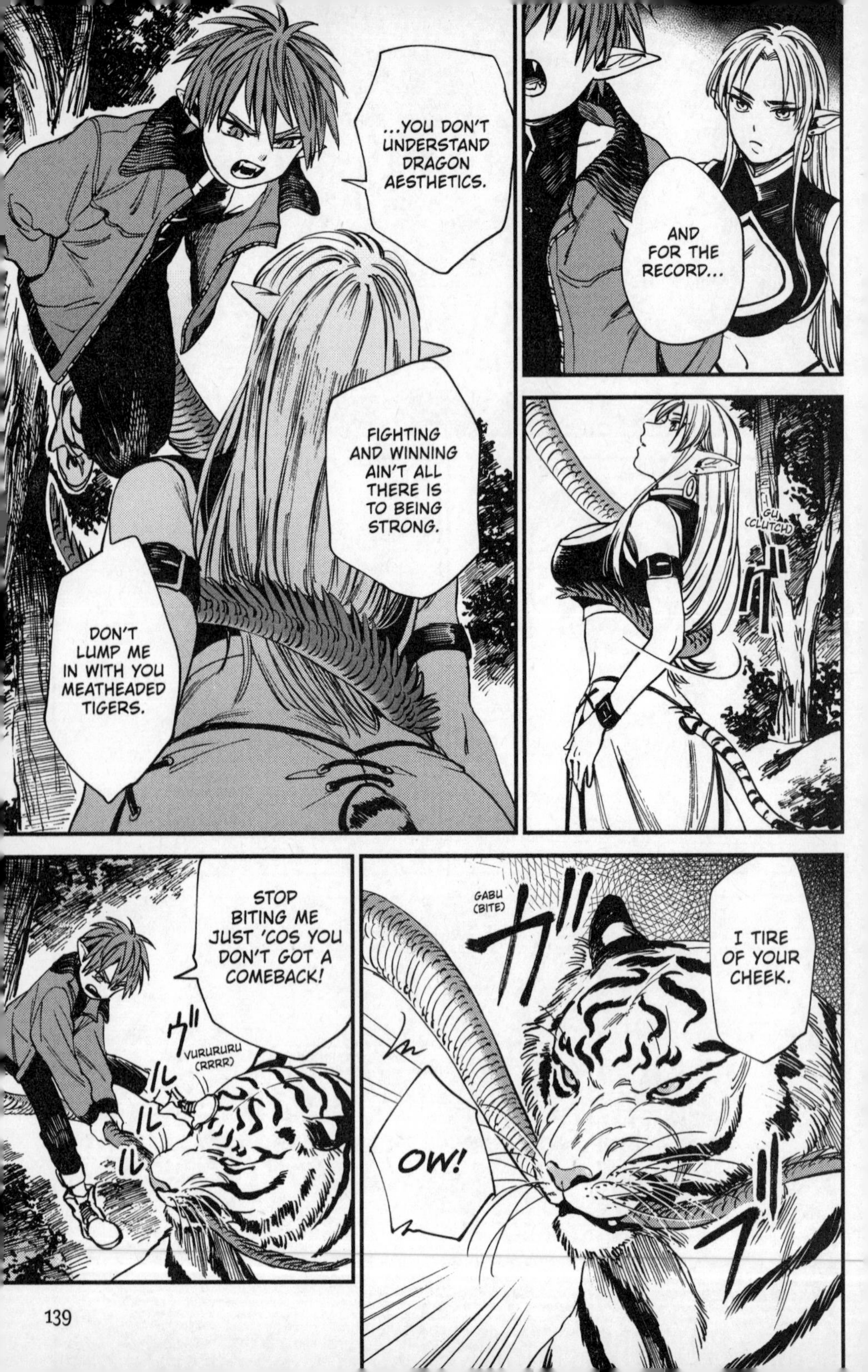
AND FOR THE RECORD...
GU (CLUTCH)
...YOU DON'T UNDERSTAND DRAGON AESTHETICS.
FIGHTING AND WINNING AIN'T ALL THERE IS TO BEING STRONG.
DON'T LUMP ME IN WITH YOU MEATHEADED TIGERS.
I TIRE OF YOUR CHEEK.
GABU (BITE)
OW!
STOP BITING ME JUST 'COS YOU DON'T GOT A COMEBACK!
VURURURU (RRRR)

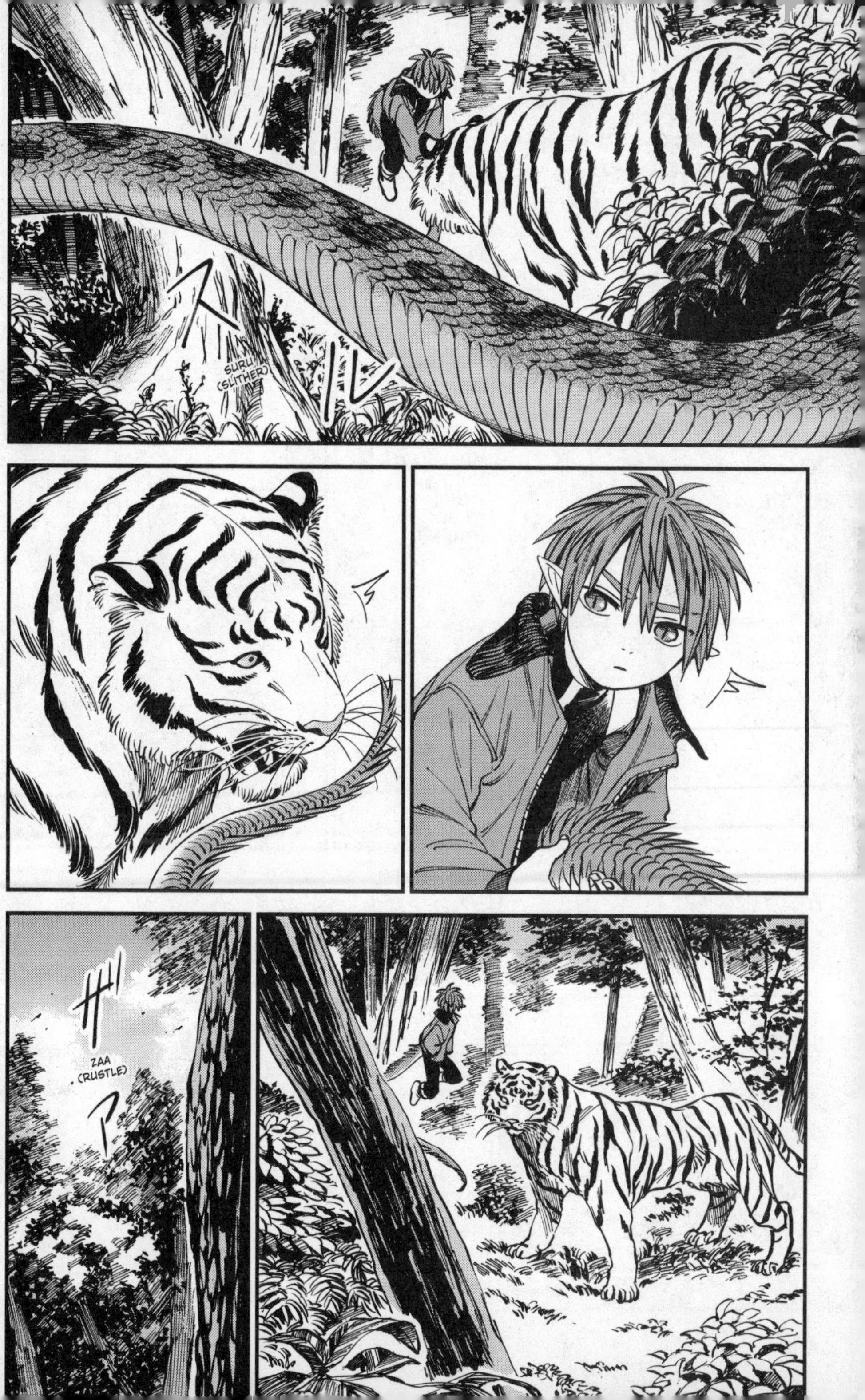
スル
SURU (SLITHER)
ザア
ZAA (RUSTLE)

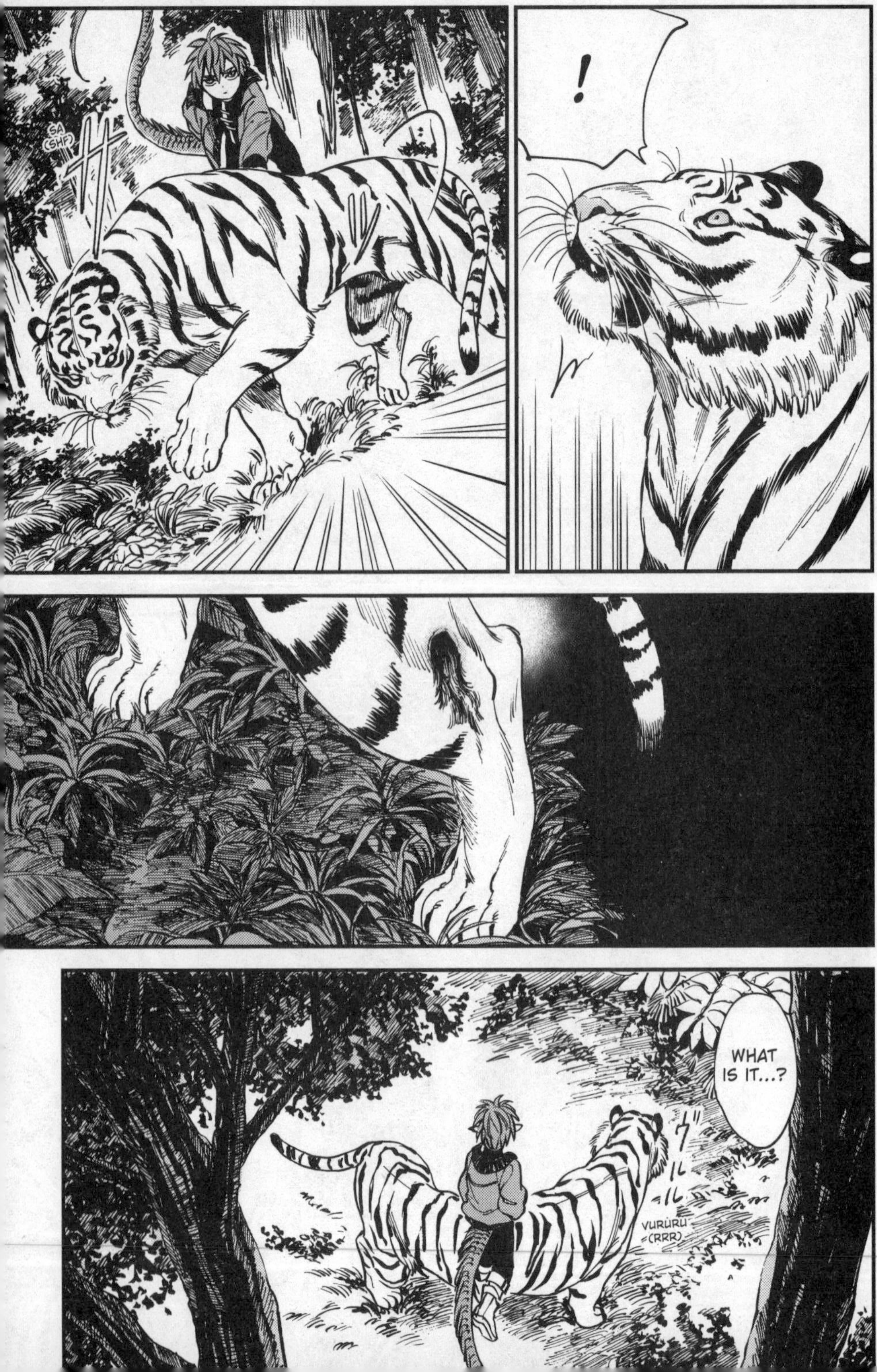
!
SA
(SHF)
WHAT IS IT...?
ヴルル
VURURU
(RRR)

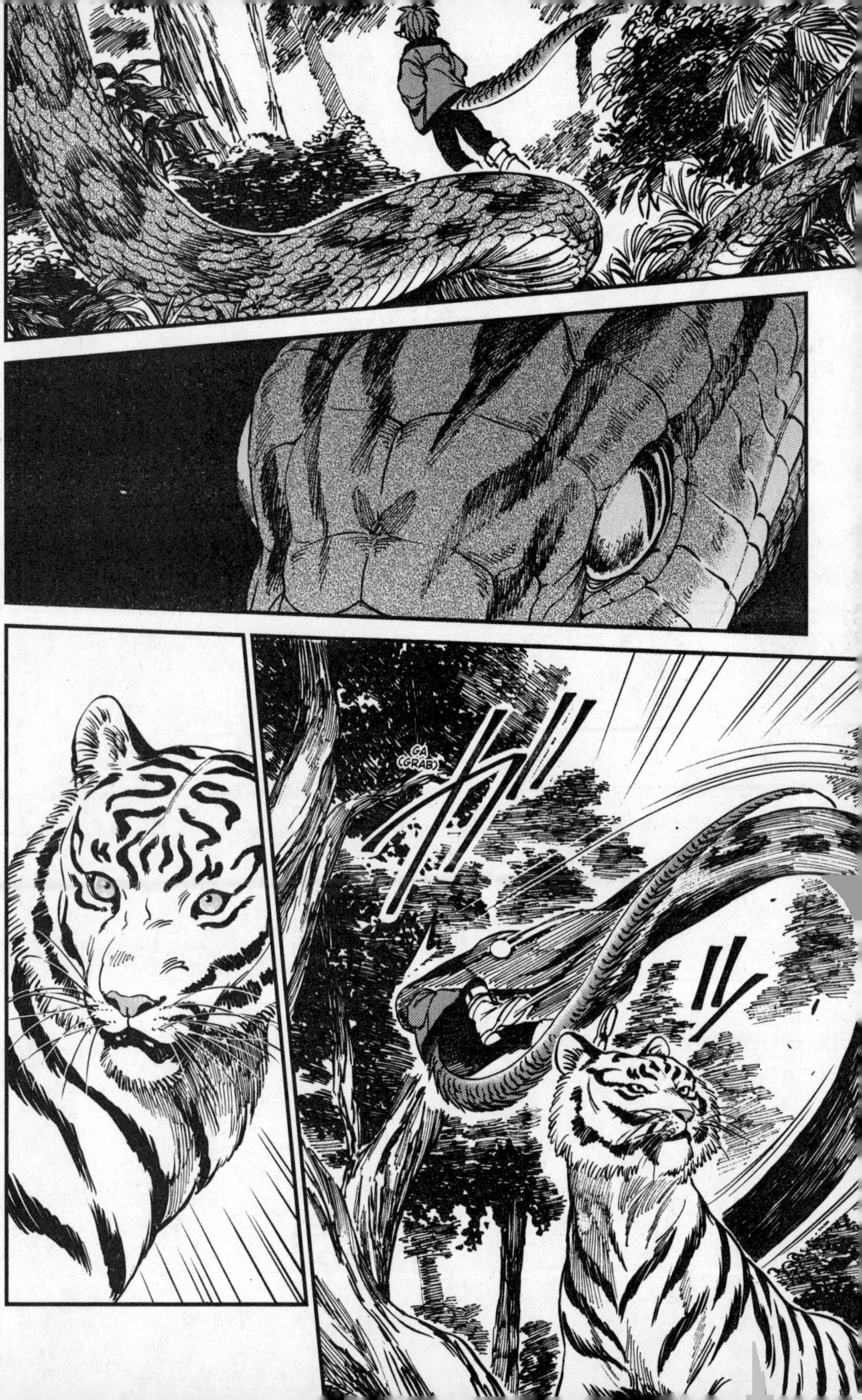
GA (GRAB)

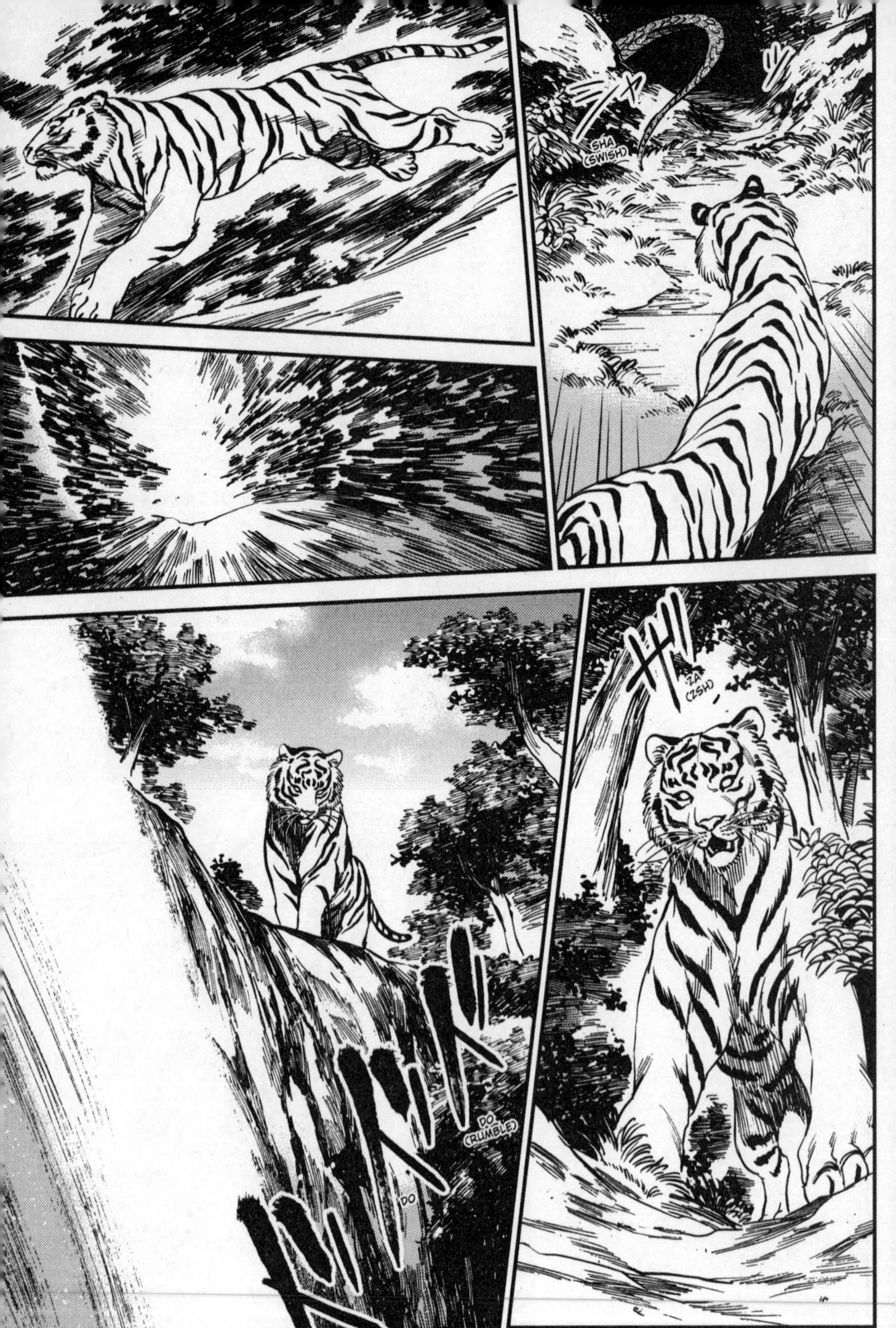
SHA (SWISH)
ZA (ZSH)
DO (RUMBLE)
DO
DO

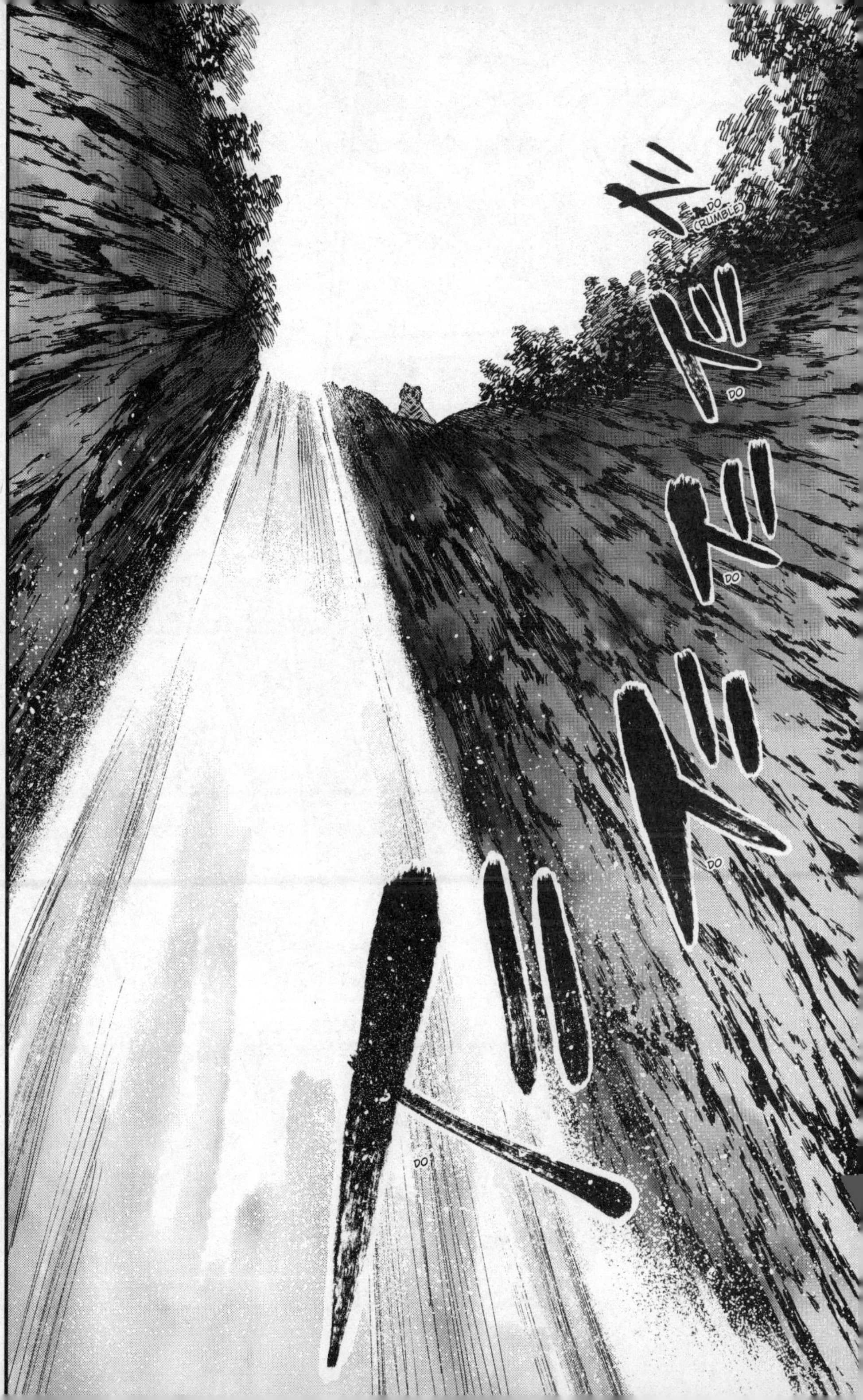

DO (RUMBLE)
DO
DO
DO
DO

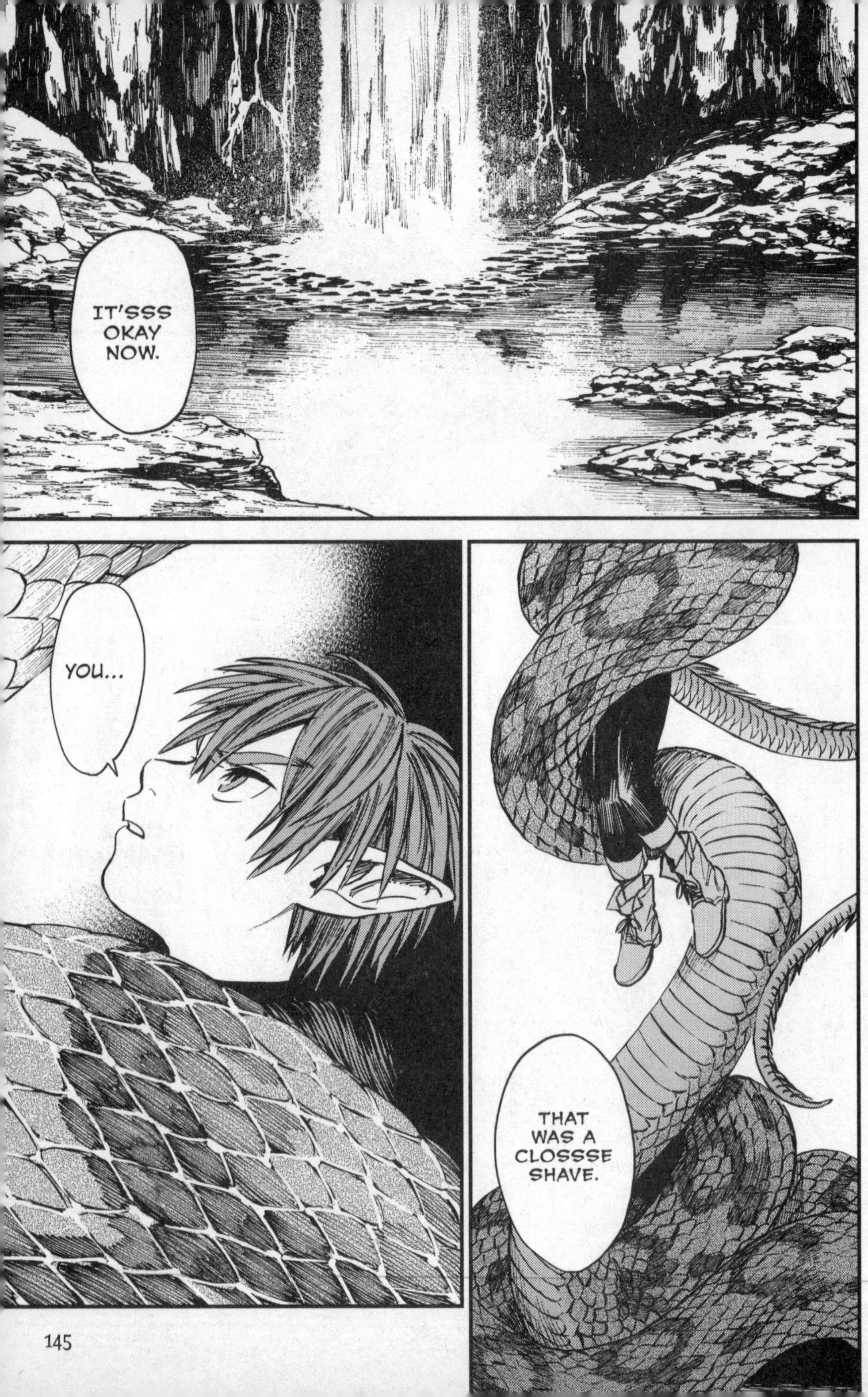
IT'SSS OKAY NOW.
THAT WAS A CLOSSSE SHAVE.
YOU...

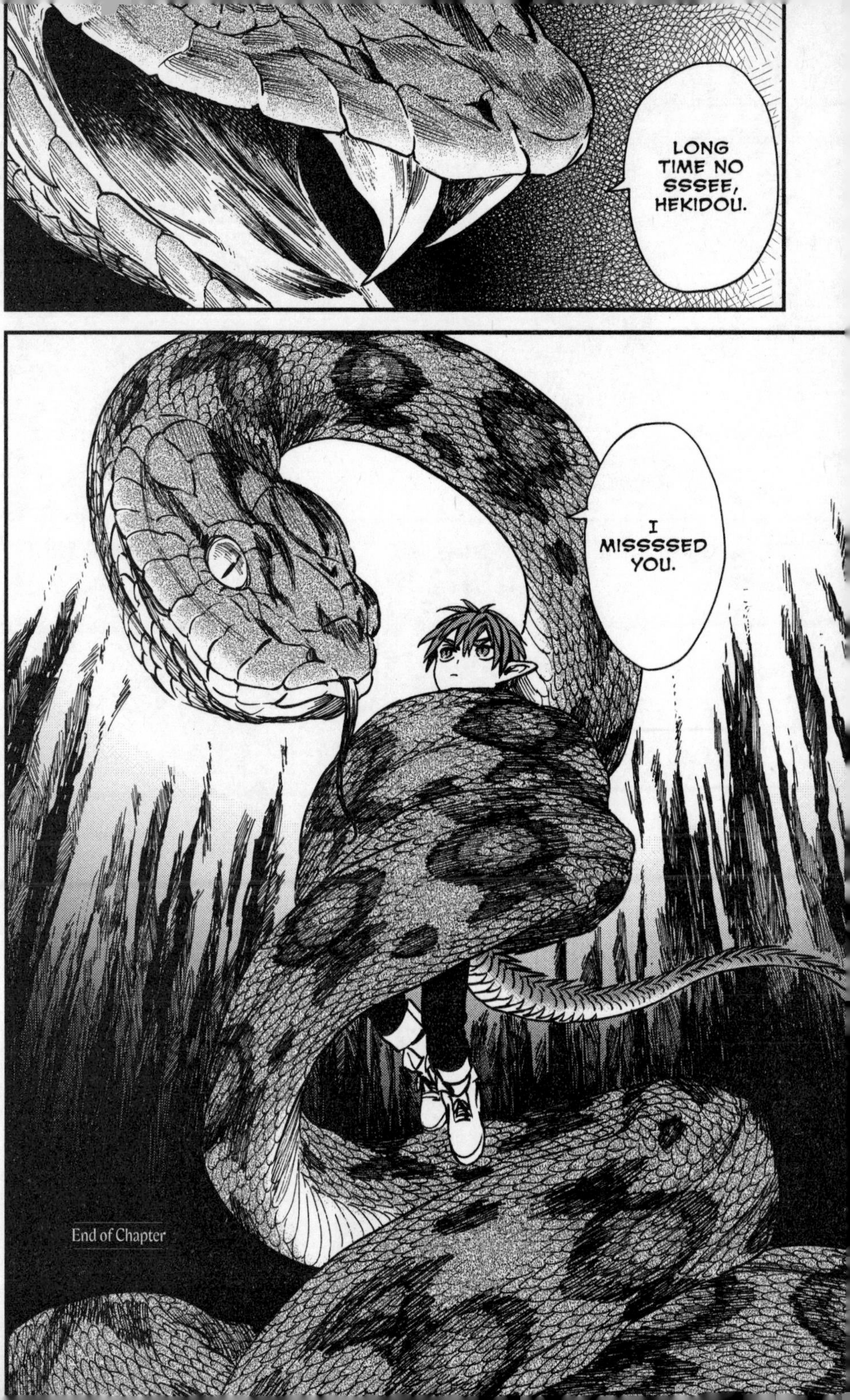
LONG TIME NO SSSEE, HEKIDOU.
I MISSSSED YOU.
End of Chapter

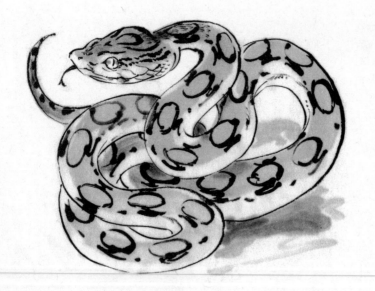

The Tiger Won't Eat the Dragon Yet

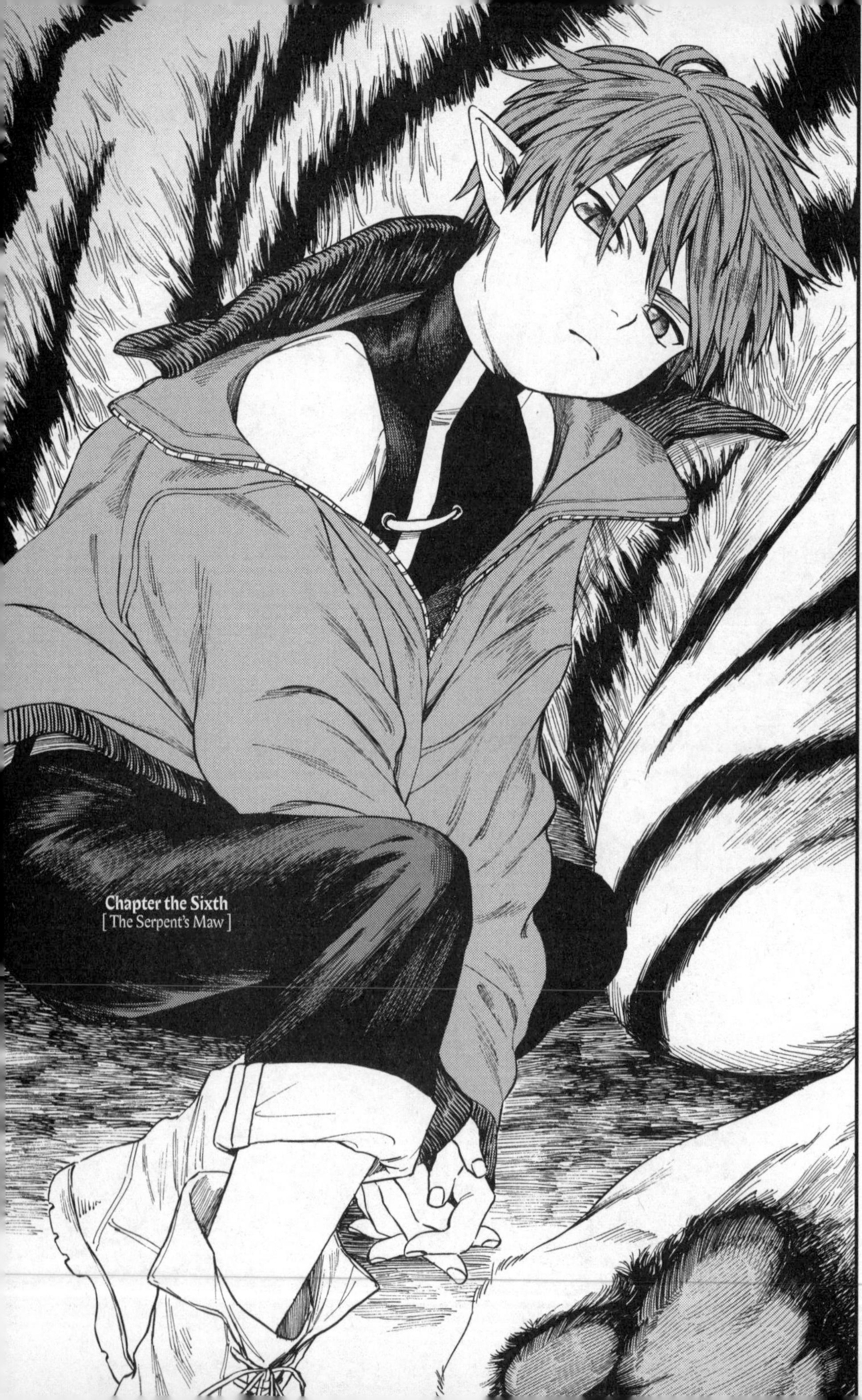
Chapter the Sixth
[The Serpent's Maw]

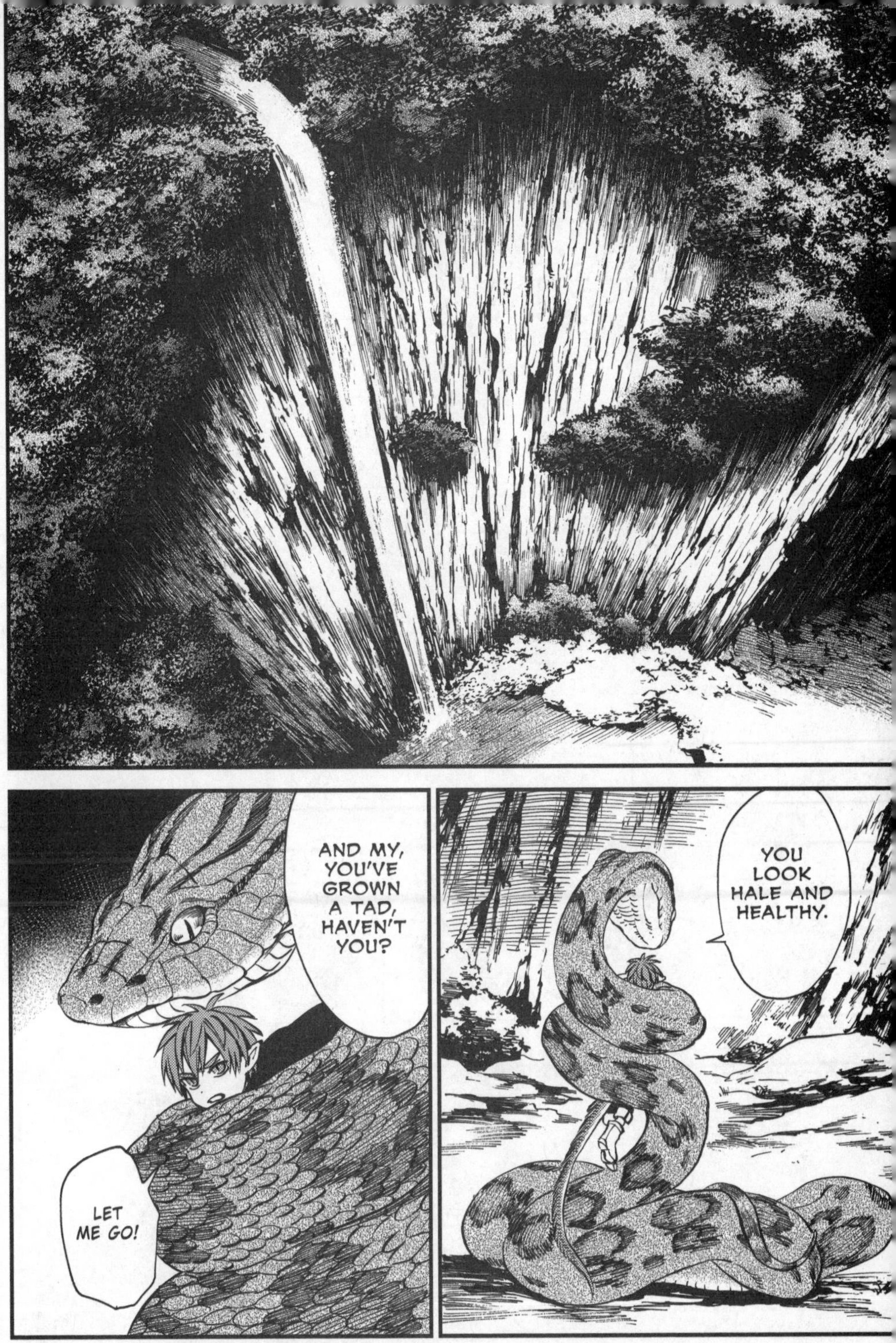
YOU LOOK HALE AND HEALTHY.
AND MY, YOU'VE GROWN A TAD, HAVEN'T YOU?
LET ME GO!

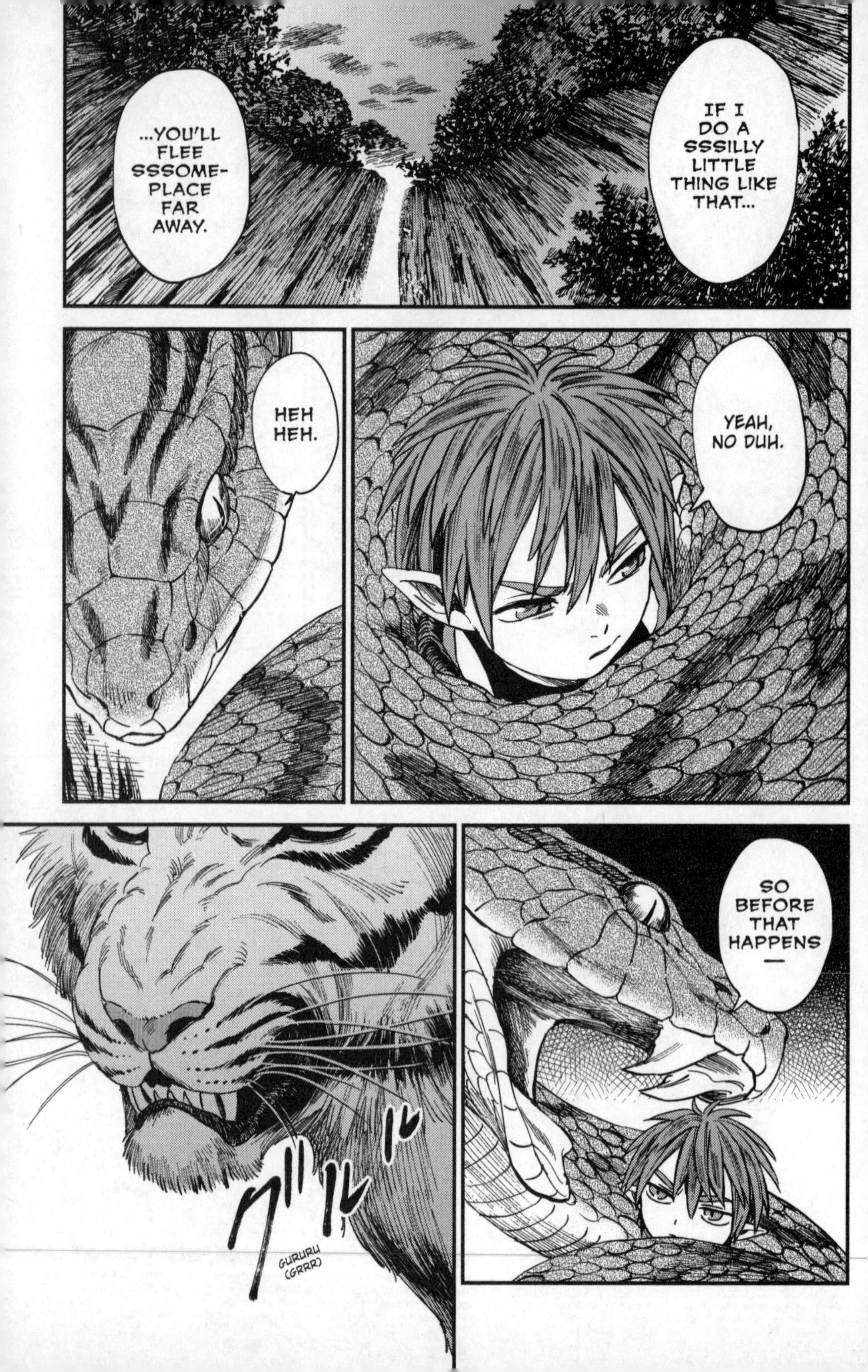
IF I DO A SSSILLY LITTLE THING LIKE THAT...
...YOU'LL FLEE SSSOME-PLACE FAR AWAY.
YEAH, NO DUH.
HEH HEH.
SO BEFORE THAT HAPPENS—
グルル
GURURU (GRRR)

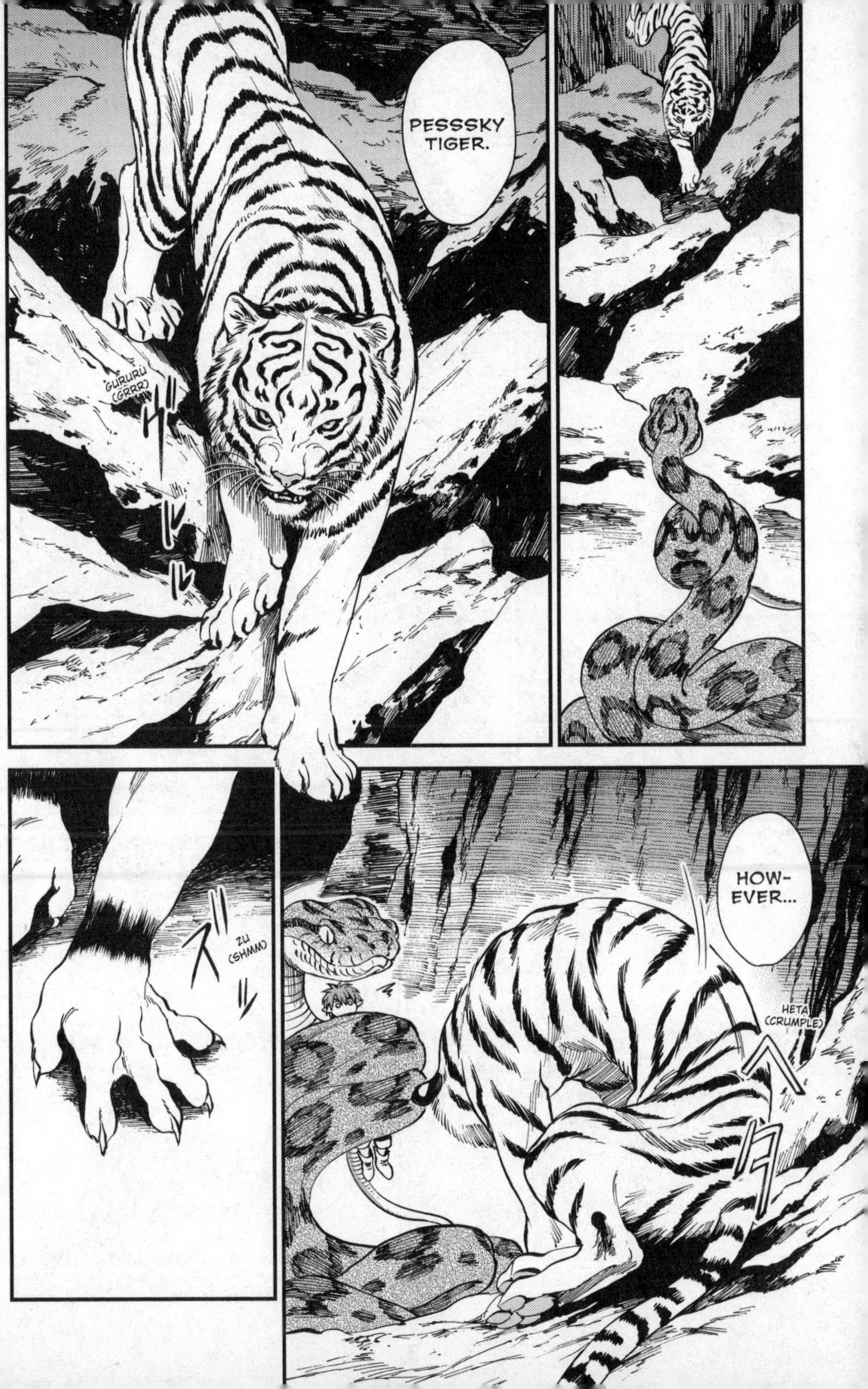
PESSSKY TIGER.
GURURU (GRRR)
HOW-EVER...
HETA (CRUMPLE)
ZU (SHMM)

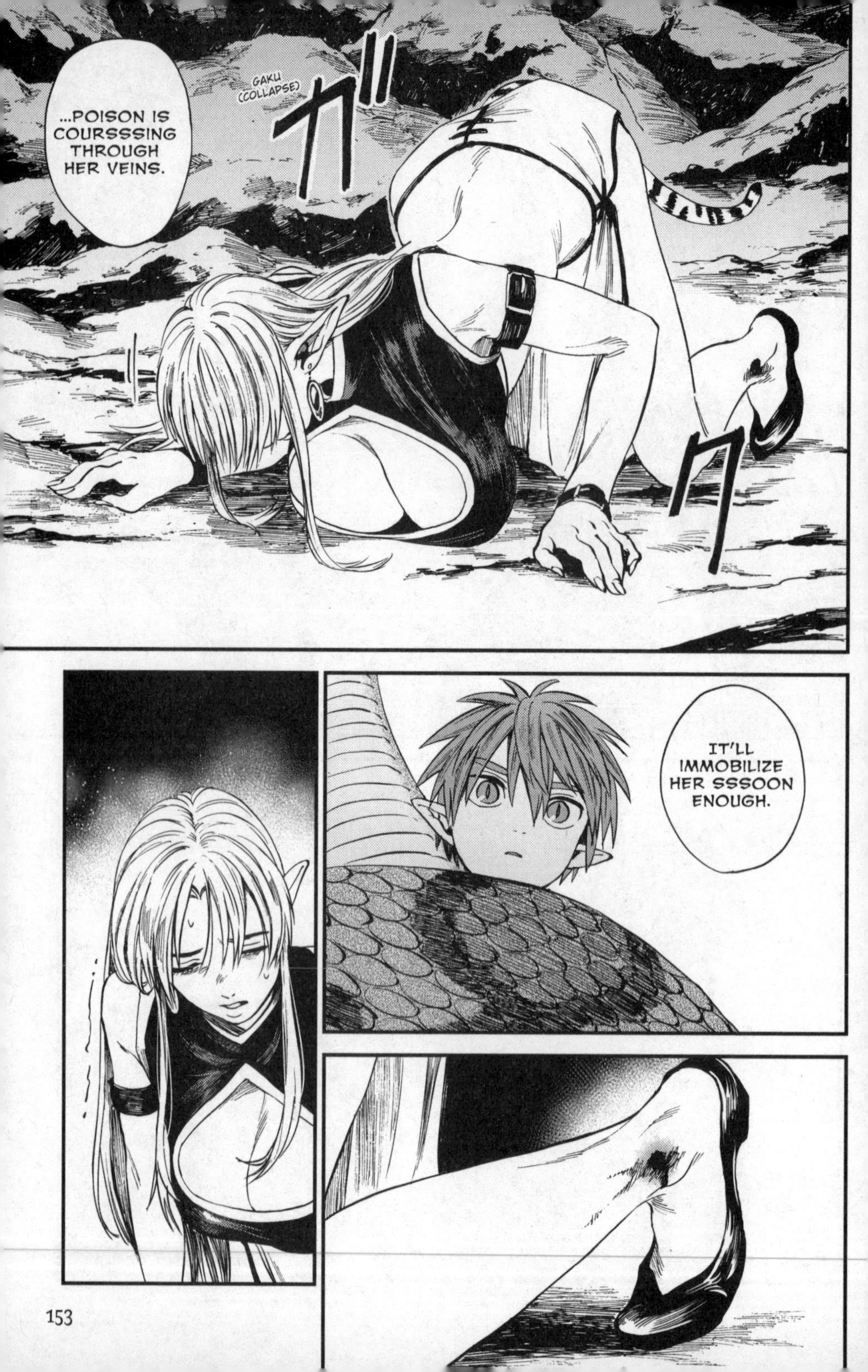
GAKU (COLLAPSE)
...POISON IS COURSSSING THROUGH HER VEINS.
IT'LL IMMOBILIZE HER SSSOON ENOUGH.

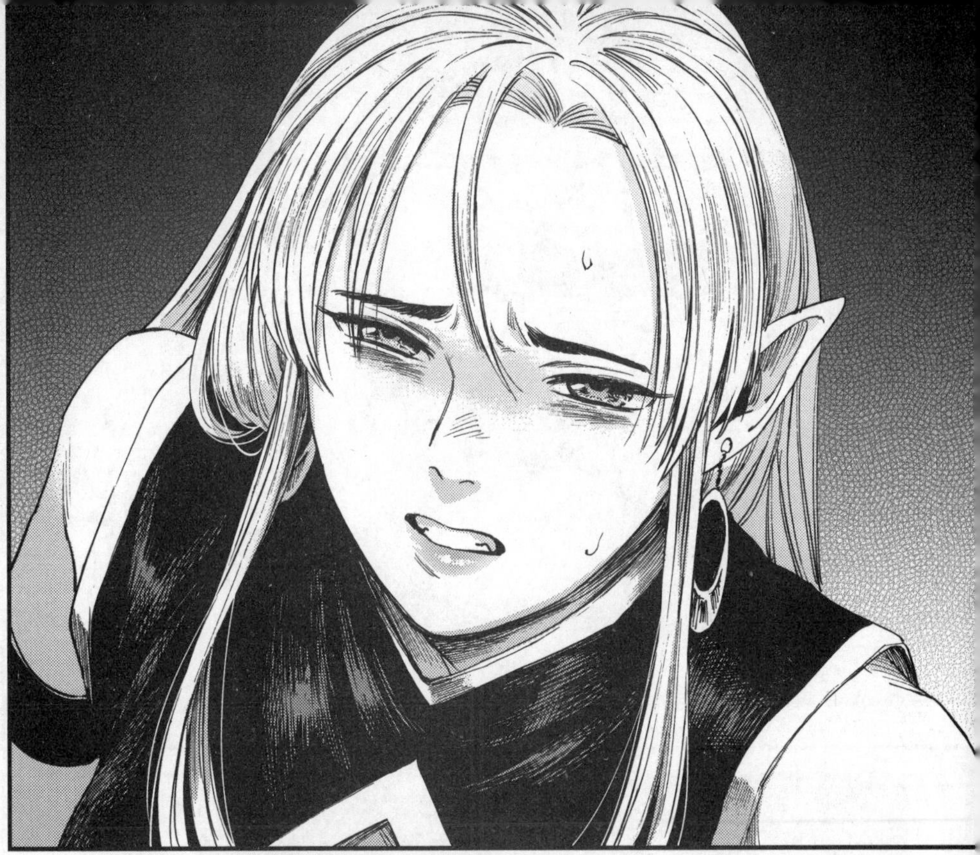

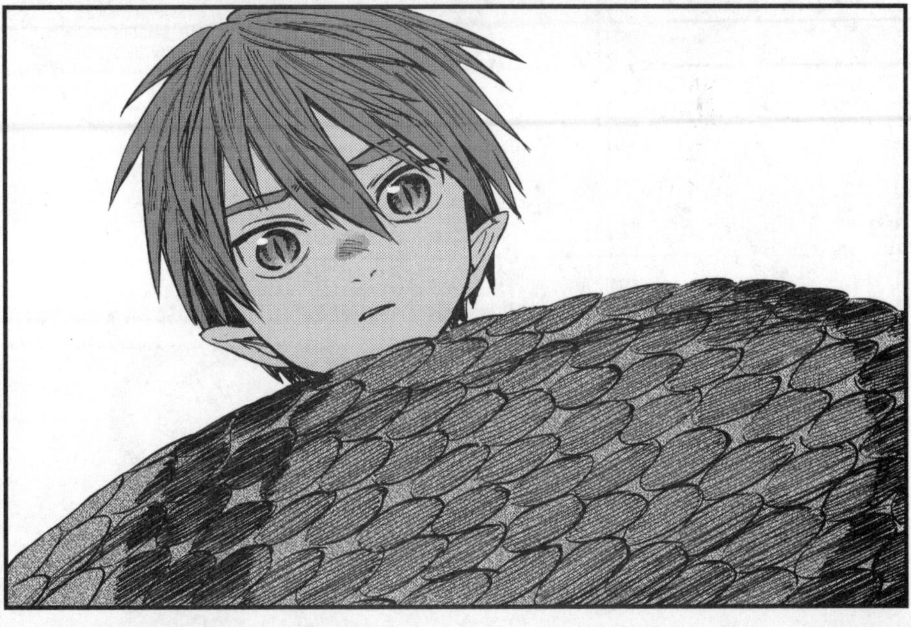

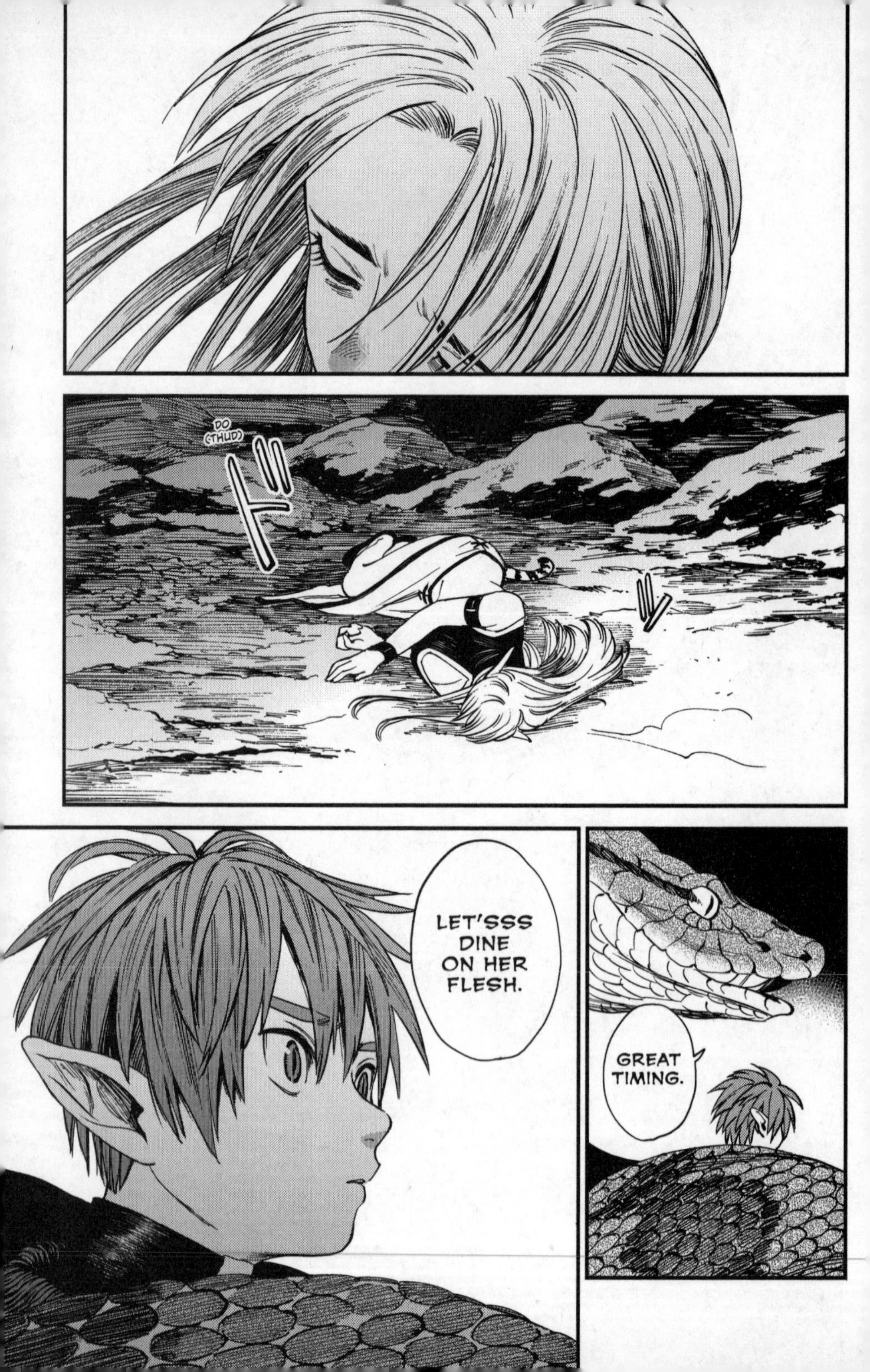
DO (THUD)
GREAT TIMING.
LET'SSS DINE ON HER FLESH.

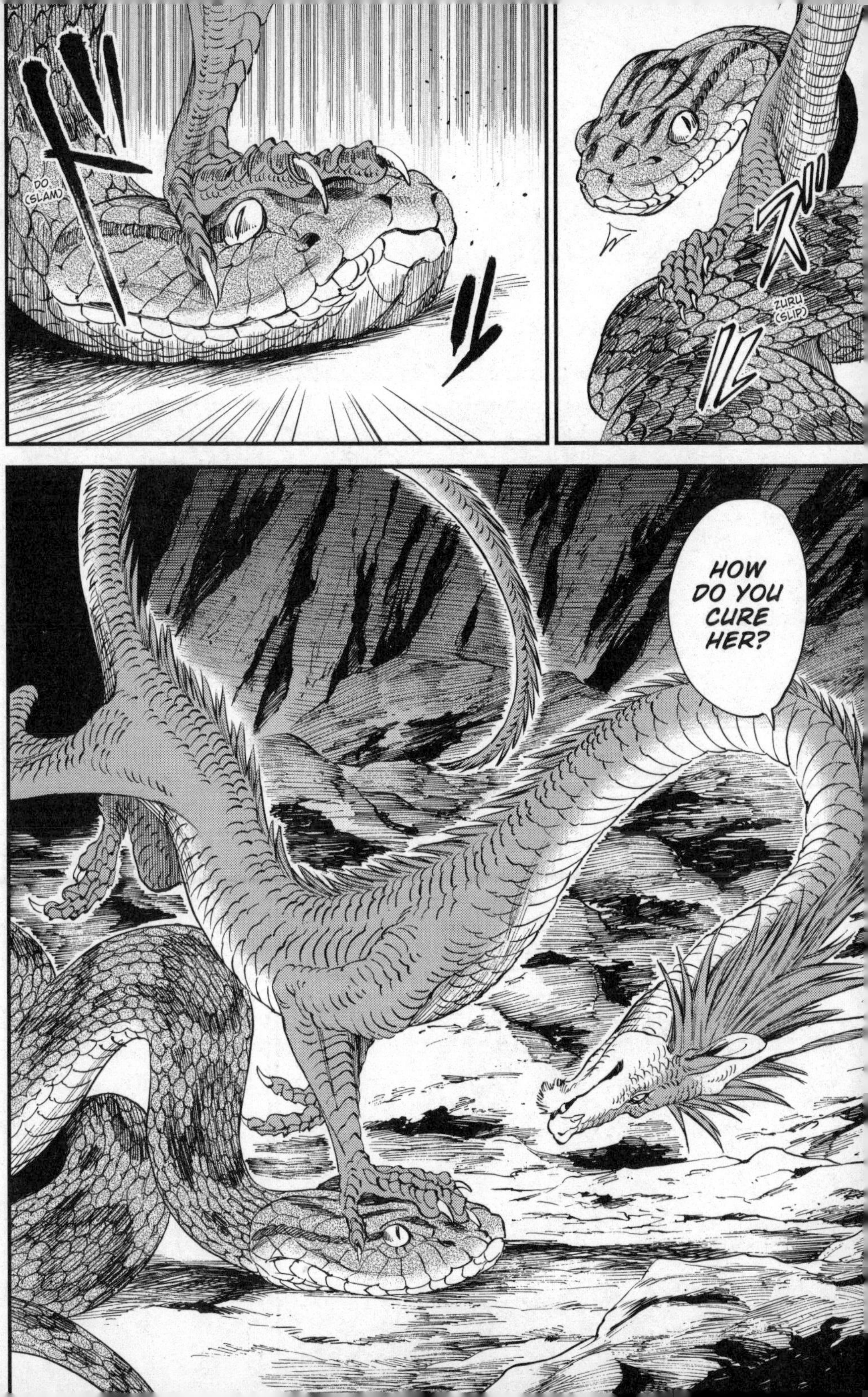

ZURU (SLIP)
DO (SLAM)
HOW DO YOU CURE HER?

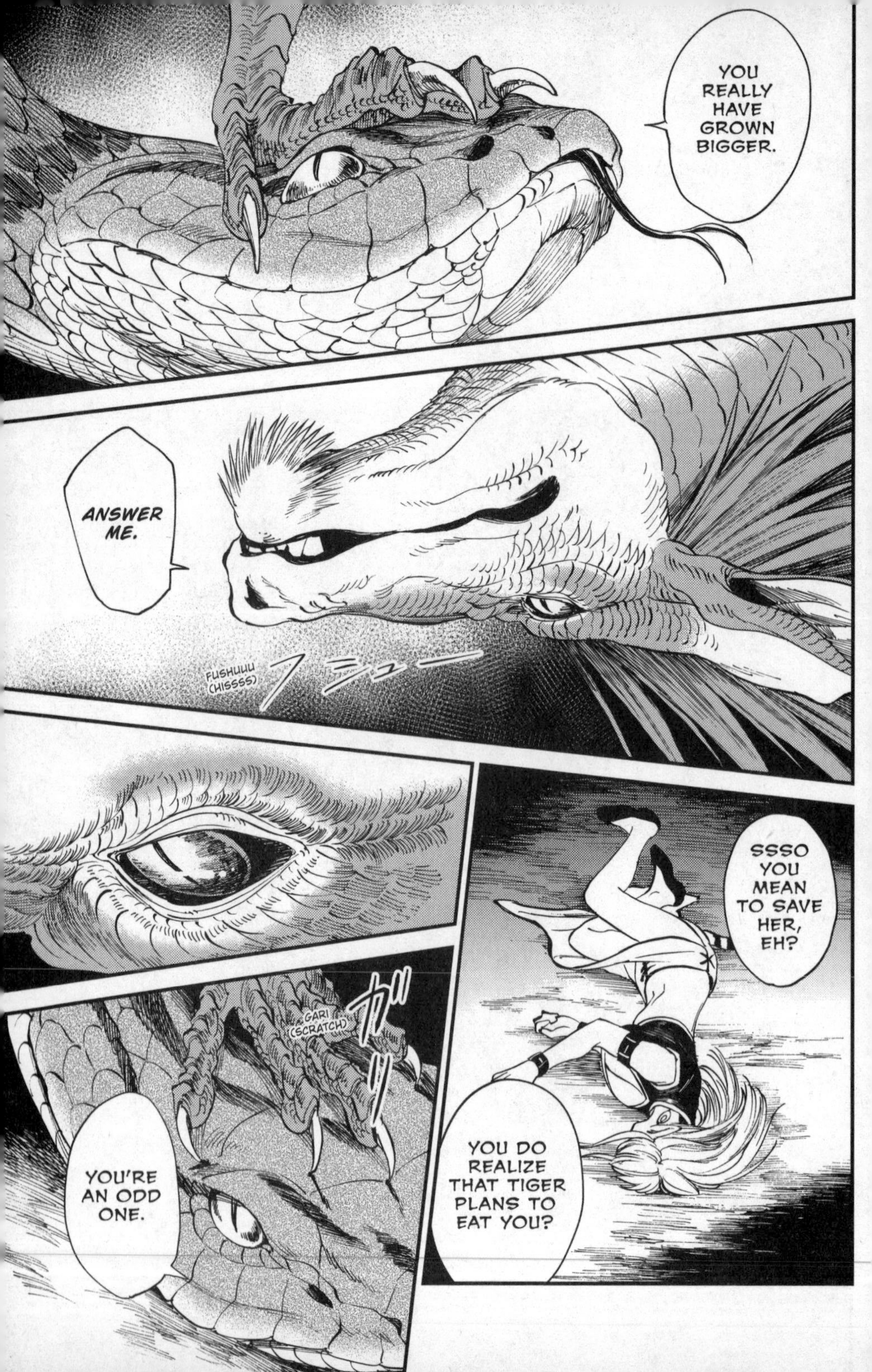
YOU REALLY HAVE GROWN BIGGER.
ANSWER ME.
FUSHUUU (HISSSS)
SSSO YOU MEAN TO SAVE HER, EH?
YOU DO REALIZE THAT TIGER PLANS TO EAT YOU?
GARI (SCRATCH)
YOU'RE AN ODD ONE.

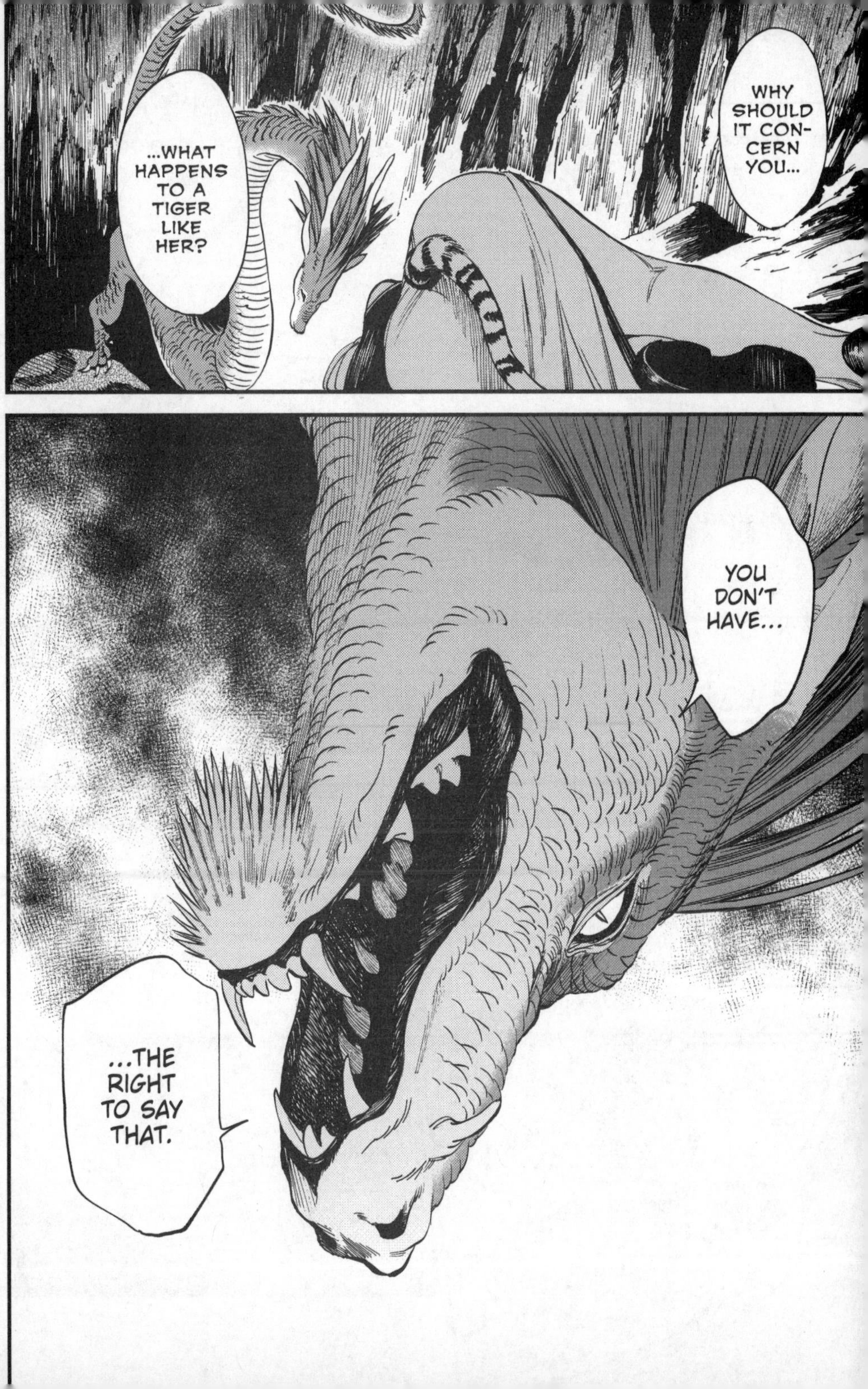
WHY SHOULD IT CON- CERN YOU...
...WHAT HAPPENS TO A TIGER LIKE HER?
YOU DON'T HAVE...
...THE RIGHT TO SAY THAT.

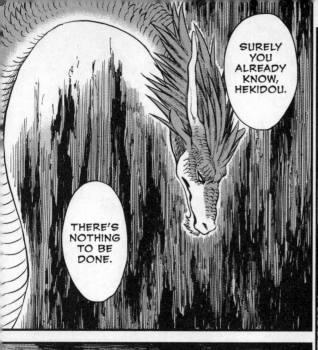

SURELY YOU ALREADY KNOW, HEKIDOU.

THERE'S NOTHING TO BE DONE.

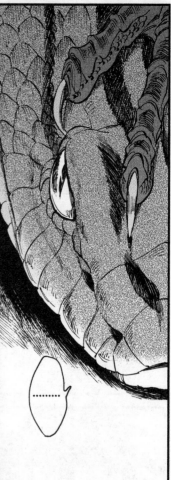

ONCE THEY GET LIKE THAT...

....

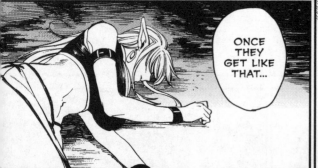

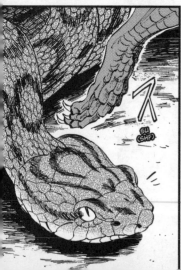

SU (SHF)

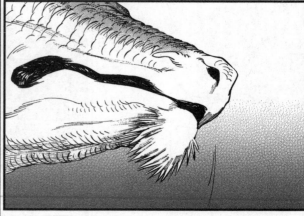

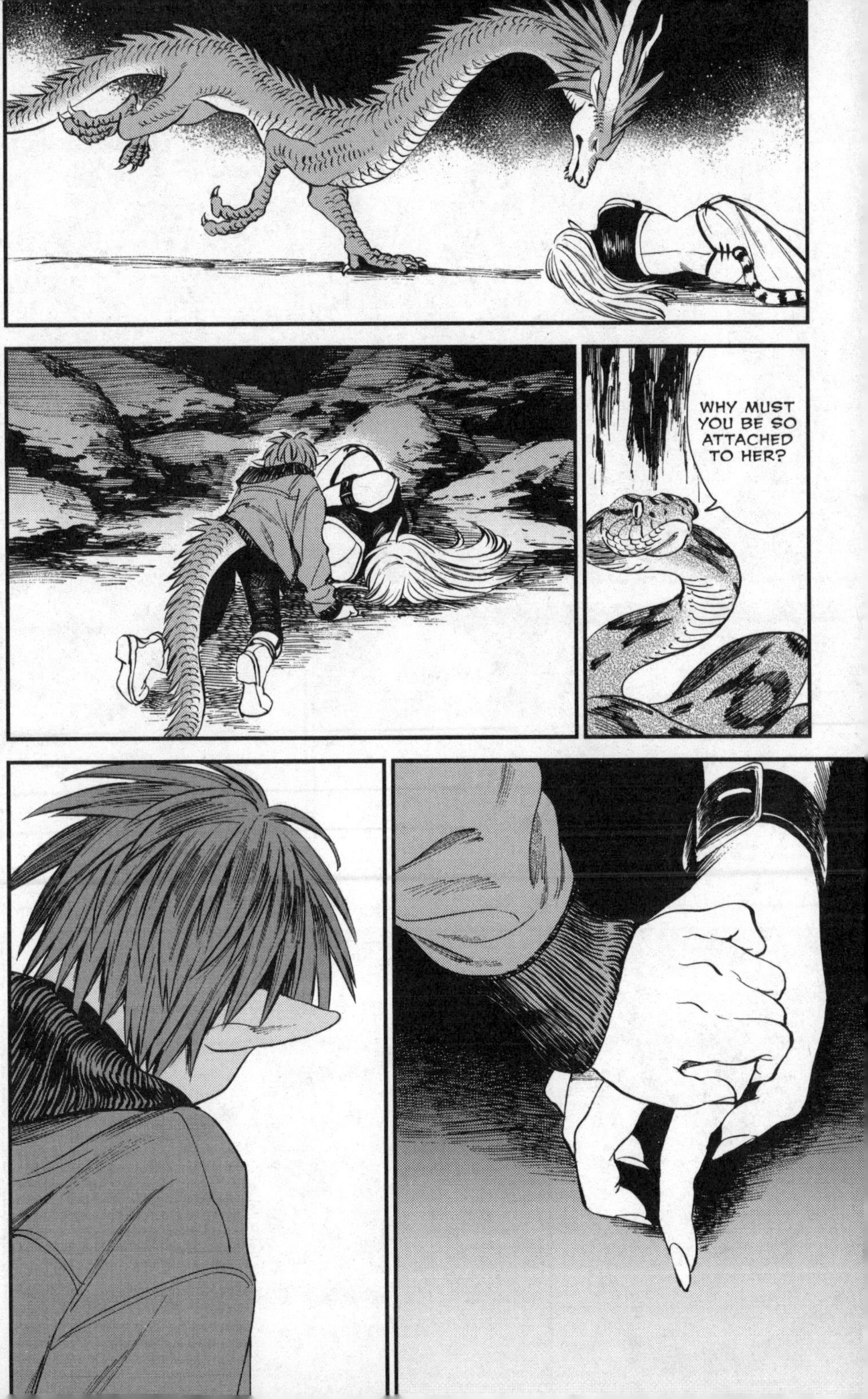
WHY MUST YOU BE SO ATTACHED TO HER?

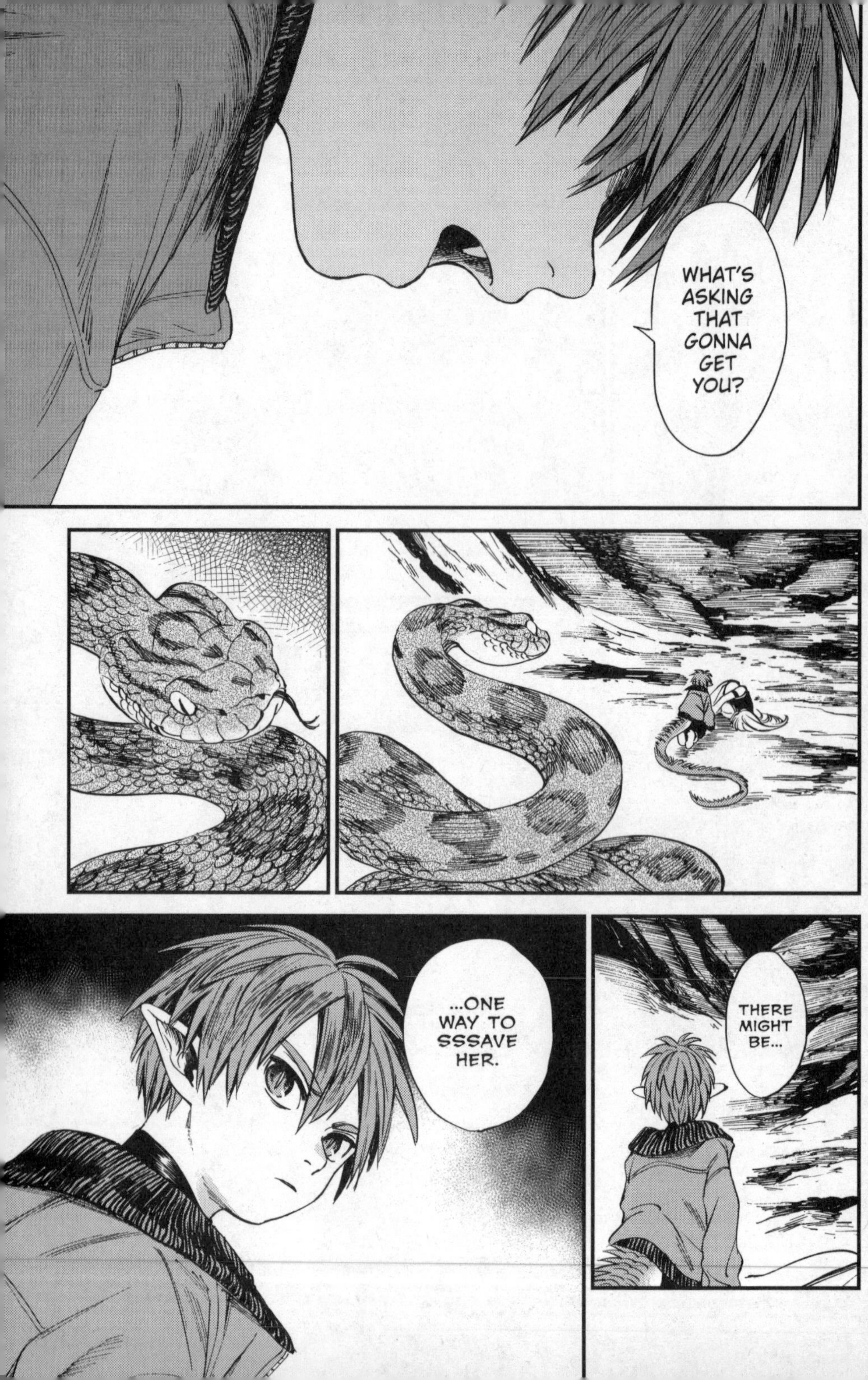
WHAT'S ASKING THAT GONNA GET YOU?
THERE MIGHT BE...
...ONE WAY TO SSSAVE HER.

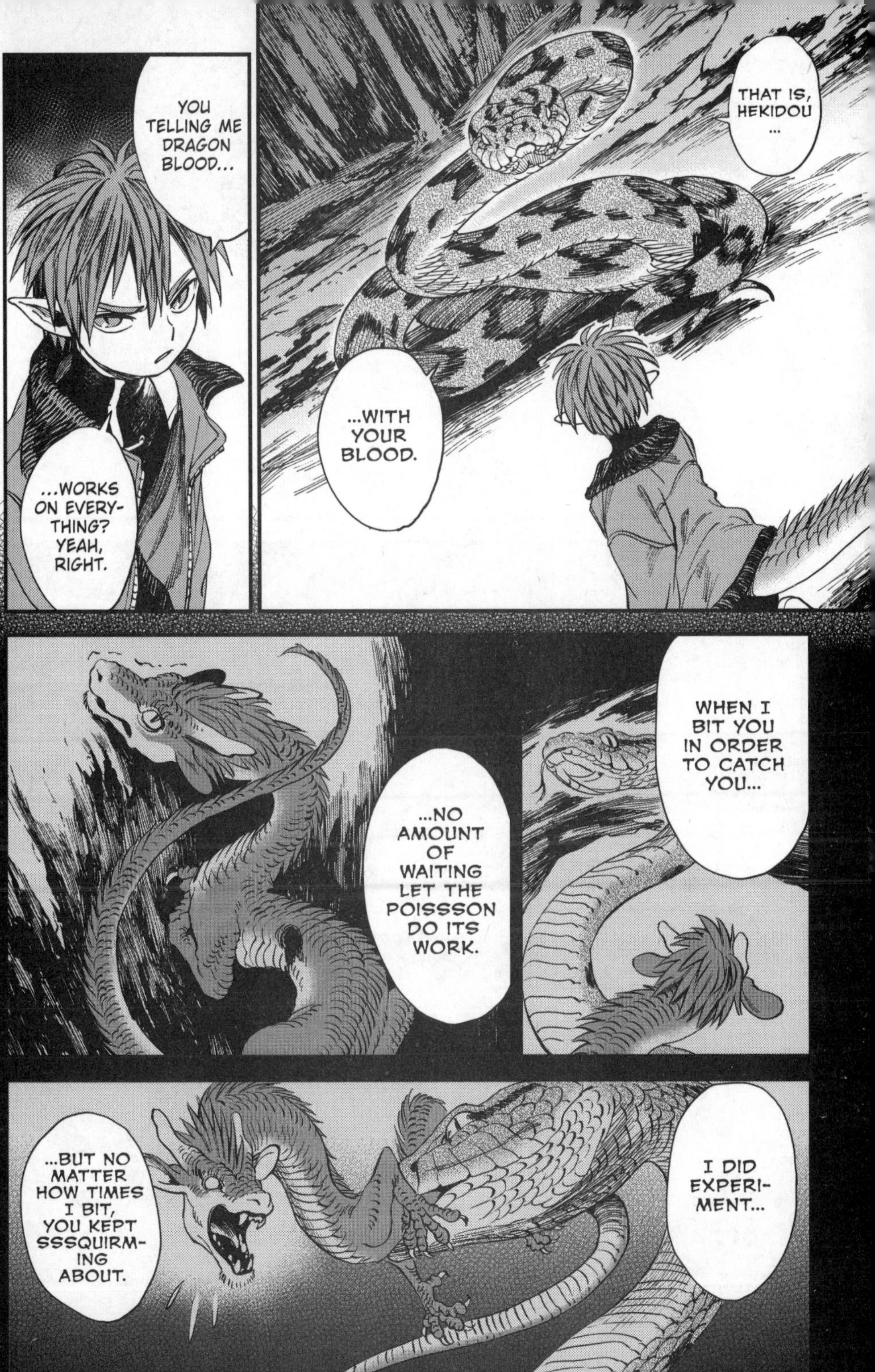
THAT IS, HEKIDOU ...
...WITH YOUR BLOOD.
YOU TELLING ME DRAGON BLOOD...
...WORKS ON EVERY-THING? YEAH, RIGHT.
WHEN I BIT YOU IN ORDER TO CATCH YOU...
...NO AMOUNT OF WAITING LET THE POISSSON DO ITS WORK.
I DID EXPERI-MENT...
...BUT NO MATTER HOW TIMES I BIT, YOU KEPT SSSQUIRM-ING ABOUT.

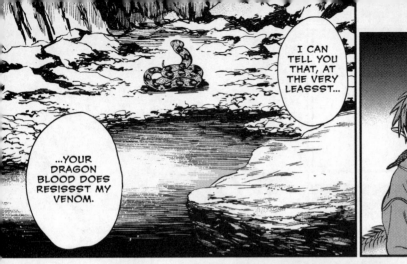

I CAN TELL YOU THAT, AT THE VERY LEASSST...

...YOUR DRAGON BLOOD DOES RESISSST MY VENOM.

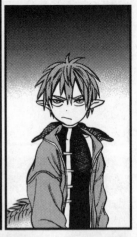

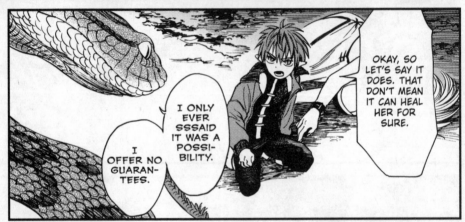

OKAY, SO LET'S SAY IT DOES. THAT DON'T MEAN IT CAN HEAL HER FOR SURE.

I ONLY EVER SSSAID IT WAS A POSSIBILITY.

I OFFER NO GUARANTEES.

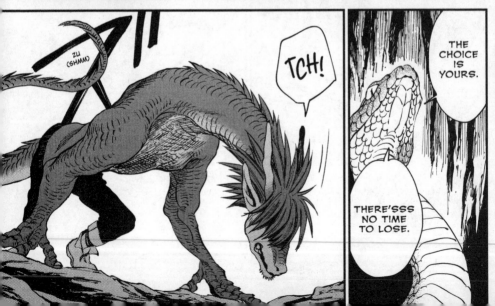

ZU (SHMM)

TCH!

THE CHOICE IS YOURS.

THERE'SSS NO TIME TO LOSE.

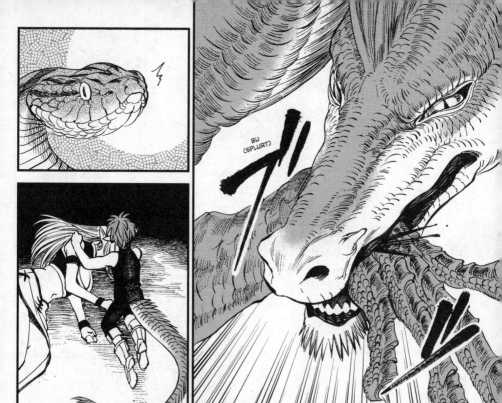

BU
(SPLURT)

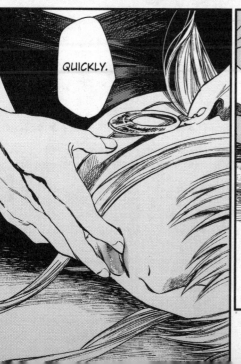

QUICKLY.

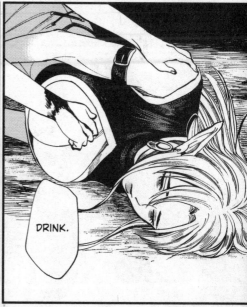

DRINK.

164

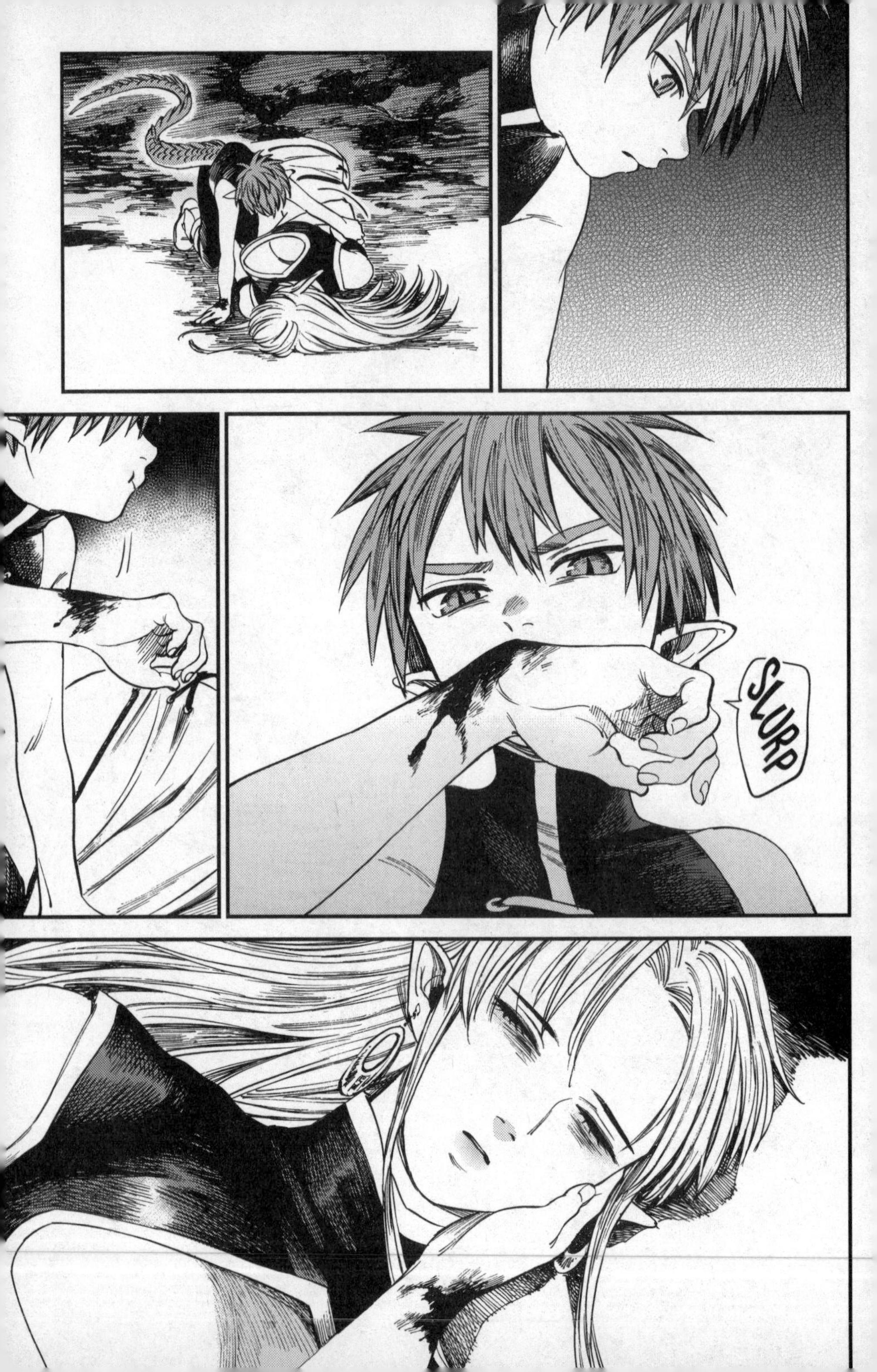
SLURP

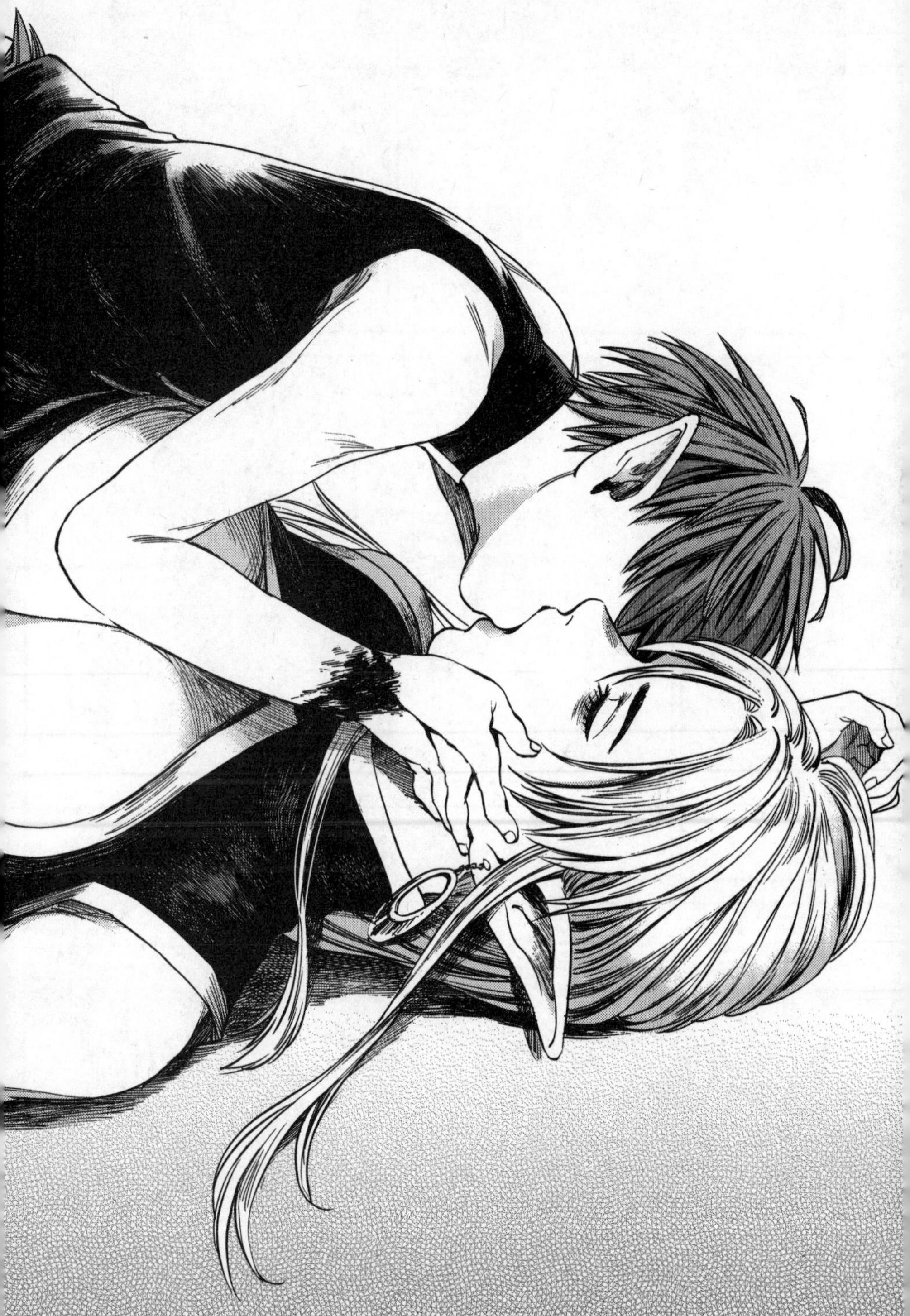

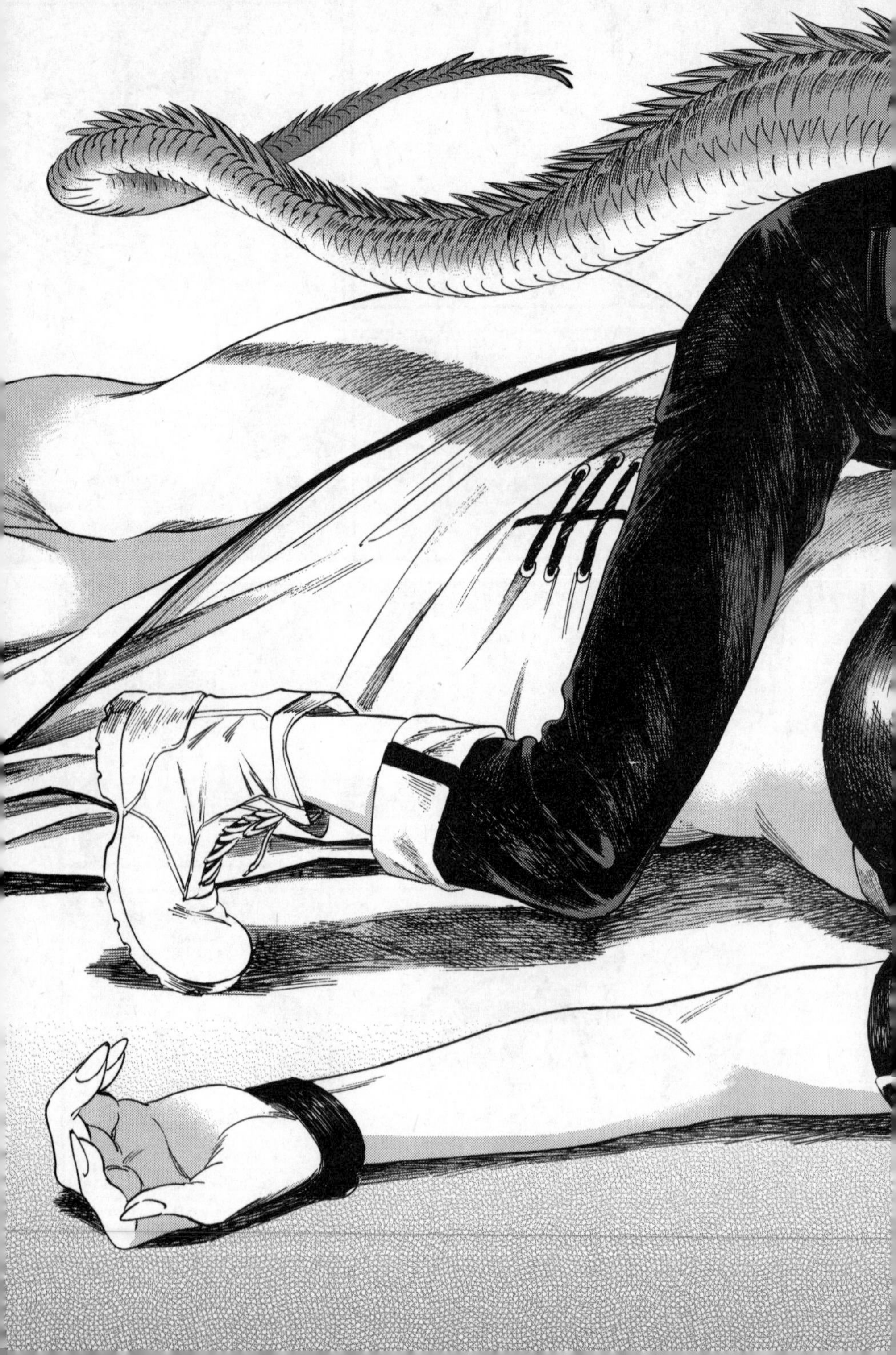

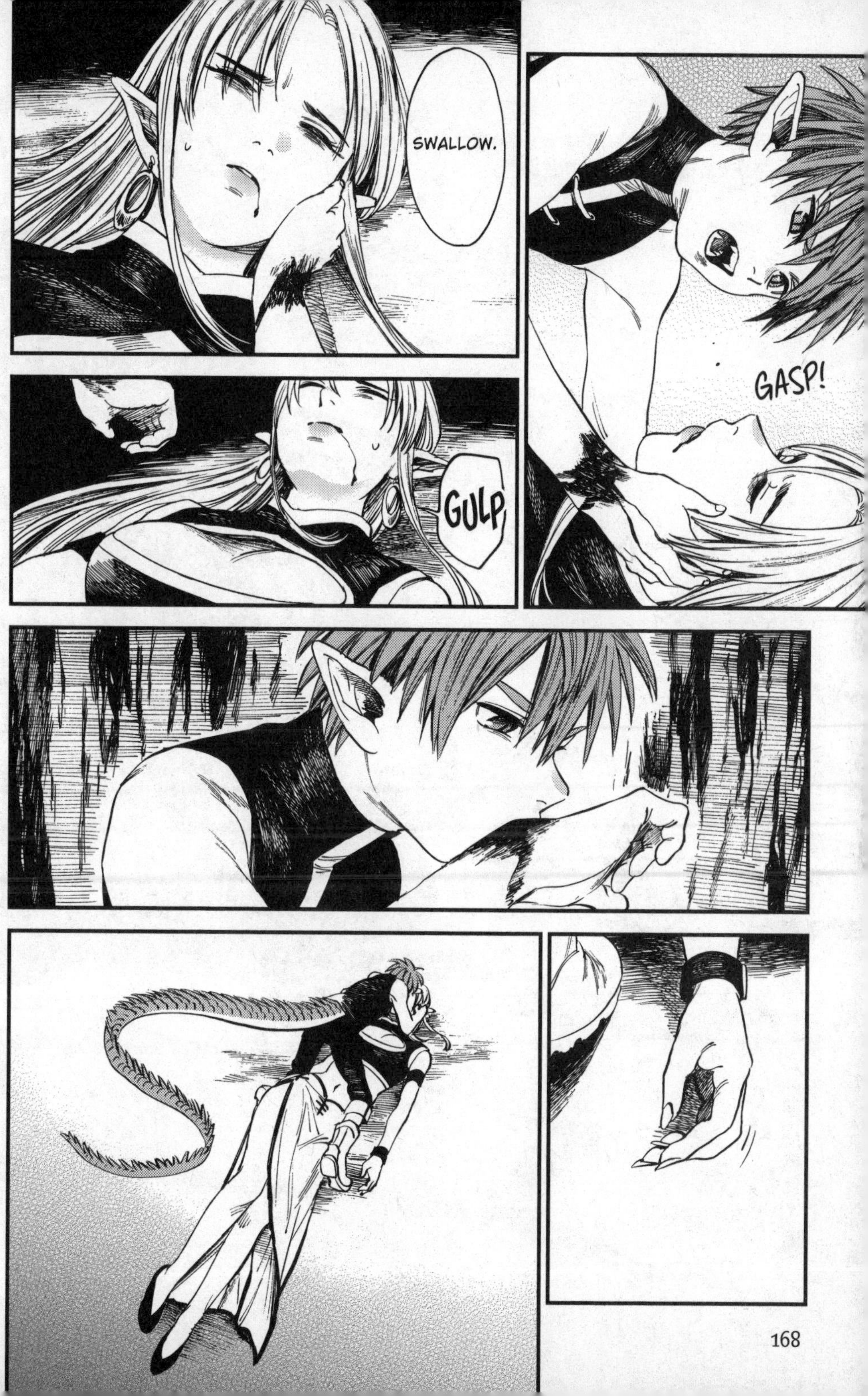
GASP!
SWALLOW.
GULP

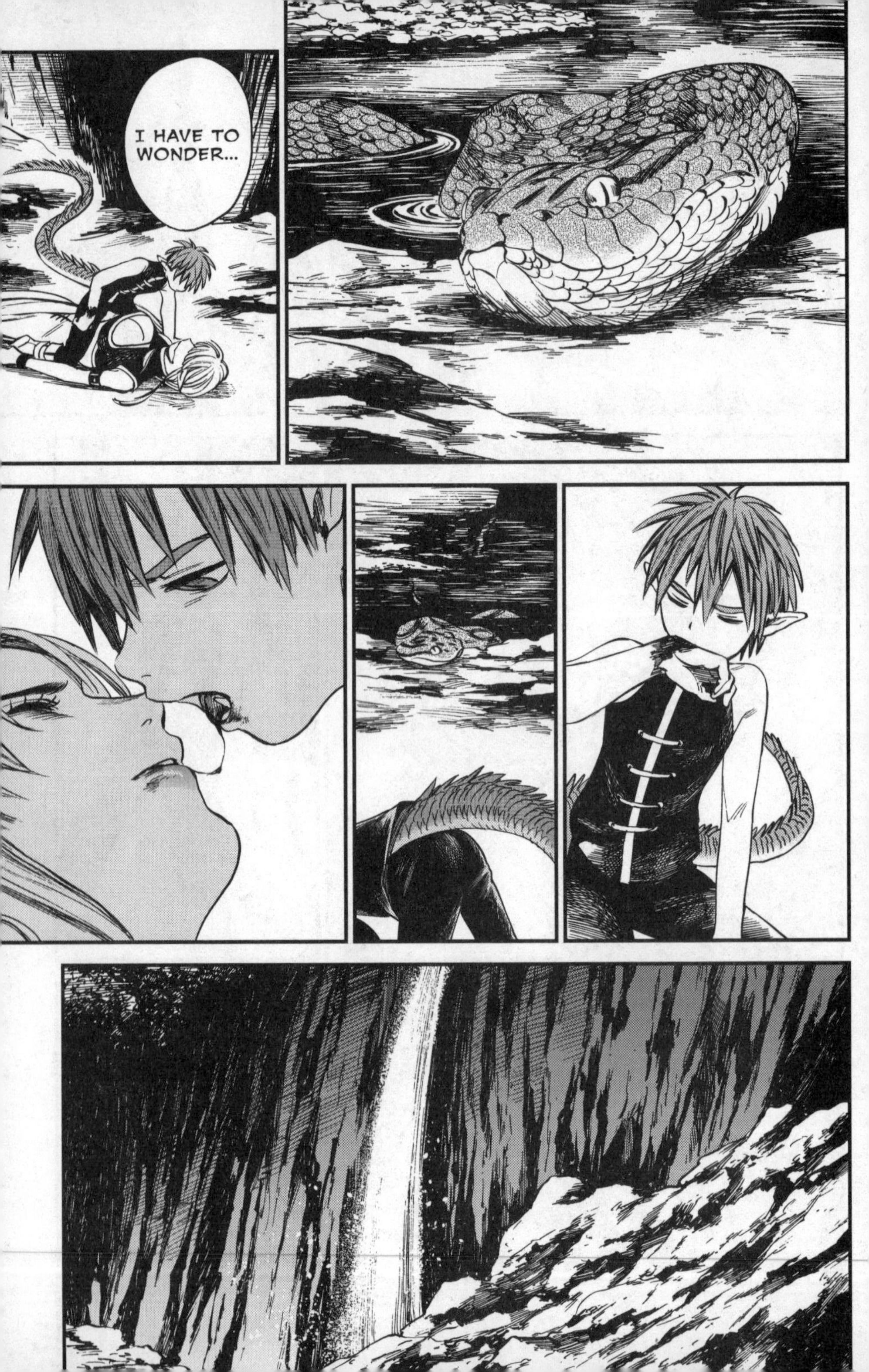
I HAVE TO WONDER...

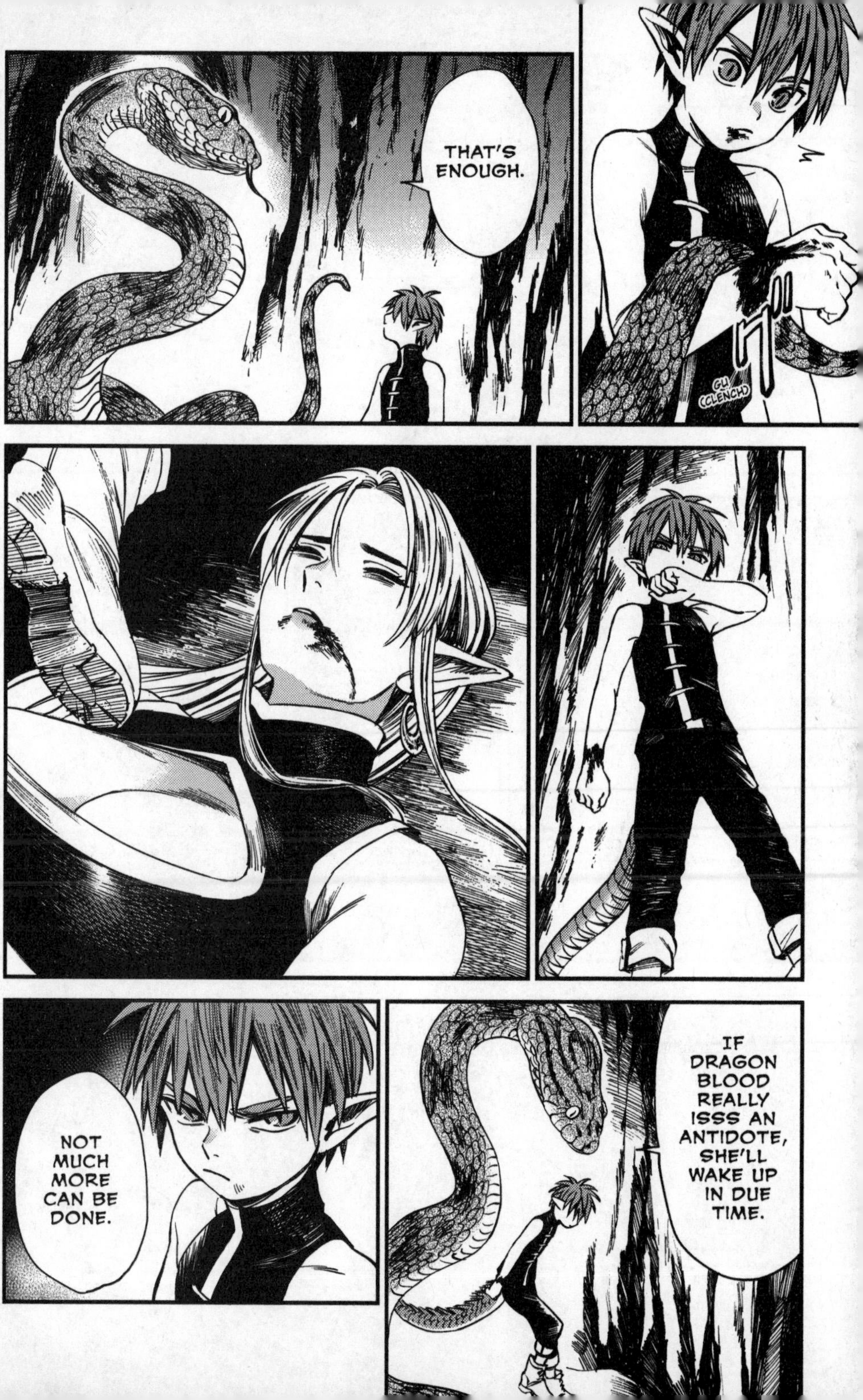
GU (CLENCH)
THAT'S ENOUGH.
IF DRAGON BLOOD REALLY ISSS AN ANTIDOTE, SHE'LL WAKE UP IN DUE TIME.
NOT MUCH MORE CAN BE DONE.

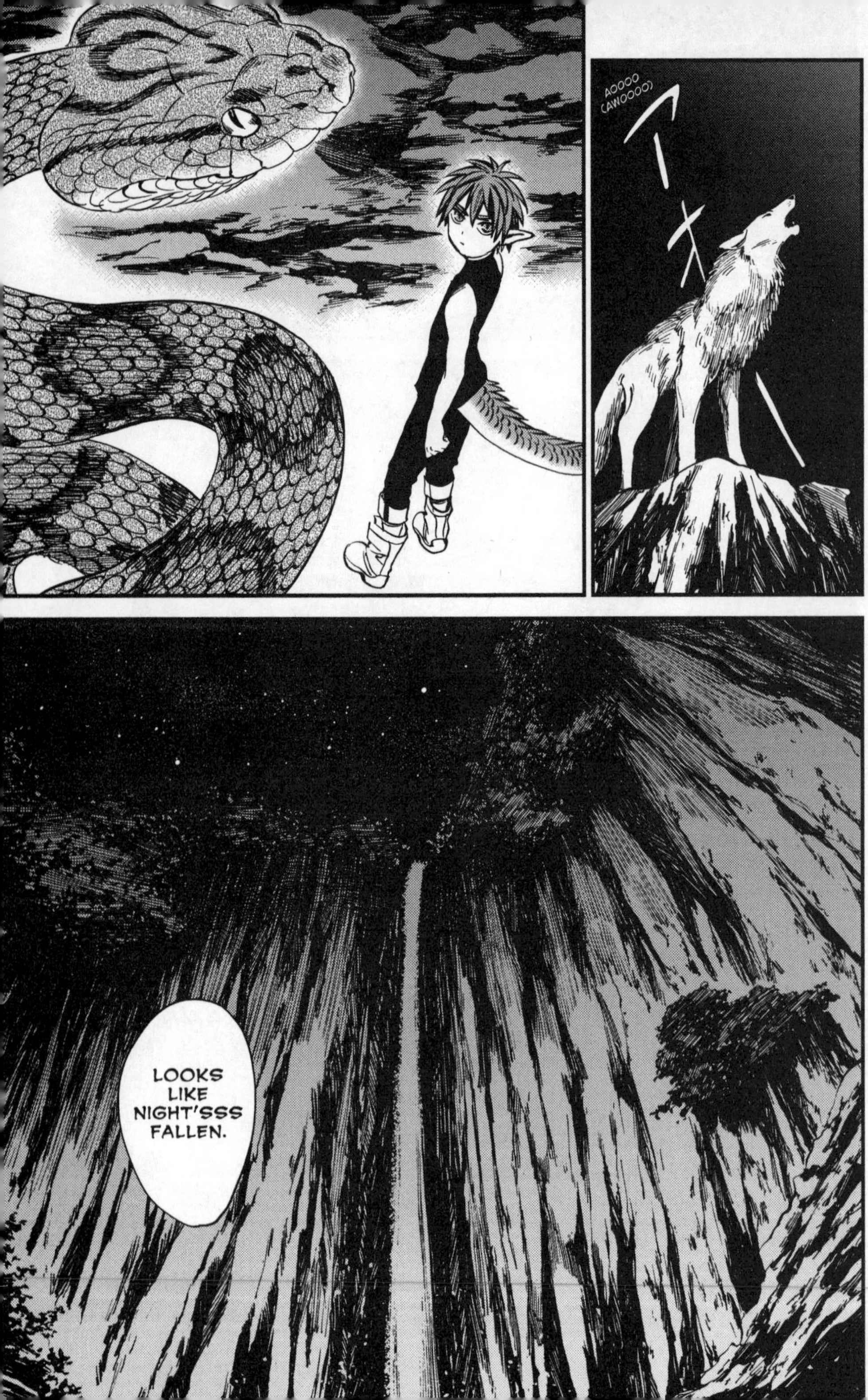
AOOOO (AWOOOO)
LOOKS LIKE NIGHT'SSS FALLEN.

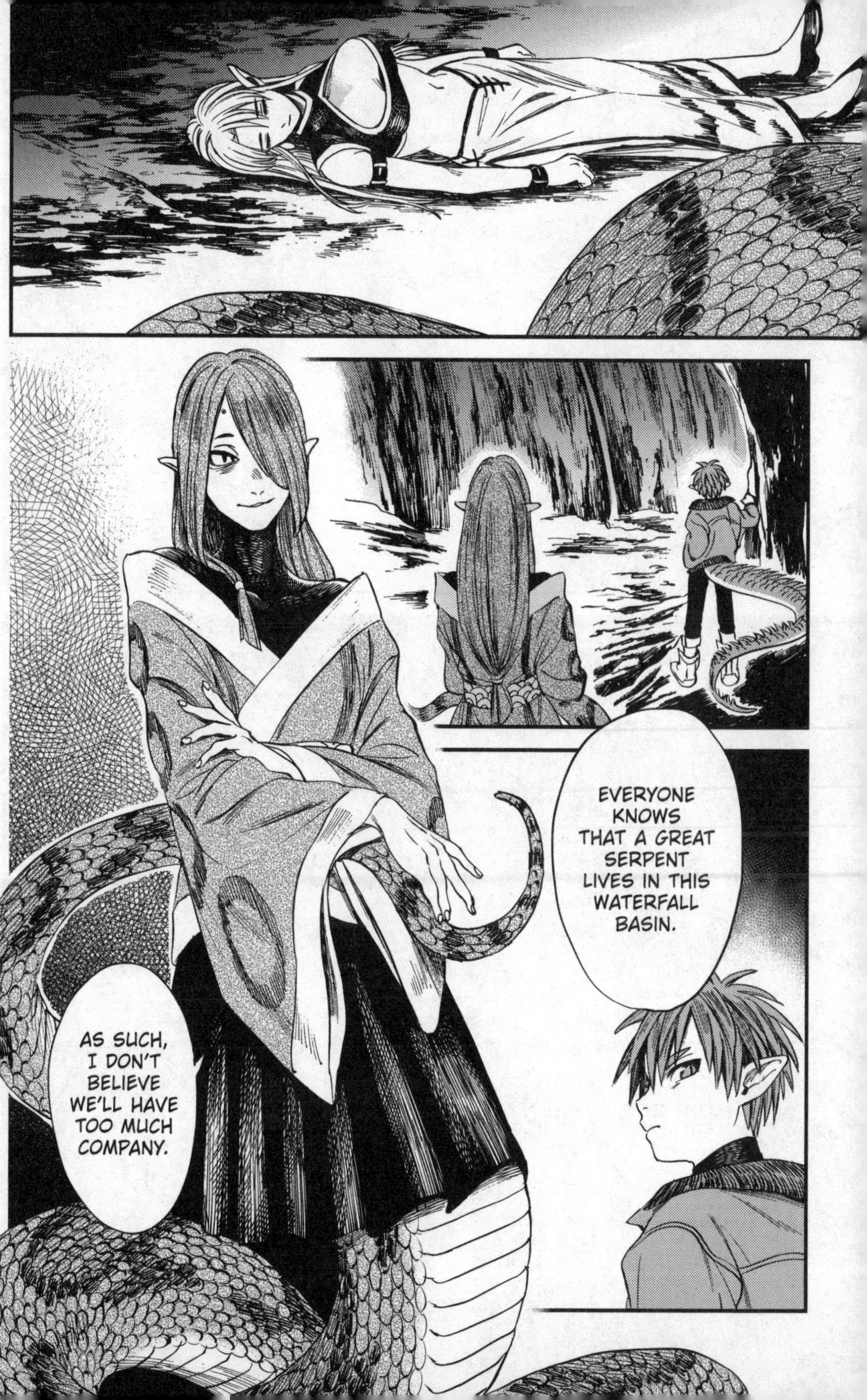
EVERYONE KNOWS THAT A GREAT SERPENT LIVES IN THIS WATERFALL BASIN.
AS SUCH, I DON'T BELIEVE WE'LL HAVE TOO MUCH COMPANY.

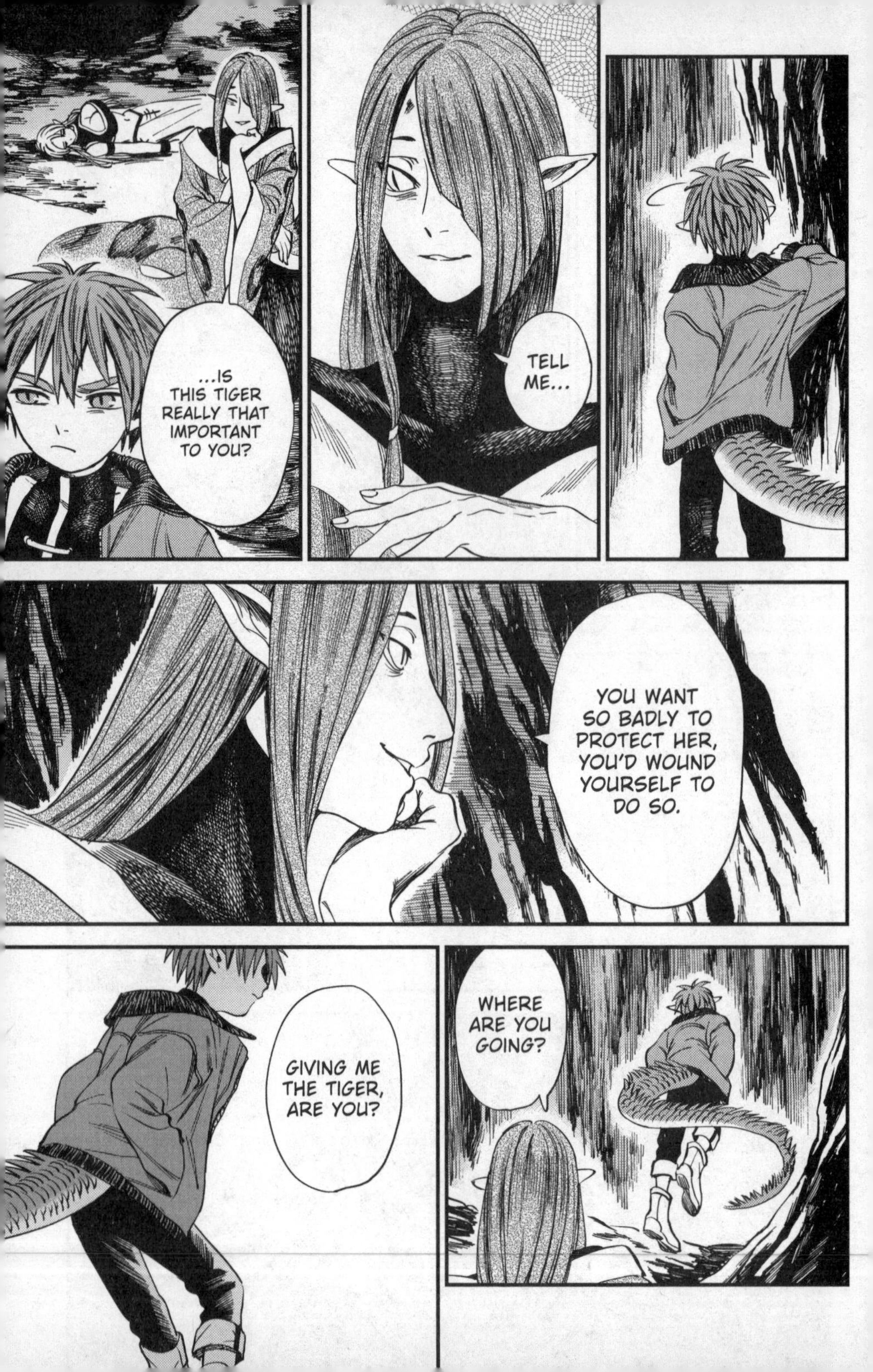
TELL ME...
...IS THIS TIGER REALLY THAT IMPORTANT TO YOU?
YOU WANT SO BADLY TO PROTECT HER, YOU'D WOUND YOURSELF TO DO SO.
WHERE ARE YOU GOING?
GIVING ME THE TIGER, ARE YOU?

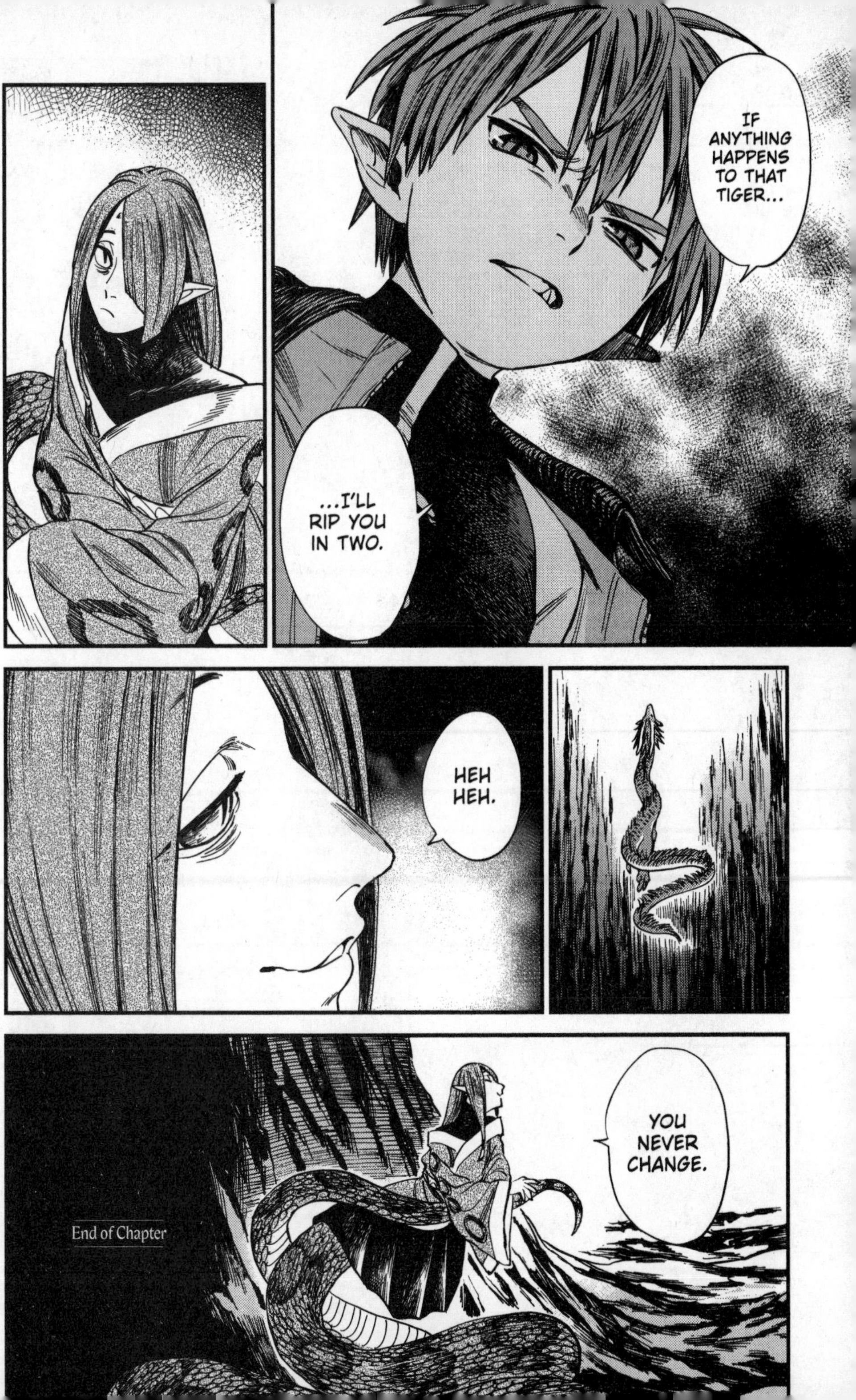
IF ANYTHING HAPPENS TO THAT TIGER...
...I'LL RIP YOU IN TWO.
HEH HEH.
YOU NEVER CHANGE.
End of Chapter

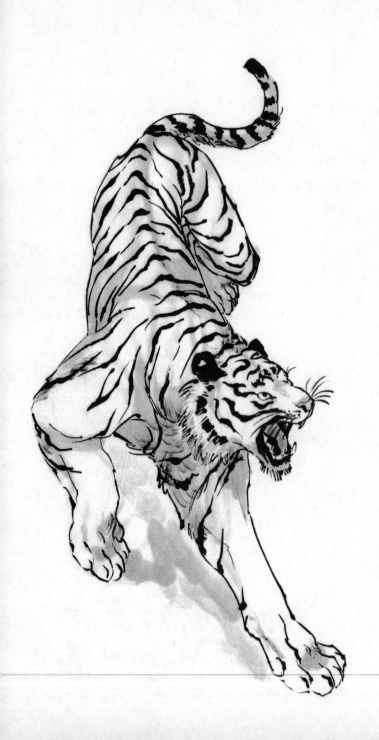

The Tiger Won't Eat the Dragon Yet

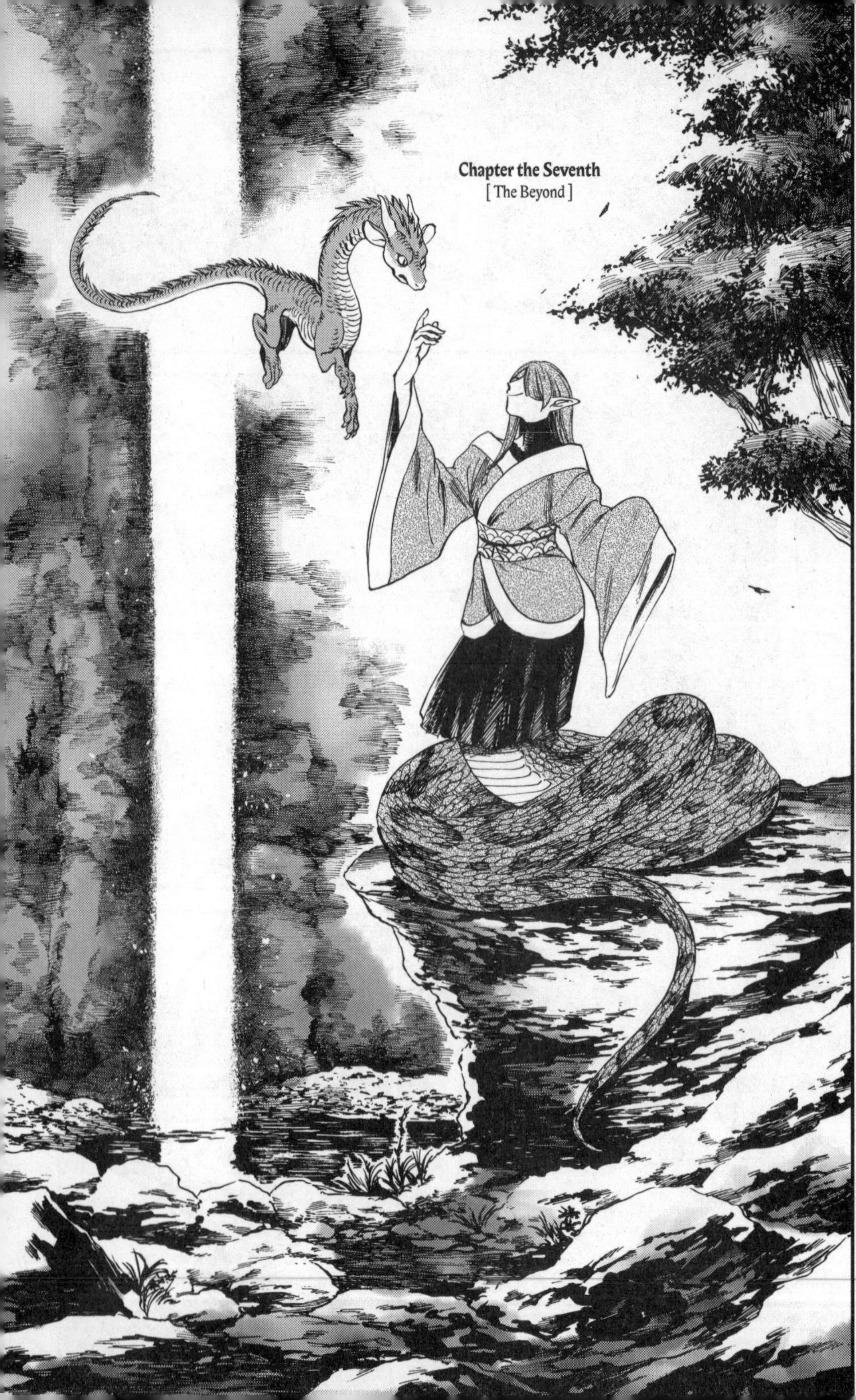
Chapter the Seventh
[The Beyond]

ペロ
PERO (LICK)
ピク
PIKU (TWITCH)

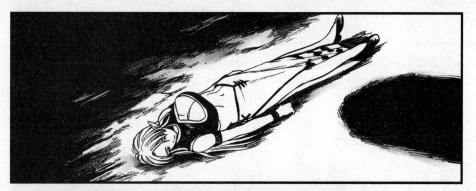

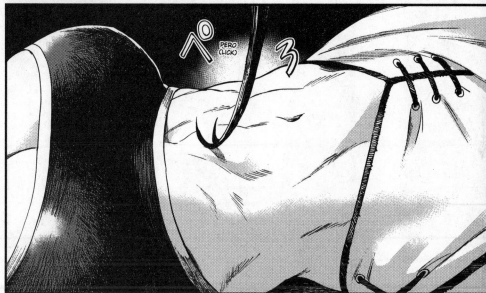

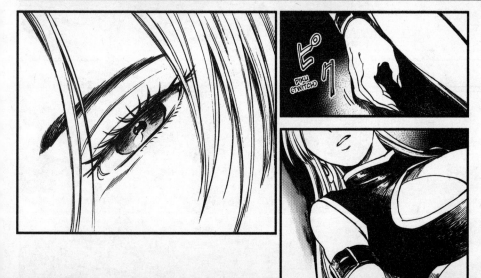

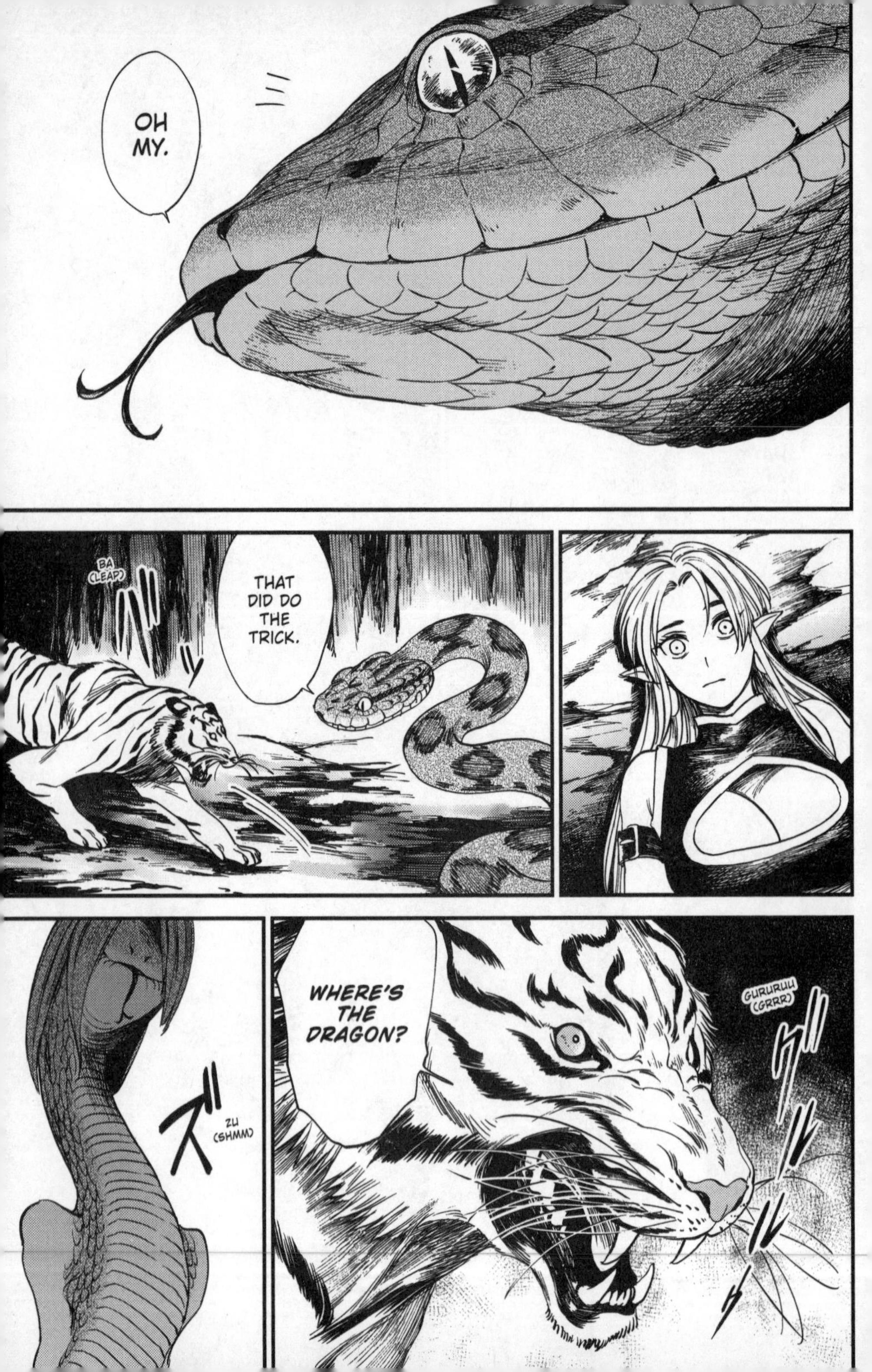
OH MY.
THAT DID DO THE TRICK.
BA (LEAP)
GURURUU (GRRR)
WHERE'S THE DRAGON?
ZU (SHMM)

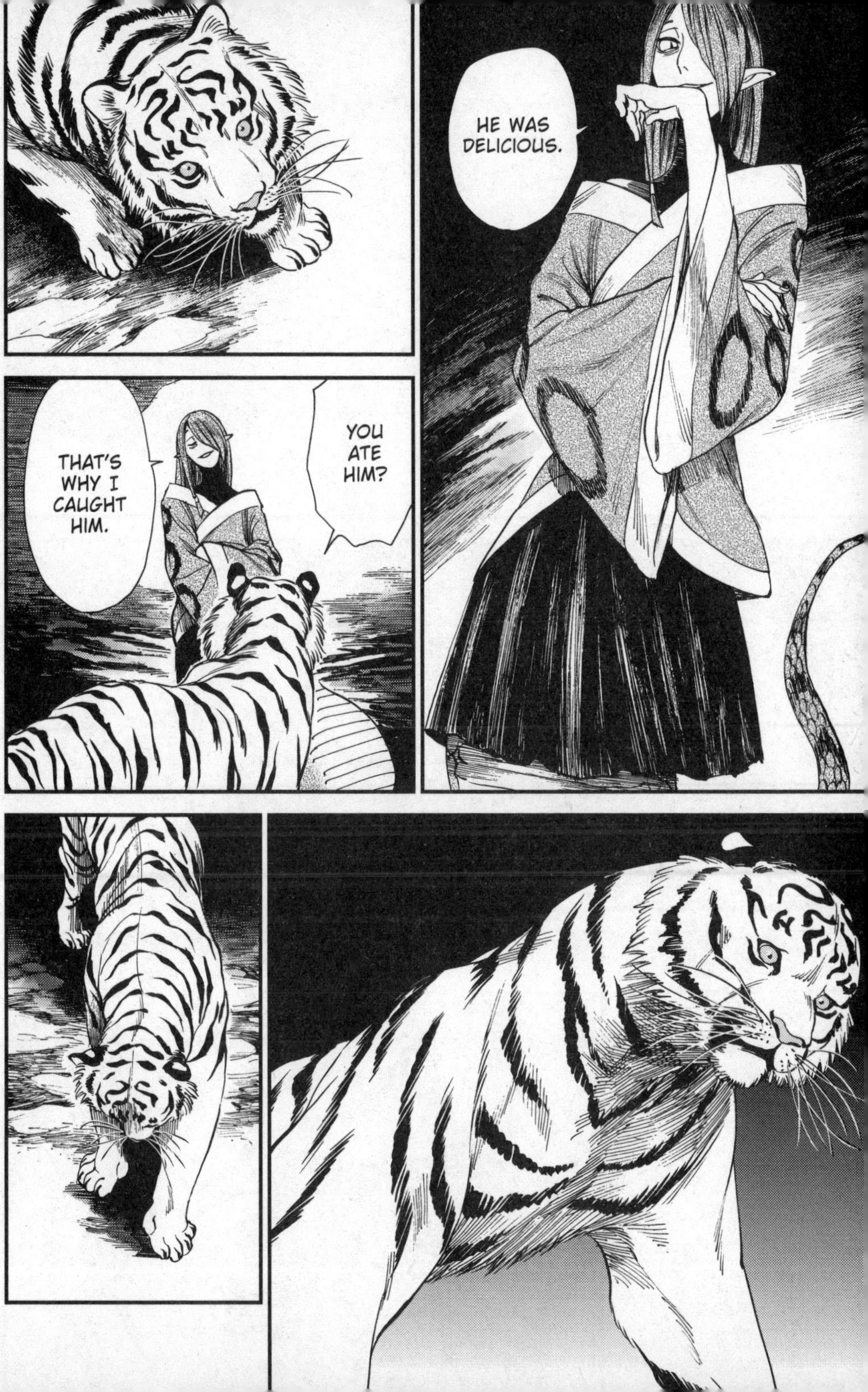
HE WAS DELICIOUS.
YOU ATE HIM?
THAT'S WHY I CAUGHT HIM.

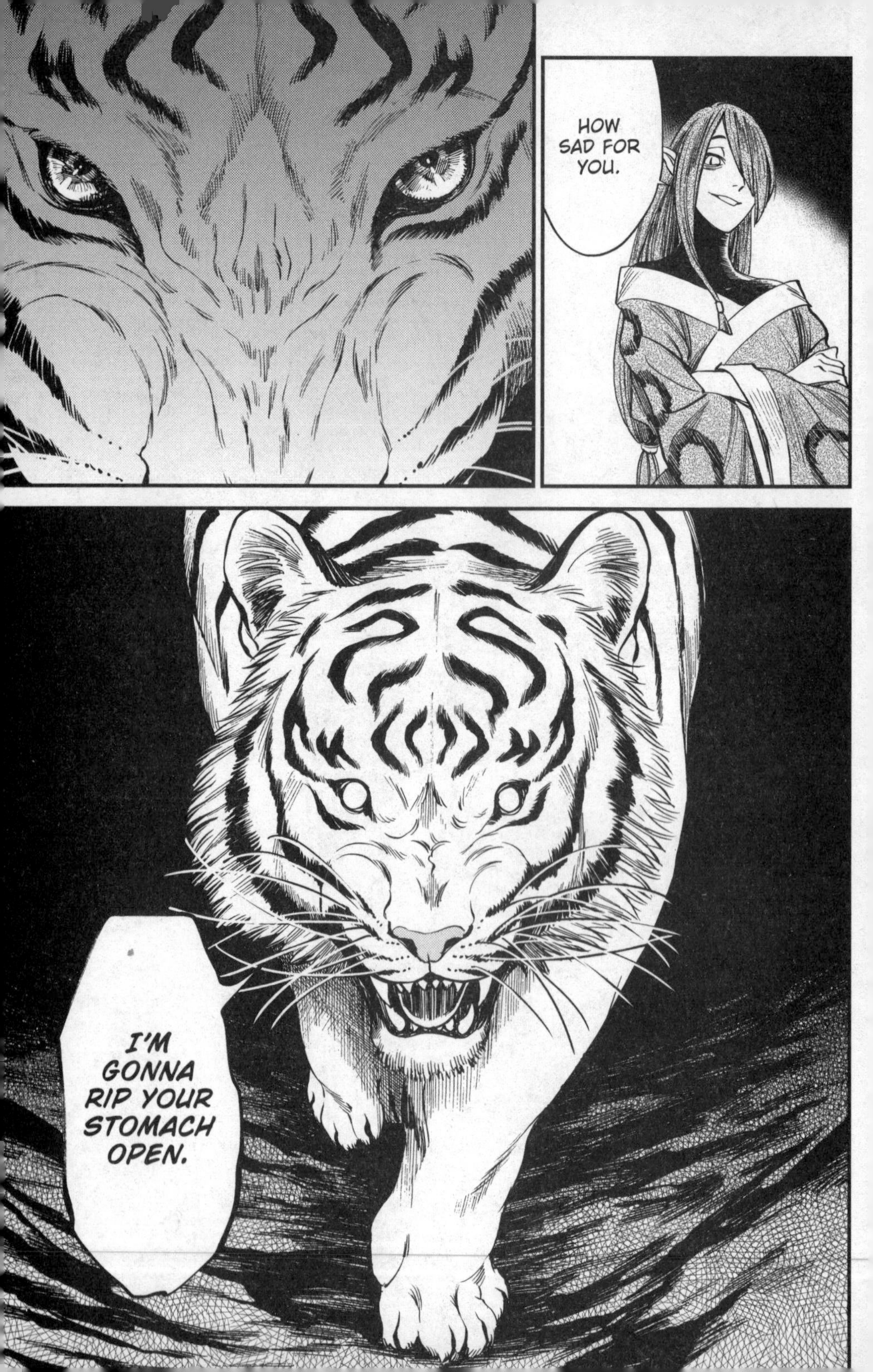
HOW SAD FOR YOU.
I'M GONNA RIP YOUR STOMACH OPEN.

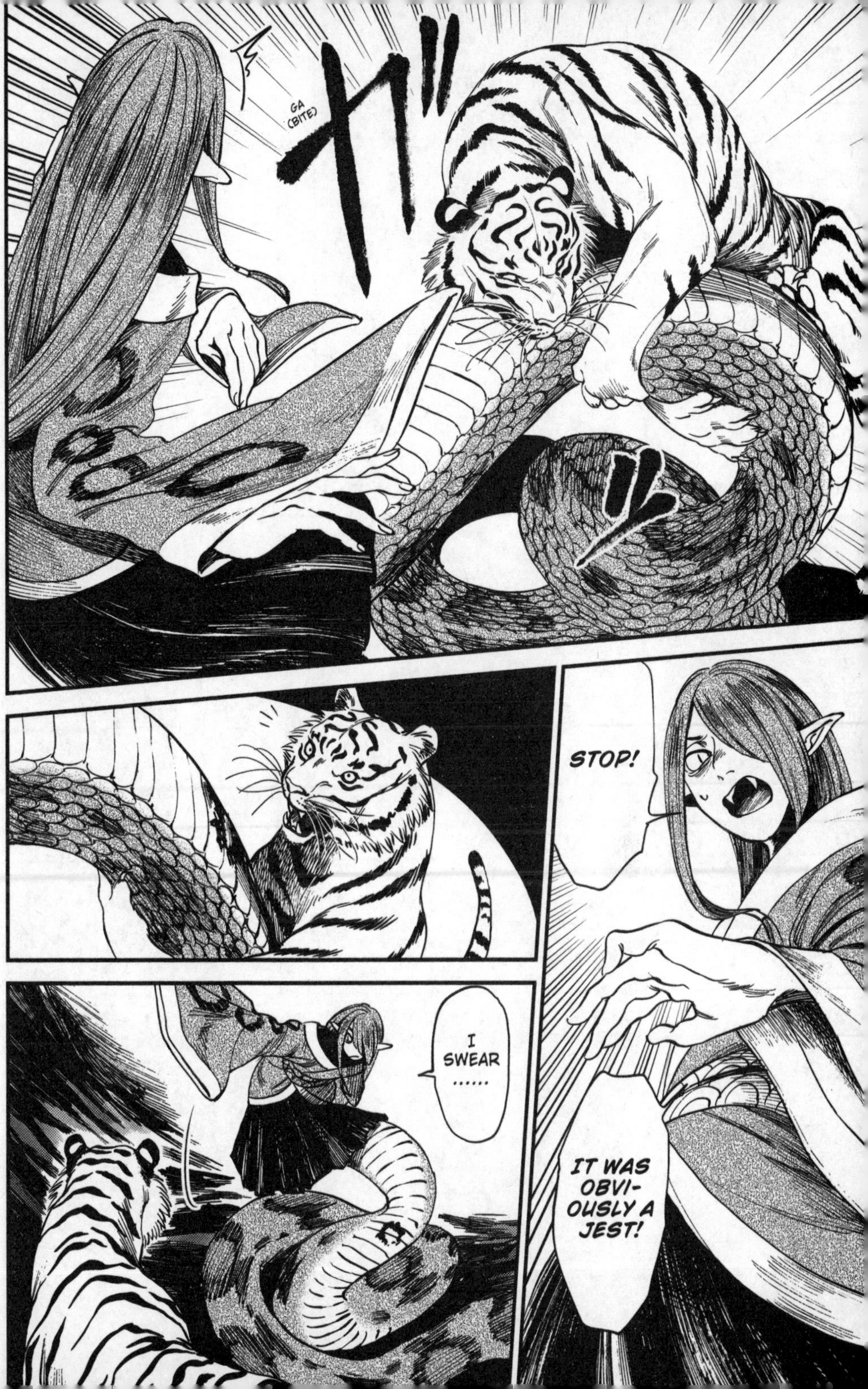
ガ
GA (BITE)
STOP!
IT WAS OBVI-OUSLY A JEST!
I SWEAR ......

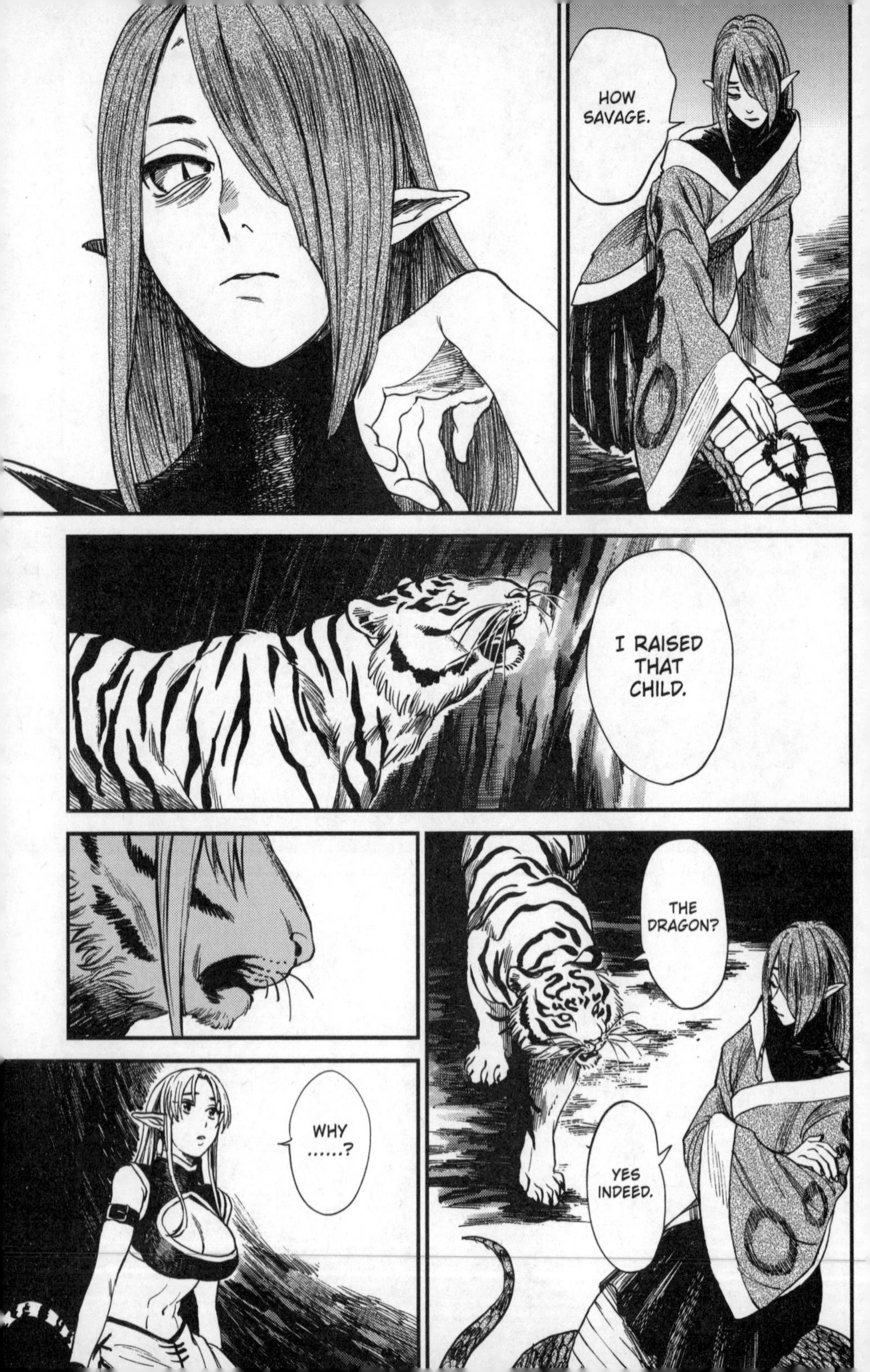
HOW SAVAGE.
I RAISED THAT CHILD.
THE DRAGON?
YES INDEED.
WHY ......?

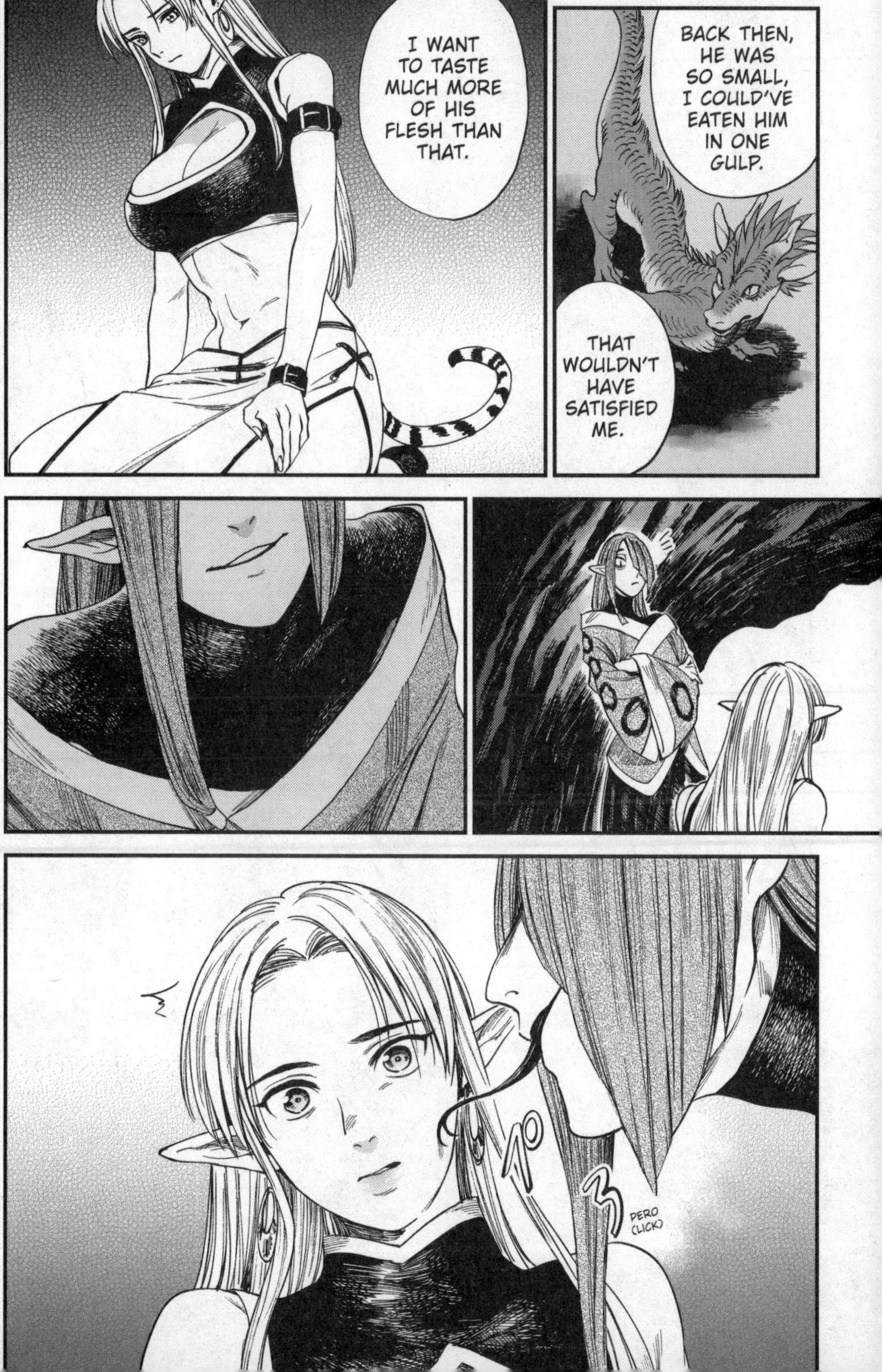
BACK THEN, HE WAS SO SMALL, I COULD'VE EATEN HIM IN ONE GULP.
THAT WOULDN'T HAVE SATISFIED ME.
I WANT TO TASTE MUCH MORE OF HIS FLESH THAN THAT.
PERO (LICK)

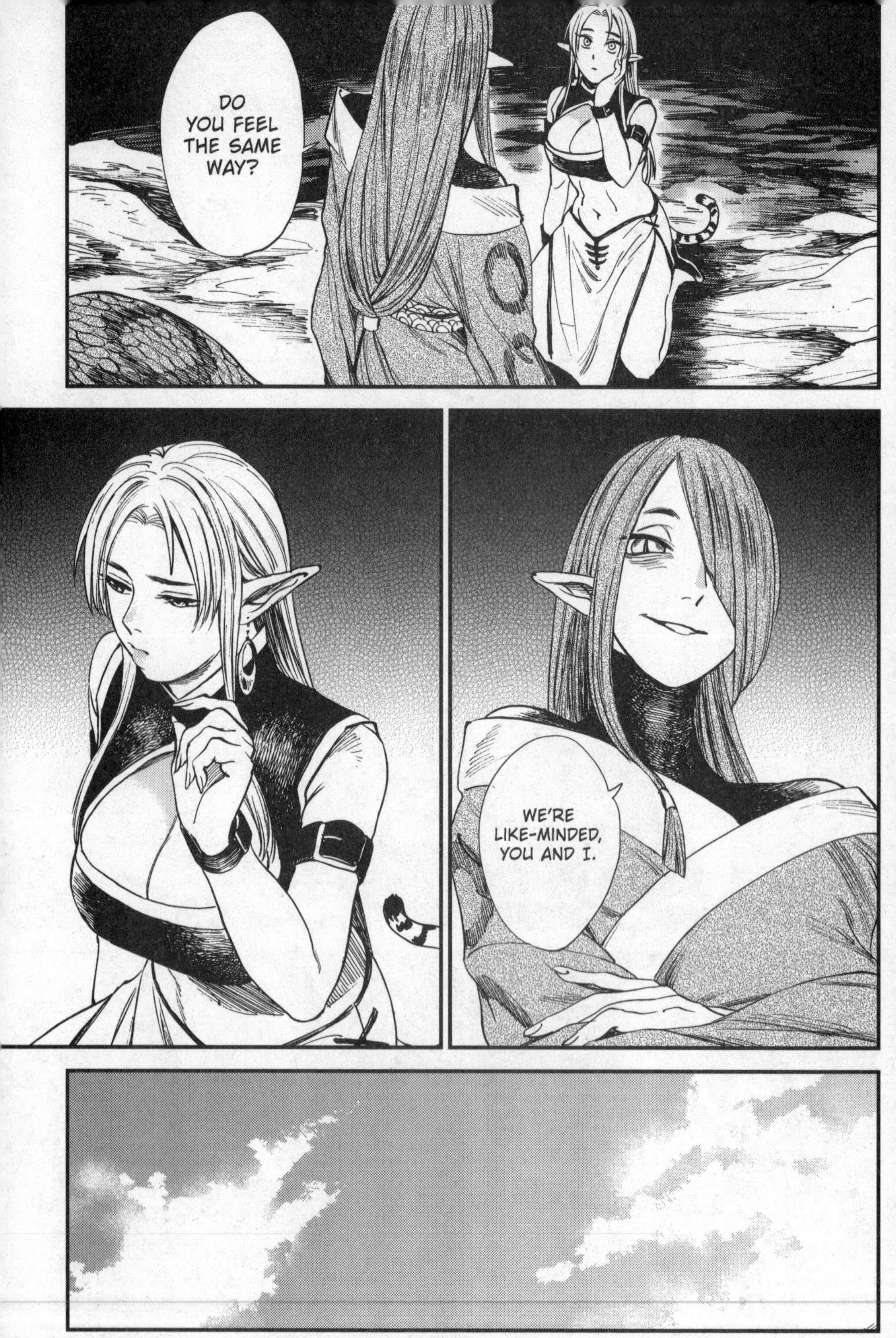
DO YOU FEEL THE SAME WAY?
WE'RE LIKE-MINDED, YOU AND I.

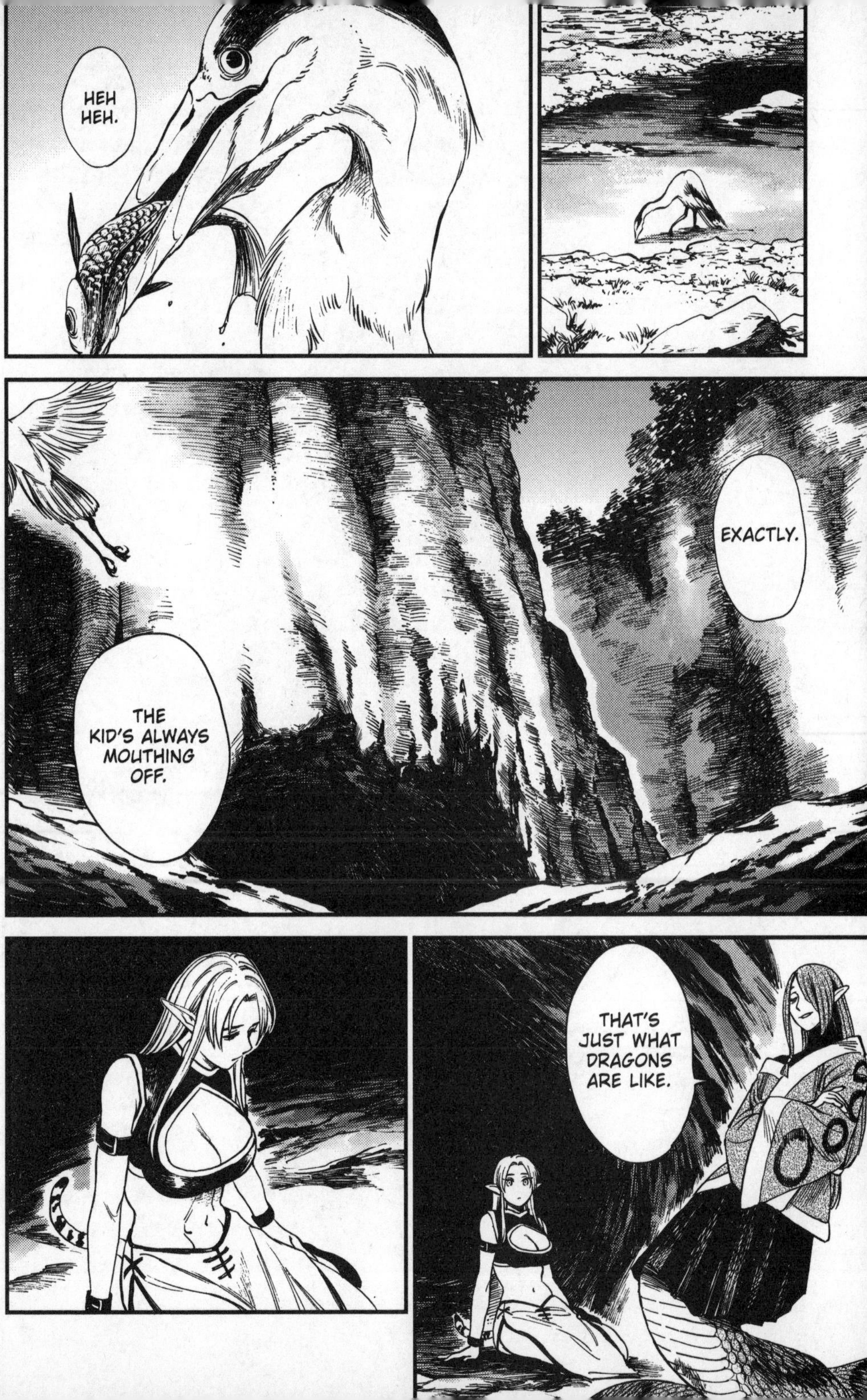
HEH HEH.
EXACTLY.
THE KID'S ALWAYS MOUTHING OFF.
THAT'S JUST WHAT DRAGONS ARE LIKE.

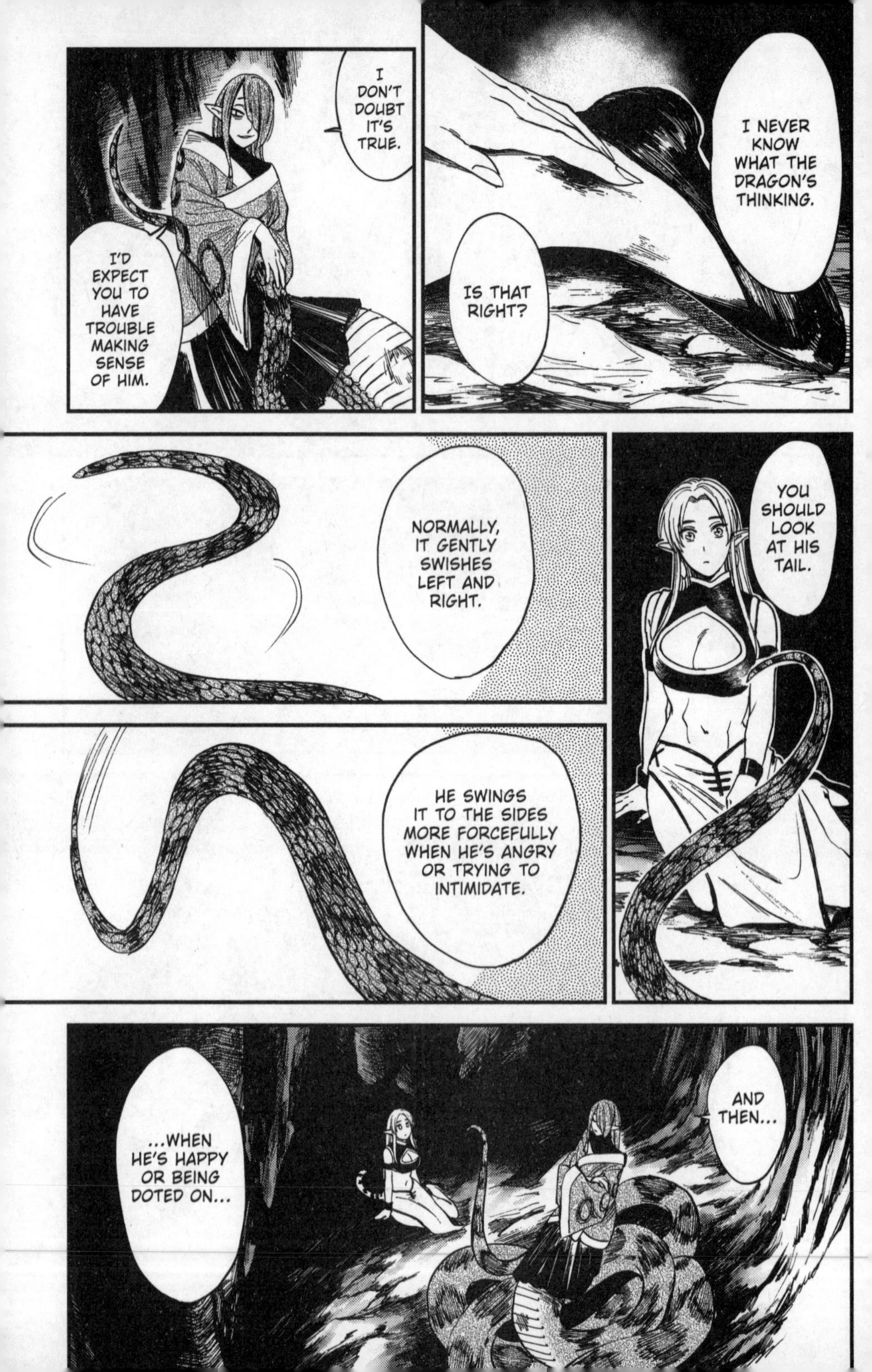
I NEVER KNOW WHAT THE DRAGON'S THINKING.
IS THAT RIGHT?
I DON'T DOUBT IT'S TRUE.
I'D EXPECT YOU TO HAVE TROUBLE MAKING SENSE OF HIM.
YOU SHOULD LOOK AT HIS TAIL.
NORMALLY, IT GENTLY SWISHES LEFT AND RIGHT.
HE SWINGS IT TO THE SIDES MORE FORCEFULLY WHEN HE'S ANGRY OR TRYING TO INTIMIDATE.
AND THEN...
...WHEN HE'S HAPPY OR BEING DOTED ON...

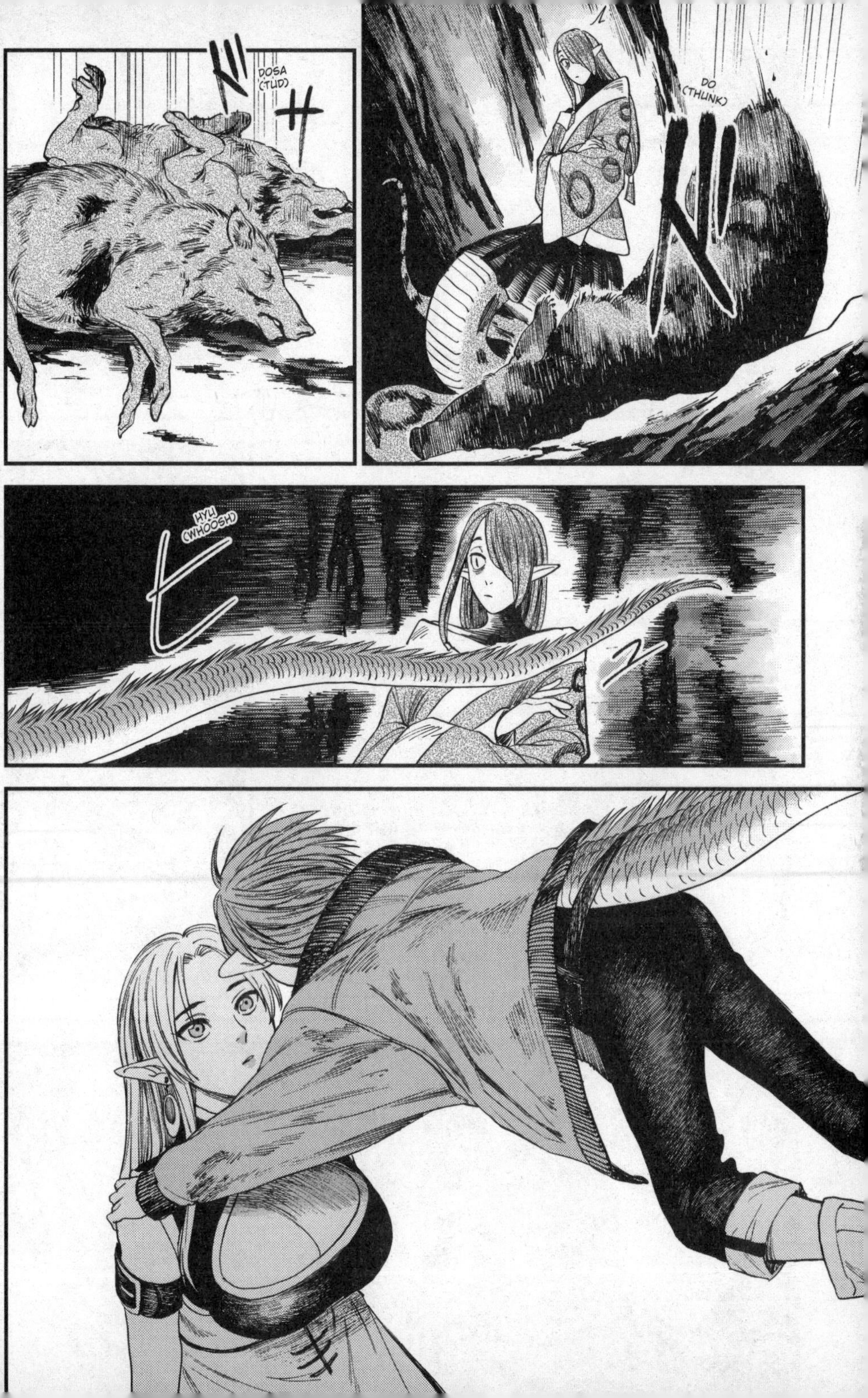
DO (THUNK)
DOSA (TUD)
HYU (WHOOSH)

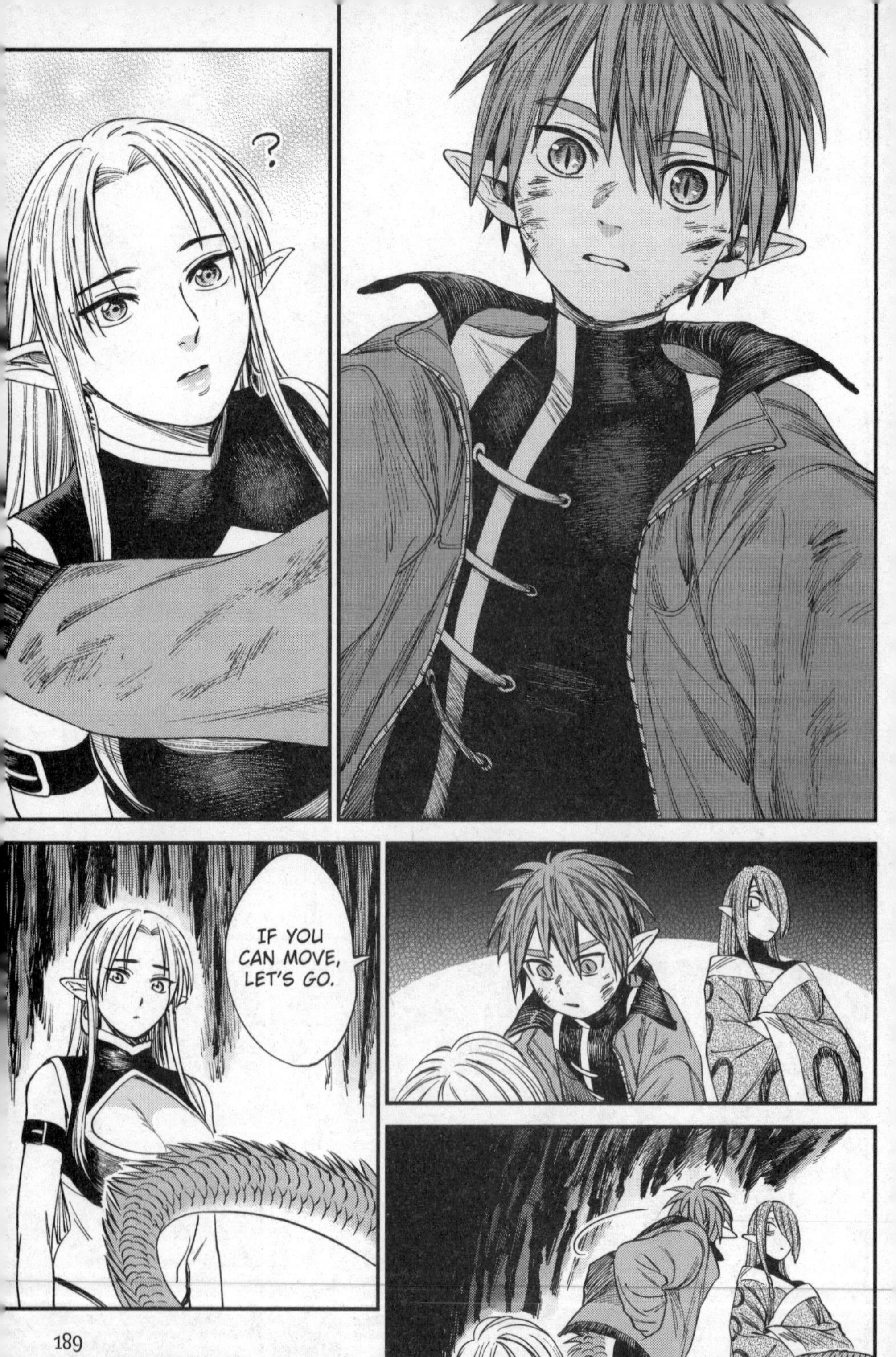
?
IF YOU CAN MOVE, LET'S GO.

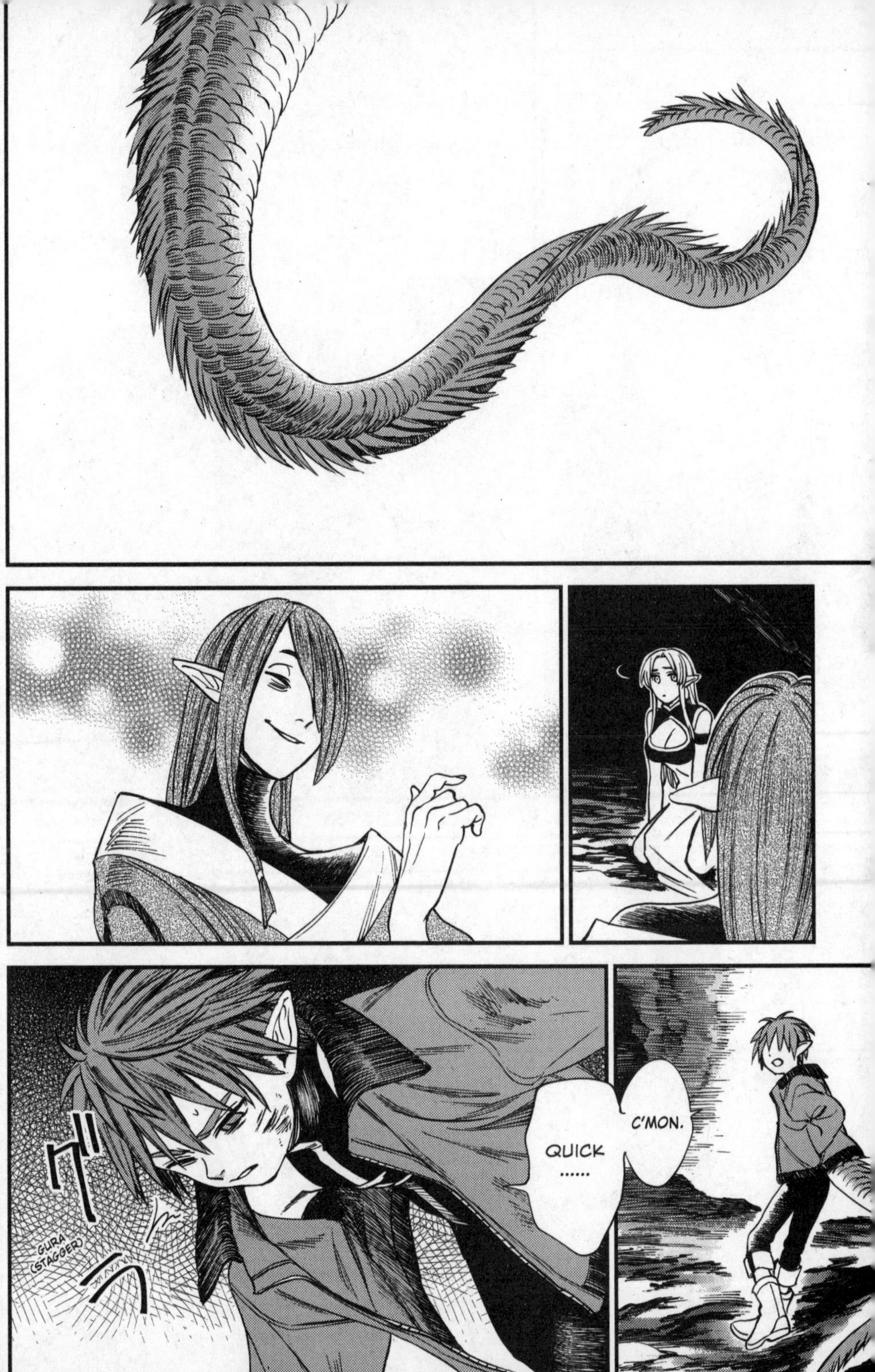
C'MON.
QUICK ......
GURA (STAGGER)

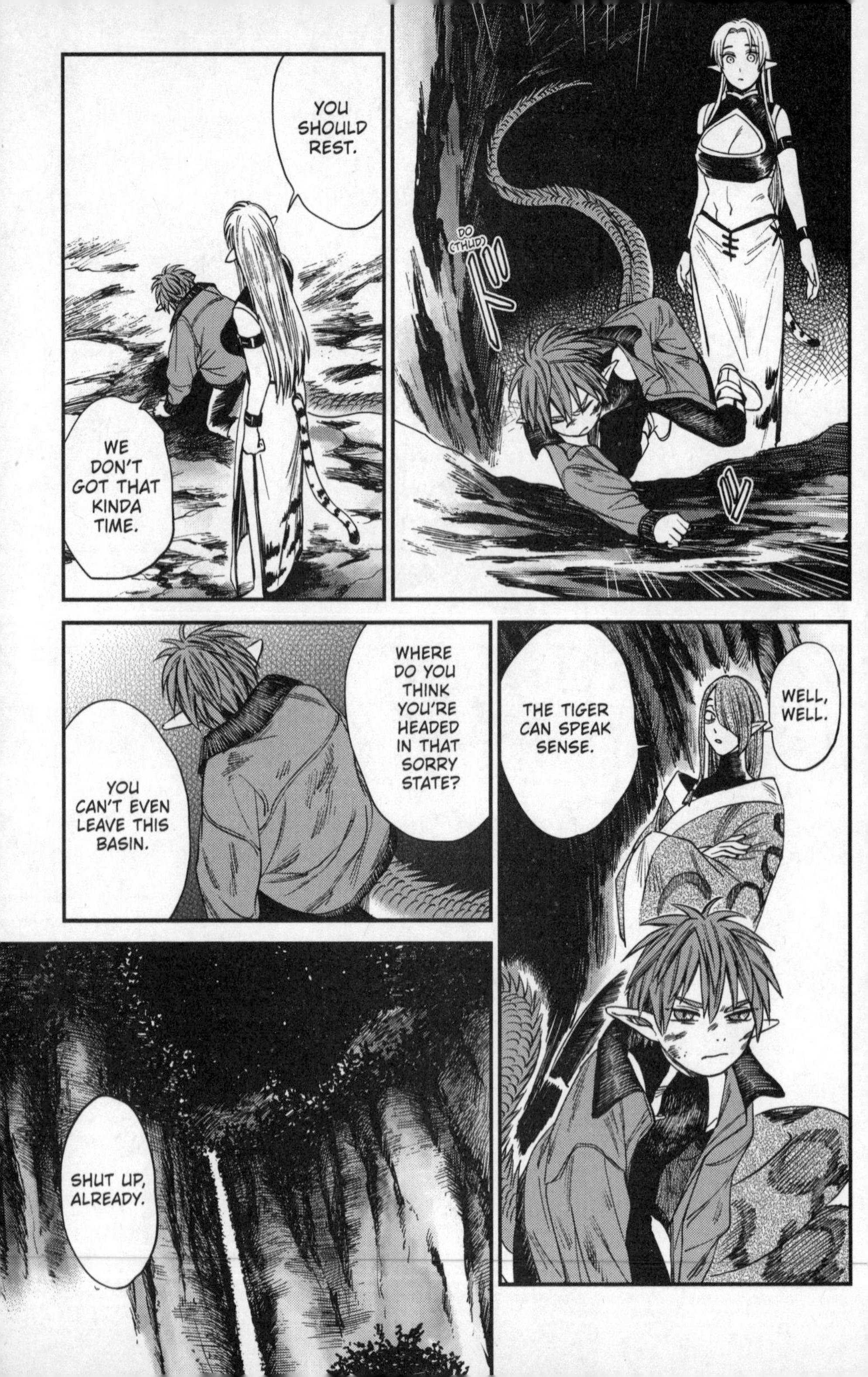
DO (THUD)
YOU SHOULD REST.
WE DON'T GOT THAT KINDA TIME.
WELL, WELL.
THE TIGER CAN SPEAK SENSE.
WHERE DO YOU THINK YOU'RE HEADED IN THAT SORRY STATE?
YOU CAN'T EVEN LEAVE THIS BASIN.
SHUT UP, ALREADY.

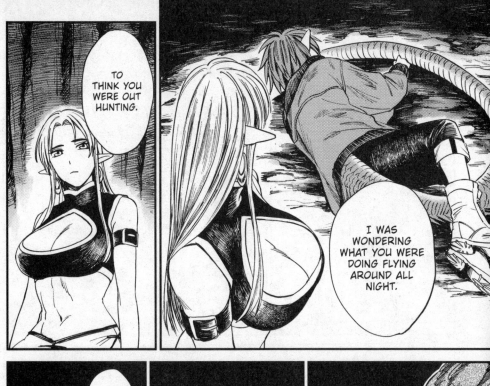

I WAS WONDERING WHAT YOU WERE DOING FLYING AROUND ALL NIGHT.
TO THINK YOU WERE OUT HUNTING.
PHEW.

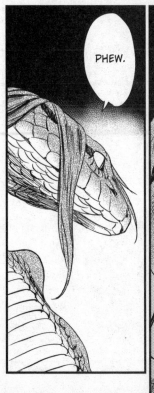

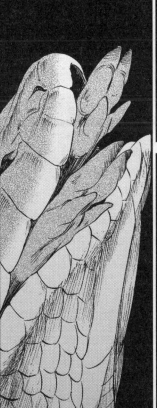

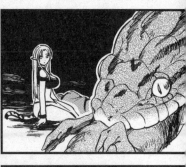

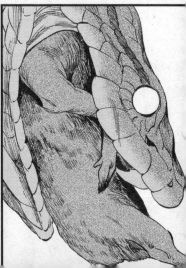

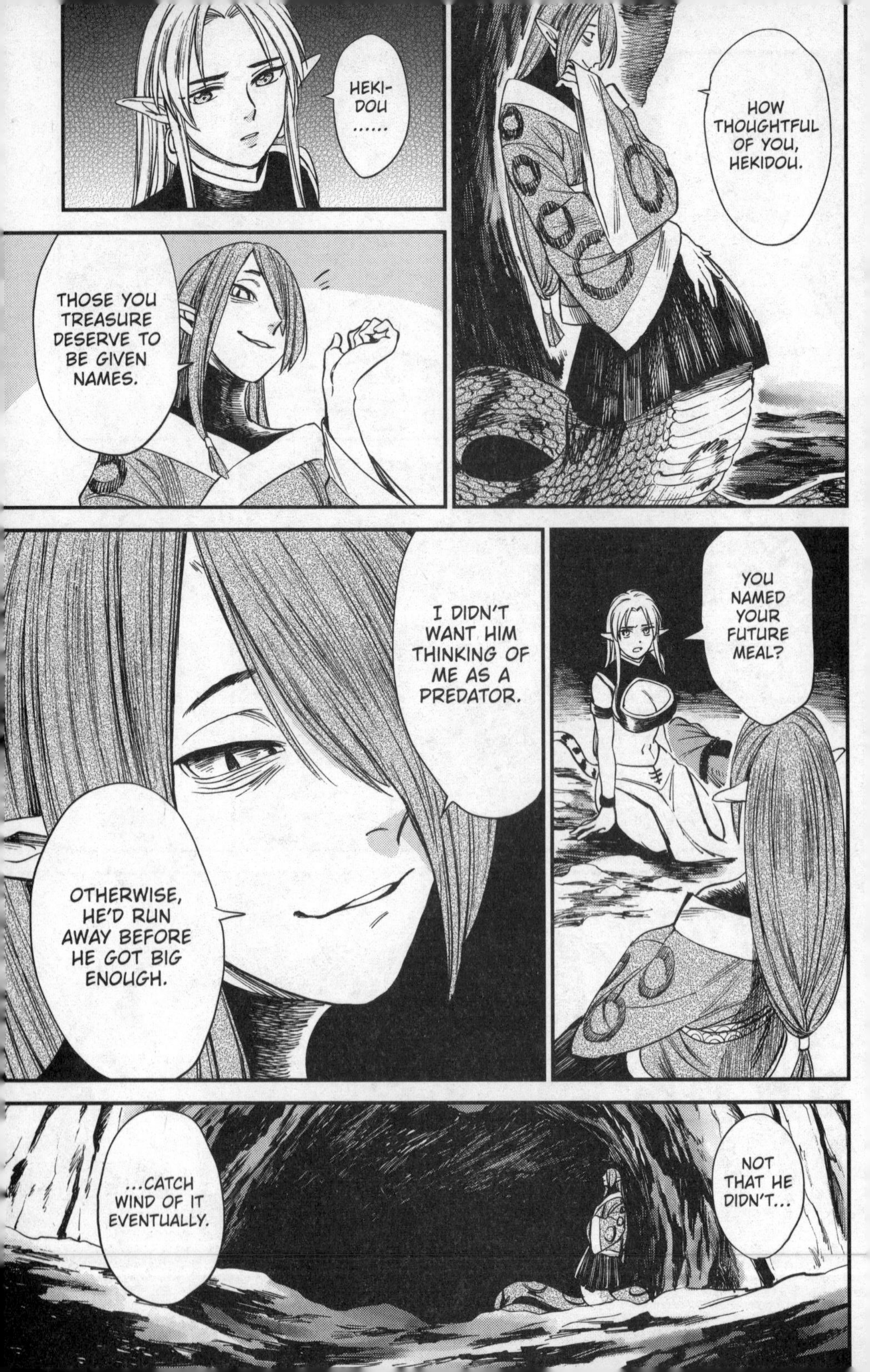
HOW THOUGHTFUL OF YOU, HEKIDOU.
HEKI-DOU ......
THOSE YOU TREASURE DESERVE TO BE GIVEN NAMES.
YOU NAMED YOUR FUTURE MEAL?
I DIDN'T WANT HIM THINKING OF ME AS A PREDATOR.
OTHERWISE, HE'D RUN AWAY BEFORE HE GOT BIG ENOUGH.
NOT THAT HE DIDN'T...
...CATCH WIND OF IT EVENTUALLY.

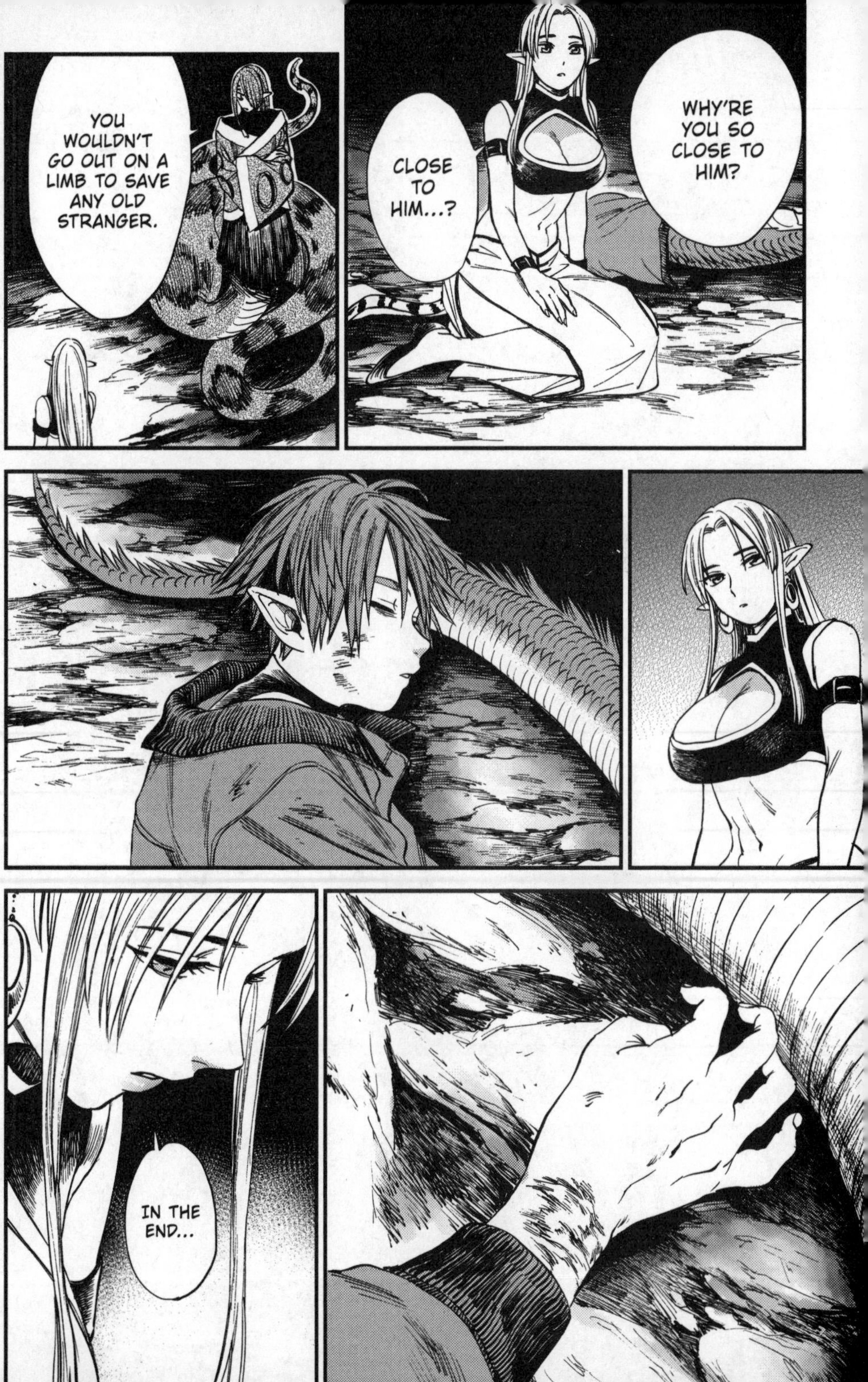
WHY'RE YOU SO CLOSE TO HIM?
CLOSE TO HIM...?
YOU WOULDN'T GO OUT ON A LIMB TO SAVE ANY OLD STRANGER.
IN THE END...

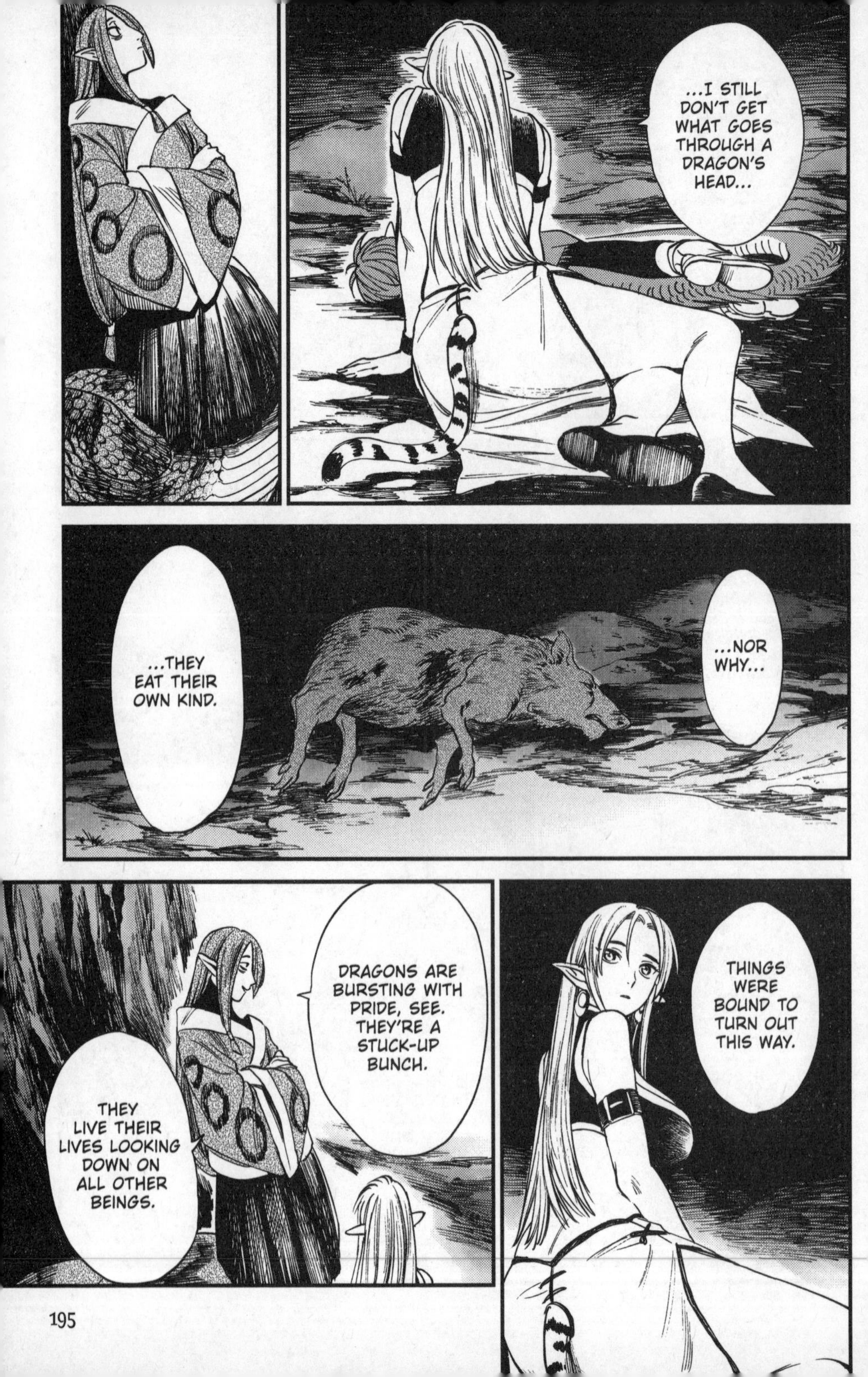
...I STILL DON'T GET WHAT GOES THROUGH A DRAGON'S HEAD...
...NOR WHY...
...THEY EAT THEIR OWN KIND.
THINGS WERE BOUND TO TURN OUT THIS WAY.
DRAGONS ARE BURSTING WITH PRIDE, SEE. THEY'RE A STUCK-UP BUNCH.
THEY LIVE THEIR LIVES LOOKING DOWN ON ALL OTHER BEINGS.

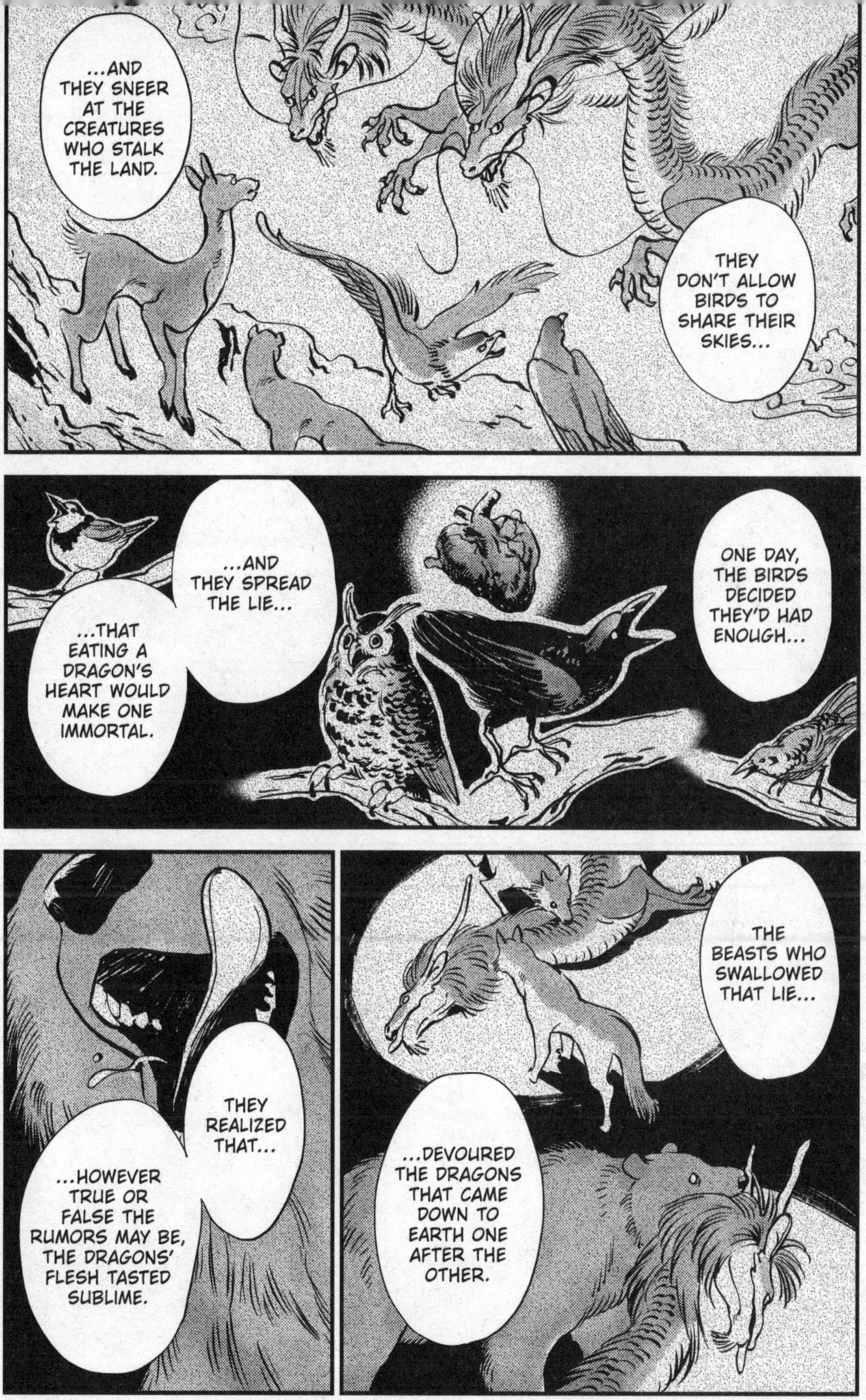

THEY DON'T ALLOW BIRDS TO SHARE THEIR SKIES...
...AND THEY SNEER AT THE CREATURES WHO STALK THE LAND.
ONE DAY, THE BIRDS DECIDED THEY'D HAD ENOUGH...
...AND THEY SPREAD THE LIE...
...THAT EATING A DRAGON'S HEART WOULD MAKE ONE IMMORTAL.
THE BEASTS WHO SWALLOWED THAT LIE...
...DEVOURED THE DRAGONS THAT CAME DOWN TO EARTH ONE AFTER THE OTHER.
THEY REALIZED THAT...
...HOWEVER TRUE OR FALSE THE RUMORS MAY BE, THE DRAGONS' FLESH TASTED SUBLIME.

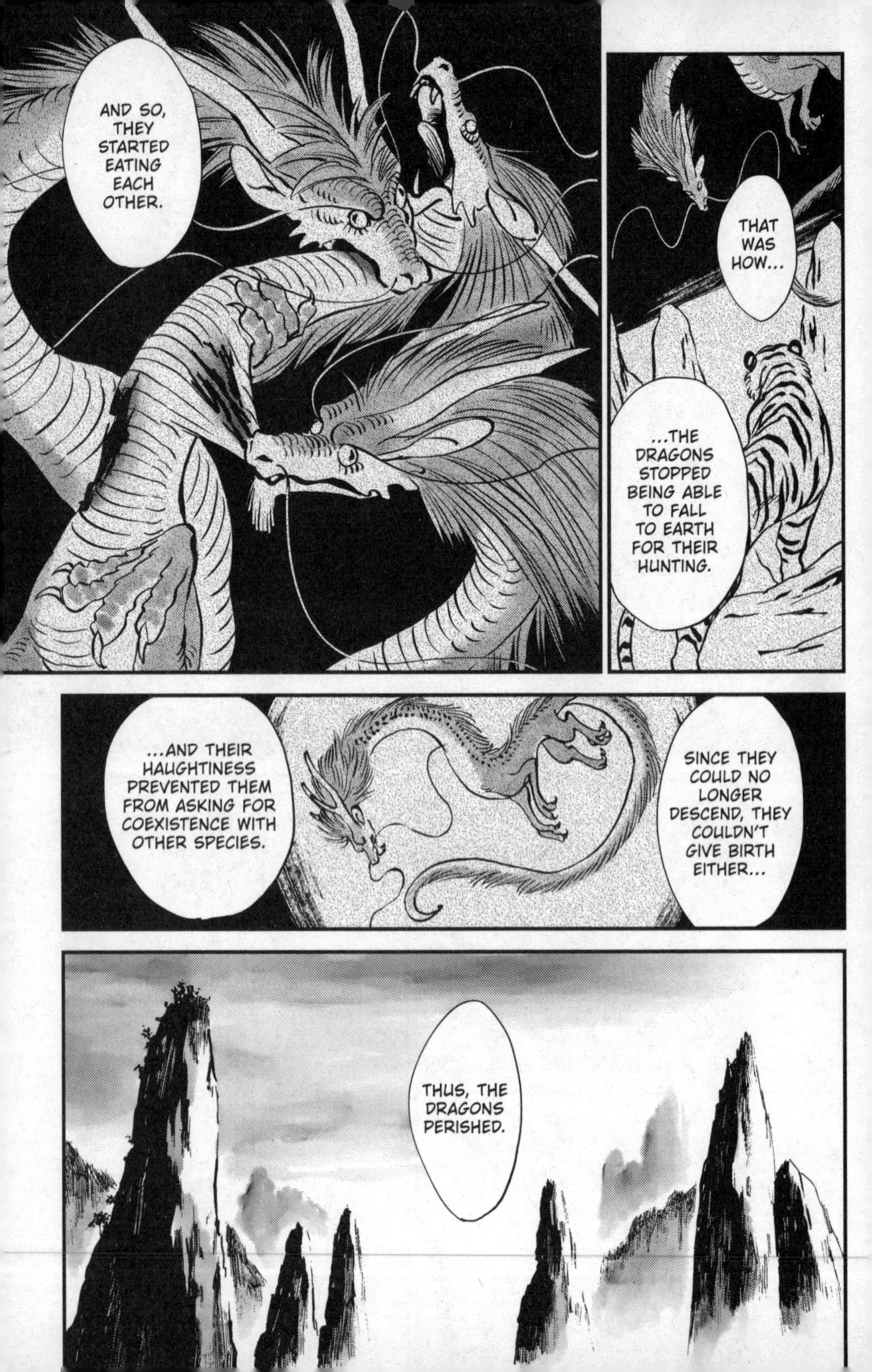
THAT WAS HOW...
...THE DRAGONS STOPPED BEING ABLE TO FALL TO EARTH FOR THEIR HUNTING.
AND SO, THEY STARTED EATING EACH OTHER.
SINCE THEY COULD NO LONGER DESCEND, THEY COULDN'T GIVE BIRTH EITHER...
...AND THEIR HAUGHTINESS PREVENTED THEM FROM ASKING FOR COEXISTENCE WITH OTHER SPECIES.
THUS, THE DRAGONS PERISHED.

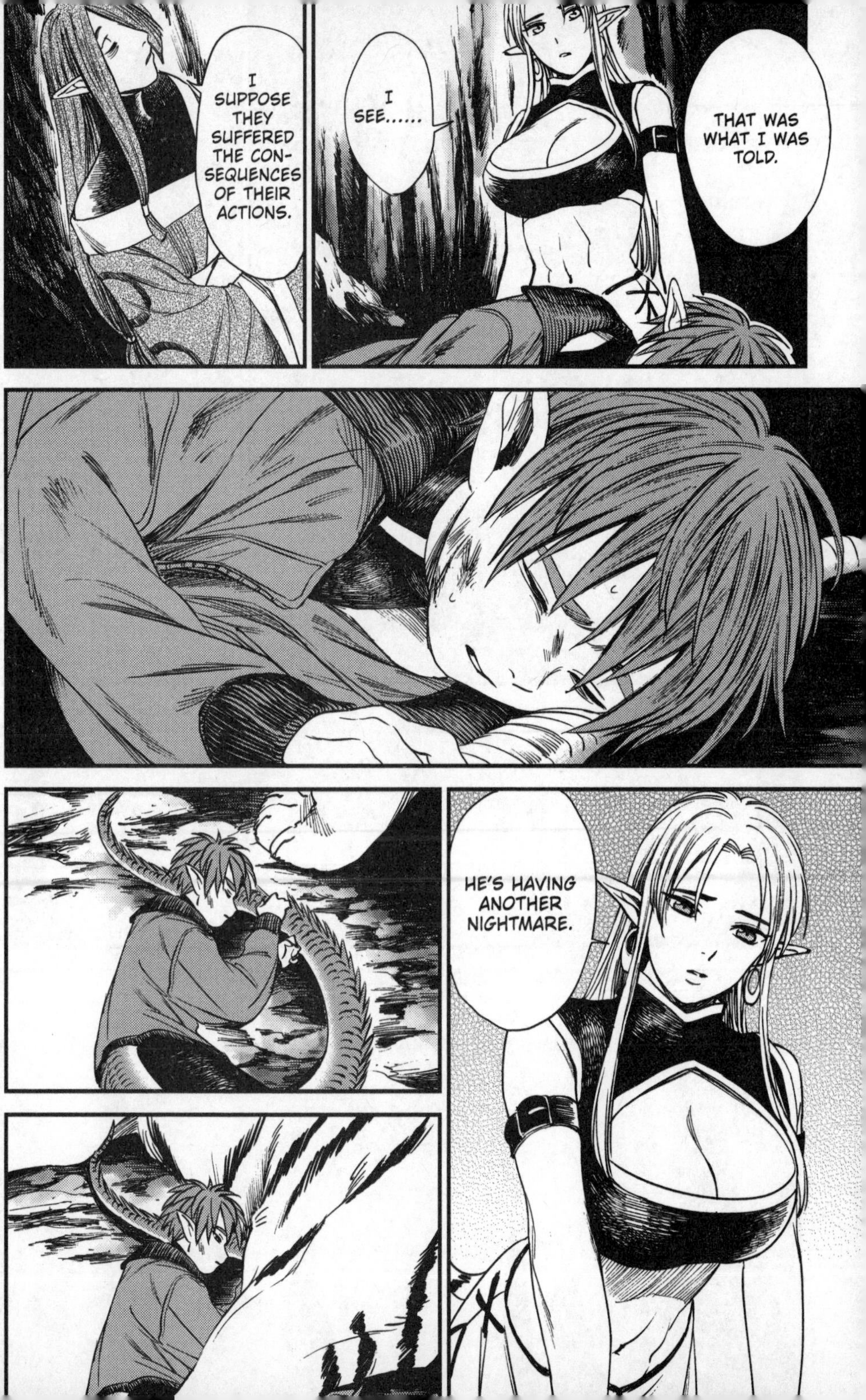
THAT WAS WHAT I WAS TOLD.
I SEE......
I SUPPOSE THEY SUFFERED THE CON-SEQUENCES OF THEIR ACTIONS.
HE'S HAVING ANOTHER NIGHTMARE.

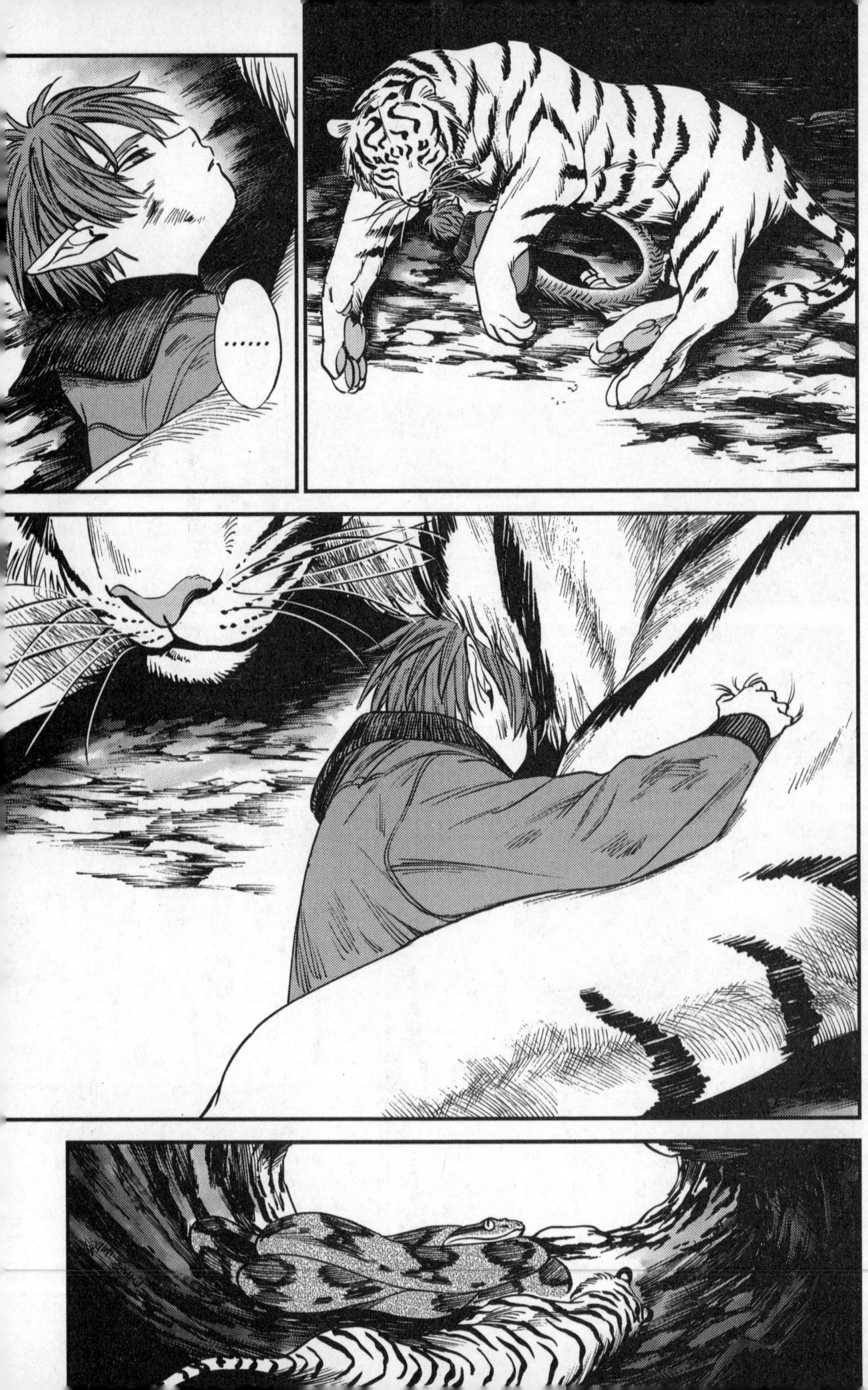
……

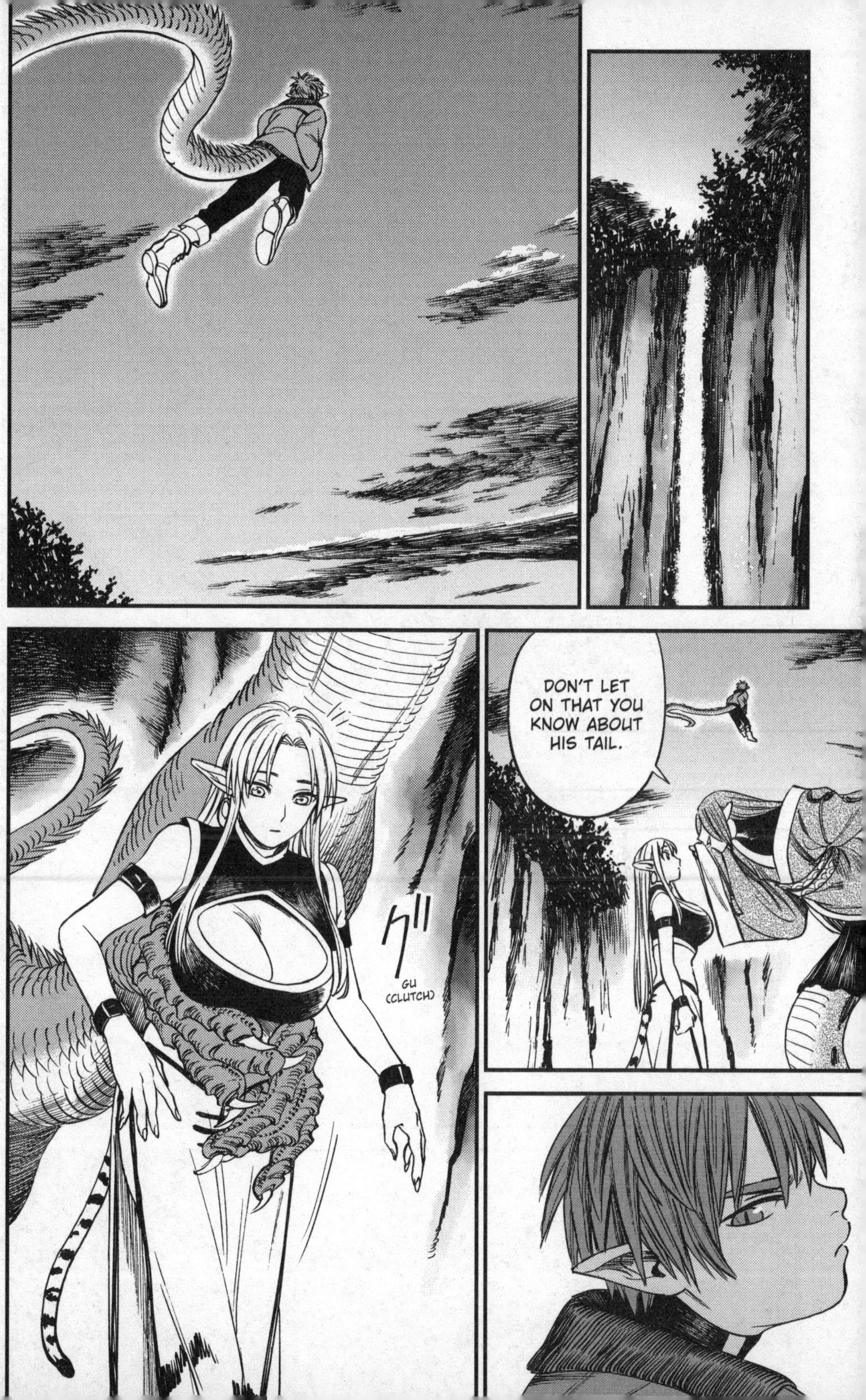
DON'T LET ON THAT YOU KNOW ABOUT HIS TAIL.
グッ
GU (CLUTCH)

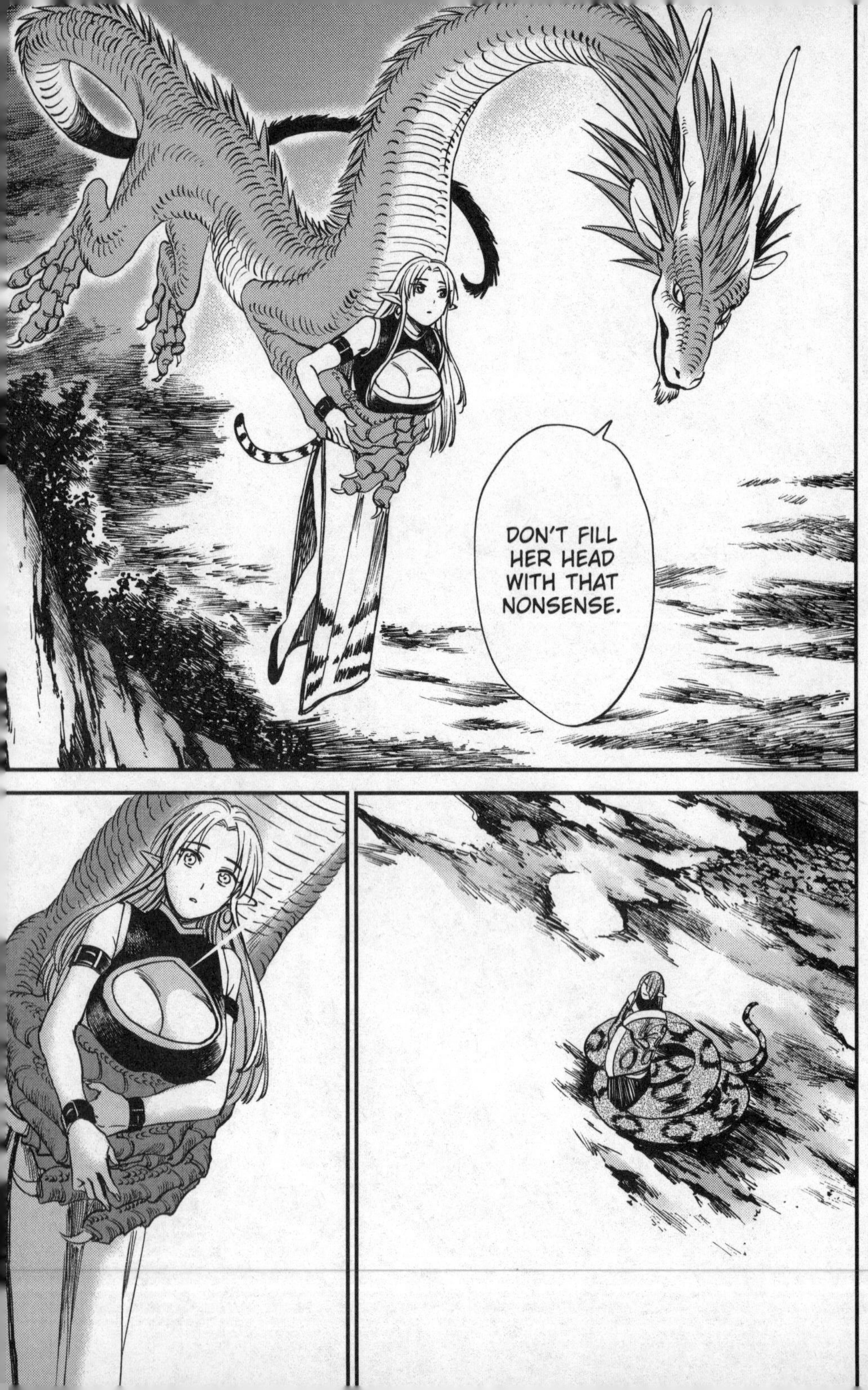
DON'T FILL HER HEAD WITH THAT NONSENSE.

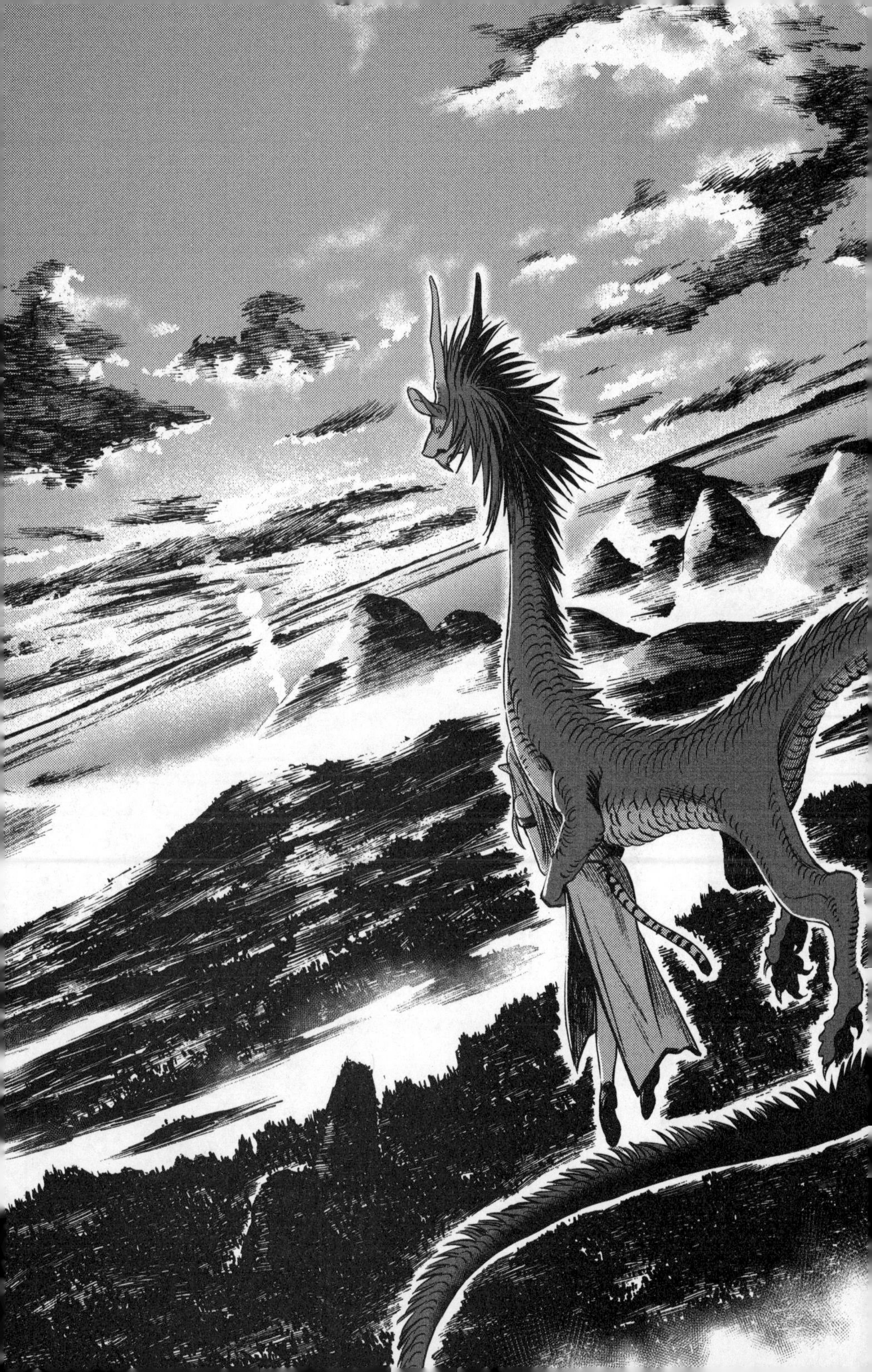

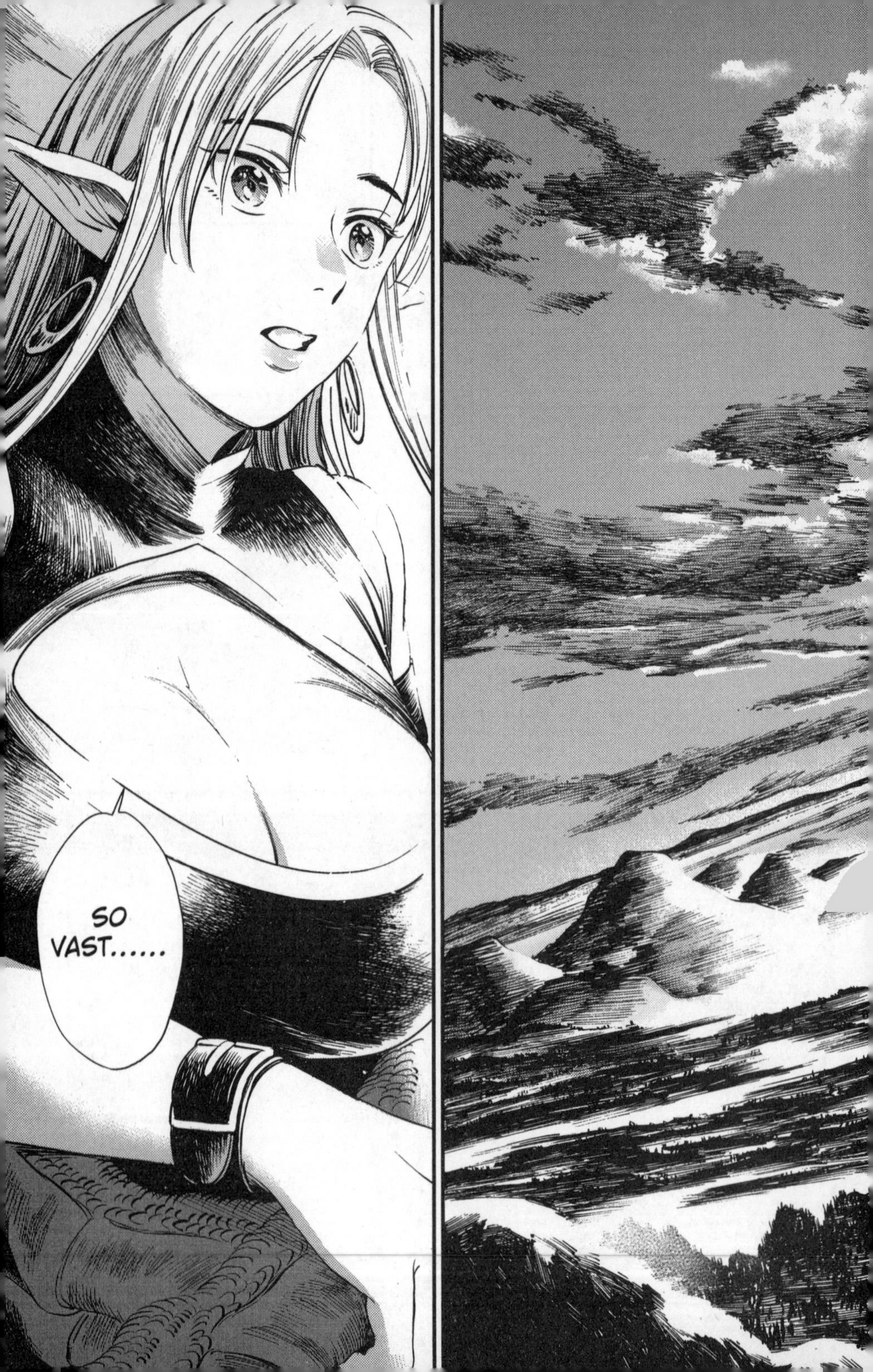
SO VAST……

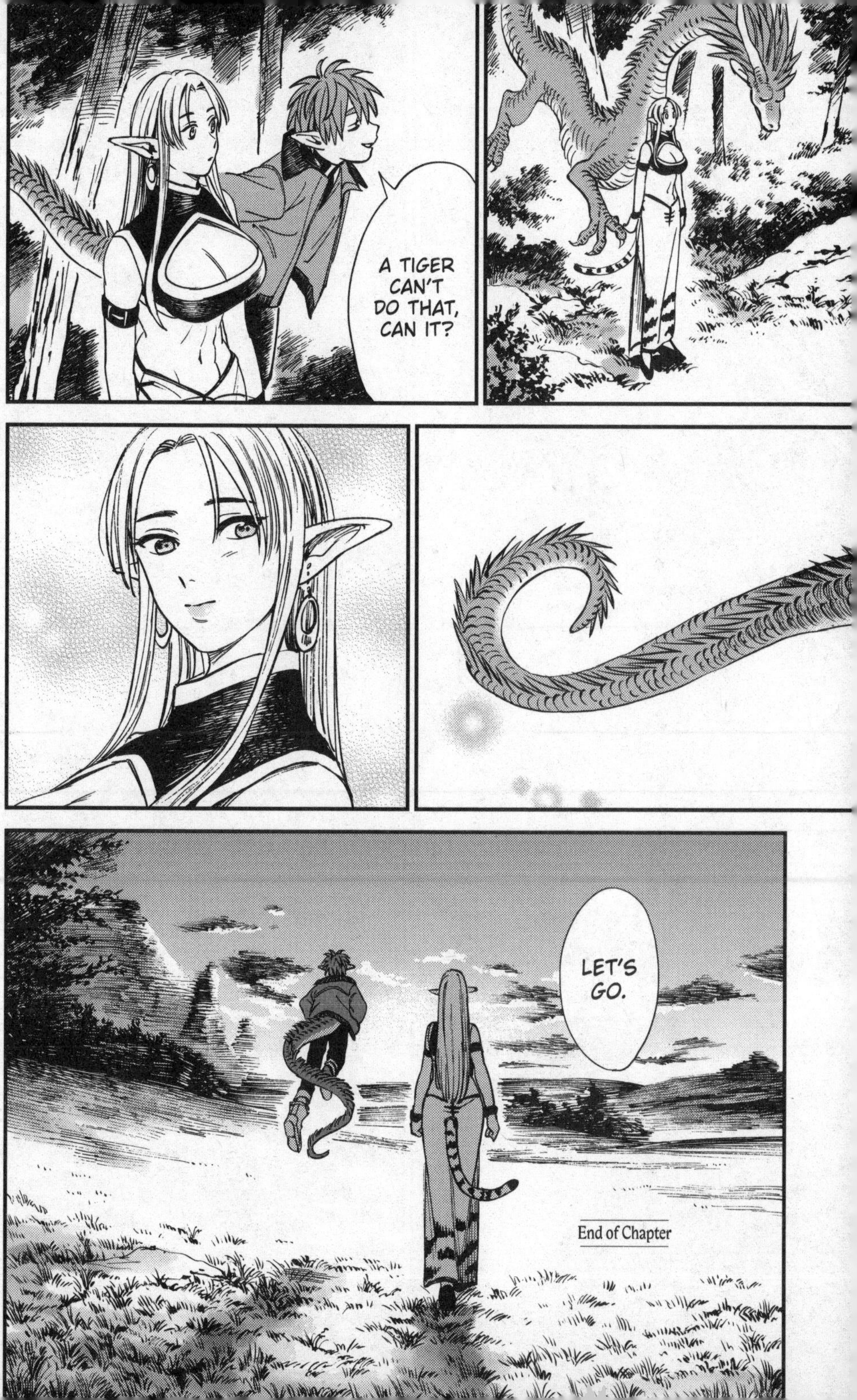
A TIGER CAN'T DO THAT, CAN IT?
LET'S GO.
End of Chapter

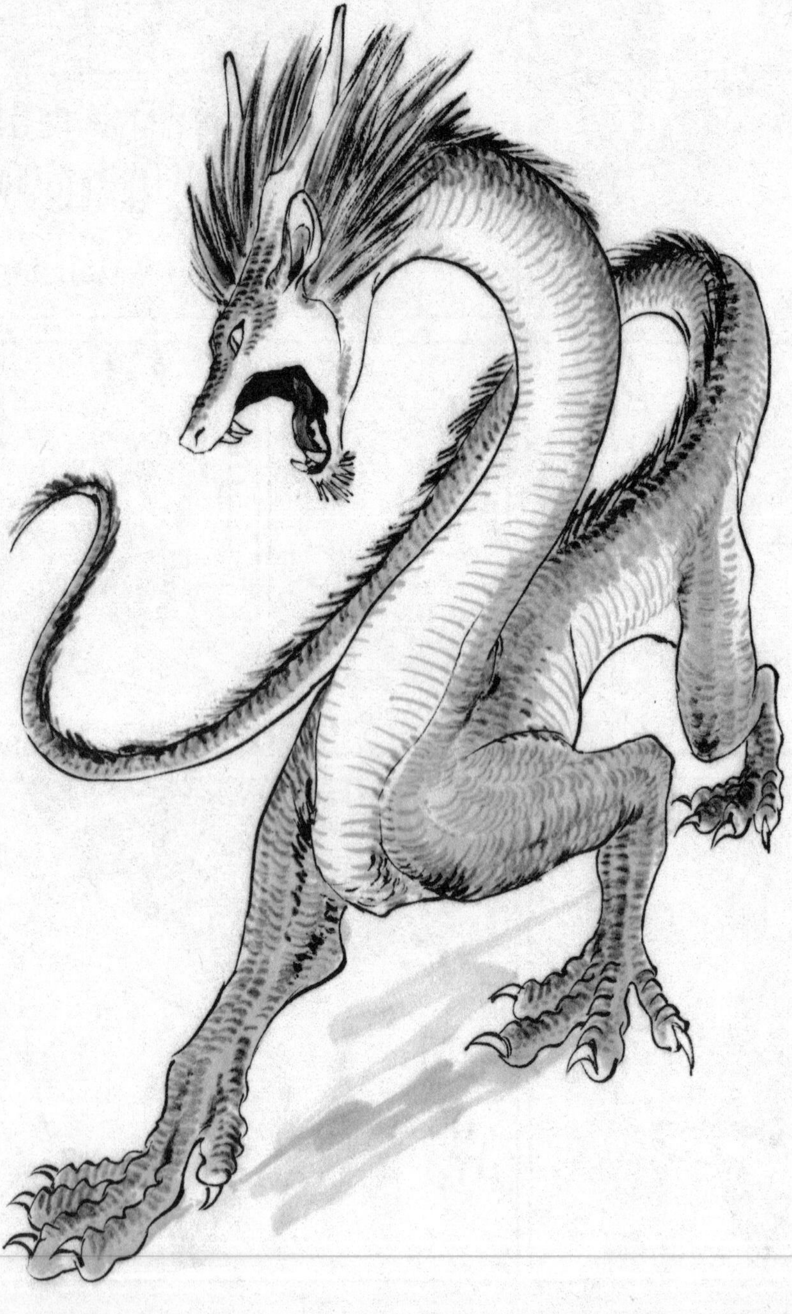

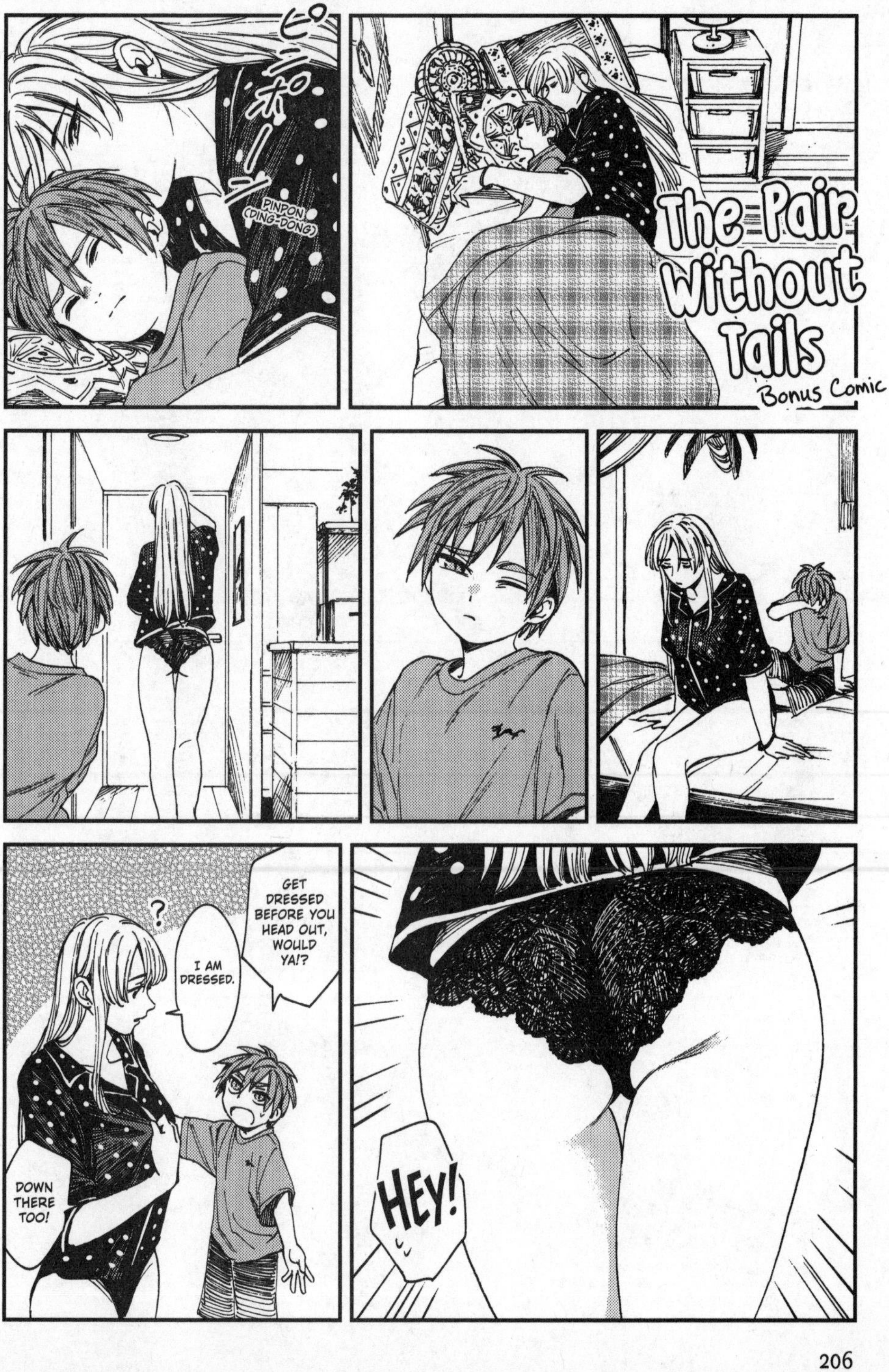
The Pair Without Tails
Bonus Comic
ピンポーン
PINPON (DING-DONG)
HEY!
GET DRESSED BEFORE YOU HEAD OUT, WOULD YA!?
I AM DRESSED.
?
DOWN THERE TOO!

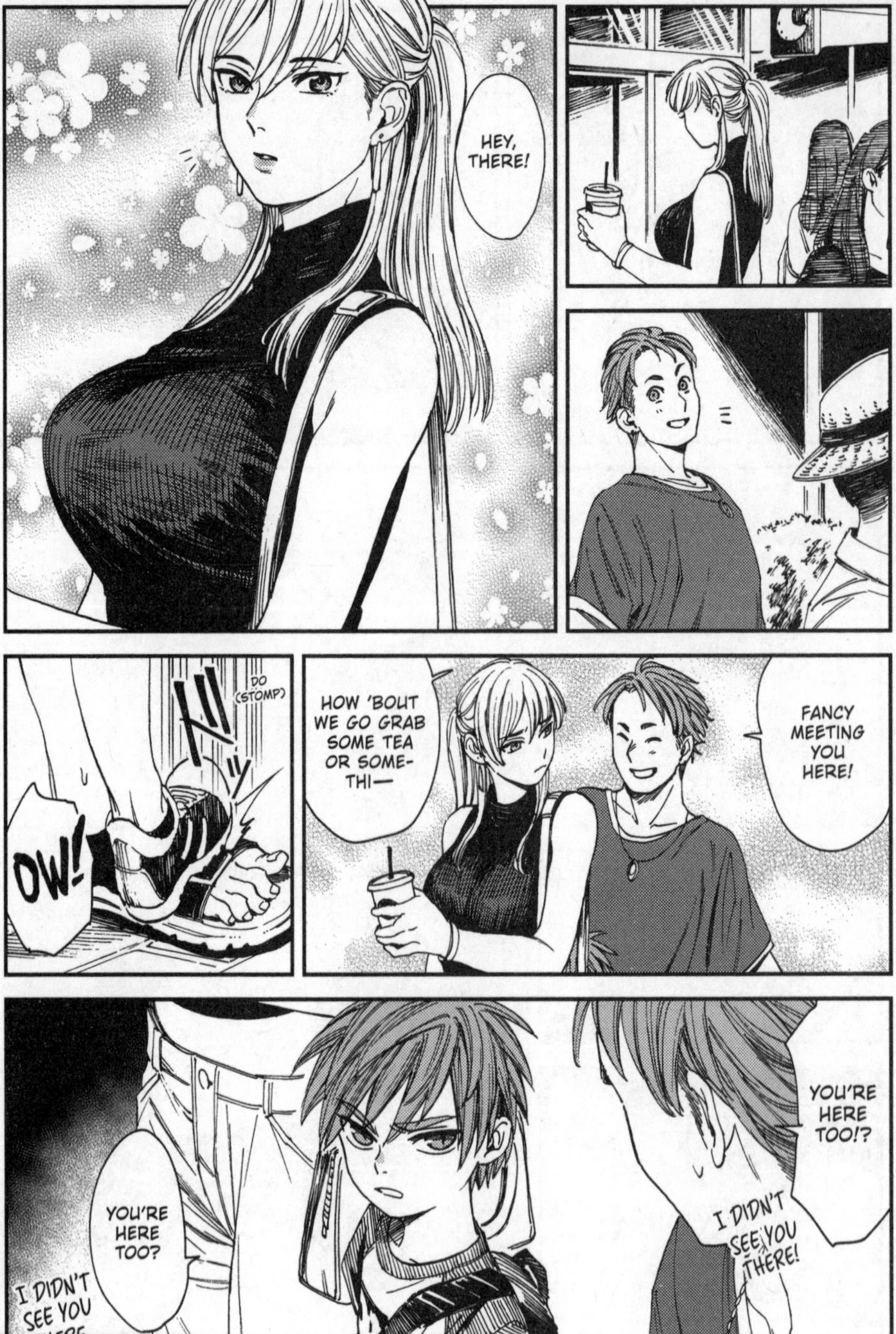
HEY, THERE!
FANCY MEETING YOU HERE!
HOW 'BOUT WE GO GRAB SOME TEA OR SOMETHI—
DO (STOMP)
OW!
YOU'RE HERE TOO!?
I DIDN'T SEE YOU THERE!
YOU'RE HERE TOO?
I DIDN'T SEE YOU THERE.

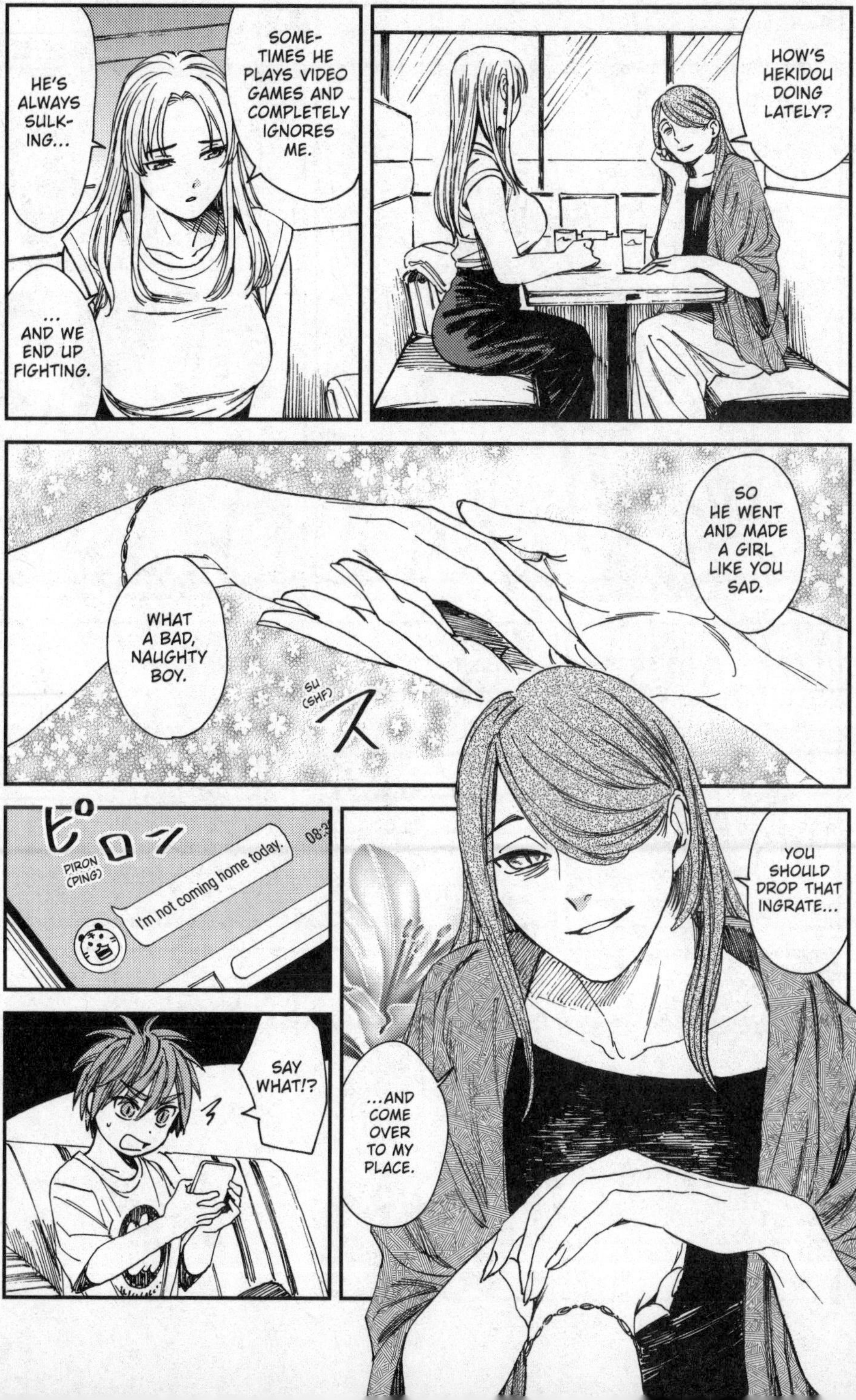
HOW'S HEKIDOU DOING LATELY?
SOME-TIMES HE PLAYS VIDEO GAMES AND COMPLETELY IGNORES ME.
HE'S ALWAYS SULK-ING...
... AND WE END UP FIGHTING.
SO HE WENT AND MADE A GIRL LIKE YOU SAD.
WHAT A BAD, NAUGHTY BOY.
ス
SU (SHF)
YOU SHOULD DROP THAT INGRATE...
...AND COME OVER TO MY PLACE.
ピロン
PIRON (PING)
I'm not coming home today.
SAY WHAT!?

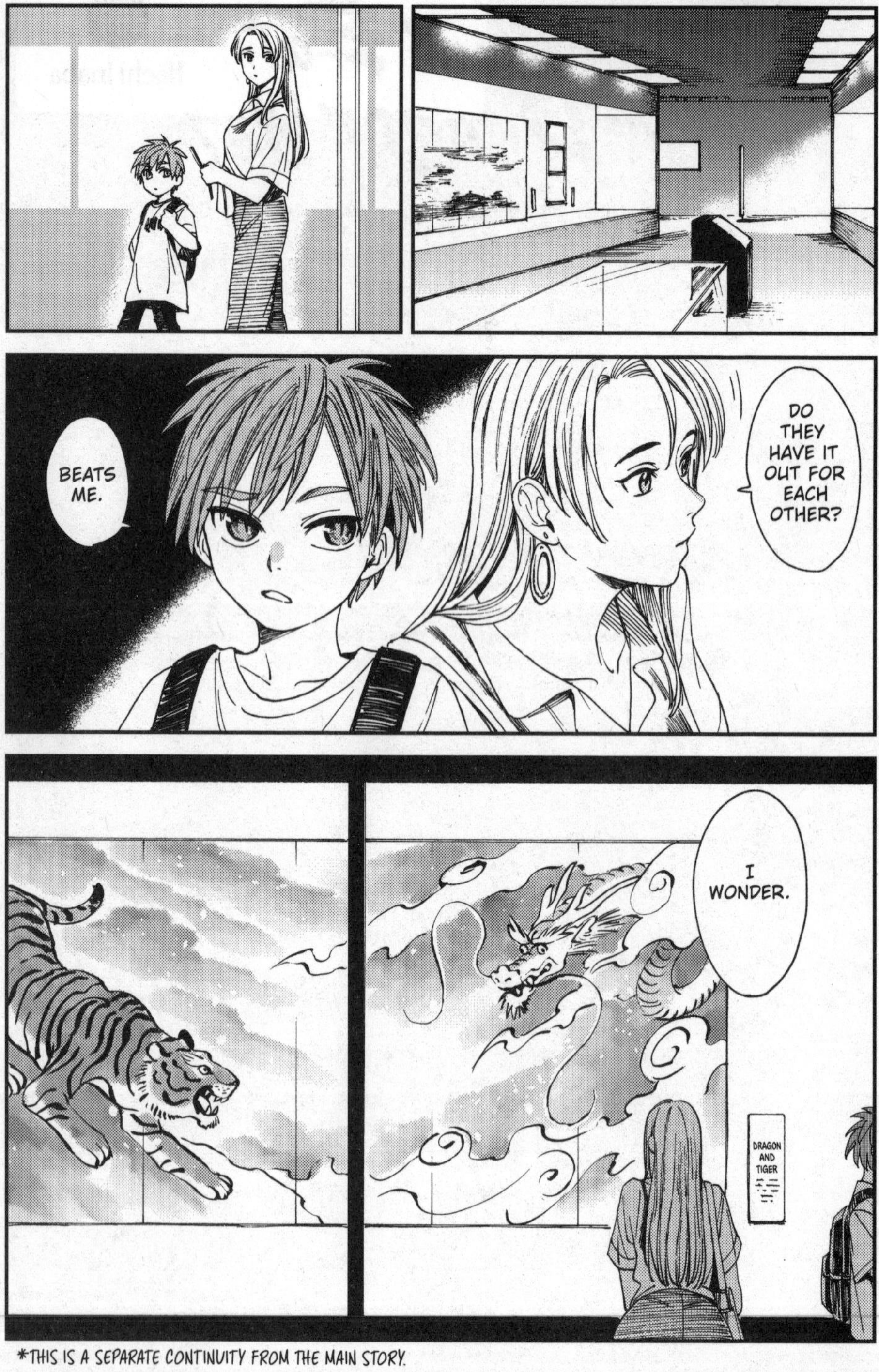
DO THEY HAVE IT OUT FOR EACH OTHER?
BEATS ME.
I WONDER.
DRAGON AND TIGER

*THIS IS A SEPARATE CONTINUITY FROM THE MAIN STORY.

Translation: Giuseppe di Martino ✶ **Lettering:** Greg Deng

TORA WA RYU O MADA TABENAI Vol. 1
© Hachi Inaba 2022
First published in Japan in 2022 by KADOKAWA CORPORATION, Tokyo.
English translation rights arranged with
KADOKAWA CORPORATION, Tokyo through TUTTLE-MORI AGENCY, INC., Tokyo.

English translation © 2024 by Yen Press, LLC

Yen Press
150 West 30th Street, 19th Floor
New York, NY 10001

Visit us at yenpress.com ✶ facebook.com/yenpress
twitter.com/yenpress ✶ yenpress.tumblr.com ✶ instagram.com/yenpress

First Yen Press Edition: March 2024
Edited by Yen Press Editorial: Ren Leon, Carl Li
Designed by Yen Press Design: Eddy Mingki

Yen Press is an imprint of Yen Press, LLC.
The Yen Press name and logo are trademarks of Yen Press, LLC.

Library of Congress Control Number: 2023951072

ISBNs: 978-1-9753-7313-9 (paperback)
978-1-9753-7314-6 (ebook)

1 3 5 7 9 10 8 6 4 2

WOR

Printed in the United States of America